OWNING RUSSIA

OWNING RUSSIA

THE STRUGGLE OVER FACTORIES, FARMS, AND POWER

ANDREW BARNES

Cornell University Press
Ithaca and London

First published 2006 by Cornell University Press

Printed in the United States of America

Library of Congress Cataloging-in-Publication Data

Barnes, Andrew Scott, 1969–
  Owning Russia : the struggle over factories, farms, and power/Andrew Barnes.
    p. cm.
  Includes bibliographical references and index.
  ISBN-13: 978-0-8014-4434-0 (cloth : alk. paper)
  ISBN-10: 0-8014-4434-9 (cloth : alk. paper)
  1. Property—Russia (Federation)   2. Privatization—Russia (Federation)   3. Wealth—Russia (Federation)   4. Real property—Russia (Federation)   5. Russia (Federation)—Economic conditions—1991–   I. Title.
  HC340.12.B39 2006
  338.947′05—dc22

                                        2005027435

Cloth printing   10 9 8 7 6 5 4 3 2 1

For Nancy
and for
Drew, Jack, and Noah

To control the production of wealth is to control human life itself.
—HILAIRE BELLOC, *The Servile State* (1912)

By right or wrong,
Lands and goods go to the strong.
—RALPH WALDO EMERSON, "Celestial Love" (1847)

CONTENTS

TABLES

ACKNOWLEDGMENTS

Expressing thanks in a book is a bit like writing invitations to a wedding. Whom can I thank/invite without offending those I don't? I have been working on this project in one form or another for over ten years, and the debts I have incurred are more than I can remember, much less acknowledge. What follows is my feeble attempt to accomplish the impossible, and many to whom I am deeply grateful will go unmentioned. I encourage them to write themselves in the margins (unless they are reading a library copy).

My advisers in graduate school, Stephen F. Cohen and Kathryn Stoner-Weiss, were constant sources of ideas, criticism, and encouragement. I am not sure that the three of us ever fully agreed on anything at any particular moment, but their suggestions and insights, as well as the examples they set in their own work, made me a better scholar. In addition, while I never had the opportunity to see Kathryn teach a class, the way Steve could capture a room, large or small, with a combination of rich historical detail, accessible stories, and thought-provoking questions heavily influences my own approach to teaching, and I thank him for that. The course I took from Stephen Kotkin opened my eyes to issues and approaches to research I had not considered before, and our conversations on the walk back across campus after class inspired me to think more boldly about what I could do as a researcher. Anna Seleny likewise shaped my early efforts at scholarship in lasting ways.

While I was an instructor and assistant professor at the University of Miami (FL), I had the great fortune to be perhaps the weakest part of an extraordinarily vibrant junior faculty, many of whose members were asking questions similar to mine about different parts of the world. I especially benefited from conversations with Marcus Kurtz about the political economy of Latin American marketization, the conduct of good fieldwork, and approaches to undergraduate teaching. I also took inspiration and moral support from Louise Davidson-Schmich, Juliet Gainsborough, J.P. and Terrie Monroe, Andrew Schrank, Kenneth Shadlen, and others who passed through the department. Our discussions of comparative political economy, American politics, hurricane preparation, child rearing, and much else made me a better scholar, teacher, and person. I am also eternally indebted to Pam Fischl and the others at UM/Canterbury for keeping my new-father neuroses from spinning completely out of control. My oldest son may not yet realize how lucky he was to have met Pam, but his mother and I do.

At Kent State, I have been welcomed into a stable, collegial department that has been the perfect home for me as I have finished the manuscript and further explored the art and science of teaching. Each member of the faculty has been remarkably patient as the scope and focus of the book continued to shift after I arrived in 2001. I am profoundly grateful to all my colleagues for their intellectual support, their familial advice, and the occasional round of golf when the snow melts.

The pages of the book would have been empty if I had not been able to take several research trips to Russia beginning in 1993; and those trips would have borne far less fruit had it not been for the innumerable people who talked with me, arranged meetings for me, and aided me at every turn. An array of language instructors, especially Alexandra Grigorievna Baker at Middlebury College and Liudmila Pavlovna Tsurikova at Indiana University, gave me the tools and confidence to conduct the research in the first place. In Moscow, where even the beginnings of a list could fill a book, a few names will have to stand in for the rest. Gennadii Bordiugov, Sergei Magaril, and Sergei Tsakunov provided assistance and friendship from the very beginning. I could not have asked for better roommates than Chris Boffey and Laura Kennedy, who were able to look on the inanities of Russian life with wry humor while still treating Russians and their experience with respect. Karen Bradbury and Andrea Littell of the American Council of Teachers of Russian (ACTR) were good friends and great advocates as I negotiated the labyrinths of official Russia. Alexandra Vacroux gave me an extensive collection of privatization clippings. In Volgograd, Dmitrii Belousov, Terri Kristalsky, Olga Naumova, and especially Elina Dobkina and her friends provided useful insights, good food, or both. In Nizhnii Novgorod,

Michael Boboshko, Valerii Borodin, Oleg Maslov, and Vladimir Nikolaev gave more of their time and knowledge than I could have hoped. In Saratov, I am particularly indebted to Sylvan Addink, Viktor Markov, and Vladimir Pashkov.

For their financial support of my research, I thank the American Council of Teachers of Russian, the Institute for the Study of World Politics, the International Research and Exchanges Board, the University of Miami (FL), Kent State University, and Princeton University's Council on Regional Studies and Center of International Studies. At Cornell University Press, I am grateful to Roger Haydon for shaping the manuscript from prospectus to final product with patience, wit, and constructive criticism. Karen Laun, Carolyn Pouncy, and Susan Barnett have been nothing but supportive, and I hope they know how much I appreciate it. I am also pleased to have permission to reprint material from articles I have published elsewhere. A significant portion of chapter 6 is adapted from "Russia's New Business Groups and State Power," *Post-Soviet Affairs* 19, no. 2 (2003), 154–86. Small parts of two other essays— "Property, Power, and the Presidency: Property-rights Reform and Russian Executive-Legislative Relations, 1990–1999," *Communist and Post-Communist Studies* 34 (March 2001): 39–61, and "What's the Difference? Industrial Privatisation and Agricultural Land Reform in Russia, 1990–1996," *Europe-Asia Studies* 50 (July 1998): 843–57 (see www.tandf.co.uk)—also appear in the text in revised form.

Many other people have offered advice, criticism, or support at key points in my career. I especially thank Hilary Appel, Harley Balzer, Laura Belin, Valerie Bunce, Timothy Frye, Stephen Hanson, Pauline Jones Luong, Philip Roeder, David Woodruff, the members of PONARS (Program on New Approaches to Russian Security), and two anonymous reviewers of the manuscript. Juliet Johnson has been a wonderful colleague and an even better friend since we began graduate school together in 1991. This book would have far deeper flaws, and indeed might not be finished, without her suggestions and her example of what first-rate scholarship looks like.

Book authors have both the special opportunity and the intimidating burden of letting their families know in public and in very few words just how much they mean to them. My father and mother, Don and Karen Barnes, taught me from very early on to ask big questions, seek real evidence, and give clear answers. They continue to set an example of curiosity, integrity, and charity that I will probably never match. My brother, Mike, challenged me in more ways than I can count; and he and his family continue to be a source of joy for me and mine. My aunt, uncle, and cousin have supported me in every task I've ever undertaken. My extended family through marriage welcomed me immediately many years ago and since then has both teased me mercilessly and supported me unquestioningly; I am grateful for all of it. Just knowing my sons—Drew, Jack, and Noah—and being part of their discovery of life is the greatest roller-coaster ride I could ever imagine. My wife, Nancy, gives me her love and her trust, has introduced me to Midwestern Thanksgiving dinners, and shows me by example what it means to be dedicated to one's work and—especially—one's family. I am a better person because of her.

NOTE ON TRANSLITERATION

The tension among accuracy, economy, and readability makes every transliteration system imperfect. With that in mind, I have used the Library of Congress system with familiar exceptions. That is, except in the footnotes, I have omitted hard and soft signs and spelled well-known Russian names as the U.S. press has popularized them.

OWNING RUSSIA

CHAPTER 1

COMPREHENDING TURMOIL

Post-Soviet Russia as a Struggle for Property

The new Russian economy is being built with pieces of the old. When the Soviet Union broke apart, countless factories continued to produce steel, cars, oil, ceramics, textiles, computers, shoes, and more. Thousands of huge farms tilled the soil of the Russian countryside. None of those enterprises—whether the miles and miles of oil pipelines, the hulking frame of the Volgograd Tractor Factory, or the innumerable pieces of a shattered agrarian sector—disappeared with the USSR. One of the most fundamental questions of the post-Soviet era was what would happen to them.

Answering that question, however, represented more than the largest privatization effort in history. It was a bare-knuckled struggle for property, in which a wide range of actors fought to wrest control over resources from the state and from one another in their attempts to build new political and economic empires. That multilayered competition for resources empowered the Russian executive at the expense of the legislature, dramatically strengthened managers vis-à-vis workers, created an array of conglomerates that went well beyond a handful of "oligarchs," and fundamentally shaped regional politics, as the line between government and business in many places was not merely blurred but erased. Raging uninterrupted since the late 1980s, the struggle for assets has proved more enduring, more intense, and more profound than many observers have recognized.

For too long, however, analysts squinted to make sense of post-Soviet Russia through the distorting lens of an interpretation that portrayed the present in terms of an anticipated future. More specifically, they viewed events, including changes in ownership, as part of a "transition to" democracy and capitalism. The Soviet system had collapsed, and a historic chance for transformation lay before those who would take it. "Political will," taking advantage of a "window of opportunity," and making reforms "irreversible" stood at the center of analyses and recommendations. Over time, especially after the 1998 Russian financial crisis, some observers lost their optimism, arguing that powerful economic interests had captured the state in Russia, perhaps permanently derailing any political or economic transition. The insights from their studies were invaluable, but the analyses suffered from shortcomings of their own. Most notably, while these analysts often believed the transition was "stalled," they still viewed change as a one-dimensional path from the old system to the new rather than an ongoing conflict over wealth that could have any number of political and economic outcomes—if, indeed, it ever came to an end. Furthermore, they were often vague about how some actors and not others came to dominate the political economy, and why some who reached the top eventually fell from their lofty positions.

By anchoring my narrative in the fate of real property, I clarify some of these processes, moving beyond earlier studies of privatization methods, political superstars, or "oligarchs" to reveal the ebbs and flows of a much broader conflict that has reshaped virtually every important aspect of the Russian political and economic landscape. I do so by identifying the major players in different phases of the struggle for real assets, their motives and strategies, and the changing environment in which they operated. My analysis thereby provides a complex but comprehensible picture of why the Russian struggle for property has been so intense and persistent and how it is likely to evolve in the future.

A LIMITING PICTURE OF CHANGE

As the Soviet Union was coming apart, many observers in the West and in the East believed the formerly communist countries had begun a journey toward a Western model of pluralist democracy and market-based economies. In this view, the young Russian politicians who pledged commitment to Western models represented the forces of progress, whereas managers and bureaucrats who feared change were obstacles to be overcome.[1] Much of the population, which Latin American experi-

---

1. Examples of this influertial argument include Aslund 1995, 2002; Shleifer and Treisman 2000; Lipton and Sachs 1990; Balcerowicz 1995.

ence suggested would not recognize the long-term benefits of short-term impoverishment, was not necessarily malicious by nature, but it could be dangerously susceptible to populist appeals by hardliners. The key to success, therefore, was to seize the moment and push through property reforms before the population had a chance to react.[2]

That conception of political and economic change is simple and inspiring, but it is flawed. Most broadly, the arguments that the "transition" framework generates center on what the system might become rather than on what it is and was. That approach inevitably leads to perpetual shouting matches between "pessimists" and "optimists," since neither side can make a definitive case regarding something that has not yet happened. Likewise, it is almost certain to generate premature declarations of "victory," "turning the corner," or "completing the transition," both because it is human nature to see one's own era as finally resolving problems of the past and because such claims can be useful in political conflicts. It encourages observers to see politics as a two-player game—one side pushes toward the desired endpoint; the other resists. From such a perspective, it is all too easy to see one side as heroes and the other as villains, when real understanding requires comprehension of a subtler blend of interests and resources. For example, knowing whether someone is a hardliner or reformer, a communist or noncommunist, or even an enterprise insider or outsider is not as useful for explaining behavior as simply knowing the extent of that person's access to key pieces of property.

Regarding property reform in particular, the unidimensional vision of "transition" suggests that the central dynamic has been one of privatization—that is, the transfer of state property into private hands—since more private property must mean progress toward the goal. That image, however, is misleading in three ways. First, aggregate statistics about state control over property in an economy are virtually meaningless, since state ownership of, say, 30 percent of the economy could mean different things in terms of majority control over particular enterprises. Inside any given firm, the state may or may not actively manage its shares— active management of a 30-percent stake may have very different implications than passive management of a 51-percent stake. Indeed, even with no ownership at all, the state can dominate an enterprise or sector through its powers of legislation and regulation.

2. For earlier statements on preempting the public, see Przeworski 1991; Haggard and Kaufman 1992; Williamson 1994. (Note that Przeworski objects to the political tactics he thinks would be necessary to carry out rapid market reforms.)

Second, privatization suggests an orderly transfer of property, or at least one associated with a formal policy. Innumerable studies of property reform in Russia have focused on the voucher privatization drive of 1992–94 and the simultaneous reorganization of large-scale farms.[3] Likewise, studies of the nefarious oligarchs have devoted many pages to the loans-for-shares plan, which was based on widely publicized auctions (Freeland 2000). In reality, Russians have witnessed not only the simple transfer of state assets to private hands but also the de facto theft of property—including what I call "privatization by exception"—because of the state's inability to monitor it. Several authors have recognized this process, calling it "nomenklatura privatization," "spontaneous privatization," or simply "corruption," but few have treated it systematically.[4]

Finally, and perhaps most important, seeing the world of Russian property as a clash between public and private sectors ignores the defining struggles over property *after* privatization. Some of the central conflicts in post-Soviet Russia, such as the violent clash over the huge aluminum complex in Krasnoiarsk, have taken place between private actors. Even after more than a decade of privatization, Russia could not escape this sort of conflict. Not only did the state still control vast swaths of desirable assets, which would take decades to sell off or otherwise distribute, but even complete privatization did not prevent significant struggles over the *re*distribution of property. Focusing on the competition over assets, rather than privatization per se, calls attention to these developments and opens the door to understanding them.[5]

By the late 1990s several scholars had begun to critique the original transition model. Without abandoning the idea that change represented movement toward or away from a predetermined endpoint, the new studies identified previously unsuspected obstacles to that transition: not the losers from economic reform but the early winners; not an overwhelming state but a captured one. Joel Hellman (1998) is perhaps the

3. For useful studies of mass privatization, see, for example, Blasi, Kroumova, and Kruse 1997; Boycko, Shleifer, and Vishny 1995; Nelson and Kuzes 1994, 1995. The last of these offers a more nuanced discussion of the political process and economic implications. On property reforms in agriculture, see Wegren 1998a; Brooks and Lerman 1994; Van Atta 1993a; Lerman, Csaki, and Feder 2004.

4. For useful, if occasionally sensationalist, studies of nomenklatura privatization under various names, see Hoffman 2002; Klebnikov 2000; Brady 1999; Goldman 2003.

5. Hellman (2002), drawing on statistical investigations of corruption and state capture in the late 1990s, likewise recognizes the potential for long-term upheaval in Russian ownership.

most widely read representative of this school of thought, which crystallized the sense among analysts of postcommunist states, especially Russia, that market reforms were not self-sustaining.[6] Rather than foster a continuously expanding coalition of beneficiaries who would support continued marketization, the new policies could create new vested interests that opposed further change. In particular, bankers, enterprise managers, and speculators reaped enormous rewards from partially liberalized economies, replete with opportunities for arbitrage and other rents.

From a slightly different perspective, other investigators focused on the importance of positive state action—rather than negative constraints on the government—in creating and sustaining a market economy. Thus, after years of concern about the ability of stubborn, powerful bureaucracies to block marketization, several observers noted that postcommunist governments may have become too weak to provide the basic institutional context that a market needs to function (Ericson 2000; McFaul 1998; Holmes 1997; Verdery 1996, 204–28). This insight had appeared in other contexts long before the fall of the Soviet Union, but in the late 1990s it also gained widespread credence in the Russian case.[7]

As important as those correctives were, however, shortcomings remained. The new outlook still implied a path from one system to another. It argued that Russia had detoured into a cul-de-sac, but the question was still how to get the transition "back on track." The answer usually lay in voting out captured politicians and strengthening the state's capacity to enforce laws, rather than defending reformers from public pressure and undercutting the state's ability to affect the economy, but the approach still tended to analyze the system in terms of what it might become—a difficult proposition at best.

Moreover, winners do not take all. Many collective farm managers, for example, while victorious in the early rounds of reform, struggled just to survive after the first few years. No one would have confused them with the financial-industrial oligarchy that seemed to dominate Russia. Conversely, some smaller economic groups, locked out of the bonanzas of the mid-1990s, pushed some of the larger conglomerates off their pedestals after the financial crash of 1998. Certainly beneficiaries of first-round reforms enjoyed significant advantages later, but they were

6. For a critique of the transition model based on a formal model and focused on the particular issue of post-Soviet Russian property, see Sonin 2003.

7. Polanyi (1944) is an especially important analysis of the state's role in market development.

not invincible. In this book I point out the advantages and highlight their origins, but I also demonstrate how changes in the political and economic environment made challenges possible. Since the post-Soviet Russian situation was volatile enough to produce several different shocks to the system, the struggle for property represented more than the Soviet elite's exchange of political for economic power or the conversion of first-round winners' early advantages into long-term dominance. Instead, new players continually challenged old ones by gaining control over key links in production chains, acquiring rights to companies' debts, forming alliances of convenience, or developing important political assets.

Finally, although the concept of state weakness served as a healthy antidote to the assumption that government involvement in the economy was the main obstacle to economic reform, it was a rather nebulous idea and could therefore be taken too far. Even under Boris Yeltsin, when the capacity of the Russian government seemed lowest, the state played a significant role in the redistribution of property. Economic interests were certainly powerful, but new rules issued by the government could significantly reshape the struggle for property. Even though policies such as the privatization program of 1992 or the bankruptcy law of 1998 never quite had their desired effects, they did change the way contestants for property battled one another.[8] By identifying both the resources available to nonstate actors and those at the fingertips of the many parts of the state, this book helps clarify both the strengths and weaknesses of government hierarchies, thereby making state capacity a more useful concept.

ORDER IN CHAOS

Rather than force history onto a unidimensional path, I argue that any particular set of circumstances, such as the fall of a superpower or a massive drop in state control over property, can produce a variety of outcomes, not just "progress" or "backsliding."[9] The constrained choices of key actors drive political and economic change and can push a system

8. For more theoretical discussions of how laws affect the behavior of economic actors in Russia, see Woodruff 2000, 2004; Hendley 1997.

9. This approach to understanding the world is most commonly known as historical institutionalism. For important developments of the theory, see Steinmo, Thelen, and Longstreth 1992; Mahoney and Rueschemeyer 2003; Ekiert and Hanson 2003. Stark and Bruszt (1998) represents an important application of the theory to

in multiple directions. Moreover, those choices can alter future constraints and therefore set the stage for a new round of competition over fundamental issues and resources.

Having abandoned the false clarity of the transition image, the casual observer might see the struggle for property in Russia as a formless mess. For years, managers, oligarchs, bureaucrats, and criminals grabbed whatever they could reach, while the state could do little to protect its own property or that owned by private actors. In practice, however, the undulating sea of property redistribution in Russia was not entirely incomprehensible. Instead, key aspects of the political and economic situation in post-Soviet Russia made a sustained struggle for property likely and influenced the shape it took. In particular, the underlying environment produced a broader range of actors, motives, and strategies than one would typically find in an established capitalist system, and periodic shocks to the system altered the context for the struggle in understandable ways.

The array of factories, farms, and other real assets that actors could pry from the state or from one another was staggeringly large, and it seemed only to grow over time. Furthermore, the development and dissolution of the Soviet system gave a wide array of actors potential claims on pieces of that property. Fairly or unfairly, the operation of a capitalist economy over time establishes rules and norms that heavily influence the types of players likely to mount a successful drive to take over important assets. Although exceptions occur, characteristics like access to financing, sectoral experience, and some sort of business plan are almost prerequisites for such an attempt, so competitors are generally limited to a small group of financiers and industrialists.[10] In the Russian case, by contrast, philosophical questions of legitimacy and practical questions of power remained unresolved, giving many more actors a real chance to participate in the clash over assets. It hardly produced an orderly, democratic, or merit-based competition for resources, but the unsettled nature of the system allowed players who would have been excluded in a more mature economy to acquire substantial networks of property.

---

the postcommunist context. Using very different language and writing about the Soviet period, Cohen (1985) likewise argues that history does not move in a straight line, and "Just as there is no iron-clad historical inevitability, there are always historical alternatives" (46–56, quotation from 71).

10. The strange world of Internet companies in 1990s America broke some of these rules, but that was clearly an exceptional environment for reasons that cannot be covered here.

In addition to the extensive collection of actors, the political and economic environment in Russia produced a kaleidoscope of motives and strategies for acquiring property. Competitors for assets were neither focused solely on maximizing profits nor reacting to ideological motivations easily labeled "reformist" or "reactionary." Instead, they responded rationally to a world full of property up for grabs, political institutions in flux, and a central state that was especially hard to predict. The context meant that real assets could do more than provide future income or wealth, and the multiple incentives helped complicate and perpetuate the struggle for property. Likewise, with rules unclear, takeover strategies ranged from the mundane to the devious to the violent. The range of tactics, however, did not reflect some Russian proclivity for lawlessness or other cultural flaw. Nor did specific choices of approaches depend heavily on whether someone was a hardliner or reformer, a communist or noncommunist, or an enterprise insider or outsider, as a progress-versus-backsliding interpretation might suggest. Instead, access to key pieces of property was a better determinant of behavior.

While the abundance of property, competitors, incentives, and tactics can help explain why the struggle for property in Russia was so protracted and intense, it cannot explain why the conflict shifted over time. Making sense of the shifts requires us to understand how events periodically shook up the system, bringing particular motives to the fore and giving certain actors and strategies advantages in the competition. In the volatile world of post-Soviet Russia, upheavals such as a financial crash, the transformation of political structures, or the emergence of new politicians and policies were virtually inevitable, and both the shocks and their aftereffects could transform the arena of competition over assets. Rather than absorbing, diffusing, or channeling such forces, the weakly defined institutions of the post-Soviet Russian political economy found themselves remade again and again. Rather than bringing the struggle for property to a close, each shake-up merely changed the ways in which it was fought, giving new competitors a chance to grab assets and pushing old ones to pursue new strategies of expansion and defense.

By examining these changes and their effects, I show which institutions shaped outcomes in which situations and why. This approach avoids the twin temptations of assuming the slate was wiped clean when the USSR broke down or bemoaning an omnipresent "Soviet legacy" when reforms produced pathological results. It also extends my analysis beyond studies that recognize the persistence of conflict over assets but explain the dynamics of redistribution by appealing to relatively constant forces—such as the perceived illegitimacy of early privatization, the conflictual incentives embedded in the mass privatization program, the relative conservatism of rural residents as opposed to urbanites, or the weakness of democratic institutions.[11] Such forces did undermine political and economic development in Russia, but they cannot account for the variation in the conduct of the struggle over time.

Actors

The first step in understanding the Russian struggle for property is to identify all the main competitors for real assets. The initial studies of privatization were simplistic in their characterization of major actors, and more recent examinations of property reform typically highlight only two or three of the main players.[12] Moreover, we must disaggregate important actors often treated as monolithic. Terms like "state" and "society," for example, can refer to several different groups that work at cross purposes, especially in a country undergoing dramatic change.[13] The same could be said for labels like "insiders" and "outsiders" or "reformers" and "rent seekers."

The full range of participants in the struggle over assets comprises workers and the general population, first- and second-tier economic groups, central and regional governments, and insiders and outsiders, each of which can be further subdivided. Their interactions are complex—just when one group seems ready to accept the status quo, another is ready to challenge it. At the same time, not all would-be contenders for property were created equal. For example, workers, agricultural laborers, and certain kinds of economic groups face severe disadvantages, and most Russian citizens have had little access to redistributed property at all. The multiplayer game is complicated, but its permutations are not infinite.

In the case of the Russian struggle for property, four sometimes-overlapping sets of participants played important roles. Most numerous, but usually least politically consequential, were the workers at individual

11. For excellent studies that point out the importance of such factors, see Hellman 2002; Woodruff 2004; Wegren 1994c; and Hellman 1998, respectively.

12. See, for example, Hellman 2002; Woodruff 2004; Sonin 2003; McDermott 2004. This focus on a few actors does not necessarily represent a flaw in the later studies, since they may be explaining something other than the struggle for property as a whole.

13. One of the strongest arguments for disaggregating "state" and "society" in studies of change came from Migdal 1988.

enterprises and members of the general population. Especially in the early debates over privatization, the interests of workers and citizens seemed to play a role in the process, as politicians and analysts wondered which groups should and would receive greater privileges during large-scale privatization and land reform. Fairly quickly, however, other actors developed strategies that left much of the population on the sidelines during property distribution and redistribution.

Second among the most famous competitors for property in post-Soviet Russia were the large economic groups that controlled assets from banks to steel plants and from farms to airlines. The biggest of these groups, known colloquially as the "oligarchs," attracted the most attention from observers, but many other conglomerates, slightly smaller in scale, created a "second tier" of economic groups that was no less important. Based in particular regions, industries, or even agriculture, members of the second tier helped perpetuate the struggle for property by threatening the dominance of the better-known oligarchs and taking advantage of such events as the 1998 financial crash to strengthen their positions. By charting the formation and behavior of conglomerates of all sizes, this book highlights a source of instability that many others miss.

Third, the Russian state played a key role in the distribution and redistribution of property in Russia, although that role is easy to mischaracterize. One common way to do so, especially in the first several years after the fall of the Soviet Union, was to look for more and less "reformist" parts of the federal government—for example, the executive versus the legislature or the Property Committee vs. the Property Fund—and attribute progress or its opposite to the successful politicking of the more or less reformist segments of the state.[14] Such voluntaristic explanations could rarely do more than tell the reader which Russian politicians happened to be in the author's favor at the time of writing.

A much more useful disaggregation of the state comes from analysts of Russian federalism, who have examined the different resources available to the central government and the dozens of regional governments that were all fighting for power, legitimacy, and economic development in post-Soviet Russia. Their studies offered enlightening and provocative explanations for the center's inability to enforce many of its decisions

---

14. Aslund (1995) is among the most widely read studies of reformist versus nonreformist factions in government.

in the regions, the regions' decisions to raise and then drop secessionist demands, and the peculiar development of center-regional relations in Russia.[15] Building on the insights in those works, I treat the federal and regional governments as independent actors in the struggle over property in Russia. I consider issues of regional implementation of central policies, but I also explore regional governments' incentives and opportunities regarding property redistribution in their own right, seeing provincial administrations as more than potential impediments to Moscow's goals.

Fourth, enterprise insiders and outsiders represented perhaps the most complicated and yet oversimplified, collection of competitors for assets in Russia.[16] For a number of analysts, the distinction between insiders and outsiders was the most important dichotomy in the struggle to transform the Russian economy. Outsiders represented the forces of progress, bringing entrepreneurship, innovation, and integrity to enterprises that had lacked all three for decades. Insiders—often known derisively as "red directors"—were portrayed as forces of resistance who longed for nothing so much as a return to central planning and state support.

Certainly the old managers of Soviet-era firms resisted efforts to remove them from power, but to place all insiders or all outsiders in the same general category is to miss a great deal of subtlety. Within the category of insiders, for example, an important but rarely noticed difference lay between the behavior of factory managers and that of farm directors. In addition, while insiders tended to fare well in the initial privatization, they did not always succeed in taking over their own enterprises, and several managed only to gain tentative control. Among outsiders, some brought positive new ideas to a firm, but others simply imported their own brand of corruption and of milking the state. Moreover, although the usual juxtaposition of insiders and outsiders envisioned the outsiders as foreign, they could also be Russian, which changed the networks and other resources available to them. Lastly, when outsiders did take over an enterprise, they became insid-

15. Among the most important works on Russian federalism are Stoner-Weiss 1997, 2004, forthcoming; Solnick 1995, 1998, 2000; Herrera 2005; Treisman 1996, 1999; Cai and Treisman 2004; Stepan 2000; Kahn 2002. For just a few of the studies that examine center-regional relations and their effects in other contexts, see Migdal 1988; Kohli 1994; Beissinger and Young 2002; Gibson 2004.

16. Insiders were factory and farm managers and, to a lesser extent, workers at the enterprises.

ers, which often changed their outlook on asset redistribution. By recognizing the variation within such groups, I am able to investigate and explain the different interests and tactics at work in a particular period of conflict, thereby rendering the struggle for property more comprehensible.

Motives and Strategies

With so many actors in pursuit of property in Russia, the motives that drove them and the strategies they employed varied widely. Of course, property is constantly redistributed in developed market economies, and it might be argued that the economic battles in Russia simply represent the rationalization of ownership through the familiar practice of mergers and acquisitions. On closer examination, however, both the causes and the mechanisms of the process in Russia differed significantly from their Western counterparts. Similarly, the conflict belied the expectations of transition-driven analyses that an extensive and transparent secondary share market would move assets from rent-seeking insiders to profit-seeking outsiders after an initial round of privatization (Boycko, Shleifer, and Vishny 1995; Blasi, Kroumova, and Kruse 1997). Instead, the incentives for acquiring property in post-Soviet Russia went beyond the pursuit of profit, and the tactics used often fell well outside the boundaries of accepted capitalist competition.

One of the forces driving the Russian struggle for property was economic actors' acquisition of assets for reasons *beyond* their current or future profitability. This is not to deny that business leaders in Russia sought increased profits when they were available, but other incentives more profoundly shaped their search for property. Even when the goal was the simple pursuit of wealth, new assets could have value beyond the potential to produce salable goods, since complicated ownership webs could hide revenues and profits. Likewise, to the extent that asset stripping was a source of enrichment in Russia, additional acquisitions could make financial sense even if the new owner had no intention of improving production lines.

Assets in post-Soviet Russia, however, served as more than a source of wealth, ill-gotten or otherwise. They were also the key to establishing, defending, or expanding one's position in the new system. Above all, since creating a brand-new enterprise would have been much harder than taking over an existing firm, it was important to grab something while it was still possible to do so—if the new system was being built with pieces of the old, actors needed to get their hands on some pieces of the old. In addition, under certain circumstances property could be an effective tool for defending or acquiring additional assets. For example, failure to control the source of one's inputs could leave a firm vulnerable to takeover by rivals. By the same token, given the right legal environment, ownership of natural resources could provide an effective tool for capturing assets further down the production chain. Considerations of commercial viability could therefore play a much smaller role in Russia than in a straightforward takeover decision in an established capitalist economy.

On top of potential economic benefits of usefulness in developing ownership empires, one other major incentive drove economic actors in Russia to acquire property: it was a source of political power. For a would-be businessperson, ownership of an enterprise could mean significant influence over politicians, especially if the firm employed a large number of people or accounted for a significant part of a regional economy. Furthermore, it could serve as an effective tool for mobilizing or demobilizing workers or other social groups. From the perspective of regional governments, involvement in an enterprise could help prevent the collapse of the local economic and social welfare systems. Like other motives in post-Soviet Russia, this one goes beyond the pursuit of profits and helps explain why the struggle for property long outlasted the major privatization programs or the concentration of key assets in private hands.

The strategies available to competitors for assets ranged from standard acquisition practices to tactics that would not be considered legitimate in any well-regarded capitalist system. When the 1998 financial crash and its aftermath made some economic groups cash rich, for example, they often used that money to buy up competitors in a fairly straightforward manner. Similarly, the mass privatization drive of 1992–94 helped create stock markets and mutual funds that performed at least some of the same functions as their Western counterparts.

Many of the techniques of property acquisition, however, skated much closer to the edge of legality. The laws in the post-Soviet era contained loopholes of grand proportions, and strategies such as insider stock issues, share registry manipulation, and transfer pricing were common. To survive and thrive in that world often required political protection, and alliances between economic actors and regional governments proved to be a key part of the post-Soviet political economy.[17] Whether because of a shared interest in protecting the local economy or because economic actors virtually dictated policy to subnational governments, regional officials tried to stave off outside attacks on "their" enterprises and weighed in on one side or the other in local disputes, often by manipulating the court system. The main players in the struggle thus shaped their strategies in the struggle for property to fit the laws on the books—and their inadequacies—as frequently as possible.

In still other cases, competitors for property in Russia simply violated the law or directly resisted its implementation. Violence and extortion were two of the most common forms of blatantly illegal strategies for acquiring or defending assets, and examples of that behavior filled press accounts of the Russian experience in the decade after the fall of the USSR.[18] Equally important, however, was the refusal by some actors, such as agricultural managers in 1992–94, to carry out policy directives as requested by Moscow. Laws and regulations had a much greater effect on competitors' behavior than one might have guessed from reading newspaper reports on Russia, but when a policy directly challenged the interests of a significant player, it stood little chance of coming to fruition.

None of these incentives or tactics came out of nowhere. Instead, an actor's position in the economy—especially his or her relationship to the property in question—significantly influenced the particular motive or strategy at play. Central government officials, for example, rarely saw the struggle for property the same way as their counterparts in the regions.

One of the clearest examples of this phenomenon came in the different behaviors of industrial and agricultural managers, especially before the 1998 financial crash. In both sectors, enterprise directors tried to outflank employees in the race for newly private assets, and they usually succeeded. Because of the different incentives and resources in the two sectors, however, industrialists and agrarians adopted divergent approaches to establishing their claims, which in turn had different repercussions for future disputes over property.

17. For four different analyses of regional economic-political alliances, see Frye 2002b; Stoner-Weiss 2004, forthcoming; Cai and Treisman 2004; Woodruff 1999.

18. For insightful analyses of illegal behavior that avoid sensationalism, see Volkov 2002; Frye 2000, 2002a.

Unfortunately, too many studies of Russian property reform focus on ownership changes in industrial enterprises and all but ignore the agrarian sector. Changes in agricultural property have usually remained the province of studies focused on Russia's rural transformation.[19] Examining change in agriculture as part of a larger struggle for property, by contrast, allows for a structured comparison with industrial change, explaining variations in the struggle for property that other studies may fail even to notice.

The Changing Context of the Struggle

Many actors competed for property in the late Soviet and post-Soviet periods, but the ones who succeeded and the tools they used changed over time, responding to shifts in the political and economic environment. In a very direct sense, the Soviet economic system made the Russian struggle for property possible. Although both deprecating jokes and serious scholarship have rightly highlighted the inefficiencies and bizarre priorities of the Soviet command economy, that system produced a complex, industrialized economy, whose physical assets long outlived the hammer-and-sickle flag. Furthermore, the government claimed ownership of virtually all those assets, and every one of its asserted privileges lay open to challenge when the regime began to fall. Chapter 2 examines what those claims were, how they evolved, and therefore what kinds of assets would be easiest to seize when the chains of command began to weaken.

Although the Soviet system of control was convoluted and vulnerable to abuse, it kept officials' misappropriation of assets within sustainable bounds for nearly seventy years. In the late 1980s, however, as chapter 3 explains, Mikhail Gorbachev's economic reforms inadvertently launched the Russian struggle for property. Resurrecting ideas from old Soviet reformers, then moving beyond them, Gorbachev intentionally loosened controls over property in hopes of sparking innovation. Unfortunately for him, the entrepreneurship he unleashed centered on pulling chunks of the state economic structure loose in order to privatize their operation and profits while avoiding concomitant responsibilities and risks. This "spontaneous privatization" undermined the economy

19. For excellent studies of post-Soviet agriculture, see Allina-Pisano 2002; Humphrey 1998, 2002; Buckley 1995; Kitching 1998a, 1998b; and the works of Stephen K. Wegren.

rather than bolstering it. Even more important for the future of the Soviet state, newly elected governments in Russia and other union republics began to assert control over state property and other resources on their territory in the latter half of 1990. While their efforts were remarkably successful, they did little to rein in managers and ministers pursuing spontaneous privatization, which continued unabated after the fall of the Soviet Union.

The context of the struggle for property, however, changed dramatically after the fall of the USSR. As chapter 4 shows, the newly independent Russian government launched programs of mass industrial privatization and farm reorganization intended to erase any remnants of the Soviet economic system, especially ministerial control of property. Although they left a surprising number of desirable assets in state hands, the programs were revolutionary in scope, as they cast thousands of enterprises upon the seas of property redistribution. In that environment, managers of factories and farms used their proximity to real assets to modify the reform programs to their own advantage during the implementation stage, establishing much firmer control over their enterprises than any other group. The differing interests and resources of industrial and agricultural managers led them to take divergent approaches in this period, with industrialists exploiting the mass privatization program in an environment of hyperinflation and agrarians resisting land reform outright. In neither sector, however, were managers' claims to property unassailable, and other actors also captured assets. Bureaucrats at various levels continued to pry segments of old ministries from state control, often more successfully than during the late Soviet era. Even a significant proportion of the general population received bits of property in the bonanza of this period, although their "success" was most evident in the rise of subsistence farming throughout the country.

Far-reaching as such changes were, none of them marked an end to the competition over assets. Instead, voucher privatization and large-scale farm reorganization simply opened the door to the next phase of the property struggle, which began in the latter half of 1994. With key assets still in state hands, with many claims to private property still contested, and with the distribution of power among formal political institutions still unclear, major economic actors remained focused on acquiring property, rather than using it more efficiently. Capturing a going concern was easier than establishing a new enterprise, and even if a firm was unlikely ever to turn a profit, it could provide political influence or serve as a fig leaf for numerous asset-transfer schemes. The years 1994–97, explored in chapter 5, represented the heyday of the infamous "oligarchs," who took control of prominent industrial and financial assets. Those high-profile groups, however, and the deals that brought them to prominence, were far from the only forces shaping the country's development. For example, smaller, geographically concentrated conglomerates developed in the mid-1990s that enjoyed significant advantages over their national compatriots when the financial crash of 1998 hit. Increasingly powerful regional governments also discovered a variety of reasons to wade deeper into the conflict over property redistribution. At the same time, the managers who had gained control over enterprises during mass privatization competed for dominance with Russian and foreign outsiders. That competition, which by that time largely excluded such rank-and-file groups as industrial laborers and farm workers, witnessed a perpetual shifting of alliances among the protagonists and looked as if it could last indefinitely.

Indeed, the distribution and redistribution of property did continue in the late 1990s. Many assets remained only weakly claimed, and myriad actors had a variety of reasons to want them, as well as multiple ways to get them. The conduct of the struggle, however, changed significantly in 1997–2002, and chapter 6 examines that transformation. Enterprise debt in the system had reached extremely high levels by late 1997; and when some companies—most notably the gas and electricity monopolies, Gazprom and UES—finally began to call in those IOUs, debtors frequently used shares in themselves to pay off the loans, ushering in a new form of asset redistribution. In 1998 two additional developments helped exacerbate that "debt roll-up." First, a bankruptcy law passed in 1998 led to a flurry of property redistribution through a practice one might call "political bankruptcy." In that process, a company could fall under the control of a well-connected rival on the pretext of bankruptcy, despite being only a few months behind on a loan of minimal size. Using the new law as a takeover tool usually required the assistance of a regional government, giving regional leaders yet another role in the struggle for property. Second, when the federal government defaulted on its treasury obligations on August 17, 1998, the ruble collapsed, severely damaging major banks. Some of them actually went under in the wake of the crash, and others were left financially weakened, exposing their industrial assets to players who escaped the collapse relatively unscathed.

Even as the effects of massive debt and financial collapse reverberated through the Russian system of ownership, a new shock hit when Vladimir

Putin rose to the presidency in 1999–2000. Putin came to power promising to strengthen the Russian state vis-à-vis economic groups, and in some ways he succeeded. For example, shortly after his election, he helped bring down two major conglomerates that had dominated the scene in the late 1990s. In addition, he forced leading economic actors to tone down their involvement in national politics. Although Putin changed the way economic actors interacted with each other and with the state, he did not bring the struggle for property completely under control. For example, the disappearance of individual oligarchs from center stage put important industrial assets back in play, and both the state and private actors quickly gobbled them up. Likewise, Russian economic leaders did not leave politics, but simply redirected their participation: although they no longer wrote laws and decrees, they still placed their supporters in the presidential administration, shared interests with the government regarding lower taxes and other reforms, and established a more direct presence in the federal legislature and regional governments than ever before. Indeed, the number of economic leaders voted into regional governorships or presidencies jumped markedly in the first elections after Putin came to power.

In response to new incentives and constraints, the most successful strategies and players in the struggle for property changed significantly from 1997 to 2002. With financial windfalls a thing of the past, major economic players needed access to real assets more than to banks. In particular, control over one's own sources of inputs was essential to prevent others from using the debt system in a takeover bid. Similarly, access to cash businesses, such as agriculture or exports, also helped fend off debt and its repercussions. Aspirants to property also needed political assistance, especially at the regional level, to defend against or take advantage of political bankruptcy. In that setting, some of the economic groups that had dominated the scene in the mid-1990s fell by the wayside. New groups took their place, agriculture became a key battleground in the fight over real assets, and groups large and small sought refuge in vertically integrated production chains or broadly diversified holdings.

By the middle of Putin's first term, the environment of the struggle for property had begun to shift yet again. A new set of laws attempted to end abuse of the bankruptcy process and liberalize the land market, but the more important change concerned the direct role of the central government in the redistribution of assets. In his first two years in power, Putin reanimated the federal government as a direct participant, but his efforts focused on reshaping other competitors' strategies for acquiring and defending property. By 2003 he moved to establish the central government as the clearly dominant player in property redistribution. The renationalization of the major production unit of the oil giant Yukos was the clearest but far from the only example of this strategy. As chapter 7 explains, the new environment benefited some formerly peripheral groups at the expense of those that had appeared dominant in 2002. Meanwhile, planned reorganizations of the electricity monopoly, railways ministry, and other state holdings threatened yet another round of knock-down, drag-out brawls among leading economic actors, second-tier groups, and various levels of government.

Well into the second decade after the fall of the Soviet Union, the Russian struggle for property raged on. The most successful competitors for assets had changed, and the strategies they employed were different from those used in the 1980s and 1990s, but property redistribution was still a far cry from normal behavior in established capitalist systems. Control of major economic assets remained unsettled, and as chapter 8 elaborates, little about the Russian system suggested a rapid resolution was likely. While some of the biggest owners had begun to focus more on defense than on expansion of their holdings, many of their strategies for doing so remained unusual, and many more aggressive competitors continued to seek new assets. A competition involving so many participants, interests, and tactics seemed unlikely to settle down naturally or easily.

From Karl Marx to Milton Friedman, and from Vladimir Lenin to Anatolii Chubais, philosophers and leaders have recognized that control over assets fundamentally shapes the economic, political, and social systems of a country. In Russia, the struggle to establish that control has been a powerful force for change, remaking the relationships among business, state, and society in unexpected ways. Rather than viewing that struggle and its surprises as detours from a well-marked path, I accept them as Russia's messy reality and explain them as the understandable result of the complex interaction of multiple players, motives, and strategies in an environment prone to change. In doing so, I offer a new way to understand one of the most tumultuous periods in Russian history.

CHAPTER 2

THE TANGLED WEB THEY WOVE

Property in the USSR before 1985

The structure of the Soviet economic system created the original environment for the Russian struggle for property. The gas monopoly Gazprom, for example, descended directly from the Soviet Ministry of Oil and Gas. Likewise, Agrokhim, a gargantuan mineral fertilizer company in post-Soviet Russia, could only emerge from a system with centralized control over the production and distribution of fertilizer. The Soviet system neither disappeared overnight nor simply collapsed under the weight of its own inefficiencies. Instead, it broke apart piece by piece along predictable lines.

To understand later developments, therefore, this chapter examines the creation and evolution of the command-administrative system, focusing on state control over property. That system did not emerge directly from the ideas of Marx, Lenin, or anyone else, and recognizing how it was constructed in practice helps one understand how it came apart later. Stalin, for example, forced centralized ownership of productive assets on the population through violence, but an explicit ideological foundation also underpinned the structure. As Khrushchev and Brezhnev each reshaped that ideology, they led crusades of amalgamation, reconfiguration, and decentralization that on the surface seemed to have little substantive impact. Although they failed to improve economic performance significantly, the reforms created the ministries, departments, associations, and other administrative organs that controlled the nation's wealth when Gorbachev came to power. Rather than a monolithic structure of unchanging authority, the Soviet command economy by 1985 was a collection of interlocking and overlapping chains of command and production that began to separate in the late 1980s.

THE FORMATION OF THE SOVIET PROPERTY SYSTEM

Before the 1930s, the future of property in the Soviet Union was uncertain. After they rose victorious from the revolutionary turmoil in Russia unleashed by World War I, Lenin and the Bolshevik Party fought among themselves about most aspects of the new regime, including what a "socialist" system of ownership would look like. Only the ascent of Joseph Stalin was able to end the debate, violently inflicting mass nationalization and central planning on society in the name of the Revolution. Whether that system represented the fulfillment of the Revolution or its betrayal, the process of its imposition followed a convoluted path and helped create the backdrop for Soviet political and economic development for more than half a century.

Property in Tsarist Russia

When the Bolsheviks seized control of the capital of the Russian empire in October 1917, they were asserting the right to rule not an established capitalist society but a feudal system barely emerged from a round of state-led industrialization and a devastating war. In the tsarist period the distribution of property had effectively been under the control of the tsar and nobility. Indeed, before Peter the Great, all lands belonged to the tsar, and even members of the aristocracy had no enforceable claim to the estates they managed. Peter made large manors heritable, so that lords could bequeath them to their heirs with confidence, but in practice the final word still lay with the monarch (Szamuely 1974, 113).

The peasants, who constituted the vast majority of the population, had even less claim than nobles to their own property. While serfs received a small amount of land after their emancipation in 1861, they still did not own it individually.[1] Instead, the land was collective property, which the village commune administered and distributed according to the medieval strip method. To ensure that all villagers had access to land

---

1. The land also came with heavy redemption payments to the lords. Rural residents were still struggling with those payments when the obligations were abolished in 1905.

of equal fertility, each family farmed a number of plots, each of a different quality. Periodically the commune reapportioned the strips to reflect changes in the village population, so that the amount of land a family worked grew with the family. Under Nicholas II Prime Minister Petr Stolypin sought to replace this inefficient system with a new one based on the private ownership of land. In 1906 he launched his "wager on the strong" by decreeing the right to leave the commune and buy and sell agricultural land. Many peasants responded to this legal change, and by 1916 they had set up about two million private farms, representing almost a quarter of the families in the forty provinces of European Russia the decree affected (Nove 1989, 13). That policy, however, prompted significant political backlash, and Stolypin was assassinated in 1911.

Some scholars argue that the distribution of political power in tsarist Russia prevented the complete transformation of ownership in agriculture, as the nobility resisted the loss of land, and the monarch forcibly prevented others from establishing strong claims to property in the empire (Macey 1995, 189; Nove 1989, chap. 1). Others point to cultural norms, especially among the peasantry, who believed that since no human had created the land, no one could claim to own it, either. The right to farm a plot in perpetuity was understandable, but buying or selling it was immoral.[2] Still others point out that the pre-Soviet ownership system may have been the logical result of economic circumstances. Thus, while strip farming and the periodic redistribution of plots do not produce an efficient commercial sector, they do make it less likely that any particular family will face disaster from a crop failure (Lih 1990, 69–72, 92–96). The alignment of political forces and ideological arguments near the end of the tsarist era combined to support a mix of large plantations, communal lands, and new private holdings.

Ownership of enterprises was mixed in the cities, as well. Under Peter the Great, for example, manufacturing owed much of its expansion to state policies—industrialization from above. By decree, the government created whole factories, including naming their managers and laborers, and the state funded entire industrial projects. During the reign of Nicholas II, Finance Minister Sergei Witte revived this practice, relying when possible on foreign capital to fund investments, and Russia began to industrialize faster than ever before (von Laue 1963). Thus, while private industry developed in the early 1900s, the state played a large

2. For examples, see Szamuely 1974; McDaniel 1988. The Slavophiles of the 1840s–60s likewise argued against a land market (Tucker 1971).

role in directing and supporting it, and parts of Russian society still challenged its legitimacy (McDaniel 1988, 17–19).

Revolution and Civil War

In that environment, the Bolsheviks struggled among themselves over the details of the society they hoped to create. Marx did not match his meticulous description of capitalism with a clear explanation of socialism and how to create it, since he assumed it would emerge naturally from the capitalist system. When it did not, the leaders of the fledgling Soviet Union fought, sometimes bitterly, about the nature of their goal and how they should pursue it. Most of them could agree that socialism and communism would rise from the ashes of private ownership—in their *Communist Manifesto*, Marx and Engels had written, "Communists can express their theory in a single phrase: the abolition of private property"—but the question of just how much private ownership to abolish was an open one throughout the 1910s and 1920s.

In the months before the Revolution, the Russian peasantry had launched a de facto land redistribution in the countryside. Peasants made up the bulk of the Russian army fighting in World War I, and with the breakdown of authority and morale at the front, they deserted in droves to claim pieces of the estates in their villages. The Bolsheviks recognized the strength of that movement and condensed their rural platform to the slogan "Land to the Peasants!" Once in power, the Bolsheviks issued the November 8 Land Decree to formalize their commitment to a peasant policy similar to that of the Socialist Revolutionaries, the party with the closest ties to the peasantry at the time. The decree condoned peasant smallholdings, tried to restrict the size of the plots, and prohibited the sale of land, which belonged to "all the people," in keeping with peasant tradition (Nove 1989, 29–30, 39–40).

The Bolsheviks' first attempt at a comprehensive economic plan after the Revolution was a short-lived experiment with "state capitalism."[3] Since five months of uncoordinated nationalization of enterprises had not helped the Russian economy recover from the Great War or the Revolutions of 1917, in April 1918 Lenin proposed something of an accord with capitalists. According to that plan, while the state would regulate the economy, particularly large-scale industrial and financial enterprises, it would not seek to abolish private property entirely.

3. The term "state capitalism" is Lenin's. See Cohen 1973, 70–78.

Instead, Soviet Russia would move toward socialism through a mixed economy.

Implementing any sort of plan, however, required political stability, which evaporated within months. Monarchists, Constitutional Democrats, socialists of various stripes, and nationalists in the border regions were not content to allow the Bolsheviks to rule uncontested, and by June 1918 the country fell into a terrible civil war. During the course of that war, another economic system began to emerge, a collection of policies that eventually came to be called "war communism" (Nove 1989, esp. 37–62).[4]

With the onset of war, the Bolsheviks tried to use state power to direct the economy toward the war effort. It was in this context that they made their first attempt at widespread nationalization of manufacturing and tried to direct most allocation of resources. In addition, they moved away from promises of worker control at the factories, as Lenin argued that collective management by labor could hamper factories' operation and therefore interfere with prosecuting the war (Sil 2002, 219). The nationalized property and state-led economic activity came under the purview of the planning agency VSNKh (the Supreme Council of the National Economy), but its control of the process was decidedly incomplete. The department went through several reorganizations, faced competition from other agencies, and repeatedly saw its plans rendered obsolete by events of war. Similarly, while some Bolsheviks believed that the state could administer all industrial assets in the name of the working class, the hierarchy for doing so only reached the largest enterprises during the first decade after the Revolution (Sil 2002, 219–20).

At the same time, with peasants reluctant to sell grain to the government at the low prices being offered, and with hunger growing more acute in the cities, the Supply Commissariat (Narkomprod) and detachments of the All-Russian Extraordinary Commission to Combat Counterrevolution and Sabotage (Cheka) began to seize grain from accused hoarders by force (Heinzen 2004). In conjunction with that strategy, the Bolsheviks also tried to combine some small peasant holdings into collective farms, both because it seemed more "socialist" and because it made grain requisitioning easier. A February 1919 decree optimistically referred to "a transition to collective farming," but in reality those efforts were largely unsuccessful, and local uprisings continued to break up larger holdings throughout the war (Nove 1989, 53).

---

4. For the central role of chaos and destruction, rather than any political party, in shaping events of the Civil War, see Lewin 1989.

Although many of the policies of war communism were unpopular with urban capitalists and rural peasants, the Bolsheviks were able to sustain them through 1921. The capital owners in the cities were not powerful enough to force a change, and the peasants feared the Bolsheviks less than their opponents (known colloquially as the "Whites"), some of whom wanted to recreate the tsarist socio-economic pyramid. By 1920, as the Bolsheviks began to enjoy military and revolutionary successes, they began to see their patchwork of policies as a viable strategy for achieving communism, especially in conjunction with the world socialist revolution they still believed was imminent.

Even at that time, however, there were signs that the system could not last. As the fear of a White victory subsided, peasant revolts became more common. Such an uprising in Tambov oblast in August–September 1920 prompted the government to replace grain seizures with a tax in kind to stave off further rebellion. When the once-loyal sailors at the Kronstadt naval base revolted in February 1921, they forced the Bolsheviks to reconsider their actions more generally. The Party's immediate response was to put down the insurrections violently, but the leaders had to admit they did not have a blueprint for achieving communism and that strategies from the Civil War seemed unlikely to take them much farther in that direction (Nove 1989, 96).

Using the Market to Build Socialism

At the Tenth Party Congress in March 1921, Lenin introduced what he called the New Economic Policy (NEP), which his associate Nikolai Bukharin continued to develop as Lenin's health faltered. Although Lenin originally presented NEP as a "retreat" from war communism, he quickly began to see it as the best way to realize the fruits of the Revolution in Soviet Russia (Lewin 1968a; Cohen 1973, 134–38). The program drew on the ideas of Lenin's state capitalism, seeking to use a mixed economy as an engine for building socialism. The early principle of direct workers' control of industry never regained its force, and indeed Lenin vigorously attacked the "Worker's Opposition" within the Party, but NEP otherwise offered a new approach to industrialization and the administration of property (Sil 2002, 220–21).

The statutes passed at the Congress condoned private trade and extended the tax in kind to most areas of the country. Over the next several months, the Party reversed many of the other hastily made decisions of the Civil War years. While heavy industry remained state property, a decree of May 17, 1921, denationalized small-scale industry. By the end of August, all enterprises—whether private or state-owned—could sell their output to private traders if they chose.

Even within the state-owned sector, central planning and control hardly resembled the command economy that emerged under Stalin. Enterprises of a sector were organized into trusts, but most of them operated relatively freely, since VSNKh directly controlled the activity of only a few. In fact, even the "plans" that VSNKh and the State Planning Committee (Gosplan) produced were not the detailed, utopian documents of the Stalin era but rather a general set of economic predictions and investment suggestions (Nove 1989, 86–92).

In agriculture NEP re-emphasized the importance of individual peasant farming and abandoned the forced collectivization of landholdings. Instead the program recommended using the peasants' self-interest to move the country toward both greater productivity and socialism. The organizations that were to harness the power of the market for socialist development were cooperatives. Lenin argued in his treatise "On Cooperation," and Bukharin reiterated throughout the 1920s, that peasants who formed credit, marketing, and purchasing cooperatives would not only improve their own living standards but also recognize the benefits of collaborative activity, which would gradually lead to collective farming itself (Cohen 1973, 195–96). Thus peasants still could not sell their land, which remained the property of all the people, but the Bolsheviks did not challenge their right to farm it as they saw fit.[5]

NEP quickly produced positive economic results. By the mid-1920s, the country had reactivated much of its economic capacity, balanced its budget, and stabilized its currency. Both heavy industry and agriculture were approaching their prewar levels of output (Nove 1989, 84, 101). Because of those successes, even discussions of policy changes assumed the maintenance of NEP's general framework (Erlich 1960). Over time, however, as the economy exhausted the potential for mobilizing damaged or idle machinery, growth slowed. Annual "grain crises" began to give Stalin the opportunity to initiate "emergency measures" against the peasantry that were reminiscent of war communism (Nove 1989,

5. The right to possess, control, and bequeath an object is captured by the Russian term *vladenie*, as opposed to *sobstvennost'*, which means "ownership" and may imply a right to sell the object as well. In the late 1980s Gorbachev sought to resurrect the idea of permanent *vladenie* of agricultural land.

141–44). Even those actions, however, did not portend the radical and violent overhaul of property that Stalin launched in 1929.

The Stalinist Onslaught

By late 1929 Joseph Stalin had defeated his chief opponents in the party leadership, and on the twelfth anniversary of the October Revolution, he announced without warning the goal of complete and rapid collectivization of agriculture.[6] The effort began with the "25,000-er" campaign, in which young, devoted urbanites went to the countryside to "educate" and "convince" peasants to abandon their claims to individual plots of land and join the collectives (Viola 1987). Thus, through a campaign of violence that caused a famine in 1932–33 and a 50-percent drop in livestock stores by 1933, Stalin and his followers completely restructured the ownership of land in the USSR. By 1935, 83 percent of peasants and 94 percent of crop lands were part of collective or state farms (*kolkhozy* and *sovkhozy*, respectively).

The early 1930s also saw the transformation of control rights over agricultural machinery. Building on experiments from the late 1920s, the Stalin administration applied the Machine-Tractor Station (MTS) system throughout the USSR (Miller 1970). Beginning in 1934, all collective farms had to turn over their agricultural machinery to the MTSs, which became the exclusive suppliers and servicers of such equipment. Furthermore, since they received payments in kind for services rendered, the MTSs became an important part of the state agricultural procurement system (Hedlund 1984, 58).

In conjunction with his rural revolution, Stalin reversed NEP in the cities through sweeping nationalization and crash industrialization (Davies 1980–89; Rosenberg and Siegelbaum 1993). Decrying the atmosphere in which "Nepmen" and "petty-bourgeois elements" flourished, he led the drive to abolish private trade and manufacture. Over the course of the first Five-Year Plan, which lasted only from 1929 to 1932, virtually all of the economy came under state control. At the same time, output of coal, oil, steel, and other heavy industrial goods jumped dramatically, and entire towns grew up around new factories.

In his *Short Course on the History of the Communist Party of the Soviet Union (Bolsheviks)*, Stalin termed this assault on private economic activity, drastic reduction in agricultural output, and construction of modern industrial

---

6. For detailed accounts of the period, see Lewin 1968b; Conquest 1986.

behemoths the "victory of Socialism" (TsK VKP(b) 1939, 342). Although his actions represented a sharp break with party policies since the Tenth Congress, Stalin justified his actions in terms many Bolsheviks could accept: "socialist" ownership of property and the central direction of economic activity were economically and morally superior to private ownership and free competition.[7] Those general beliefs, however, could underpin widely varying policies, including both NEP and its abolition. The question was how one defined "socialist" ownership, and thus the appropriate degree of centralized economic control.

In the Stalinist vision, socialist ownership consisted of three major categories of property. The first and by far the largest was "state property" (*gosudarstvennaia sobstvennost*), which Stalin equated with "all-people's" (*obshchenarodnaia*) property. As part of his rejection of the Marxist-Leninist teaching that the state would wither away under socialism, Stalin declared that, since the state embodied the will of the population, state ownership was the closest approximation of communist property relations possible in a socialist country. With this reasoning, he closed debate over private ownership of virtually all the productive forces of the country, including all heavy industry, most light industry, the assets of state farms, and the land of both state and collective farms.

The 1936 (Stalin) Constitution condoned a second category of socialist property, ideologically inferior to the first but nonetheless preferable to private ownership, called "cooperative-kolkhoz" (*kooperativno-kolkhoznaia*) property. The assets of collective farms—aside from land—and the property of producers' cooperatives fell under this rubric, although the latter group was small and contributed a mere 3 percent of industrial output by 1960, when such enterprises were abolished (Schroeder 1988, 180). Possessions of this type were nominally the property not of all members of society but of all members of the enterprise (the "collective"). Nonetheless, in practice, citizens had little more freedom in deciding how to use cooperative-kolkhoz property than state property.

Even in the Stalin Constitution, however, tension was evident between the alleged desirability of state ownership and control, on one hand, and the political and economic necessity of some decentralization, on

7. Ball (1987), esp. 55, 60–62, shows the uncertainty among Bolsheviks in the 1920s, even those who supported NEP, about how far to allow marketization to go.

For the Stalinist statement of the virtues of socialist ownership of the means of production, see esp. Article 4 of the 1936 Constitution; on the benefits of state planning, see esp. Article 11.

the other. "Personal" (*lichnaia*) property, the third category in the Stalinist hierarchy, reflected this tension. This label referred to the fruits of
collective or individual production that citizens could claim as their own,
such as clothing, food, and other small possessions, as well as auto-
mobiles and even some housing. The most famous example of personal
property in the USSR, however, was the produce from the so-called
"private plots" of the Soviet era. The Model Kolkhoz Statute of 1935
stipulated, and the Stalin Constitution of 1936 confirmed, that kolkhoz
workers could till a small plot of land adjacent to their homes and sell
what they grew at an approved market. The peasants did not actually
own these little gardens, but freedom in disposing of output was incentive enough that the tiny parcels accounted for large proportions of
Soviet production of several fruits, vegetables, and animal products.
Throughout the Soviet era, the plots accounted for at least 20–25
percent of such products, and in the aftermath of the collectivization
disaster, they produced more livestock and dairy products than the collectives, along with most of the potatoes, vegetables, and fruit in the
country (Nove 1989, 233).[8]

Despite the importance of this personal-plot sector, the vast majority
of property in Stalin's USSR fell into the first two categories, state and
collective, and an enormous administrative elite developed to manage
those assets. During NEP, the Bolsheviks had come to a truce with special-
ists from the old regime, but a show trial of "bourgeois wreckers" in 1928
launched a drive to train workers, who were presumably more reliable
than holdovers from the previous era, to fill management positions in the
economy (Fitzpatrick 1992, chaps. 6 and 7). By 1931–32 this drive to
educate had leveled off, but the cohort that had entered higher education
during the intervening years began to fill posts in the government, Party,
and enterprise management, especially during the Great Purges of
1937–38. Many of these new leaders thus owed their positions to Stalin's
violent elimination of their predecessors. They were not immune from
future purges themselves, however; and after Stalin's death, one of the
principal desires of the elite he had created was stability, which later
influenced the course of Soviet elite politics and economic policies.

The state apparatus that these new leaders entered expanded dramatically and grew increasingly complex throughout Stalin's rule. In
December 1929 VSNKh coordinated the activities of thirty-five "associa-

---

8. For more data on nonstate agriculture in the USSR, see Wädekin 1973, 43–80;
Grossman 1977, 25–26.

tions" of enterprises throughout the country (Nove 1989, 203–7). As more property was nationalized, however, and as planning and central control permeated more of the economy, this system of individual associations became unwieldy. In 1930 two of Stalin's closest associates, Sergo Ordzhonikidze and Viacheslav Molotov, took over VSNKh and the Council of People's Commissars (i.e., Council of Ministers), respectively. In 1932 they launched the creation of the ministerial system that would oversee the Soviet economy through 1991 and heavily influence post-Soviet Russian economic development. They abolished VSNKh and replaced it with three commissariats—Heavy Industry (under Ordzhoni-kidze), Light Industry, and Timber—which came under the direct control of the Council of People's Commissars (Tucker 1990, 107). At about the same time, the state planning agency (Gosplan) was also subordinated to the council, and its directives became legally binding. Over time, continued subdivision made the organizational chart of the system more complicated—for instance, there were twenty-one industrial commissariats by 1939 (Nove 1989, 258)—but the principles of hierarchy and centralization persisted.

As the Stalinist state expanded to administer property in all sectors of the economy, it also redistributed authority from the local level to the center. The federal structure of the USSR was a complicated one. Since its official creation in 1923, the Soviet Union was made up of union republics (the Russian Federation, Ukraine, Kazakhstan, and so on), republics within those areas, regions (oblasts, okrugs, and krais), districts (raions), and cities. From the beginning, Stalin fought to subordinate all those entities directly to the government of the Russian Federation, but Lenin disagreed, and the 1924 Constitution established ministries at the all-union, union-republic, republic, regional, and local levels (Pipes 1992). Stalin's 1936 Constitution retained those distinctions, but in practice, the lines of authority ran directly back to Moscow and the USSR Council of People's Commissariats.[9] All-union ministries were directly responsible for segments of the economy deemed especially important, including heavy industry and the defense industry. Union-republic ministries had nominal responsibilities for other segments, including light industry and agriculture, but in reality they had to answer to ministers at the all-union level. Likewise, republic and local administrators were to monitor local industry and the municipal

---

9. See the 1936 Constitution, Articles 14, 74–78, and 83–101; Fainsod 1957, 335–39.

economy, but they were to do so under the guidance of the ministers above them.

The key to staffing this hierarchy, from the highest levels of bureaucracy all the way down to individual enterprises, was the "nomenklatura system." Party committees maintained lists of important posts and reliable candidates to fill them, and they used those lists to approve or reject appointments by the state bureaucracy (Hough 1969, 114–16; Berliner 1957, 13). Managers of the most important factories fell under the jurisdiction of the Central Committee of the CPSU itself, while collective farm chairmen, for example, were the responsibility of district party committees (Hough and Fainsod, 1979, 431; Conquest 1968, 89). Under Stalin, the system was yet another mechanism of control for the dictator, who as general secretary sat atop the appointment process.

The Stalinist system of ownership and control of property was thus remarkably extensive and coherent. Although built on violence, it also enjoyed popular support as the engine of growth that industrialized a feudal society and underpinned the victory over Germany (Kotkin 1995). Furthermore, the murderous Stalin himself was virtually deified (Daniels 1972; Tucker 1990). Even under Stalin, however, central control was incomplete, as managers had to violate some rules to fulfill production quotas, and state and party administrators sometimes colluded with managers for protection from higher layers of supervisors (Berliner 1957, 248–63). Perhaps more important, the system could not sustain the levels of growth from the 1930s in the decades after the war. While the economy continued to expand, it did so at slower and slower rates, while the economies of the West began to recover after the Great Depression and World War II. Stalin's successors had to decide again and again how and whether to remake the economic system he had bequeathed them, and their answers helped reshape control over property in unexpected ways.

POST-STALIN REFORMS: NEW HIERARCHIES ON TOP OF OLD

After Stalin died in 1953, the next two Soviet leaders, Nikita Khrushchev (1953–64) and Leonid Brezhnev (1964–82), repeatedly tried to coax better performance out of the Soviet economy, sometimes to increase the supply of consumer goods, at other times to achieve military parity with the West, and always to demonstrate the economic superiority of Soviet socialism to Western capitalism. They faced the unenviable task

of confronting the shortcomings of Stalin's system without his administrative or personal authority. Several important studies have examined
Khrushchev and Brezhnev's leadership styles, the relative radicalism or
conservatism of their policy goals, and the aspects of the Soviet system
that constrained their efforts to reform it (Bialer 1980; Breslauer 1982;
Bunce 1981; Cohen 1985; Colton 1984; Hough and Fainsod 1979;
Linden 1990 [1966]; Tatu 1968). The cumulative effect of their reforms
on real control over productive assets in the USSR, however, has received
far less attention.

Khrushchev and Brezhnev differed markedly in their personalities
and approaches to politics. If Khrushchev was combative and flamboyant, Brezhnev was conciliatory and plain. Where Khrushchev launched
a campaign of de-Stalinization as part of his attempt to chip away at the
system Stalin had created, Brezhnev partially rehabilitated the tyrant as
part of his. Nevertheless, both leaders dealt with similar problems in the
realm of economics. That is, while the economy continued to grow at a
respectable pace until at least the early 1980s, leaders grew increasingly
frustrated with the interference of ministries in the micro-level decisions
of enterprises and with the failure of firms and bureaucrats to cooperate
across ministerial lines. Several Soviet scholars and policy makers argued
that Stalin's hyper-statization had perverted socialism and needed
significant reform.[10] Over the next thirty years, therefore, new policies
sought to free parts of the economy from the stultifying control of the
state by restructuring the mechanisms of administration inside enterprises and in the bureaucracy. The reforms failed to rejuvenate the
economy, and several of them were reversed within a few years, but they
slowly remade the system of control over property in the USSR.

Reforming Enterprises and Bureaucracies

In attempting to redraw the lines of economic command etched by
Stalin, Khrushchev and Brezhnev focused attention both on individual
enterprises and on the overarching administrative system. Farms and
factories, they and their administrations argued, could produce better
goods more efficiently if managers and workers were allowed to make
more independent decisions and had to face monetary consequences
for the outcomes of those decisions. At the same time, an increasingly

---

10. Lewin (1974), esp. 300–333, examines the connection between those proposals and a reconsideration of NEP.

complex economy demanded better communication between ministries and enterprises and more cooperation across sectoral lines. The two leaders pursued those goals in different fashions, but their policies were not always contradictory, stemming as they did from a similar understanding of the shortcomings of the economic system.

In one of his most famous enterprise-level changes, Khrushchev supported what became known as the "link" system of farming, aimed at increasing production and decreasing ministerial interference. Under that system, a small group of collective-farm workers took responsibility for a distinct tract of land within the larger farm (Yanov 1984, esp. 23–64). The group cared for the land from tilling to harvest and was paid according to output, rather than hours worked. The state still owned the land, but the policy significantly altered who controlled the property, and the links consistently delivered higher yields than state and collective farms in the early 1960s.[11]

Brezhnev significantly reduced support for the link reforms, while at the same time easing restrictions on the size of private plots, but his enterprise-level reforms did not simply represent a return to the past. Largely at the insistence of Prime Minister Aleksei Kosygin, Brezhnev introduced changes in industry that sought to limit ministries' control over state property and give more authority to enterprise managers. Thus a 1965 decree handed managers greater authority to make production and pricing decisions, decreased the number of compulsory directives from the ministries, and set plan targets in terms of goods sold, rather than goods produced (Nove 1989, 367).

At the ministerial level, Khrushchev's clearest attack on the power and influence of the state nomenklatura came in his abolition of central economic ministries and creation of regional economic councils (*sovnarkhozy*). Arguing that Moscow was too far removed from the daily workings of factories to provide effective guidance, Khrushchev and his supporters claimed that the new councils would function as better monitors and directors of state property (Nove 1989, 337). This particular restructuring of ministries appeared to have little real effect, as many of the bureaucrats from the supposedly disbanded ministries joined an expanded Gosplan or the Moscow offices of the sovnarkhozy, never moving and never changing the essence of their jobs (Whitefield 1993,

---

11. Even as he supported the link system, Khrushchev's policy on collective farmers' personal plots was ambiguous. He eliminated compulsory deliveries for the plots, but he also restricted their size and limited peasants' rights to raise livestock. See Wädekin 1973, 274–301.

27). Furthermore, conservative elements of the government successfully pressured Khrushchev to begin consolidating the sovnarkhozy into larger units almost immediately after his initial decentralization campaign (Linden 1990 [1966], 105). The issue of reducing negative bureaucratic influence, however, never disappeared. When Brezhnev confronted the question, he decided that the sovnarkhozy were a mistake, and he abolished them in 1965, recreating the central economic ministries. Nevertheless, he tinkered with the ministerial structure in 1973 and again in 1979, never seeking to upend the Stalinist system as Khrushchev had but instead hoping to refine it.

One type of reform on which Khrushchev and Brezhnev largely agreed was enterprise amalgamation, which had implications for both enterprise management and ministerial control. For Khrushchev, the focus was on agrarian enterprises. Since the end of collectivization, the Soviet government had encouraged state and collective farms to consolidate into ever larger entities, and Khrushchev continued that trend. By the mid-1960s, individual collective and state farms often included thousands of hectares of land and typically produced a wide array of outputs, ranging from field crops to livestock to fruits and vegetables (Laird and Laird 1970, 40). Moreover, beginning in 1961, Khrushchev began to create Territorial Production Administrations that coordinated the activity of several farms in a geographic area under the direction of party committees (Hedlund 1984, 72; Laird and Laird 1970, 45). Creating these larger entities established both a potential counterweight to Moscow bureaucrats and a new hierarchy of control at individual farms.

In the 1970s the Brezhnev leadership also began to integrate industrial enterprises into larger organizations. Over 10,000 firms were merged with others as part of this campaign, reducing the number of independent enterprises from 47,858 in 1970 to 36,630 in 1980 (Gorlin 1985, 362). Ostensibly, the newly integrated units—variously called industrial associations, interbranch organizations, territorial-production complexes, and other names—could improve coordination among participating enterprises, reduce the need to communicate through ministries, and thus diminish bureaucrats' power to meddle in the affairs of firms (Gorlin 1985, 362–63).

In addition to industrial integration, the Brezhnev government continued to pursue both horizontal and vertical integration in agriculture. After 1976 horizontal integration took the form of "interfarm associations" (*mezhkhoziaistvennye obedineniia* [MKhO]), of which there were more than ten thousand by 1985 (Litvin 1987, 66–67). Those organizations combined three to ten adjacent farms into a single unit, which then received aggregate plan targets, rather than goals for each individual farm. In principle, then, if one kolkhoz enjoyed a comparative advantage in producing potatoes and another in producing grain, the two could form an MKhO, and overall output would increase because of specialization. At the same time, vertical integration led to "agro-industrial associations" (*agropromyshlennye obedineniia* [APO]), which united farms with processors and other related enterprises (Litvin 1987, 69). After experimenting with the system for a few years, the administration in 1982 extended the APO program to the whole country, creating an APO in each raion and then uniting those organizations under a regional hierarchy, all in the name of improved coordination (Litvin 1987, 125).

Crossed Lines of Control

None of these reforms radically transformed the Soviet economic system or significantly increased economic growth rates. Instead, the periodic creation of new kinds of hierarchies established an increasingly complex system of overlapping and conflicting means of control over property, in which even the largest networks of newly amalgamated firms still found themselves embedded.[12] At the same time, enterprise managers grew increasingly powerful at their own enterprises as they successfully resisted reforms that challenged their authority and took advantage of the limited increases in their power. Most important, they and individual bureaucrats exploited the absence of a coherent command structure to enrich and empower themselves.

From the time of Lenin, Soviet leaders complained about the over-bureaucratization of the system, but their complaints rarely produced demonstrable results. Thus, while there were three ministries in the USSR in 1932, by 1980 there were thirty-six. Indeed, since the administrative system also included a panoply of departments, committees, and other ministry-like organizations, over a hundred organizations issued commands to enterprises (Gorlin 1985, 354). In theory, the command economy operated on the "branch principle" of ministerial organization, where each ministry or similar hierarchy dealt with a separate sector or subsector of the economy (Whitefield 1993, 54). In practice,

12. For more on the resiliency of the ministerial system, see Whitefield 1993.

however, such a system was impossible to maintain, given the intricacy of a modern economy, and the lines of authority became hopelessly convoluted. Even in 1939 the Soviet government recognized 39 official branches of the economy, and by 1971 the number had risen to 162 (Gorlin 1985, 354). Such complexity meant that producers and users of a good often came under different ministries, and even a single production process could cross ministerial lines, terribly complicating issues of product design, schedule, and delivery (Fortescue 1992, 152).

An examination of the agrarian sector illustrates the complexity of the administrative web. By the end of the Brezhnev era, an astonishing array of political and economic actors wielded de jure control rights over assets related to agriculture (see Table 2.1). Within the sector's "first sphere," which supplied inputs to farms, six major state organizations held responsibility for production and distribution. The result could be a coordination nightmare. For example, while the Ministry of Agricultural Machinery oversaw production of fertilizer-spreading equipment, it did not make fertilizer. The production of fertilizer sometimes far outpaced the production of spreaders, while the spreaders were sometimes the wrong size for the fertilizer granules (Hedlund 1984, 176; Litvin 1987, 29).

The Ministry of Agriculture played the main role in governing the "second sphere" of Soviet agriculture—the producers. That organiza-

TABLE 2.1
Major administrative structures for the Soviet agro-industrial complex by the early 1980s

First sphere (inputs)
Ministry of Tractor and Agricultural Machine Building
Ministry of Machine Building for Animal Husbandry and Feed Production
Ministry of Mineral Fertilizer Production
Selkhoztekhnika (for supplying production equipment for agriculture)
Selkhozkhimiia (for supplying agricultural chemicals and related equipment)

Second sphere (producers)
Ministry of Agriculture (multiple subdivisions)
State Committee for Forestry

Third sphere (procurement, processing, and large-scale storage and distribution)
Ministry of Procurement (grain; "technical crops," such as oilseeds)
Ministry of the Meat and Dairy Industry (milk, livestock, and poultry)
Ministry of the Food Industry (fruit, vegetables, and potatoes to be processed)
Ministry of Trade (fruit, vegetables, and potatoes to be sold fresh, largely produced in suburban areas)
Tsentrosoiuz (fruit, vegetables, and potatoes to be sold fresh, largely produced in rural areas)

Sources: Litvin 1987; Hedlund 1984.

tion, however, included subdivisions for poultry, livestock, industrial crops, animal husbandry, grain crops, and more (Litvin 1987, 62–63). Because so few farms focused on just a few crops—by 1985 over 90 percent of kolkhozy and sovkhozy had plan targets for cattle production, 87 percent for grain, 90 percent for milk, 80 percent for potatoes, and 75 percent for vegetables—the potential for conflicting orders just from the Ministry of Agriculture was significant (Litvin 1987, 66).

The "third sphere" of the Soviet agro-industrial complex covered after-farm activities, such as procurement, storage, processing, and distribution. Again, multiple hierarchies tried to direct those exchanges, and the lines between them were frequently blurred. The Ministry of Procurement itself was the largest single piece of the system, buying most of the grain from kolkhozy and sovkhozy and managing all state grain resources, including their storage and utilization (Hedlund 1984, 22–23). In addition, above-plan production from the large farms, as well as about one-quarter of marketed produce from personal plots, went to the ministry, which paid a premium for it (Hedlund 1984, 98). The Ministry of Procurement also supervised the centralized storage facilities and processing for the goods it collected (Litvin 1987, 41–42).

As large as it was, however, the Ministry of Procurement represented a small part of the system overseeing the third sphere. The Ministry of the Meat and Dairy Industry, for example, performed similar functions for most of the milk, livestock, and poultry produced in the country (Litvin 1987, 42). In addition, the Central Union of Consumer Cooperatives (*Tsentrosoiuz*), while technically not part of the state, bought potatoes, fruits, and vegetables, as well as some livestock, usually in rural areas (Hedlund 1984, 23).[13] By the early 1980s about one quarter of marketed produce from personal plots went through Tsentrosoiuz, while collective and state farms could also sell above-plan output through the agency for a commission (Hedlund 1984, 153, 98). Tsentrosoiuz performed relatively little processing but sold its goods through its own network of stores, which were concentrated in rural areas (Van Atta 1993a, 12; Hedlund 1984, 152).

Finally, about half of marketed output from personal plots, as well as some above-plan output from collective and state farms, was sold through the "kolkhoz market" system (Hedlund 1984, 23, 153). Anyone who legally produced food could participate in the system, which in 1980

13. The Ministry of Trade purchased produce and livestock from personal-plot farmers around the cities (Litvin 1987, 41).

included about 5,700 outdoor markets across the country with stalls for about 1.5 million sellers (Hedlund 1984, 107). Turnover stood at about 7.4 billion rubles, but it represented a shrinking proportion of all food sold in the country. In 1950 the markets had accounted for 30 percent of the total; in 1965, 10 percent; and by 1980, only 5 percent, although the markets continued to serve as an important source of quality perishables like fruit, vegetables, and potatoes (Hedlund 1984, 107, 158 n. 76).

From the perspective of individual ministries, two strategies could help alleviate the problems of such overlapping chains of command, but neither was particularly desirable for the system as a whole. First, they could try to issue orders to enterprises that also fell under the jurisdiction of another ministry. Second, and more common, they could create firms, or shops within existing firms, with functions outside their nominal areas of responsibility (Whitefield 1993, 55). Official Soviet literature derided this second tendency as *vedomstvennost*—literally, "departmentalism"—since the creation of such autarchic fiefdoms was economically and administratively inefficient. The criticism had little practical effect, however, as ministries developed more and more capacity outside their area of expertise. By the early 1980s about 20 percent of total output came from firms outside their ministries' specialization, and for some products the proportion was much greater (Gorlin 1985, 354; see also Tables 2.2 and 2.3). Conversely, many different ministries and departments—sometimes several dozen—produced the same types of goods, again rendering production inefficient and administration difficult.

TABLE 2.2
Specialization of Soviet industrial ministries, early 1980s

Product	Percent of output produced under the ministry nominally in charge of the product
Tractors	75
Compressors	75
Machine tools	87
Instruments and automation equipment	57
Trucks	64
Bricks	62
Construction materials	37
Light industry products	86

Source: Gorlin 1985, 355, Table 1.

TABLE 2.3
Number of Soviet industrial ministries and departments
producing specific products

Product	Number of ministries and departments
Sawn timber	70
Building materials	60
Light industry products	over 20
Logging and wood processing	35

Source: Gorlin 1985, 355, Table 2.

The apparent solution to such compartmentalization of authority was to establish overarching bodies that could coordinate the activity of the myriad subunits. Indeed, from very early on, three committees held responsibility for such oversight: Gosplan set production targets; the State Committee for Procurement and Supplies (Gossnab) oversaw supply; and the State Committee on Pricing (Goskomtsen) established prices. In reality, however, lines of authority were less clear. In the early 1980s, while Gosplan decided on production and exchange targets for about two thousand specific goods, and Gossnab directed trades of about fifteen thousand, individual ministries coordinated transactions for about fifty thousand (Gorlin 1985, 356). Likewise, a single ministry in the machine-building sector set over two thousand prices in the late 1960s (Whitefield 1993, 40). Furthermore, the different spheres of agriculture fell under different planning and supply structures. Spheres I and III received their quotas from Gosplan and their inputs from Gossnab, while producers received their orders from the Ministry of Procurement and their supplies from Selkhoztekhnika and Selkhozkhim-iia (Litvin 1987, 40).

Below the top of the system, the administration periodically tried to reemphasize the coordination powers of a particular ministry within a sector. For example, the Ministry of Light Industry and the Ministry of the Gas Industry both received the designation of "head ministry" (*golovnoe ministerstvo*) in the Brezhnev era, meaning they were given final say over the production, supply, and distribution of goods in their sectors, regardless of which other ministries had responsibility for individual firms (Whitefield 1993, 62). In practice, of course, such designations often remained largely on paper. The Ministry of Ferrous Metallurgy, for example, tried and failed to claim authority over the production of tableware; and on a much larger scale, the Ministry of the Petroleum

Industry proved unable to enforce its legal right to coordinate all construction in the sector (Whitefield 1993, 62–63).

Even creating new amalgamations of enterprises, which aimed to reduce conflict among ministries and simplify the operation of enterprises, failed to resolve questions of authority over property. First, the new giants remained embedded in the old networks of supply and procurement Stalin had created. For example, even after Khrushchev abolished the MTS system in 1958, claiming that farms were large enough to own and operate their own equipment, machine repair still took place at central points under the auspices of the state organization Selkhoztekhnika (Litvin 1987, 3; Hedlund 1984, 95). Unsurprisingly, repairs frequently took too long, came at inconvenient times of the season, and lacked real quality control (Hedlund 1984). Furthermore, since planners evaluated Selkhoztekhnika by the volume of services provided, it preferred to sell large pieces of equipment rather than small parts, and it forced farms to take unwanted pieces along with the ones they had ordered (Van Atta 1993a, 12). Finally, all new farm equipment came through Selkhoztekhnika, thus cementing its position as a virtual replacement for the MTSs in Soviet agriculture (Hedlund 1984, 102).

Second, the amalgamation drives emphasized yet another administrative hierarchy, one based on geographic region rather than production process. That decision compounded the coordination problems of a command economy, rather than resolving them, since production and processing capacities within regional economic structures often failed to match. For example, in the Kubanvino APO, located in Krasnodar krai, the grape-growing sovkhozy could only supply the APO's processors with half the raw materials they needed, while other former suppliers fell under the direction of a different APO (Litvin 1987, 122). Integrating enterprises also tended to increase, rather than decrease, the number of ministries with nominal responsibilities for goods produced in the organization, thereby increasing the possibility of interministerial turf wars (Whitefield 1993, 57).

Within this increasingly jumbled network of command and control, managers and bureaucrats expanded their de facto power at enterprises under their direction. Amalgamation drives, for instance, placed ever greater resources under the control of individual managers, such as the director of the dominant farm in an agricultural group (Litvin 1987, 68). In addition, the Ministry of Agriculture reversed a policy dating from collectivization and allowed APOs to construct about two thousand small processing facilities on their own land by 1980, increasing the autonomy of those directors (Van Atta 1993a, 12; Litvin 1987, 124).

In the realm of policy making, as well, enterprise directors strengthened their positions, blocking unfavorable reforms and modifying others. The link policy, for example, never moved far beyond the experimentation stage, despite evidence of success, because managers resisted the loss of land and authority it entailed. The Kosygin reforms, by contrast, withered on the vine not because of managerial resistance, but because of opposition from party leaders who feared the policy would be incorporated into a broader platform of political reform, as had occurred in Czechoslovakia's Prague Spring of 1968. Regardless of the de jure rollback, however, managers often retained their increased influence over production decisions, while still avoiding consequences for running losses.

Most fundamentally, however, the Party and the government steadily lost their ability to monitor enterprises and the lower levels of administration responsible for guiding them. The bureaucracy itself simply grew too large and complicated for the Party or the Council of Ministers to manage; indeed, they could not even agree who had the authority to regulate or punish bureaucratic infractions (Gorlin 1985, 356). Furthermore, with Brezhnev's emphasis on stability in the system and trust in the people who ran it, the Party lost control over the nomenklatura system. In its place developed informal norms that hid quality managers and administrators in low-level positions, promoted inferior ones instead of firing them, and even allowed members of the nomenklatura to pass their positions on to their children (Whitefield 1993, 83–86; Voslensky 1984, 101–2). In that environment, administrative officials and enterprise managers increasingly used state resources for individual profit—taking bribes, embezzling funds, selling goods on the black market, even using parts of state factories as their own private workshops—further clouding the lines of ownership and control in the system (Vaksberg 1991; Simis 1982, 144–79).

A CLUNKY MACHINE STILL CHUGGING ALONG

No one believed more strongly than the Soviet leaders that ownership relations underpinned any political and social system, and throughout their time in power they sought the most effective way to govern property in the USSR. None of their multiple experiments proved wholly successful in stimulating economic performance, especially by the 1970s, and the system's perverse results have been the subject of many deservedly derisive analyses. To stop there, however, is to miss two essential points regarding the control of assets in the USSR that had implications for the late Soviet and post-Soviet eras.

First, while none of the property reforms allowed the Soviet economy to overtake the West, neither did they destroy it. The economy continued to function in the late 1970s and early 1980s, despite slowing growth rates, manifest inefficiencies, and violations of the system's own rules. Nothing in Soviet economic performance preordained either the reforms Mikhail Gorbachev would undertake in the second half of the 1980s or the fall of the USSR in 1991.

Second, and more important for the future of the Soviet Union and Russia, while the various reforms never seriously challenged the principle of universal state ownership of property, they did significantly restructure the mechanisms for enforcing it. Those new mechanisms, in turn, affected the way the system broke down in the late 1980s and thereafter. They did not cause the structure to come apart, but they marked the edges of large pieces that were likely to break off in the face of a seismic shift. That process began in 1985 with a leadership change in the Communist Party, and it only accelerated through the end of the USSR and the first years of the post-Soviet era.

CHAPTER 3

LET THE GAMES BEGIN, 1985-91

The tumultuous period from 1985 to 1991 was one of high hopes, immense changes, and excruciating disappointments in the Soviet Union. What began with promises of political, social, and economic renewal ended with the dissolution of the USSR, the repudiation of state socialism, and an economy in turmoil. During the intervening years, in the context of economic reforms that undermined macroeconomic stability and weakened state control over real assets, the struggle for property began in earnest.

These disastrous results made it easy to paint Mikhail Gorbachev as too timid in his economic reforms and to credit union-republic leaders, especially Boris Yeltsin in Russia, with advocating more rapid reforms in opposition to Soviet "hardliners." In practice, the Gorbachev reforms of ownership laws were generally very radical and certainly did not lag far behind the Russian offerings. The reforms failed to achieve their goals not because of their tentativeness but because of their many unforeseen consequences. This chapter details the process by which new entrepreneurs, managers, and ministers used legal changes and declining supervision to pry assets from the grip of the Soviet state. Their strategies ranged from low-level embezzlement to widespread "privatization by exception," which gave well-connected individuals special permission to reorganize their enterprises or ministries just enough to enjoy the benefits of private ownership without the risks.

In the final years of the Soviet Union, however, the key forces in the struggle for property were the union-republic governments, especially Russia, and the elections that gave them independent political legitimacy. Citizens in most union republics chose legislatures in 1990 and presidents in 1991, and those new governments began to lay claim to ever larger pieces of union property on their territories. By examining that process, this chapter helps explain both the role of property in the fall of the USSR and how the competition for assets could continue and even intensify after 1991 without breaking up the Russian Federation. When the union republics dissolved the USSR at the end of 1991, they eliminated the Soviet state as a player in property redistribution, but the other competitors remained in place, and several new ones emerged. Misappropriation of resources by managers, ministers, and others weakened the Soviet Union but did not cause it to fall. By the same token, when Soviet authorities acquiesced to the union-republican takeover of state assets, their decision did not end the struggle for property. It merely shifted the battleground to Russia.

AUTHORITY GIVEN AND AUTHORITY TAKEN

Innumerable authors have criticized Gorbachev for failing to abandon his commitment to socialism and therefore not pursuing economic reforms sufficiently radical to overcome his country's economic malaise. In reality, while Gorbachev and his supporters couched their advocacy of reforms in the *language* of Soviet socialism, the property laws and decrees of that period represented a radical break with traditional Soviet positions on ownership. "Socialist ideology" proved flexible enough that leaders could bend it to support either the elimination of private property or its expansion.

State control of the means of production, however, was not the only pillar of the Soviet economy. The system also rested on a planning bureaucracy that set targets for all enterprises and monitored the flow of money and products among them. In response to what he saw as the over-bureaucratization of Soviet life, Gorbachev sought to decentralize that system of planning and control. That process empowered not only enterprise managers and other economic actors but also the governments of the union republics, which made huge leaps in legitimacy through legislative and presidential elections in 1990 and 1991. Union-level officials continued to expand the legal bounds of private economic activity, but quarrels over the distribution of political power undermined the ability of either level of government to deliver on promises of a better economy.

Rewriting the Rules: "Socialist" Justifications for Private Property, 1985–89

When he became general secretary in 1985, Gorbachev was well aware of the Soviet system's strengths and weaknesses, and he responded by launching a series of reforms designed to give new freedoms to economic actors. That strategy included devolving authority to enterprises and allowing new players to enter the system. He saw himself in the mold of Vladimir Lenin and Nikita Khrushchev, two earlier Soviet leaders who had decried the stultifying effects of bureaucracy, and his reforms represented a sustained attack on the system of administrative control over property in the Soviet Union.

Preparing for that attack required admitting publicly the problems of the Soviet economic system and rehabilitating arguments from the Soviet 1920s that justified changing property relations. In April 1985, at the first Central Committee Plenum after his selection, Gorbachev announced that, while all Soviet citizens should be proud of such economic achievements as a guaranteed right to work and a cradle-to-grave welfare system, they also needed to admit that the USSR lagged behind most advanced countries in technical and productive capacity (*Materialy plenuma* 1985, 7).[1] At the Twenty-seventh Party Congress in February–March 1986, he claimed the problem lay in slavish adherence to the Stalinist economic model. He directly challenged the Stalinist hierarchy of ownership forms, which heavily favored state ownership, declaring to the assembly that "Socialist property has a rich content; it includes a multi-faceted system of relations" (*Political Report* 1986, 50). Pushing his argument further, and making clear its connection to Lenin's New Economic Policy, he stated that *cooperative* property—which official pronouncements since Stalin had only grudgingly tolerated—"has far from exhausted its possibilities in socialist production and in providing better satisfaction of people's needs."[2] Gorbachev was trying to resurrect Lenin's

1. Even official statistics, which did not take account of population increases, reported annual economic growth from 1981 to 1985 at 3.6 percent, or about a quarter the rate between 1951 and 1955 and less than half that from 1966 to 1970. Given the tendency to over-report performance in the Soviet system, and knowing that unwanted heavy machinery made up much of the economy's output, some scholars conclude that real economic growth was probably negligible or negative by 1985. See White 1993, 104–5.

2. *Political Report* 1986, 51. Some Western scholars have argued that NEP was not a "golden age" worthy of reviving, and even if it were, the 1980s were so different from the 1920s that such resurrection would have been impossible. (See, for example, von Hagen 1990.) Those arguments, however, did not keep NEP from serving as a fertile source of economic reform ideas in the late 1980s.

idea of cooperatives to justify employing market forces to improve economic performance.

That approach produced its first major legal change in 1986, in the form of the Law on Individual Labor Activity.[3] Under its provisions, individuals and their families could operate small-scale businesses outside the purview of the plan, in hopes that they would meet consumer demands that the official economy could not.[4] The law restricted such private economic activity to a few sectors of the economy, prevented entrepreneurs from hiring outside their families, and prohibited most citizens from working in the enterprises full-time. Nonetheless, it was a critical part of the attempt to undermine the Stalinist legacy of ministerial control of property in the USSR.

At the January 1987 Central Committee Plenum, Gorbachev pushed still harder for property reform, asserting that "Leninist postulates on socialism have been treated simplistically," and as a result, socialist property "has not infrequently . . . become 'no one's,' free of charge and without a real owner" (*Materialy plenuma* 1987, 8, 9). A Western microeconomist would scarcely have framed the problem differently. Shortly after the plenum, two USSR Council of Ministers decrees approved the creation of cooperative enterprises in the food and consumer-goods sectors, and the first cooperative restaurant appeared in Moscow shortly thereafter.[5] The new decisions dropped the familial limits of the Law on Individual Labor Activity, allowing unrelated citizens to own and operate cooperatives and hire outside labor. The decrees required all members of the cooperative to be co-owners, so that the enterprise was technically not private, but even that thin veneer of collectivism evaporated in the coming years.

In July 1987 the Soviet legislature passed the Law on the State Enterprise (Association), the single most far-reaching legal change regarding control over state property in the Gorbachev era.[6] In that decision, enterprises received rights of possession, use, and disposition (*vladenie, polzovanie,* and *rasporiazhenie*) over their assets, including the right to

3. For the text of the Law on Individual Labor Activity, see *Pravda*, November 20, 1986:3.

4. A brief discussion of the law appears in Hanson 1990, 83–84.

5. Postanovleniia soveta ministrov SSSR "O sozdanii kooperativov obshchestvennogo pitaniia" and "O sozdanii kooperativov po proizvodstvu tovarov narodnogo potrebleniia," *Sobranie postanovlenii pravitel'stva SSSR,* no. 10 (1987), 195–222, signed February 5, 1987.

6. For an extensive discussion of the debates surrounding the Law on the State Enterprise, see Christensen 1993, esp. chap. 5.

transfer those assets to virtually any other enterprise or person. The law also allowed enterprises to integrate sectorally, regionally, or according to other principles, and the resulting associations would have the final say in allocating assets among subdivisions. Furthermore, enterprises received explicit permission to engage in foreign trade, conduct their deals through ministerial foreign trade associations, and maintain hard-currency bank accounts to facilitate international economic transactions. Finally, the decision allowed state enterprises, not just individual citizens, to form cooperatives. In fact, the law often granted such rights directly to the *manager*, constrained only by principles of workplace democracy, which in practice could be very weak.

In conjunction with a set of resolutions from the June 1987 Central Committee Plenum, the Law on the State Enterprise also had implications for the way the agrarian sector operated in the USSR. Agriculture had traditionally been the most regulated part of the Soviet economy, but the new decisions declared that farms should have greater autonomy in deciding what to grow. Furthermore, plan targets would become less onerous, and farms could make their own decisions about selling surplus produce to processors or directly to consumers. At the opposite end of the production chain, farms received permission to choose their own input suppliers, although the concentration of the Soviet economy often made such freedom irrelevant in the short run (Cook 1990, 143).

By May 1988, when the legislature passed the USSR Law on Cooperation, cooperatives had become private enterprises in all but name. The new law removed most remaining legal obstacles to the operation of cooperatives by lifting limits on their size and vastly extending the list of products and services they could provide.[7] In addition, the law set cooperatives on the same doctrinal pedestal as state-owned enterprises, reflecting the complete ideological resurrection of cooperative ownership.

One section of the law also contained a provision that would develop into the legalization of publicly held corporations, called "joint-stock companies" (*akstionernye obshchestva*). It allowed members of a cooperative or of a state-enterprise labor collective to own "shares" (*aktsii*) in their firm, although the shares had a fixed rate of return and implied no right to influence corporate activity, making them similar to bonds

---

7. The law was signed on May 26, 1988, and published in *Izvestiia*, June 8, 1988:1–4. As other authors have noted, it probably took its name—"On Cooperation," rather than "On Cooperatives"—from Lenin's article of same title, one of NEP's founding texts.

in Western parlance. Leonid Abalkin, Gorbachev's head of the Institute of Economics of the USSR Academy of Sciences since 1986, defended the socialist nature of this apparently capitalist form of ownership by arguing that the income from shares would not be large and could come under the heading of "personal" property (Hanson 1990, 89). This argument demonstrates the almost limitless flexibility of "socialist ideology" and the concomitant difficulty in arguing that it significantly constrained Gorbachev.

In 1989 two processes that had little to do with property reforms—the loss of the East European satellite states abroad and competitive elections to a national legislature at home—contributed to an increasingly tumultuous political environment in the USSR.[8] Despite his declining control of the Party and other political activity by early 1989, Gorbachev continued to marshal support for legalizing the market-oriented ideas he and his team championed. For example, on the eve of the March 26 elections to the USSR Congress of People's Deputies, the Central Committee Plenum of the Communist Party resolved that creating "peasant farms" (*krestianskie khoziaistva*) should be a vital part of efforts to stimulate agricultural output.[9] The farms marked yet another change in the control of agricultural property, a step beyond the rental contracts already in operation, since the farmers could receive additional land free of charge from unprofitable collective and state farms that faced "reorganization or liquidation." The peasant farms would also be freer than the large enterprises to decide what to produce and how much to charge for their goods. They represented the next step in a series of property-reform laws that would have been unthinkable in the Soviet Union just four years earlier.

Administrative Devolution

As one set of reforms eased restrictions on enterprises, the basic units of the economy, Gorbachev also challenged the overarching administrative hierarchy that governed—some would say, "suffocated"—the system as a whole. Within the Communist Party, for example, he radically reshaped the Secretariat, which oversaw the state ministerial structures. In an attempt to undercut the power of Yegor Ligachev and other poten-

---

8. On the election campaign and the new Congress of People's Deputies it created, see Fish 1995, esp. 35–38.

9. The resolution on peasant farms appeared in *Sel'skaia zhizn'*, April 1, 1989.

tial adversaries within the Party, Gorbachev reorganized the Secretariat into an unwieldy mass of commissions under the leadership of different Politburo members (Kotkin 2001, 77).[10] In doing so, he succeeded in erecting considerable barriers to any opponents who hoped to use the Secretariat as a base of power. At the same time, however, the reform weakened the administrative structure of the Party itself, hampering its ability to ride herd over the sprawling executive bureaucracy of an enormous, nominally federated state.

Decentralization of authority within the bureaucracy had far-reaching consequences for the territorial integrity of the USSR. The process of devolution in agriculture, which was much more explicit and extensive than in industry, began in March 1986, when a decree "On Further Improving the Economic Management Mechanism in the Country's Agro-industrial Complex" transferred partial authority for managing the agrarian sector to regional administrations (Cook 1990, 140). The decision in some ways smacked of Khrushchev's many bureaucratic reorganizations, but in this instance it served as the first step toward completely eliminating the all-union government's control over the distribution of food in the USSR.

The March 1989 Central Committee Plenum took another major step in that direction when it abolished Gosagroprom. Gorbachev had created this superministry in 1985, combining the Ministry of Agriculture, the Ministry of the Food Industry, the Committee for Agricultural Machine Supply, and several other entities (Litvin 1987, 127). Gosagroprom's replacement was a much weaker State Committee for Food and Purchasing, which continued to operate the union-level food fund (Chotiner 1992, 166–67). Many of its planning, procurement, and supply functions, however, moved to union-republic and oblast governments, which received responsibility for ensuring the food supply on their own territories, as well as keeping the union-level food fund supplied (Van Atta 1993b, 57; Chotiner 1992, 167; Cook 1990, 143–44). Thus, far from another insignificant administrative reshuffling, this reorganization essentially eliminated the union government's role in most of the agro-industrial complex.

Gorbachev hoped that the decentralization of administrative authority would improve the distribution of food products in the country (Brooks 1990, 31). Lines at retail stores were growing in 1989, even

---

10. The reorganization of the Secretariat was also a part of a broader effort to reduce the Party's direct management of the economy (Gill 1994).

though production was not dropping significantly and, in fact, was rising for a number of goods. Reformers therefore wanted republican, regional, and local leaders to find solutions to their food-supply problems that did not rely on the center. In practice, however, the new freedom simply allowed those leaders and the managers of state and collective farms to avoid making their required deliveries to the all-union food fund (Brooks 1990, 31). It was the kind of conflict between levels of government that would only grow worse.

USSR versus RSFSR: A Question of Power, not Economic Reform

Authors who contend that Gorbachev's reforms were too timid to solve the problems facing the Soviet Union in the late 1980s often contrast him with Boris Yeltsin, who, along with a few other union-republic leaders, had the foresight and political will to undertake the difficult, unpopular reforms necessary to revive the Russian economy. In that view, 1990 serves as a watershed in Soviet history because it was the year that Yeltsin became Speaker of the Russian parliament, the position from which he launched his attack on the foot-dragging Gorbachev. Certainly the union-republic legislative elections of 1990 changed Soviet politics forever. Those votes imbued the union-republic governments with a legitimacy that Gorbachev and his government, who had not competed in free elections, could not duplicate. The ensuing battles between the Russian and Soviet leaderships represented a competition for the right to rule—indeed, for the right of the Soviet Union to exist. It is important to recognize, however, that the world was not witnessing union "hardliners" in combat with Russian "reformers" over how best to transform the economy. In truth, the two groups were not far apart on matters of economic policy—they were at loggerheads over power.

During and after the Russian elections, the Soviet leadership continued to liberalize property laws and lay the foundations for a regulated market economy. The USSR Law on Ownership, passed in March 1990, officially abandoned the Stalinist hierarchy of ownership types, stating that the Soviet Union must be based on a multiplicity of ownership forms, each receiving equal treatment under the law.[11] While the law did not use the term "private property," which many deputies still condemned as the exploitation of man by man, it did introduce the category

---

11. See Block 1991. The property law itself appears in *Izvestiia*, March 10, 1990:2.

of "citizen's property," which could include ownership of the means of production.[12]

In the wake of the Law on Ownership came several other decisions aimed at undermining the dominance of state property. In June 1990, for example, the Law on Enterprises replaced the Law on the State Enterprise. Where the old statute had repeatedly portrayed state enterprises as the "fundamental link" in the socialist economic system, the new one consistently asserted the equality of all enterprises under the law, regardless of ownership form.[13] In the same month, the USSR Council of Ministers allowed shareholders in joint-stock companies to receive dividends based on the firm's performance and the number of shares held.[14] The resolution also provided for the outright privatization of state-owned enterprises: "A state enterprise," the document read, "may be converted to a joint-stock company," and "the shares may be distributed by open tender," rather than simply turned over to workers and managers at the firm.[15]

Finally, in August 1990, the USSR Council of Ministers issued a decision "On Means for Creating and Developing Small Enterprises."[16] In an attempt to boost the supply of goods and services and to combat monopolism, the decision allowed citizens and legal entities to set up small enterprises "based on any form of ownership" in any sector of the economy unless expressly prohibited by another law. The state was not to interfere in product selection, goods distribution, or profit disbursement in the new firms. The new businesses also received a profit tax exemption, as well as state assistance in acquiring inputs, constructing places of business, and other activities. So favorable was this treatment, in fact, that many cooperatives changed their registered form to "small enterprise" in the following months.

By contrast, when the Russian legislature, under the leadership of Boris Yeltsin, met in June 1990 to choose a prime minister, the most important attribute of the candidates appeared to be their willingness

---

12. For examples of legislators' concerns about private ownership, see *Izvestiia*, February 16, 1990:1–2, translated in *Current Digest of the Soviet Press* 42:7, 5.

13. The Law on Enterprises was published in *Ekonomika i zhizn'*, no. 25 (1990): 19–21.

14. "Polozhenie ob aktsionernykh obshchestvakh i obshchestvakh s ogranichennoi otvetstvennost'iu," printed in *Ekonomika i zhizn'*, no. 29 (1990):12–14.

15. Ibid.

16. The decision on small business appeared in a supplement to *Ekonomika i zhizn'*, no. 33 (1990):4.

to take on the all-union government rather than their commitment to radical economic reform. As part of his campaign for the post, deputy Mikhail Bocharov presented a revised version of a plan in circulation at the time for a rapid shift to a market economy. It proposed beginning with macroeconomic stabilization and de-monopolization, proceeding through widespread privatization, and concluding with price liberalization, thus creating the basis for a capitalist system in five hundred days.[17] Yeltsin initially supported Bocharov, but gaining approval for him promised to be difficult at best, and Yeltsin soon threw his support behind the candidacy of Ivan Silaev, who then won handily. Silaev's proposal struck a balance between state management and free market forces, similar to the proposal of the allegedly "conservative" USSR prime minister, Nikolai Ryzhkov.[18] Silaev's plan, however, differed from Ryzhkov's in two important respects. First, Silaev argued that price increases were *not* essential except on goods whose sales were increasing, and in that way he was actually less inclined to plunge the country into a market economy than Ryzhkov. Second, and more important in securing the post of Russian prime minister, Silaev detailed the freedoms the RSFSR deserved from the union government, including the right to decide what state property within Russia the union government could control.

Just days before, on June 12, the parliament had preceded its selection of Silaev—whom Ryzhkov called a "fervent opponent of everything all-union"—with a declaration of sovereignty from the USSR, asserting the supremacy of RSFSR laws on Russian territory (Ryzhkov 1995, 431). Gorbachev later characterized the declaration as the "first nail in the coffin of the Union state" (Gorbachev 1996, 345). It also had direct implications for the distribution of property in the USSR, as control over economic resources became one of the central battlegrounds in the war between the Soviet Union and Russia. On one side, the union government fought to retain control over the national wealth that could provide the resources for effective governance. On the other, control over assets on Russian territory formed an essential part of

17. Bocharov's presentation appears in a stenographic report in *Sovetskaia Rossiia*, June 16, 1990:5–6. The other "Five-Hundred-Day Plan," the result of a USSR-RSFSR working group under Stanislav Shatalin and Grigorii Iavlinskii, appeared as *Perekhod k rynku* (1990a, b).

18. For the Ryzhkov plan in circulation at the time, see "Ob ekonomicheskom polozhenii strany i kontseptsii perekhoda k reguliruemoi rynochnoi ekonomike," *Izvestiia*, May 25, 1990:1–4.

Yeltsin's strategy to pull Russia out of the USSR, so he and the Russian leadership promised lower taxes and less regulation to those "concerns" and "associations" that declared their allegiance to Russia, rather than the Soviet Union.[19] Barring a change of heart by the Soviet or Russian government, the USSR was on a path toward violence or disintegration.

THE FIRST GREAT GRAB

Gorbachev's reforms assumed that giving economic actors greater flexibility to set and pursue output goals would improve the performance of the system. Observers at the time, both inside and outside the USSR, often feared that party and state loyalists would strangle the new private sector, not allowing it to work its magic. In practice, managers, ministers, and others used the new freedoms for what William Baumol has called "destructive entrepreneurship"—activities that benefit only those who engage in them rather than the economy as a whole. Contrary to some expectations, the new freedoms were very real, and the presumed representatives of the old system—such as the Committee for State Security (KGB), local law enforcement, and regional administrators—did not work systematically to stop private economic activity. Instead, they sought to turn it to their advantage, which meant that success for an economic actor lay not in adhering to increasingly unclear planning directives but in bribery, protection, theft, or some combination thereof.

In the context of repressed hyperinflation and weakened planning authority, the new laws encouraged the destructively entrepreneurial to siphon money from the system wherever possible. In addition, imaginative directors and creative bureaucrats exploited the legal changes to pull assets from the grip of the state. Managers of state and collective farms tended to resist the redistribution of farmland, but otherwise the privatization of state assets gathered speed, often creating quasi-state monopolies beyond the control of government or society. Even so, the Soviet state retained some control over the vast majority of its resources until the August 1991 coup attempt, after which the union-republic governments effectively eliminated the USSR as a state by laying claim to those resources.

19. For more on using taxes to sway enterprises' loyalty, see, for example, Deliagin 1991; Sluzhakov 1991.

Embezzlement, Arbitrage, and Transfer Pricing

The most straightforward method members of the Soviet elite used to take advantage of their changing environment was simply to embezzle funds. In some cases, they redirected the state budgets for which they were responsible to create new businesses, as when Vladislav Sedlenek of the Communist Youth League (Komsomol) founded an employment agency with 20,000 Komsomol rubles in 1987 (Kotz and Weir 1997, 121).[20] On a much larger scale, many state enterprise managers siphoned money directly from the state through so-called "pocket banks." Vague language in the 1987 Law on the State Enterprise and the 1988 Law on Cooperation allowed enterprises such as the Volgograd Tractor Factory or the car maker AvtoVAZ to set up banks using very little capital and then to borrow money from the Central Bank at subsidized rates.[21]

The decrees and laws on cooperatives also allowed a new wave of entrepreneurs to enter the pilfering game by creating trading companies. Since there were few restrictions on what cooperatives could do for money, one of the most popular strategies was to buy goods whose prices were regulated and resell them at market prices. Future oligarch Boris Berezovskii, for example, made his first major foray into business in 1989 by forming the company Logovaz, technically a joint-venture with an Italian firm (Klebnikov 2000, 33–34). Though the company was allegedly created to provide advanced technology to Russian car maker AvtoVAZ, it made its money reselling AvtoVAZ cars it had bought below cost or with credits that would never be repaid (Klebnikov 2000, 35, 91–95).

One particularly notorious trading firm was ANT. Former KGB officer Vladimir Riashentsev created the company in 1987 as a cooperative, and it received support from the highest levels of power (Timofeev 2000, 214–21; Jones and Moskoff 1991, 88–89). In May 1989, for example, Prime Minister Ryzhkov granted the cooperative permission to barter with international partners and purchase above-plan output from Soviet enterprises, including those in the defense industry. In October of the same year, Deputy Prime Minister Vladimir Gusev allowed it to export goods without obtaining a license for each shipment. Even Yegor Ligachev, the ideologically conservative second-in-command in the Soviet Communist Party, offered words of support for ANT: "In my opinion, these guys are building the kind of socialist cooperative Lenin

---

20. For a rich analysis of the unofficial privatization of Komsomol assets, see Solnick 1998, esp. 101–24.

21. For more detail on banking maneuvers, see Johnson 1994, esp. 977–79.

dreamed of" (Timofeev 2000, 216). We will never know Lenin's dreams, but ANT folded in disgrace when authorities inspected one of its export shipments and discovered a load of Soviet tanks.

Many of the firms created under the new laws, however, were not separate entities engaged in trade or production. Instead, a growing number of directors of industrial firms turned parts of their enterprises—such as a particular shop or the accounting office—into "cooperatives" with which the original firms did business. Creating cooperatives within state enterprises served several purposes, some of which may have benefited workers inside the firm, but none of which provided much stimulus to the economy as a whole (Burawoy and Hendley 1992, 380–81). First, cooperatives gave management more flexibility in setting wages, which in the late Soviet context usually meant *higher* pay for workers. Employees at individual firms obviously benefited from these increases, but the aggregate effect was to fuel inflation (Woodruff 1999, 65–66). The second purpose of an internal cooperative was to serve as an outlet for the large firm's goods, since cooperatives could set much higher prices for their outputs. Even when the state imposed a maximum markup on goods, managers of state enterprises could set up a chain of cooperatives and resell a product several times in order to achieve market-level returns. Finally, these internal structures could help the main enterprise avoid taxes. The initial laws taxed cooperatives at a dramatically lower rate than state enterprises, so managers had every incentive to use transfer pricing to realize profits in the cooperatives, even if they intended to return those profits to the main enterprise.[22]

Even relying on official statistics, which probably understated the impact, the number and economic activity of cooperatives exploded between 1987 and 1990 (see Table 3.1). At the end of that period, nearly a quarter of a million cooperatives employed 4.4 percent of Soviet workers and accounted for more than 6 percent of the country's gross domestic product (GDP). It is impossible to know exactly how many of those cooperatives were legitimate production or trading units and how many were designed to bleed resources from the state, but the majority of them operated in close connection with state-owned enterprises. In 1988 such cooperatives accounted for 37 percent of the total and 57

22. For other examples of how managers used these laws to their own benefit, see Kotz and Weir 1997. At the time, however, most Western scholarship focused on the failure of the enterprise law to grant managers complete authority to run their firms and on bureaucratic resistance to cooperatives. See, for instance, Heymann 1990; Tedstrom 1990.

TABLE 3.1
The Soviet cooperative sector, 1987–90

	1987	1988	1989	1990
Production, trade, and service cooperatives (1000s)	14	80	193	245
Workers employed (1000s)	200	1,500	4,855	6,000
Value of production (bn rubles)	0.35	10.3	40.3	67
Share of GDP (%)	no data	no data	4.4	6.1

Source: Radygin 1994, 149.

percent of the sector's output (Tedstrom 1990, 127). By late 1990, at the end of the "cooperative boom," more than 80 percent of cooperatives operated inside state enterprises (Radygin 1994, 26–27).

Forming a cooperative was not the only way to create a well-connected business, however, and many industrial managers exploited the new leasing laws in similar ways. Beginning with the 1987 Law on the State Enterprise, and developing further over the next two years, this legislation allowed managers and workforces to lease sections of their firms from the main enterprise or from the supervising ministry.[23] Leased enterprises tended to be much larger than cooperatives: the twenty-four hundred that existed in the USSR at the beginning of 1991 employed 1.5 million workers and produced 5.2 percent of total industrial output (Filatotchev, Buck, and Wright 1992, 275). They did share some similarities with cooperatives, however. While performance data suggest that leased enterprises grew faster and fulfilled their state orders more reliably than traditional state enterprises, closer investigation revealed that those supposedly independent firms "[had] been set up to exploit through arbitrage the difference between state input prices . . . and uncontrolled prices for the finished goods and services" (Filatotchev, Buck, and Wright 1992, 276–77).

All the reforms just discussed in the industrial context—trade liberalization, cooperatives, and leasing—applied to the agrarian sector as well. For example, the 1988 draft model charter for collective farms increased

---

23. "Arenda gosudarstvennogo predpriiatiia trudovym kollektivom," *Ekonomicheskaia gazeta*, no. 36 (1988):17; "Osnovy zakonodatel'stva Soiuza SSR i soiuznykh respublik ob arende," *Ekonomicheskaia gazeta*, no. 49 (1989):14–15. See also Hanson 1990, 89.

their autonomy to plan their own operation and finances, including engaging in trade (Wegren 1998a, 64). Likewise, Gorbachev argued that cooperatives could help stimulate agricultural production, and he advocated allowing production brigades to operate as cooperatives, which could open their own bank accounts, lease their equipment from the farm, and use it as they saw fit (Van Atta 1993a, 16). His government also encouraged the development of processing, supply, procurement, and retail cooperatives within the large farms (Van Atta 1993a, 17). Finally, the reforms allowed families and groups to lease plots of land from the collective and state farms in order to operate more independently and, advocates hoped, more efficiently (Hanson 1990, 88–90).[24]

Large farm managers, however, did not exploit the new rules in the same way as their industrial brethren. Instead, they tended to react much as analysts had *feared* industrial managers would: by using their positions to thwart would-be entrepreneurs. Many farm directors, for example, resisted leasing altogether, simply refusing to rent out "their" land (Van Atta 1993a, 17). The Soviet government responded in 1989 by offering to cancel the debts of farms that adopted leasing contracts, but the debt reduction simply fueled inflation, and the leasing arrangements usually remained on paper (Wegren 1992a, 11, 15; Brooks 1990, 39). When managers did allow small groups to set up enterprises with land and equipment from the large farm, they tended not to use the small farms as off-book centers for arbitrage and embezzlement as industrialists did. Instead, they used their own positions as monopoly suppliers of inputs and monopsony buyers of outputs to squeeze the small farms for all they were worth (Brooks 1990, 38, 41). Located far from export markets and facing a de facto monopsony buyer in the state, managers of the large farms feared the loss of land, and therefore productive capacity, more than they relished the chance to set up networks for selling their goods at slightly higher prices on the sly.

Ownership and control of the production units in agriculture (i.e., farms) therefore did not change spectacularly in the last years of the Soviet era. Post-Soviet Russian land reform bore some striking similarities to the Soviet version and therefore faced many of the same obstacles, as the next chapter shows. Even the experience of agriculture, however, demonstrates that economic elites in the Soviet period reacted rationally to constraints and opportunities. The next section examines how they

24. For a discussion of small-scale experiments with leasing in Orlov oblast as early as 1985, see Stroev, Zlobin, and Mikhalev 1998, 10–11.

took advantage of their environment to pull entire enterprises and more out of state hands.

Firms, Networks, and Ministries

The shenanigans just described chipped away at the capacity of the Soviet state over time. Inflationary wage increases and backdoor loans, as well as the diversion of state income and tax revenues, all impeded the government's efforts to fund itself and its vast array of social programs. Even greater repercussions, however, stemmed from a phenomenon I call "privatization by exception": the ever widening stream of decisions from the Council of Ministers to approve privatization of individual enterprises, networks of firms, or entire ministries.

Such privatizations often began as leasing arrangements, since many leases included a provision for management and employ buy-outs. The Moscow Ventilator Factory (Moven), for example, followed this path, having become a cooperative and leased its assets from the state in 1989 (Filatotchev, Buck, and Wright 1992, 278; "Privatisation in the Soviet Union" 1991). In 1990 the management of the company borrowed about 6.5 million rubles (around $3.6 million at the official exchange rate) from its customers, especially the Svetlana association in Leningrad, to purchase a controlling stake in the company. The loan was interest-free and could be repaid over ten years, which meant inflation was likely to reduce its real value to zero.[25]

This strategy was also prevalent in the agro-industrial sector, where managers of processors and enterprises of similar structure took advantage of the new environment—when they could privatize without losing control of land, agrarians were ready. For example, in 1989, the collective at the Ust-Labinskii Sugar Factory in Krasnodar krai leased the assets of the factory with the right to buy them early. They purchased the factory outright on December 26, 1990 (Kuz'minskii 1991, 9). In another instance, the labor collective of the Rossiia Breeding Factory in Cheliabinsk oblast received ownership of its enterprise at no charge in July 1990 (Grigor'ev 1991, 7–8). Likewise, an administrative decision launched the privatization of the Stavropolskoe Broiler Association at about the same time (Grigor'ev 1991, 8).

---

25. Clarke et al. (1994) saw essentially similar processes at a garment factory, a coal mine, and a chemical factory between 1989 and 1991, although management sometimes bought the company using retained earnings rather than cheap loans.

Privatization by exception extended not only to individual firms but to much larger networks and associations as well. For example, in the late 1980s a group of about twenty-five firms associated with the Altaiselmash Agricultural Machine-building Plant converted themselves into joint-stock companies, each with an individual account in the state banking system (Kokorev and Tolstov 1995). In 1991 the group formally became a "concern," in which the member firms owned pieces of one another, and they pooled their resources to create Altaibiznes-bank to serve as their pocket bank.

Examples of such transformations abound. In May 1988, for instance, thirty-three enterprises in Leningrad withdrew from their ministries and formed the associations Energomash and Tekhnokhim (Johnson and Kroll 1991, 289). The Saratov Aviation Plant (SAZ) is another much-studied example, and the truck-building association KamAZ and the auto-making behemoth AvtoVAZ also followed this path.[26] All these changes required permission from the USSR Council of Ministers, and it was forthcoming. Prime Minister Nikolai Ryzhkov himself, for example, signed off on the creation of Reforma, a fund made up of seventy-two organizations, including parts of KamAZ. The management of the fund included Soviet Finance Minister Viktor Pavlov and State Bank (Gosbank) Chairman Viktor Gerashchenko (Nemtsov 1990b).

Even the privatization of networks, however, was not the most impressive example of the surreptitious transfer of assets out of state control in the late Gorbachev era. The combined forces of experimental marketization, newly unshackled greed, and increasingly limited state authority achieved their full expression in the redistribution of the assets of entire ministries or subdivisions. That process, which began in 1989 and accelerated through the end of the Soviet Union, combined a desire to expose state institutions to market pressures with an inability to monitor or regulate the newly created entities (see Table 3.2). While they probably would not have spelled the end of the USSR without a strong push from the Russian Federation, the enormous conglomerates created in this fashion dramatically weakened the Soviet state's remaining controls over asset use.

The rules governing the creation of these new entities were murky at best. Officially, they were part of a strategy to improve ministerial

---

26. On SAZ, see Hendley 1992, 1998; McFaul and Perlmutter 1995. On KamAZ, see Christensen 1999, 50–54. On AvtoVAZ, see Kryshtanovskaya and White 1996, 721.

TABLE 3.2
The transformation of Soviet ministries, 1989–91

	Ministry of	New entity
Pre-coup (1989–1991)	Production of Mineral Fertilizers + parts of Gosagroprom	Agrokhim
	Construction Materials	State Association of the Industry of Construction Materials
	Metallurgy	Norilsk Nickel
	Natural Gas Industry	Gazprom
	Construction of Enterprises for the Oil and Gas Industry	Neftegazstroi
	Water Industry Construction	State Concern for Water Industry Construction
	Chemical and Petroleum-Refining Industry	A series of corporations and concerns
Post-coup (Aug.–Dec. 1991)	Automobile and Agricultural Machine-Building	Automobile and Agricultural Machine-Building Holding Association
	Heavy-Machine-Tool Making (parts of it)	Transport Machinery Concern
	Electrotechnical Industry	Inter-republican stock company
	Petrochemical Industry	Inter-republican stock corporation
	Metallurgy	Roschermet and Rostsvetmet
	Defense (parts of it)	Corporations and concerns
	Glavalmazzoloto	Rosalmazzoloto
	All-Union Wood Ministry	All-Russian Wood Concern

Sources: Whitefield 1993; Kroll 1991; Fortescue 1993; Hough 1997: Burawoy and Krotov 1992.

performance by exposing the organizations to market pressures. Soviet Prime Minister Nikolai Ryzhkov appointed the academic Leonid Abalkin to head a new State Commission on Economic Reform in the summer of 1989 (Abalkin 1991, 25–26). The commission included many well-known figures in Soviet economic reform, including Abel Aganbegian, Stanislav Shatalin, Boris Milner, Evgenii Yasin, Grigorii Yavlinskii (who did not remain long), and S. Assekritov (who became the director of the USSR State Property Fund in 1991) (Abalkin 1991, 54–60). In addition to making broad recommendations about Soviet economic reform, the commission approved the conversion of several ministries and subministries into "state-owned concerns" that were to compete in the marketplace for consumers, workers, and profits. In practice, however, many of the approvals were retroactive, while the commission's instructions were imprecise and incomplete (Whitefield

1993, 230). The transformations on the ground typically resulted from individual Council of Ministers decisions or decrees of the ministerial elites themselves.

In this environment, the Ministry of the Production of Mineral Fertilizers transformed itself into the State Agro-Chemical Association (Agrokhim) in 1989, drawing many of its parts from Gosagroprom, which was abolished at the same time (Whitefield 1993, 229). In the same year, the Ministry of Construction Materials was reorganized into eight separate concerns, which together formed the State Association of the Industry of Construction Materials (Whitefield 1993, 228). The two most prominent examples of reorganization in 1989 were the non-ferrous metals conglomerate Norilsk Nickel and the natural-gas giant Gazprom, both of which were formed on the basis of previous ministries (Kroll 1991, 153–54). This process continued in 1990, as the USSR Council of Ministers approved converting the Ministry of Construction of Enterprises of the Oil and Gas Industry into the state concern Neftegazstroi; the Ministry for Water Industry Construction into the State Concern for Water Industry Construction; and the Ministry of the Chemical and Petroleum-Refining Industry into a series of corporations and concerns (Whitefield 1993, 228–29). In the last case, the minister resigned during the reorganization, only to re-emerge in the management of the new enterprises (Whitefield 1993, 228).

The managers of many of these organizations insisted that they were running self-financed businesses, but such claims were usually a myth. Instead, while they had greater control over their financial and other resources than they had enjoyed under the old system, they still faced soft budget constraints. That is, they continued to receive funding from the state, and there was no indication that it would be cut off because of poor business performance. Furthermore, individual enterprises within the giant conglomerates actually lost some of the autonomy in allocating resources or establishing contracts that they had acquired as part of earlier reforms (Whitefield 1993, 230–31). While the leaders of the new entities could now direct resources wherever they liked, including into their own pockets, they hardly represented progress toward a functioning market economy.

The privatization of ministries and ministerial departments continued to accelerate through the end of 1990 and the beginning of 1991. Between November 1, 1990, and April 30, 1991, for example, the number of concerns in the USSR jumped from 73 to 164; the number of consortia from 66 to 92; and the number of associations from 842 to

1,790 (Whitefield 1993, 227, Table 6.1). Most of them represented direct descendants of ministerial organizations.

Even in the face of such apparent decay, the Soviet government still included nearly eighty ministries and state committees by the time of the August 1991 coup attempt (Whitefield 1993, 254, 257). Most property remained in the Soviet government's hands until the final months of the USSR. With the putsch, however, the nature of the struggle over property changed, as the governments of the union republics, especially Russia, stepped fully into the fray as rulemakers and eventually property takers.

Shortly after the coup attempt, Yeltsin pressured Gorbachev to create the USSR Committee for the Operational Management of the Economy, the membership of which suggested Russia's new strength. Russian Prime Minister Ivan Silaev chaired the committee, which included three deputy chairmen: Arkadii Volskii, an industrialist with long-standing connections to Gorbachev; Grigorii Yavlinskii, an economist favoring more rapid reforms than Gorbachev; and Yurii Luzhkov, deputy mayor of Moscow (Hough 1997, 451). In practice, even that stacked roster understated the Russian government's role, since the committee almost always approved decisions of the Russian Council of Ministers, which took control of conversions. By the end of August, the Russian government claimed jurisdiction over the operations of all union-level ministries on Russian territory. Soon thereafter, ostensibly to allow greater flexibility in negotiating the unpredictable rapids of the transition to a new political and economic order, it granted blanket approval of ministers' decisions on most issues, including ministerial conversions (Whitefield 1993, 257).

The ruling hastened the metamorphoses of Soviet ministries to quasi-state organizations under Russian jurisdiction. For example, the Ministry of Automobile and Agricultural Machine-Building became the Automobile and Agricultural Machine-Building Holding Association, while a network of enterprises inside the Ministry of Heavy-Machine-Tool Making became the Transport Machinery Concern (Fortescue 1993, 36). In a similar fashion, the Ministry of the Electrotechnical Industry transformed itself into an "inter-republican stock company," including assets outside Russia (Hough 1997, 452–53). The Soviet subministry for diamonds and gold (Glavalmazzoloto) became the Russian diamond and gold company Rosalmazzoloto, while the All-Union Wood Ministry became the All-Russian Wood Concern (Whitefield 1993, 260; Burawoy and Krotov 1992). In October 1991 the Russian Council of Ministers converted the Ministry of Metallurgy into two separate corporations, Russian Ferrous Metallurgy (Roschermet) and Russian Nonferrous Metallurgy (Rostsvetmet) (Fortescue 1993, 36n2).[27] In the defense sector, the Russian leadership in November formally dissolved several defense-ministry organizations and revived them as corporations and concerns (Whitefield 1993, 260).

With the Soviet bureaucratic hierarchy largely a figment of its own imagination in the wake of these takeovers, the Committee for the Operational Management of the Economy pledged to abolish all union-level ministries except for those in foreign affairs, internal affairs, railways, power, atomic energy, and customs (Whitefield 1993, 254). At the same time, Yeltsin used his newly awarded powers of issuing decrees on economic questions to cut off Russian funding for central organizations, and the Russian government officially laid claim to all USSR ministerial property, organizations, and enterprises on Russian territory (Whitefield 1993, 255). Finally, on November 28, 1991, Yeltsin issued a decree establishing the outlines of the post-Soviet Russian executive apparatus.[28] All that remained of the Soviet Union were its international obligations and privileges, which Russia assumed in the weeks between the creation of the fig-leaf Commonwealth of Independent States on December 8 and the resignation of Mikhail Gorbachev on December 25.

PROPERTY, THE END OF THE USSR, AND THE NEXT STAGE

In the Soviet Union, if you knew what someone thought of Stalin's time in power, you could easily guess how that person evaluated everything that came after. In the words of the period, "Tell me your opinion about our Stalinist past, and I'll know who you are" (Cohen 1985, 93). In post-Soviet Russia, one can tell a great deal from how someone explains the fall of the USSR. A new version of the old adage might read, "Tell me why you think the Soviet Union collapsed, and I'll know how you understood all that followed." Likewise, making sense of the struggle for

27. See also the decree "On the Work of the Metallurgical Industry on the Territory of the RSFSR" from October 15, 1991. The former minister of metallurgy, Nikolai Gugis, became the vice president of Russian Ferrous Metallurgy, and the former deputy minister took charge of Rostvetmet (Whitefield 1993, 260).

28. Ukaz prezidenta RSFSR no. 242, "O reorganizatsii tsentral'nykh organov gosudarstvennogo upravleniia RSFSR," November 28, 1991. Available at fpf.referent.ru:4005/security/1/1275/1; last accessed July 22, 2003.

property in the post-Soviet era depends heavily on understanding how conflicts over assets at the end of the Soviet period did and did not contribute to the dissolution of the USSR. More than a decade of research has produced a range of explanations for the breakdown of the Soviet Union, but two schools of thought in particular have focused on the role of economic performance and policies in the collapse and what that has meant for Russian development since.[29] While each offers useful insights, they sometimes conflate the causes of economic decline and those of political fragmentation and therefore hinder our understanding of the post-Soviet Russian political economy and the struggle for property that permeated it.

One of the most widely promulgated explanations for the fall of the Soviet Union holds that poor economic performance, which grew especially bad in 1990 and 1991, undermined the stability of the political system, eventually allowing the Soviet people to throw off their increasingly inept oppressors. This argument implies that post-Soviet Russian leaders needed to liberalize all facets of the economy as rapidly as possible in order to defeat the temporarily disoriented hardliners. It produced prescriptions of economic "shock therapy," a sense of Western (especially American) triumphalism, and a running debate over which Russian leaders were real "reformers" who deserved international support and which were not (e.g., Aslund 1995; Lipton and Sachs 1990).

No one should underestimate the macroeconomic imbalances in the late Soviet economy or their effects on daily life in the USSR. The reforms of *perestroika* weakened state controls over the emission of money in the Soviet system in four important ways. First, cooperatives allowed enterprises to raise wages, which increased the cash money supply. Second, the "pocket banks" funneled money from the Central Bank to their affiliated enterprises, effectively offering negative real interest rates. Third, the state continued to lend money without restraint. The Law on the State Enterprise explicitly stated that a firm that ran short of money and could not obtain loans elsewhere would receive either cash or loan guarantees from its supervising agency. Meanwhile, the direct production subsidy to agriculture stood at about 11 percent of GDP by the end of the 1980s, and subsidies to the agro-industrial

---

29. The many important studies of the fall of the USSR that emphasize causes other than ownership include Bunce 1999; Beissinger 2002; Roeder 1993; Suny 1993; Hale 2004, 2005; Kotkin 2001.

complex as a whole in 1989 and 1990 were higher than the total budget deficit in those years (Brooks 1990, 35; Liefert 1993, 31). Such lending practices led both to exploding budget deficits and to the fourth major cause of over-active monetary emission: debt forgiveness. In both 1989 and 1990, for example, the state wrote off approximately 70 billion rubles of bad loans in agriculture alone, essentially printing money (Brooks 1990, 34; Wegren 1992a, 12). All these forces put enormous upward pressure on prices, most of which the state refused to free. Instead, it periodically promised to raise prices in the future, which led to panic buying and hoarding. Lines for basic goods were widespread in the late Gorbachev era, and they shaped many perceptions of the Soviet political economy as a whole.

Scholars need to be cautious, however, in drawing conclusions from the late Soviet Union's miserable macroeconomic condition. First, leaping from an observation about poor economic performance to an argument that the government had to collapse is questionable at best.[30] Countless regimes—including the Bolshevik government after the 1917 Revolutions, the Soviet Union during World War II, and Russia in the 1990s—have survived crushing economic downturns, including hyper-inflation. Second, while the macroeconomy clearly needed some kind of radical fix, it does not follow that the state had to abandon control over *property* as rapidly as possible.[31] Instead, weakening state control over property in the USSR often bred additional problems—analysts must be wary of offering a wide set of prescriptions and interpretations based on observations as narrow as macroeconomic data.

A more convincing attempt to tie changes in the Soviet economy to the administrative breakdown that brought down the USSR centers on the shift of state property from government to private control. One version of this argument holds that economic elites, recognizing that they could enjoy even greater privileges under capitalism than under Soviet socialism, threw in their lot with Boris Yeltsin in his struggle against Gorbachev and union-level authorities (Kotz and Weir 1997). A more compelling version—indeed, one that many analysts take farther than its author seemed to intend—argues that events were not so well

---

30. Attributing poor performance to inherent flaws in the Soviet model is also analytically dubious, given the extent of the reforms that preceded the troubles of the final years.

31. Woodruff (1999) has argued very effectively that the usual prescriptions for the macroeconomy—price liberalization and tight monetary policy—also were probably misguided.

planned. According to that view, as entrepreneurs, admirable or not, absconded with more and more assets, they undermined state capacity to the point that the USSR collapsed. The government could not collect the revenues to perform basic monitoring functions; individual bureaucrats and managers saw their colleagues successfully pilfering and wanted a piece of the action, which led to a "bank run" on state-owned property; and soon civil servants had collectively "stolen the state" itself.

The bank run metaphor comes from Steven Solnick (1998), and it captures much of what happened to real assets in the late Soviet era. The analysis in this chapter is generally consistent with it: there can be little doubt that bureaucrats and managers appropriated more and more property as the Soviet system weakened and that their actions further undermined state capacity. Solnick's strongest claims, however, are about the decline or transformation of hierarchies in the area of Soviet youth policies; he is much more circumspect in his arguments about industrial property or the Soviet system as a whole. When his images are used in common discourse on property and the fall of the USSR, they can oversimplify that set of events and leave the analyst unable to explain what came next. First, in analyzing the run-up to the fall, the stealing-the-state argument can hide the heterogeneity of actors and strategies for appropriating assets. For example, it can overstate the role of managers and mid-level bureaucrats and the unintended consequences of Gorbachev's reforms while underemphasizing the actions of top-level administrators and the wholly intentional results of the policies of "privatization by exception." In addition, when applied to industrial property, the bank-run analysis tends not to investigate the different methods of asset misappropriation in the late Soviet period, assuming instead that they are simply additive. In practice, a range of actors with varied interests and resources controlled property at the beginning of the post-Soviet period.[32]

The image of a bank run can also, if applied carelessly, exaggerate the breakdown of control over state property in the Soviet Union. As discussed above, dozens of ministries remained under state direction until the final months of the Soviet period, and at that point they shifted to Russian control rather than to complete independence. The associations, concerns, and other such conglomerates also never broke entirely

---

32. The main case analyses in Solnick's study are quite subtle, but as he points out, his brief treatment of the theft of industrial property is only meant to be suggestive and cannot allow for many nuances. It is those nuances that help explain events after the fall, and I build on Solnick's insights by exploring them.

from the state but instead positioned themselves to be ready whether the Soviet administration dominated, the Russian bureaucracy took over, or neither could govern effectively. Many individual enterprises remained at least partially embedded in their ministerial hierarchies. It is a mistake, therefore, to see the post-Soviet Russian struggle for property simply as a matter of converting de facto ownership developed in the late Soviet period into de jure property rights. Enterprise managers represented a powerful force in asset redistribution in Russia, but they competed with other potent interests, and the property at stake extended far beyond what managers had claimed in the last years of the USSR.

Finally, if the countless acts of individual expropriation examined here actually caused the disintegration of the USSR, they should have either ended with the Soviet Union or brought down the Russian Federation as well. Instead, Russia remained intact, and most of the pathologies regarding property in the late Soviet period continued or worsened in the post-Soviet era.[33] The solution to this paradox is to recognize that the asset theft that undermined the state's ability to govern was separate from the union republics' takeover of property which spelled the de facto end of the Soviet Union. Thus the fall of the USSR resolved only the competition between the Soviet and union-republic governments. Although the competition over assets after 1991 took place in a new arena, most of the important issues remained unchanged. The details of economic reform were still unclear, political institutions and authority remained open to challenge, and members of the economic elite continued to secure property for themselves. At the same time, the vast majority of Russian assets remained within the state's sphere of influence, and those that had slipped into the private sector would be hard to defend in the face of a rival's attack. The struggle for property was just getting underway. The next chapter explores what happened when the Russian government employed a strategy of destruction in pursuit of a new economy.

33. See also Solnick 1998, 252–53, 328n30. It is not Solnick's analysis but careless extrapolations from it that display the shortcomings noted here.

CHAPTER 4

THE NEXT BIG THING

Property in the Era of Mass Privatization and Land Reform, 1992–94

The fall of the Soviet Union did not end the struggle for property. The Russian state laid formal claim to most property in the country, but it had no more resources to monitor it than the late Soviet government did. The status of newly private and quasi-private assets also remained unclear, as no one could be sure how those recently established claims would stand up to challenges. In that context, political and economic actors continued to pursue whatever property was available. None of that changed simply because Gorbachev resigned.

What did fundamentally alter the redistribution of property were massive privatization drives in both industry and agriculture. By virtue of the fall of the Soviet Union, the Russian government became a national administration trying to maintain the state, rather than a sub-national one trying to undermine it.[1] On the question of administering property, the most important initiatives from the newly independent leaders came in the form of two major privatization programs, which reached their peaks between 1992 and 1994. Touted as solutions to the problems of both command economics and the multiple versions of nomenklatura privatization, the new policies turned over more assets to the private sector faster than any reform had ever done, changing the owners of thousands of factories and farms in only a few years. In addition, as part of the new state's attempts to avoid Soviet-style

1. As another scholar put it, "All at once, Russian authorities found themselves in the position of governing a territory they had sought to render ungovernable" (Woodruff 1999, 80).

dismemberment, the programs clearly delineated which level of government would control which property in the country.[2]

In that changed environment, competitors for property adopted new
strategies to complement the ones developed at the end of the Soviet
era. Most notably, managers of industrial and agricultural enterprises
exploited their respective mass privatization programs; and although
they took different approaches in doing so, both proved enormously
successful. Regional governments also played a role in property redistribution in this period, although less by dragging their feet on privatization, as some reformers had feared, than by allying themselves with the
regional and local managers trying to take advantage of the new laws.
Workers, farmers, and other citizens also sought to own a piece of the
wealth they had helped create, but they enjoyed few of the advantages
of managers, and their influence declined as time passed. Their greatest
impact came in the rapid growth of microfarming in Russia. In the midst
of it all, bureaucrats and their allies continued to pursue the general
strategy of "privatization by exception" developed in the late Soviet era,
albeit in new ways that took advantage of the opportunities of the
period.

As major reform initiatives launched during the height of post-Soviet
euphoria, industrial and agricultural privatization programs have hardly
lacked for scholarly and journalistic coverage.[3] Although useful, most of
these studies have seen the reforms as part of a transition rather than a
more general struggle for property, which presents four obstacles to
understanding the period.[4] First, it views policy making as a conflict
between "reformers" and "hardliners," often arguing that reformers
needed to win that battle at all costs. In reality, the allegedly reactionary
legislature had been moving toward mass privatization and agrarian
reform since it was elected in 1990, and its recommendations came out

2. The Russian Federation avoided the fate of the Soviet Union for several reasons
beyond the scope of this study, but the Russian leadership itself seemed to think the
federalization of property control was an important task.

3. For a variety of analyses of mass privatization that nonetheless shared several
characteristics, see Boycko, Shleifer, and Vishny 1995; Aslund 1995; Radygin 1994;
Blasi, Kroumova, and Kruse 1997; Frydman, Rapaczynski, and Earle 1993; Blanchard
et al. 1993; McFaul 1995. On agrarian reform, see Van Atta 1993c; Csaki et al. 2002;
Prosterman, Mitchell, and Rorem 1997; Prosterman, Rolfes, and Mitchell 1994; and
some of the works of Stephen K. Wegren.

4. For works that avoid a number of these pitfalls, see Nelson and Kuzes 1994,
1995; Christensen 1999; Clarke 1996; and Hough 2001 on industry and Allina-Pisano
2002; Kitching 1998a, 1998b; and Humphrey 2002 on agriculture.

of negotiations among proponents of reconcilable approaches to the reforms. Second, the transition-oriented approach usually sees disappointing outcomes—such as managers' success in taking over their enterprises or small farmers' failure to rejuvenate agriculture—as the result of hardline strength or reformist weakness in the policy-making bodies. In practice, the key to those outcomes lay in the implementation stage of the reforms, where interested players had day-to-day influence over real assets that policy makers could only discuss in theoretical terms. Third, by focusing observers on the privatization policies and their results, the transition lens diverts attention from the significant changes in ownership that occurred outside those formal programs, as privatization by exception evolved in response to the changing environment. Paradoxically, that approach overstates the effect of the industrial privatization program and understates that of agrarian reforms. Finally, transition studies have in practice rarely compared changes in industry and agriculture where factory and farm managers operated in significantly different legal, economic, and political contexts. Their distinctive approaches to the common goal of controlling physical resources helped set the struggles for property in the two sectors on divergent paths for years.

This chapter examines industrial privatization and agricultural land reform in the early 1990s in the context of an ongoing struggle for property. It documents the sources of the reform programs, as well as their results on the ground, without relying on a narrative of white hats versus black hats. It also shows that, while the privatization and land reform programs represented the dominant forces in the period, they were far from the only sources of property reform, as groups and individuals throughout society sought to make the best of the new era. The interaction of the major policies with responses from below thoroughly transformed the system of ownership in Russia, even if that transformation differed from what most observers expected.

INDUSTRIAL PRIVATIZATION: GREAT CHANGE, BUT LESS THAN ADVERTISED

As the institutional infrastructure of the Soviet Union crumbled in 1990 to 1991, one of the myriad questions facing the newly elected Russian legislature was how best to reform the state's role in administering industrial property. By that time, most deputies agreed Russia needed to develop some kind of market economy, and they recognized that the unregulated de facto privatization occurring at the time was unfair to the bulk of the population. They therefore agreed the country needed a large-scale privatization program to regularize the transfer of state assets to private hands (Nemtsov 1990b; Glaz'ev 1991). Aside from that general agreement, however, Russian policy makers differed on such fundamental questions as whether to give away enterprise shares or sell them, whether to limit participation to members of the enterprise, and how much to restrict the resale of shares. Over the next several months, legislators negotiated agreements on each of these questions to create a set of privatization laws. Subsequently, Yeltsin and his supporters added provisions to the program to accelerate some of its effects, but in doing so the administration also began to chip away at the legitimacy of the legislature as a branch of government.

Three men came to be identified with the major proposals at the time: Grigorii Yavlinskii, who had helped author the Five-Hundred-Day Plan; Mikhail Malei, head of the Russian government's State Property Committee (GKI); and Petr Filippov, a member of the parliament's committee on economic reform. Yavlinskii, who believed that industries should be de-monopolized before privatization, argued for selling state enterprises, rather than giving them away. In addition, he opposed restrictions on participation or limiting the resale of shares. He contended that his approach was more market-oriented than the others', since it gave stockholders a real stake in their enterprises' performance, and therefore it was more likely to produce an efficient and growing economy.

Malei agreed with Yavlinskii that privatization should make citizens stockholders, but he pointed out that only a few members of society would have the funds to pay for shares (Paniushkina 1991). He therefore advocated selling some shares for vouchers to allow broader participation. Citizens would be allowed to use the vouchers only to buy shares; and they could not resell the shares for five years, a restriction Malei argued would prevent a speculative frenzy in the first years of the new economy (Sluzhakov 1991). In addition, Malei argued, since it was the workers who had built the enterprises up to their current value, 30 percent of each firm's shares should go to its labor collective for free ("Programma" 1991). The collective would then have the right to buy more shares from GKI at a discount and to decide whether to lease the remaining shares from GKI or sell them to the general public. Finally, GKI and the labor collective would always control at least 51 percent of the shares in an enterprise.

Filippov's plan was similar to Malei's on the questions of sale and resale of shares: he argued for vouchers, since few citizens had much money, and he wanted a three-year moratorium on reselling shares, in order to stabilize the market (Filippov 1991a and 1991b). At the same time, he opposed giving shares directly to workers. He agreed with Pavel Bunich, president of the Union of Lessees (*arendatory*) and Entrepreneurs of the USSR, who pointed out that all Russians—not just factory laborers—had helped create the nation's wealth (Bunich 1991). Malei's plan would have left out workers who were not employed at profitable enterprises or in productive industries, such as teachers and doctors. In addition, Filippov argued that Yugoslav experiments with worker self-management in the 1970s and 1980s showed that worker control bred inefficiency. Therefore, instead of transferring any shares to the workers for free, Filippov's plan offered the collective a 30-percent discount on shares it purchased.

The Russian parliament reached a decision on the privatization question in July 1991, passing the laws "On Privatization Accounts" and "On Privatization." The system of "privatization accounts" transferred some state property to the population for free, but the majority of shares were to be sold. Citizens could use their accounts only for buying shares, and they could not resell the stocks for three years, but during that time they could exchange shares in one firm for those in another. The privatization law did not allow workers to receive their entire enterprise for free but gave them a 25-percent nonvoting stake at no charge, with the opportunity to buy voting shares at a discount. Several months later, in February–March 1992, the legislature added another option for workers and managers: if the labor collective chose not to receive any free shares in its enterprise, it could purchase a sizable (at the time not precisely determined) voting stake in the enterprise before the rest of the public was allowed to bid (Berger 1992).

Although the laws of 1991 represented an acceptable compromise for most leading politicians in Russia the time, one faction remained frustrated. Boris Yeltsin, who had been elected president in June 1991 from his seat in the legislature, and advisors like Yegor Gaidar and Anatolii Chubais focused much of their attention on the perceived need to destroy the remnants of the Soviet economic system so that a market economy could grow in its place. In particular, they argued that the economic ministries would resist losing control over property, so the most effective privatization would wrench enterprises from the ministries' clutches as quickly as possible and prevent replacement hierarchies from forming (Boycko, Shleifer, and Vishny 1995; Aslund 1995; Gaidar 1995; Blasi, Kroumova, and Kruse 1997; Blanchard et al. 1993; World Bank 1992, 96).[5]

In November 1991, to accelerate the legislative process, the parliament granted Yeltsin decree powers on economic questions for one year, with the stipulation that no decree could contravene existing law, and Yeltsin began to use that authority to speed up the dismantling of ministerial control. His first effort appeared to reduce the size of the Russian government dramatically, although in the end it contained more flash than substance. After slowly claiming authority over governmental functions on Russian territory after the August 1991 coup attempt, Yeltsin issued a decree on November 28, 1991, creating the structures of the new Russian executive apparatus.[6] The decree cut the number of ministries and state committees from forty-six to twenty-three, but in practice many of the former branch ministries survived as departments in the new configuration, including at least fourteen within the new Ministry of Industry (Huskey 1992, 258; Whitefield 1993, 258; World Bank 1992, 72). Furthermore, to the extent that the reorganizations represented a streamlining of the ministerial system, progress evaporated in the first few months of 1992 as agencies, committees, and other bureaucracies proliferated within the government and presidential administration. The number of ministries also began to rise soon after the initial reorganization (Whitefield 1993, 259–60; Huskey 1999, 102, 113). These early moves were supposed to signal a decisive break with reform efforts of the past, but on the question of real property they were less radical than what had come before.

In January and June 1992 Yeltsin dealt a more significant blow to the system of ministerial control. In particular, he issued decrees establishing a procedure for "commercializing" enterprises—that is, performing the legal and accounting process that would turn the firms into joint-

---

5. The World Bank was a more sophisticated observer on this question than some others. It recognized that new hierarchies such as holding companies were not meant to replicate the central planning system, but it thought they might have significant leverage over the state in lobbying for subsidies and be inclined to redistribute resources toward underperforming firms in the holding. That interpretation, however, still conceives of the purpose of ownership networks too narrowly, as this book demonstrates.

6. Decree no. 242, "On the Reorganization of the Central Organs of State Administration of the RSFSR," November 28, 1991.

stock companies with shares to be sold later.[7] The decrees specified that firms should commercialize individually, rather than as entire ministries or subministries, and that the new joint-stock companies were immediately freed from the administrative hierarchy of their previous ministry, department, or local administration, regardless of when the privatization actually took place. The structure of this reform was clearly aimed at breaking up connections between firms and reducing ministerial control over enterprises.

When the Russian legislature passed the State Privatization Program in June 1992 it incorporated most of the approaches just outlined. In particular, the commercialization decrees and the system of privatization accounts remained intact, and the program included three types of privileges for managers and workers at privatizing enterprises. The first option reflected the initial agreement of 1991: workers and managers received 25 percent of the shares for free but were unable to vote with them. The proposals of February–March 1992 were refined into a second option, allowing labor collectives to purchase up to 51 percent of their enterprise's shares—all of which would have voting rights and none of which would be free—at 70 percent over "book value."[8] The third option was a complicated variant that involved a promise to restructure the enterprise and did not apply to large firms; labor collectives rarely chose it.

For the rapid-reform faction, however, the negotiated program would not transfer industrial assets to strong private owners fast enough. In a subsequent interview, the economics editor of a Russian newspaper known for its support of democratization and marketization expressed frustration when he said of the program, "It wasn't reform; it was compromise" (Zasurskii 1994). On August 14, 1992, with the parliament out of session, Yeltsin negated these compromises by signing a decree initiating the Russian voucher program. That system would give every citizen a certificate that he or she could either sell or use to buy a handful of shares in an enterprise or a mutual fund, effectively eliminating the system of privatization accounts and the moratorium on share resale discussed

7. Decree no. 66 (January 29, 1992) "On Accelerating Privatization of State and Municipal Enterprises"; and Decree no. 721 (June 1, 1992) "On Organizational Measures for the Transformation of State Enterprises and Voluntary Associations of State Enterprises into Joint-Stock Companies."

8. "Book value" (*nominal'naia stoimost'*) was determined in an appraisal and was not indexed to inflation. As noted below, the absence of indexing was key to insiders' success at retaining control of enterprises.

above. Faced with this populist fait accompli, the parliament did not reverse the decree, and the vouchers were distributed by October.[9]

With the new decree, the Russian system of mass privatization was in place: managers and workers would have early access to some shares, the state would retain a minority position, and the public would bid on the rest of the shares using fully transferable certificates they had received essentially for free. In Yeltsin's words, the approach would "transfer . . . state property to the citizens of Russia and attract broad strata of the population to the process of privatization" (Decree no. 914, 1992). Whether or not the decree accomplished those lofty goals, it provided the backdrop for the struggle over industrial property in 1992–94.

Mass Privatization in Action

From an administrative perspective, mass industrial privatization in Russia was astonishingly successful. In less than two years, thousands of medium- and large-scale enterprises across the country created millions of stock certificates, distributed large numbers to managers and workers, and transferred still others to citizens through voucher auctions. Precise statistics are unavailable, both because of errors in reporting and because some enterprises conducted multiple voucher auctions, but the program clearly reached vast swaths of the economy and society. Over the course of the program, more than twenty thousand enterprises became joint-stock companies (Radygin 1994, 153; "Svodnyi otchet" 1994, 53). Most of the population, or almost 150 million Russians, received vouchers, and nearly all those certificates were eventually invested in privatizing firms or in voucher funds (Boycko, Shleifer, and Vishny 1995, 99–100; Radygin 1994, 154; Aslund 1995, 255). By June 1994, when the program ended, about fifteen thousand enterprises employing over seventeen million workers had held voucher auctions (see Table 4.1). Those firms represented nearly two-thirds of the industrial workforce at the time, and they encompassed a range of subsectors from both heavy and light industry (see Table 4.2). Carrying out such a program was no mean feat.

---

9. Although the Supreme Economic Council of the Supreme Soviet did not overturn the program, it did object to its approach and to the way it was introduced (Nelson and Kuzes 1995, 51). Although it is not the focus of this book, the increasing reliance on decrees to change property laws over the objections of the legislature helped weaken the formal institutions of government in Russia in the early 1990s (Barnes 2001).

TABLE 4.1
Voucher auctions, December 1992–June 1994

	Enterprises sold	Thousands of employees	Charter capital sold (millions of rubles)
December 1992	18	43	513
January 1993	108	188	676
February	197	200	1,685
March	450	556	5,266
April	611	837	6,294
May	576	598	5,194
June	909	821	7,115
July	916	782	8,193
August	895	830	7,010
September	811	826	7,432
October	959	910	8,151
November	1,005	906	9,007
December	1,054	1,026	8,814
January 1994	738	664	9,137
February	779	1,285	13,703
March	975	1,072	16,647
April	1,084	1,283	16,469
May	1,212	1,170	16,398
June	3,165	7,822	137,165
TOTAL	16,462	21,819	284,869

Source: Blasi, Kroumova, and Kruse 1997, 192, Table 3.
Note: Figures may be overstated because of multiple voucher auctions at the same firm. Aslund (1995, 256), based on statistics from the Russian State Property Committee and the Russian Privatization Center, gives a figure of 13,832 enterprises sold through voucher auctions by the end of June 1994. Boycko, Shleifer, and Vishny (1995, 106–7) report 15,779 enterprises sold. According to *Russian Economic Trends* 4, no. 1 (1995), 97, the total stood at 15,052.

TABLE 4.2
Proportion of formerly state-owned enterprises privatized by July 1, 1994

Sector	Percent privatized
Light industry	48
Food processing	47
Construction	35
Construction materials	46
Automobiles and repair	42
Wholesale trade	47
Retail trade	55

Source: Radygin 1994, 155.

Alongside the auction process itself, the voucher privatization rules also spawned a new form of economic institution, the voucher investment fund (VIF). A much-heralded part of the 1992–94 industrial privatization drive, VIFs were supposed to resemble Western mutual funds, giving individual investors a collective voice in the operation of privatized firms.[10] Politically, they aimed to help popularize privatization by allowing individual investors to benefit from the expertise and buying power of a larger firm. As with voucher auctions themselves, VIFs proliferated rapidly and seemed to bring large swaths of the population into the process. The number of licensed VIFs rose above 600 during 1993 and stood at 596 when the voucher program ended in June 1994 (Pistor and Spicer 1996, 8; Kogut and Spicer 1999, 39). All told, the funds collected about forty-five million vouchers, representing nearly a third of the certificates in the country (Boycko, Shleifer, and Vishny 1995, 100).[11]

For all its administrative and statistical achievements, however, mass privatization's substantive effects on ownership in Russia differed from its authors' promises in important ways. The VIFs, for example, largely failed to spread effective ownership to the bulk of the population. Instead, they were rarely strong enough to restructure firms, used what power they did have to enrich their own managers, and left most Russians who invested in them with nothing to show for their efforts. When it came to exerting influence over firms, most funds began with small holdings and no resources with which to expand. In particular, their only avenue for raising capital was to sell off shares they had bought for vouchers. Unfortunately, the Russian stock market was highly illiquid at the time, so the shares they could sell were usually in the firms with the greatest potential for future returns.[12] Thus, VIFs could bring in a one-time cash infusion, but they were unlikely to parlay that into increased influence (Spicer 1998, 72–73). By the fall of 1996, analysts estimated

10. Among the many discussions of what these funds could be expected to achieve, see Anatolii Chubais's periodic contributions to *Panorama privatizatsii* from 1992 to 1994.

11. Note that this does not mean that the remaining vouchers were invested by their original recipients. Many Russians sold their vouchers for cash (or exchanged them for goods), so that only about 28 percent of the Russian population owned shares at the end of the voucher program, as opposed to 80 percent of Czechs (Kogut and Spicer 1999, 39).

12. According to a 1994 survey of over three hundred funds, only about 11 percent of funds' trades took place on an official stock market, with the rest occurring as private trades between individuals (Spicer 1998, 73).

that only twenty to thirty funds in Russia still had active investment strategies and long-term prospects (Pistor and Spicer 1996, 8, 13).

While they failed to achieve their ostensible goals, VIFs did provide their managers with several paths to enrichment. Chubais and others resisted calls to regulate the funds, which made them useful vehicles for milking an unsuspecting population. For example, some funds inflated management costs—which could legally reach 10 percent of the fund's assets and which state agencies rarely monitored—to siphon cash from the funds (Spicer 1998, 79). In other instances, fund managers sold real assets to associates or to dummy corporations at enormous discounts (Spicer 1998, 80). Catching perpetrators of such scams proved virtually impossible.

Beyond the official voucher investment funds, as many as two thousand unlicensed firms collected vouchers and cash from the population, and their performance differed little from that of the VIFs (Kogut and Spicer 1999, 19). Such firms, which attracted $5–7 billion from more than eighty million Russians by the end of 1994, provided some of the most spectacular scams in which ordinary Russians lost their savings (Spicer 1998, 62, 65). The Tibet fund, for example, brought in as much as $3 million (3 billion rubles) in investments with its promise of returns of 30 percent a month or more than 2,000 percent a year. Instead of delivering on the promises, the president of the company disappeared in 1995, leaving his more than 600,000 investors empty-handed (Kogut and Spicer 1999, 21). In an even bigger scandal, five to ten million Russians had bought shares in the MMM fund by early 1994. A classic pyramid scheme, MMM collapsed in July 1994, as share prices fell from $62 to $0.50 in two days (Kogut and Spicer 1999, 22). The story was repeated again and again at such companies as Russkii Dom Selenga, Khoper, and several others.

In a few cases, the otherwise minimally influential funds did purchase significant property, although the acquisitions failed to enrich most of the population. In one example whose repercussions far outlasted mass privatization, Kakha Bendukidze, a biologist from Georgia, acquired firms in the industrial sector using both cash and vouchers. He established a trading company called Bioprotsess in 1988, and in 1991 he created the People's Oil and Investment-Industrial Eurasian Corporation (NIPEK) to collect investments from the population (Miloslavskaia 2001). Most observers believe that when NIPEK folded in 1993, its assets went to Bioprotsess and Bendukidze, who used them to buy up vouchers and then shares in enterprises, especially the Uralmash Machine-tool

Complex. He had acquired 18 percent of Uralmash's shares by the middle of 1993, and by the end of the year he had raised his stake to over 40 percent ("Russian Industry" 1993; Blasi, Kroumova, and Kruse 1997, 156; Miloslavskaia 2001).

In a less controversial example, the Alfa Kapital Fund, managed by Mikhail Aleksandrov, bought stakes in companies that became part of the Alfa Group's assets, including 25 percent of the famed Bolshevik Biscuit Factory, the first to go through the voucher auction process (Spicer 1998, 77; "Russian Industry" 1993). Some regional governments followed a similar strategy, creating voucher funds to buy up shares in enterprises. The Uralskie zavody ("Urals Factories") conglomerate, for example, established in 1993 in Udmurtia, included the republican VIF, along with several factories, a bank, and other enterprises (Slider 1997b, 108, 111). Such examples of activity were the exceptions, however, and even in those cases the VIFs failed to achieve their stated goals of establishing effective private governance from the outside.

The main role of the funds thus seemed to be to abscond with the money and hopes of citizens rather than dramatically affect property distribution; and after the initial fanfare surrounding their creation, they largely disappeared from the story of Russian property reform. A second unexpected result of the mass privatization drive, however, troubled analysts, advisors, and policy makers more deeply—the success of enterprise managers in taking over their own firms. Option 2 in the program, which allowed the labor collective to purchase 51 percent of an enterprise at a fixed price, proved far more popular than Options 1 or 3. Indeed, by the time voucher privatization ended, nearly three-quarters of the enterprises sold off had chosen the second option.[13] Nominally, of course, Option 2 did not give control to management alone, but to the labor collective as a whole. Indeed, workers had reason to support managers in their efforts both to free the enterprise from ineffective state control and to protect it from takeover by unpredictable outsiders (Christensen 1999, 134; Sil 2001, 223–26; Clarke 1993, 218). Nonetheless, the directors were usually clearly in charge, as they enjoyed great advantages in share concentration, access to information, and coercive power relative to workers.

13. By January 1, 1993, over 63 percent of privatizing enterprises had chosen Option 2, and by April 1 that proportion was up to 74.2 percent (Radygin 1993, 60). Overall, 73 percent of enterprises selected Option 2; 25 percent chose Option 1; and only 2 percent picked Option 3 (Blasi, Kroumova, and Kruse 1997, 41).

The first shareholders' meeting of the Volgograd Ceramics Factory produced typical results. Although workers—rather than managers— owned 51.5 percent of the shares, a journalist at the meeting observed that it bore a strong resemblance to a labor collective assembly in the Soviet era. The only candidate for general director was Mikhail Shulzhenko, the director of the factory for the past three years, and he was not asked a single question from the floor. Nine of the ten places on the board of directors went to members of the firm's upper management (Vdovin 1993).[14]

In other instances, enterprise managers were able to gain explicit ownership and control of large portions of their own firms. In one common scheme, directors retained control of their enterprises by convincing workers to turn over their vouchers, which they promised to use to buy up shares of the enterprise for the collective as a whole. The shares, however, were registered only in the director's name (Abramovich 1993). In another example, the director of GAZ, an enormous auto factory in Nizhnii Novgorod with more than 100,000 workers at the time, used about $30 million in tax credits earmarked for the development of a new truck to purchase nearly 30 percent of the shares in the company for himself (Boulton 1994). The director, Boris Vidaev, used fifteen proxy firms to buy up privatization vouchers and used the vouchers to purchase shares in the company (Rutland 1994, 1118).

Finally, not only did old directors not turn over control of their enterprises in most cases, but the changes they did make often exacerbated declines in production while allowing managers themselves to reap extraordinary profits. A report by a commission from Yeltsin's office on the behavior of directors of newly privatized firms in Volgograd oblast described several abuses (Tsygankov 1994). The emblematic Tractor Factory, for example, was in desperate straits: it had produced only a thousand tractors in five months, operated only two days a week, and paid its wages late. The 88,600 rubles a month that its workers earned was one-third less than the oblast average. Nonetheless, the director Valerii Khvatov was receiving 716,200 rubles a month, plus 3.2 million rubles in dividends from his shares in Traktor eksport, of which he was a founder. The situation at the Tractor Parts Factory was similar. The enterprise was four months behind in its wage payments at the time of

---

14. The tenth spot went to a representative of an investment fund that had acquired 5.72 percent of the firm's shares.

THE NEXT BIG THING 81

the study, and it had lost 203 million rubles in the first three months of the year. The director, however, received 5.5 million rubles in dividends from Rosagromet, which was affiliated with his factory. Finally, when the Volzhskii Pipe Factory built new housing for its workforce, most of it was for upper management, rather than the laborers who bore the brunt of the economic decline.

Insider ownership, of course, did not always doom a firm to stagnation or asset stripping.[15] Furthermore, the practical alternative to insider privatization was a greater role for voucher funds and similar intermediaries. Given the unsavory role VIFs and related organizations played in the Russian experience, preventing more managers from taking over their own firms may simply have given funds the opportunity to fleece more people.[16]

Nevertheless, since managerial dominance was more widespread than anticipated, and since it entailed more direct control of real assets than VIFs, it captured the attention of many scholars and advisers. The most common explanation for the phenomenon held that industrialists virtually dictated privatization policy to the government in the early 1990s (McFaul 1995; Boycko, Shleifer, and Vishny 1995; Aslund 1995; Blanchard et al. 1993). As overseers of most of the Soviet Union's material wealth, industrial managers commanded enormous resources, and for decades they had engaged in informal lobbying at the highest levels (Berliner 1957; Hough 1969, 35–79; Hardt and Frankel 1971). They therefore seemed well-positioned to take advantage of political liberalization in the USSR and Russia. In May 1990 the industrialist Arkadii Volskii created a faction within the Soviet legislature; and after the breakup of the USSR, he reconstituted it as the Russian Union of Industrialists and Entrepreneurs (RUIE) (Lohr 1993; White, Gill, and Slider, 1993). The RUIE was instrumental in forcing Yeltsin to include the industrial leaders Vladimir Shumeiko, Grigorii Khizha, and Viktor Chernomyrdin in his government after the Sixth Russian Congress of People's Deputies in April 1992. Soon thereafter, the RUIE seemed to grow even stronger when it formed an umbrella group called the Civic Union together with the People's Party—Free Russia, under Russian Vice President Aleksandr

15. Hough (2001) emphasizes this point, perhaps overplaying his hand but providing an important corrective to the assumption that all Soviet-era managers were incompetent, corrupt, or both.

16. The Czech experience also highlights the dangers of relying heavily on voucher investment funds during mass privatization (Brom and Orenstein 1994; Kenway and Klvačová 1996; Barnes 2003).

Rutskoi, and the Democratic Party of Russia, led by the popular politician Nikolai Travkin (McFaul 1993).

In practice, however, Option 2 did not come directly from the pens of the Civic Union but was the result of understandable policy negotiations that included compromises by both the government and the managers. For example, while Option 2 allowed insiders to acquire up to 51 percent of their enterprises at the closed auction, that was a far cry from the 100 percent they had requested. Also, they had to pay for the shares. Finally, since enterprises would not be allowed to form closed joint-stock companies, in which only insiders could own stock, a secondary market for shares could dilute insider control of enterprises. All these stipulations appeared in the final version of the 1992 Privatization Program.

Thus industrialists did not simply foist a privatization scheme on the government and exploit it as planned. Instead, they opposed the program but later took advantage of it to an unexpected degree. Ironically, it was the government team's own insistence that privatization proceed quickly, not any "dilution" of the program in consultation with the managerial lobby, that gave managers the best opportunities to exploit. For example, the 1992 decrees on "commercialization" left thousands of enterprises in a kind of ownership limbo reminiscent of the late Soviet period. In particular, the decrees specified that enterprises converting to joint-stock companies immediately gained their freedom from ministerial oversight. Thus, while the government still owned the companies, the decrees destroyed its apparatus for monitoring them, opening wide the door to managerial abuses.

In addition, the government's focus on speed inadvertently helped managers take advantage of Option 2 (Sutela 1994; Rutland 1994). The fixed price for the shares available to insiders was calculated according to 1991 prices—that is, before the price liberalization of 1992. Legislators and industrialists argued that enterprises should be reappraised in the wake of liberalization, but the reform team saw those requests as efforts to slow or stop privatization altogether and therefore refused to recalculate the "book value" of enterprises as they underwent privatization. As a result, the fixed share price available to labor collectives under Option 2 proved to be relatively tiny.

Industrial managers' frequent success in establishing de facto ownership of their enterprises thus depended more on their strength during the implementation of mass privatization than on their ability to affect the legislative process, a fact that has several implications. First, managers behaved like rational economic actors, given the context in which they operated, rather than the mindless hardliners their opponents sometimes tried to make them out to be. Second, managers were likely to retain whatever authority they had on the ground and therefore affect the distribution of property in Russia even though their lobbying group, the Civic Union, had lost a great deal of its power by the end of 1993. Finally, since their success in the mass privatization program depended on the particular legal and economic circumstances at the time, their tactics for affecting ownership relations, either at their own firms or elsewhere, were likely to change after the program ended. The program thus shaped the strategies of competitors for property, even when its effects did not match the expectations of its authors.

Property beyond Mass Privatization

Even in the era of mass privatization, significant transformation of industrial ownership took place outside the major campaign. The Privatization Program of 1992–94 was not just smoke and mirrors; it transferred unprecedented amounts of property from state to private control. It was, however, less extensive than it appeared, since it contained significant restrictions that kept important assets out of the reach of ordinary Russians. In most privatized enterprises, for example, 29 percent of the shares remained with the state, whether to retain government influence at the firms, leave the state an opportunity to raise cash later, or both.

Potentially more important than minority holdings in privatized enterprises, a surprising array of assets remained entirely outside the auspices of the program. Six pages early in the program document enumerated which objects could not be privatized at all, which required special permission from the Council of Ministers or the State Property Committee (then under Chubais), and which would be subject to mandatory privatization. The assets excluded from privatization included television and radio centers, the pipeline system, local infrastructure, and assets of the natural gas sector that had "all-Russian or interregional significance." The Council of Ministers had to sign off on privatization of several types of assets, including those in the fuel and energy complex, the communications sector, and international trade associations run by ministries and departments. The list of property under the jurisdiction of the State Property Committee (GKI) was particularly wide-ranging, including enterprises for rail, air, sea, and river transport; firms with "all-Russian significance" in the construction sector; factories producing alcoholic beverages or baby food; and parts of the system for petroleum distribution. In addition, GKI determined whether or not to privatize enterprises with more than ten thousand workers or a value of over 150 million rubles as of January 1, 1992, a category that included dozens of enterprises employing tens of thousands of workers in such sectors as fuel, metallurgy, chemicals, petrochemicals, and engineering (World Bank 1992, 83, Table 6–1). Finally, GKI received authority over firms occupying "dominant positions" in national or regional markets. Given the intentional construction of regional and national monopolies in the Soviet period, that provision gave GKI a role in deciding the privatization of nearly every industrial enterprise of significance in Russia.[17]

By contrast, the range of assets slated for mandatory privatization was strikingly narrow, even if it encompassed a large number of enterprises. This category of property included enterprises significantly "affecting the formation and functioning of the market infrastructure of the Russian economy," as well as those "whose ineffective performance is slowing the pace of economic growth and the formation of a market in Russia." The list of assets meant to clarify this ambiguous description included wholesale and retail trade networks, some construction assets, most of the agro-industrial complex, and "unprofitable enterprises." For all of its impact on the redistribution of property in Russia, therefore, the program specifically left most of the valuable property in the country to be privatized through channels that could be closed to most Russians.[18]

With so much property still owned by the state, and with the state itself continuing to fragment and lose the ability to monitor its assets, the spontaneous privatization of the preceding years did not stop. Instead, the "privatization by exception" described in the previous chapter morphed and accelerated. In late 1992, for example, Yeltsin issued a series of decrees converting major state-owned associations and ministerial property into joint-stock companies. On August 14, 1992, the same day as the voucher decree, he declared that the privatization of

17. In 1989, of the 7,664 "product groups" distributed by the USSR State Supply Committee (Gossnab), 77 percent were produced by a single enterprise (World Bank 1992, 82, Box 6–1).

18. In a further irony, the assets of the Soviet-era trade unions—the buildings, vacation areas, and finances that arguably represented the common heritage of all workers—were turned over to the Russian successor of those unions, thus excluding most laborers. After first threatening to redistribute the holdings, Yeltsin acquiesced in the face of the union's support in the legislature and the fact that he needed the union to help garner support for his policies (Christensen 1999, 109–10; Cook 1995, 33–34; Sil 2001, 214–16).

enterprises in the fuel and energy complex would take place according to presidential decree.[19] Then, with decrees on August 15 and November 5, he converted the successors of the Soviet electrical power industry into a single company, called Unified Energy System (UES).[20] Also on November 5, a decree converted the gas monopoly Gazprom into a joint-stock company.[21] Similarly, the coal monopoly "Ugol Rossii" became "Rosugol" on December 30.[22] Nor was this process confined to the energy sector. The Alrosa Joint-stock Company, for example, was created from the diamond-mining assets in Sakha (Yakutia) in 1992; and in November of that year, a presidential decree (no. 1481) gave it a near monopoly on the export of unfinished diamonds from Russia. In similar examples, gold-mining assets in Magadan oblast came under the control of a single, forty-three-firm holding company; the Sakha administration transferred shares in various firms to Sakha-Invest; and the Moscow government turned over management rights in several enterprises to Menatep Bank (Rutland 1994, 1120; Gorbatova 1995, 28).

In the oil sector, this process, which laid the groundwork for over ten years of political and economic conflict, was especially complicated because of the fragmented nature of the sector. In the Soviet period enterprises at different stages of the oil-production process fell under the authority of separate ministries. For example, Minnefteprom oversaw extraction, Minneftekhimprom refining, Gossnab distribution, and Soiuznefteksport the export of petroleum products. Compounding the problem of control, as the Soviet state crumbled, most authority for operating the enterprises fell to managers, directors, and some regional leaders (Lane and Seifulmulukov 1999, 15–17). The most notable example of this devolution of authority was the creation of LUKoil, a vast holding company established in 1990 under Vagit Alekperov, a deputy minister in the USSR Ministry of Oil and Gas (Kotz and Weir 1997, 122–23).

The issue of control over oil assets remained unresolved in the first years after the Soviet Union fell. As part of the conversion of Soviet ministries to Russian ones, Vladimir Lopukhin and his deputy Mikhail Khodorkovskii formally took over oil-related assets in the name of the Russian Ministry of Fuel and Energy (Lane and Seifulmulukov 1999, 16; Rutland 1994, 1119–20). On November 17, 1992, a presidential decree

19. Decree no. 922.
20. Decrees no. 923 and no. 1334.
21. Decree no. 1333.
22. Decree no. 1702.

again tried to clarify authority over oil resources by creating a state conglomerate called Rosneft and three holding companies: Yukos, Surgutneftegaz, and a re-registered LUKoil (Sagers 1993b; 1998, 298). The pipeline system remained separate from the other enterprises and came under the jurisdiction of two state-owned companies, Transneft for crude oil and Rostransnefteprodukt for processed goods (Sagers 1993b, 355). On paper, the decree reasserted the state's right to own, operate, and dispose of assets in the sector.

In practice, however, the decision did not prevent further privatization by exception. In the short run, the state continued to own all shares in the newly created companies, but over the next several years, it sold off parts of them, often to managers or former bureaucrats in the oil sector. For example, when the state sold 8 percent of Surgutneftegaz for vouchers and cash in 1993, local officials ran the auction and allowed Surgutneftegaz itself to buy most of the shares. Likewise, the government directly transferred 7 percent of the shares to the company in hopes that the Surgutneftegaz management could use them to raise cash via the stock market. In the summer of 1994, the Surgutneftegaz-owned Neftinvest Company received another 40-percent stake at an investment auction (Lane and Seifulmulukov 1999, 32).

Even creating the holding companies at all, especially Rosneft, proved difficult. For example, several enterprises, including a group in Siberia calling itself the "Eastern Oil Company" (VNK), tried to remain outside Rosneft (Sagers 1993b, 354). While Rosneft gained authority over those enterprises in the short run, privatization deals in the mid-1990s sold them off separately. More immediate challenges to Rosneft's authority came from republics within Russia, especially Komi, Bashkortostan, and Tatarstan (Sagers 1993b, 354–55). By the end of 1994 those governments had received permission to operate their own oil sectors largely independently from the center (Sagers 1998, 299n8). None of this struggle took place under the auspices of the mass privatization program, but it helped decide the fate of great swaths of the most desirable property in Russia.

All these changes indicate that, as important as mass privatization was in 1992–94, its impact has been misrepresented in several ways. In particular, by seeing it as part of a transition to a market economy instead of a struggle for property, observers have overstated the drama of policy conflicts and the sweep of the program itself. In doing so, they have drawn attention away from the vast reorganizations of property that took place outside the structures of the mass privatization program.

Unfortunately, such shortcomings have not been confined to studies of industrial privatization. Although few students of post-Soviet Russia systematically compared asset redistribution in industry and agriculture, and although each of these realms had distinct features, the interpretive lens of "transition" caused many observers to take the same misguided shortcuts to understanding the transformation of both sectors. The next section places the agrarian reforms of the early 1990s in the context of the broader struggle for property in Russia.

AGRARIAN REFORM: REVOLUTION FROM ABOVE, SURVIVAL FROM BELOW

Even before they took up questions of industrial privatization in 1990, Russian legislators broached the subject of agricultural land reform. As thorny a problem as farm privatization eventually became, politicians at the time believed it would be simpler and potentially more popular than restructuring industry. In particular, since there were already thousands of farms in the country that could compete with one another, agrarian reform would not have to address the question of de-monopolization, or so the argument went (*Perekhod k rynku* 1990a, 166). In addition, distributing land to those who worked it had been the promise of Russian reformers since Alexander II freed the serfs in 1861.

With those thoughts in mind, and in pursuit of a more efficient agricultural sector, the Russian parliament passed laws in late 1990 similar to those passed in the USSR the year before. The laws laid the groundwork for individual farmers to take land from the large enterprises and strike out on their own. Near the end of 1991, in a move similar to his decisions regarding industry, Yeltsin issued decrees intended to break up the large farms quickly and make the sale of land and the formation of new farms easier. Taken together, the new regulations created a framework for the rapid privatization of agricultural land. In practice, agricultural managers were even more effective than their industrial counterparts at reshaping privatization during the implementation stage, but land reform did have a real effect on property distribution in Russia, creating both real owners and a land market of sorts.

To the extent that Russian agriculture received political or scholarly attention in the early 1990s, most of it focused on the process of breaking up large farms and creating new, smaller ones, but major changes in the sector took place outside the land-reform program as well. Large parts of the input supply chain and the output procurement system were eventually privatized through several channels, including the mass privatization program and a number of individual government decisions. At the same time, as the reforms from above splintered the networks of the old economy, managers, farmers, and traders created new ones that could help them survive the changes. The policies for redistributing agrarian property in the early 1990s bore a surface similarity to those in industry, but the opportunities available to the major participants during implementation produced considerably different results.

Conflict over Rules

As it eventually developed, the program to remake agricultural landownership in Russia embodied two major components. The most visible part sought to create small, family farms—usually called "private" or "peasant" farms—and legislation in late 1990 took significant steps in that direction. Contrary to the Russian legislature's popular image as an unrepentant obstacle to change, in December 1990 it passed two laws that Boris Nemtsov, who would later become Russia's most famous local reform leader as the governor of Nizhnii Novgorod oblast, called the "most radical since the Stolypin reforms" of the early 1900s (Nemtsov 1990a).[23] That legislation allowed peasants to leave collective or state farms, take with them a plot of land they could own privately, and even sell the land after ten years, all without obtaining the permission of the large farm.

As in industry, however, when Yeltsin brought his "change team" of Gaidar, Chubais, and others to power in late 1991, they sought to speed up the process and circumvent possible resistance, especially from farm managers. To achieve that goal, Yeltsin issued a decree introducing the second major facet of land reform: all collective and state farms would have to "reorganize." That is, they would have to calculate the value of their assets and choose an ownership form that would make future privatization possible, much like "commercialization" in industry.[24] In addition, another decree required that farm managers issue paper certificates to workers that represented an amount of land (although not its specific location) those workers could take with them if they left the collective to start a family farm.[25] The new private farmers could then

---

23. The new laws were called "On the Peasant Farm" and "On Land Reform."

24. Presidential decree "On the Procedure for the Reorganization of Collective and State Farms" (December 29, 1991).

25. Presidential decree "On Urgent Measures for the Implementation of Land Reform in the RSFSR" (December 27, 1991).

supplement that land either with acreage from a regional land fund, to which the large farms had to contribute, or by leasing additional land from the large farms or from individuals.[26] Furthermore, while it violated the ten-year moratorium of the 1990 laws, the decree allowed rural residents to buy and sell land certificates from anyone who did not need them, such as "a pensioner or a rural teacher" (Pishchikova 1992a). Supporters of the reforms saw the new mandates as providing a "mechanism" for breaking up the state and collective farms and creating a class of small private farmers who would lead Russia out of its agricultural morass.[27] That is, the decrees gave recalcitrant local authorities direct, specific instructions on how to carry out land reform.

Yeltsin and his government, however, continued to push for a completely unrestricted market in agricultural land. After branding even potential moderates as pawns of a self-interested elite in mid-1992, the government called for a referendum on land reform.[28] Whether because they feared Yeltsin's ability to manipulate the outcome of the vote, or because they believed many Russians wanted a freer land market, the deputies at the Seventh Congress of People's Deputies (December 1992) lifted the moratorium on resale of some plots of land, thereby heading off the referendum drive. The changes amended the constitution to permit a free market for land used for dacha construction, orchards, and private gardening, although not for full-scale farming.[29] Thus reform of large farms would still require converting them to private entities and allowing individual farmers to take pieces and strike out on their own.

Throughout the early 1990s the parliament continued to resist the idea of an unrestricted market for farmland, and the Yeltsin team continued to believe that the absence of such a market impeded useful property reform in agriculture. The government issued numerous

26. As early as 1994, most of the land in the regional funds that had not been leased by new private farmers was being leased back to the large farms from which it had originally been taken (Prosterman, Rolfes, and Mitchell 1994, 11–12; Prosterman, Mitchell, and Rorem 1997, 1383).

27. See Agricultural Minister Viktor Khlystun's praise for the edict in Pishchikova 1992a.

28. For an example of such comments, see governmental statements during a threat to resign ("S″ezd" 1992). For a fuller discussion of policy making on land reform, see Barnes 2001.

29. The amendment, which was part of the "Zakon ob izmeneniiakh i dopolneni-iakh Konstitutsii Rossiiskoi Federatsii–Rossii," was passed on December 9, 1992, and referred to land "dlia vedeniia lichnogo podsobnogo i dachnogo khoziaistva, dlia sadovodstva i individual'nogo zhilishchnogo stroitel'stva." It appears in *Sobranie aktov prezidenta i pravitel'stva Rossiiskoi Federatsii*, 1993, 2:92–101.

decrees in an attempt to circumvent the legislature on the land question. The two most dramatic decisions came in October 1993, shortly after Yeltsin's dissolution of the parliament and the resulting violence in the streets of Moscow. First, on October 26, 1993, he and his international advisors unveiled a land reform program that became known as the "Nizhnii Novgorod model." The approach, which grew out of an earlier attempt by Yeltsin to use regional leaders to circumvent the federal legislature, effectively transferred the authority to make land reform policy to regional executives. The Nizhnii Novgorod version was developed in cooperation with the International Finance Corporation, and it used a complicated system to break up collective and state farms into smaller entities on a case-by-case basis, providing subsidies from the oblast government to the new enterprises (*Zemel'naia reforma* 1994; Wegren 1994b).

The day after announcing the new program, Yeltsin signed another decree allegedly removing any remaining legal obstacles to the creation of a free land market in Russia.[30] The decision reiterated an earlier requirement that collective and state farms issue shares to their workers, and it stated unequivocally that those shares—and the plots they signified if the farmer left the collective—could be bought and sold at any time, although the land itself could only be used for its originally designated purpose. The decree also abolished the Land Code that the old parliament had passed, since that code prohibited the immediate resale of farmland. As discussed below, however, even with parliament physically removed from the scene and with Yeltsin able to promulgate laws virtually at will, the new rules did not produce the expected changes in landownership.

Land Reform in Practice

As a campaign, large-farm reorganization proved remarkably successful, much like mass privatization in industry. Approximately two-thirds of farms had reorganized by the original deadline of January 1, 1993, about 90 percent by July 1, and nearly all of them by January 1, 1994 (Wegren 1993, 45; Zhurek 1994, 260). The large farms also issued land certificates as required, despite some efforts at foot-dragging. Such numerical successes, however, hid disappointing results. On the question of farm

30. Decree no. 1767, "On the Regulation of Land Relations and the Development of Agrarian Reform in Russia" (October 27, 1993).

reorganization, for example, most farms retained some form of collective ownership. By mid-1993, about 35 percent remained collective or state farms outright, and more than half became closed joint-stock companies or limited partnerships, in which outside ownership was prohibited and where the director of the farm still held sway over operations (Wegren 1993, 45–46; Novikov 1995, 22). According to Anatolii Cherniaev, a senior Russian scholar on agricultural production in the Volga region, the reorganization drive represented just one more fruitless reform drive in a line of many. Pointing out that 23 percent of reorganized farms in Volgograd oblast kept their original status and 68 percent simply adopted some other form of collective organization, he argued that the program did not change internal relations on the farms nor among farmers (Cherniaev 1994, 3, 39).

Further evidence that the reorganization drive was another Russian reform "from above" without much impact on the operation of agricultural enterprises comes from a poll of directors at 111 agricultural enterprises in Volgograd oblast, representing 21 percent of all such enterprises (Zakahrova and Antonova 1995). The survey found that the impetus for reorganization came from the labor collective in only 14 percent of the cases. Sixteen percent of the time it came from the leadership of the collective or state farm, and in 70 percent of the cases it came from above. Furthermore, by far the most common action for large farm members regarding their land certificates was to lease them back to the collective (Wegren 2000, 251; Allina-Pisano 2002). In a survey of 358 large farms in 10 oblasts, members leased all of their shares back to the farms in 110 instances and more than 90 percent of their shares in another 121 cases.[31] At the regional level, approximately 65 percent of land shares were leased back to the collective in Kirov and Volgograd oblasts, over 80 percent in Orel oblast, and about 90 percent in Nizhnii Novgorod and Rostov oblasts (Wegren 2000, 251). For all these reasons, the conventional wisdom held that the reorganization campaign had simply "changed the signs on the doors" at state and collective farms—the Lenin Collective Farm had become the Lenin Joint-Stock Company.

For advocates of market-based land reform, however, reorganization was not an end in itself, but merely a prelude to the creation of small private farms, a process that began in earnest at the end of 1991. Yeltsin's

---

31. Similarly, an average of 86 percent of property shares were leased back to the farms (Wegren 2000, 251).

December decrees initially seemed to have the desired effect, as peasants left the larger farms to create their own private holdings in 1992 in greater numbers than in any other year since Stolypin's time. The number of small farms jumped to nearly 183,000, a 250-percent increase over 1991 (see Table 4.3). The amount of land under cultivation in the private sector expanded even faster, from 2 million to 7.8 million hectares. The peasant exodus from the large farms continued in 1993, and Russians had created 270,000 private farms by the end of the year.

If the reorganization drive achieved only superficial success, however, the private farmers' movement failed to reach even that goal. The initial burst of private-farm creation in 1992, for example, did not signify an extensive restructuring of agriculture in favor of private farming. By the end of the year private farms cultivated less than 2 percent of Russian agricultural land, and they produced only about 1–2 percent of the country's food (Pallot 1993). When the rate of increase in the number of private farms fell in 1993, even former champions of private farming began to question how much such enterprises could contribute to Russian agricultural production.[32]

After the shelling of the parliament in October 1993, Yeltsin issued a new decree to speed up the transformation of landownership, but rural dwellers added fewer than ten thousand new small farms in the next year. In addition, some of the provisions of the October decision hurt the private farmers' cause. In the name of tightening the money supply, Yeltsin eliminated subsidized credits to small farmers. With the entire agricultural sector facing unfavorable terms of trade with industry, many rural dwellers chose to expand and work harder on the private plots they had received during the Soviet era, rather than striking out on their own.[33] Urbanites also used the private farm legislation to expand their garden plots, and most of the new "peasant farmers" in Russia by 1993 turned out to be city residents receiving land from the regional land funds (Wegren 1992b, 119; Craumer 1994, 329; Prosterman, Rolfes, and Mitchell 1994, 13n11).[34] The "farmers' movement" was even less significant than official statistics suggested.

32. See, for example, Agricultural Minister Viktor Khlystun's comments in July 1993, cited in Craumer 1994, 339–40.

33. In the first nine months of 1993, agricultural prices rose by 6.6 times, while those of industrial goods and services went up by 10.4 times. For inputs to agricultural production in particular, prices went up by twelve to sixteen times. (See Komitet po sel'skomu khoziaistvu administratsii Volgogradskoi oblasti, n.d.)

34. A decree in December 1993 ended the practice of giving land to urbanites for free, except for private farming (Wegren 1998a, 159).

TABLE 4.3
Number of farms and size of landholdings

	1991	1992	1993	1994
Large farms				
Number (thousands)	25.5	26.6	26.9	26.9
Land farmed (million hectares)	186.3	162.8	157.9	155.8
Avg. size (hectares)	7,306	6,120	5,870	5,792
Percent of total ag. land	**97.2**	**93.9**	**91.1**	**89.0**
Personal plots				
Total				
Number (millions)	39.4	40.7	39.1	38.9
Land (million hectares)	5.253	8.510	7.646	7.892
Percent of total ag. land	**2.7**	**4.9**	**4.4**	**4.5**
Subsidiary farming plots				
Number (millions)	17.6	19.3	16.6	16.6
Land (million hectares)	3.654	6.826	5.825	6.062
Avg. size (hectares)	0.21	0.35	0.35	0.37
Gardens or orchards (*sady*)				
Number (millions)	12.2	13.5	14.3	14.7
Land (million hectares)	0.930	1.083	1.167	1.209
Avg. size (hectares)	0.08	0.08	0.08	0.08
Vegetable gardens (*ogorody*)				
Number (millions)	9.6	7.9	8.2	7.6
Land (million hectares)	0.669	0.601	0.654	0.621
Avg. size (hectares)	0.07	0.08	0.08	0.08
Peasant farms				
Number (thousands)	4.4	49	182.8	270.0
Land (million hectares)	0.181	2.068	7.804	11.342
Avg. size (hectares)	41.1	42.2	42.7	42.0
Percent of total ag. land	**0.1**	**1.2**	**4.5**	**6.5**

Sources: Rossiiskii statisticheskii ezhegodnik 2001, 402–4, except for the following: data on personal plots in 1991 are from Shaw 1992, 554, and those in 1992–94 are from Rudnev and Borobov 2000, 106–7. When direct comparison with the official statistics of Rudnev and Borobov was possible, Shaw's data overstated the number of personal plots, which suggests that the jump in microfarming between 1991 and 1992 is probably understated in this table.

Like managers' success in taking over industrial firms during mass privatization, the anemic development of private farms cried out for explanation. Some observers argued that Anatolii Chubais ran a tighter and more committed administrative hierarchy at GKI than his counterparts at the Russian Land Committee, allowing him to force the pace of reform more effectively (Aslund 1995, 315; Medvedev 1994). In reality, the land-reform bureaucracy pushed through farm reorganization at almost exactly the same pace as mass privatization. Conversely, no one should overstate the successes of mass privatization, which failed to achieve several of its goals.

A second possible explanation for the relatively slow pace of private farm creation was the strength of conservative values among the rural population. Perhaps the peasantry—depleted and terrorized by Stalin's collectivization and further drained by subsequent out-migration—simply did not want the land and the responsibility it entailed. Or perhaps some believed the land should not be owned by anyone, since it was a "bozhii dar"—a gift from God—as Russian tradition had held for centuries (Szamuely 1974; McDaniel 1988; Tucker 1971). Large-farm managers and their political lobby group, the Agrarian Union, frequently offered such explanations, and televised images of an elderly peasant shouting angrily across a fence at her upstart neighbors seemed to lend credence to them.

While it is certainly plausible that the countryside was, on the whole, more conservative than the cities, two factors weaken the argument that a rural culture of timidity undermined agricultural land reform. First, independent private farming is extraordinarily difficult in the best of circumstances, and the Russian environment of the early 1990s was far from ideal. Since failure can be life-threatening, reluctance to leave the large farm may have been evidence of prudence, rather than culturally conditioned fear. Second, the development of a private farming sector does not require universal participation in family farming, and Russia had an active core of private farmers and would-be private farmers in 1992–94. Their failure to realize the high hopes of land-reform advocates was not due to conservatism or timidity (Barnes 1998).

Instead, the main resistance to the creation of independent private farms came from farm managers and their allies in local government. Whereas industrial privatization allowed factory managers to privatize their enterprises without losing control over them, creating private farms required agricultural managers to give up physical assets. Some farm directors may have sincerely believed they could best feed the country and protect the peasants' interests by blocking the dissolution of the large farms, and some Russian scholars agree that there was more hope in restructuring large agricultural enterprises than in breaking them up into tiny private farms (Cherniaev 1994, 51). Other agrarians were almost certainly making cynical attempts to preserve their own wealth and prestige, as several Western scholars have emphasized (Van Atta 1993c). Regardless of motive, however, whereas industrial managers exploited their environment to encourage a particular form of privatization, farm directors used their considerable resources to block property reform outright.

In the first months of the land reform program, the easiest strategy for managers was to withhold land certificates from members of the collective. In a memo to the deputy head of the oblast administration, for instance, Aleksandr Vorobev of the Volgograd oblast land committee wrote that agricultural managers, such as the director of the Komsomo-lets state farm in Sredneakhtubinskii raion, were refusing to distribute land and property shares to members of the collectives (Vorob'ev 1992c, 4). The refusals had continued despite warnings from the local land committees to dozens of farm managers, and a fine of three months' pay in the case of the Komsomolets director (Vorob'ev 1992a, 4; 1992b, 1).

Issuing paper shares was only the first step toward transferring real land to would-be private farmers, and directors could delay such trans-fers in other ways. For example, many of them ignored an explicit legal requirement that they specifically identify the land to which a land share referred (Vorob'ev 1992c, 5). Such failures of identification often led to long disputes when a farmer wanted to leave the collective and take the land to which he or she was entitled. Similarly, managers could drag their feet in signing the proper forms to prevent would-be private farmers from leaving the collective ("Reshenie" 1993, 1).

Even when the new entrepreneurs won permission to break away from the larger units, the directors of the collective and state farms could undermine their efforts to develop viable enterprises. For example, managers determined both which plots of land a new farmer could claim upon leaving the collective and which land would go into the regional fund from which farmers could expand their holdings. According to Vorobev, the funds in Volgograd oblast, especially in areas around larger cities, contained a disproportionate amount of poor-quality and incon-veniently located land (Vorob'ev 1992c, 3). Furthermore, some heads of raion administrations regularly transferred the better land back to collective and state farms, arguing that it should not lie unused while the legislature waited for a private farmer to ask for it (Kazannik 1993). Through this process, the agricultural elite could ensure that private farmers received land that was far from populated areas, of low quality, too small to be practical, or in need of extensive investment.

Even if the new farmers left the collective with usable land, they could not be certain of keeping it. In a story that would be repeated across the country, a farmer in Krasnodar krai signed a forty-year lease with the local state farm but lost his land after a little more than a year—the sovkhoz took him to court for "not using the land properly" and was able to confiscate it (Pishchikova 1992b). In Volgograd, oblast land committee chief Vorobev consistently argued that, taking into account the low quality of land the new farmers usually received, they produced at least as well as the collective enterprises, but his arguments often went unheard (Vorob'ev 1995, 2).

In addition to all the roadblocks they could set on the road to obtaining and retaining land, the large-farm managers could block access to processing facilities, markets, and even inputs intended for private farms. Typically, that strategy involved lobbying against special privileges for new farmers; and it began with a litany of the difficulties plaguing the entire agricultural sector, including decreasing yields, insufficient funds for investment, and plummeting terms of trade with the industrial sector.[35] According to the argument, since the large farms actually had the greatest productive potential, and since all of agriculture was suffering, it made little sense to earmark assistance for small private farms. The campaign met with some success, as in Tiumen oblast, where equipment set aside for private farmers in 1993 was sold to collective and state farms instead. Likewise, in Saratov oblast, private farmers did not receive the credits they were owed in order to purchase parts and fuel, while the large farms did (Kazannik 1993). Given the multiple options available to large-farm managers who wanted to prevent the establishment of new private farms, the creation of 270,000 such farms in an environment of macroeconomic disorder and trade disruption was perhaps all that could have been expected.

The most important effects of land reform in 1992–94, however, lay not in creating a quarter of a million family farms against long odds. The farm reorganization drive created a group of real landowners, albeit not the ones reformers wanted, and their success actually slowed the development of the small-farmers' movement. As discussed above, many rural citizens turned their land shares over to the large farms during reorganization, either through a leasing arrangement or by depositing their certificates in the "charter capital" of the new entity. In either case, the manager of the large farm—not a family farmer or the state—became the de facto or de jure owner of the land. The arrangement made further transfers difficult, since the government's legal right to require them had become less clear.

35. For but one example of such claims, see Sovet Agrarnogo soiuza Volgogradskoi oblasti, 1993.

Moreover, the new rules of the game allowed a land market of sorts to develop. While law and circumstance blocked outright sales of land, owners of land certificates could lease them to others, and small farms often used this method to expand (Kliamkin and Timofeev 2000, 32–33). The leases could take several forms, but usually they incorporated some kind of barter exchange. For example, a farm in Rostov oblast paid 300 kilograms of grain and 100 kilograms of sunflowers per land certificate. Similar arrangements developed in Riazan oblast, Novgorod oblast, and elsewhere (Kliamkin and Timofeev 2000, 28–29). In such transactions, just as in the first stages of land reform, the managers of large farms often proved to be the dominant players, since they represented the only realistic lessor in an area. They could decide which plots to lease out, who would be allowed to take them, and what the payments would be (Kliamkin and Timofeev 2000, 31). In practice, they could virtually dictate the terms of the lease agreement even after it had been signed (Allina-Pisano 2002, 310–11). The problem for the peasant farmer, however, was not that real property rights for land did not exist but that the managers of the large farms had effectively claimed them. That arrangement helped shape the redistribution of land long after the main land-reform drive came to an end.

More than Farms

Land reform understandably attracted great attention in 1992–94, as it represented an age-old, unfulfilled promise and a repudiation of Bolshevism. Furthermore, most authors and readers see private farmers as sympathetic figures. There is more to agriculture than land, however, and more to Russian agrarian reform than breaking up farms. In particular, the agrarian sector also contains suppliers of farm inputs and purchasers of agricultural outputs. In both subsectors in 1992–94, some assets were distributed through the mass privatization program, while others worked their way out of state control through other channels.

In the USSR, a broad array of enterprises under various ministries produced inputs for agriculture; and as the Soviet state crumbled, many of them created large-scale associations. After the fall of the Soviet Union, mass privatization pulled individual producers of fertilizer, farm machinery, and so on out of these associations and transferred them to new owners. Indeed, the first nationwide voucher auction in Russia included the Volgograd Tractor Factory (Esliamova 1993). As such, the sale of input suppliers enjoyed all the successes and endured all the failures of mass privatization.

At the procurement end of the system, the processing plants, which bought produce directly from farms, also privatized in accordance with the program. That is, they became independent joint-stock companies and sold their shares to insiders and outsiders. Firms that privatized earlier tended to follow Option 1, but by the end of the process the vast majority had chosen Option 2, with its privileges to management and the workforce. Thus, in Briansk oblast, by January 1, 1995, insiders owned over 66 percent of the shares of privatized food-processing plants, while another 24 percent were dispersed among several producers (Vas'kin 1996, 29). Even after a policy to increase farms' ownership stakes in processing companies, producers held majority stakes in only 14 percent of the privatized processors in Russia by the end of 1996 (Wandel 2000, 370).

Not all food processors privatized using Option 2. The Vostok agro-industrial formation, for example, established in 1993 in Novosibirsk oblast, consisted of a meat-processing firm in which three cattle and hog producers owned 90 percent of the shares, while the workforce of the processor owned the remaining 10 percent (Novikov 1996, 74). Indeed, the entire Republic of Chuvashia followed its own plan for privatizing food processors, hoping to give producers a more significant ownership stake. The approach banned the use of Option 2 in selling processors, required the privatized enterprises to become open joint-stock companies, and sold to producers any shares remaining after the closed sale to insiders. Groups of producers were guaranteed a controlling stake in the processors to which they supplied inputs (Ivanova 1995, 17–18). Experiments like these, however, were clearly the exception to the rule that held in most of the country.

Although Option 2 and insider ownership were issues for all enterprises in the mass privatization program, they evoked additional political consternation in the case of food processors. In a pinch, farms can operate with old machinery or without fertilizer, so when property reform changed the relationship between suppliers and farms, it raised some objections, but not enough to change the policy. Processing, however, is an integral part of agriculture—without it, produce simply rots—and advocates of large producers in Russia frequently blamed insider privatization of processing plants for the dire straits of the farms. Thus, whereas radical reformers decried insider ownership throughout the economy, agrarian leaders particularly objected to insider ownership of processors, and their arguments helped frame property debates in the sector for the next several years.

In addition to the enterprises that passed through the mass privatization program, significant pieces of the input and procurement systems followed strategies in the "privatization by exception" vein. Agrosnab, for example, the main distributor of agricultural inputs, did not reorganize in the late Soviet era. Instead, it converted to joint-stock-company status only in 1992, much like the enterprises of the electricity or oil sectors discussed above. The lines of ownership in the new organization were very complicated, as the regional branches owned the national association, now called Rosagrosnab ("Ob AO 'Rosagrosnab'" 2001). In the early 1990s the state sold off pieces of the structure, but in doing so it turned a state monopoly into a de facto private monopoly (Wegren 1996, 162–63). The network of suppliers remained the sole source of key inputs for many farms.

The rural procurement and distribution agency Tsentrosoiuz was privatized in 1992–93 in much the same manner as Agrosnab. Tsentrosoiuz had been responsible for most retail outlets in rural areas under the Soviet system. In addition, the network served as a major part of the procurement system, purchasing potatoes, fruits, vegetables, and some livestock from rural producers and sometimes processing them in its own plants. Beginning in 1992 the government began to sell off pieces of the Tsentrosoiuz system, usually breaking up the hierarchy along regional or local lines (Wegren 1996, 155).

The behemoth of Russian agricultural procurement, however, was Roskhleboprodukt, which purchased grain from farmers, stored it in elevators, and passed it along to processing plants. Because of its centrality to the system, redistribution of this asset took a slightly different path from the other pieces. Specifically, the immediate elimination of the entire state procurement system for grain would have been politically, and probably culturally and ethically, impossible. It is one thing to argue that market mechanisms will eventually develop and allocate machine tools or concrete efficiently; it is a far different matter to ask people to sit quietly while the traditional source of their daily bread is dismantled. For that reason, even though more and more farms had become private, the government feared chaos if it left the grain market entirely to chance, and it continued to require deliveries from farms, using Roskhleboprodukt to collect them. In 1992 it converted this monopoly—which included over three thousand enterprises—into a joint-stock company, placing Leonid Cheshinskii, former chair of the Russian branch of the ministry at the end of the Soviet period, in charge (*Kto est' kto* 1993, 709).

In the context of continued mandatory state grain purchases, the distribution of assets led to contentious politics, unbalanced supply and demand, and a series of state experiments with both procurement policy and the ownership of Roskhleboprodukt. By the middle of 1992, for example, official prices for produce had lost half their value relative to important agricultural inputs (Wegren 1994a, 200). In response, the Agrarian Union organized eighty-five strike committees throughout the country that withheld grain from the state to try to force higher procurement prices or greater subsidies to agricultural enterprises (Van Atta 1993b, 63; Hahn 1993, 44). With procurement levels at about 50 percent of the previous year's numbers, the Russian government raised the state's offering price in August 1992. At the same time, Yeltsin issued a decree allowing the state to confiscate the proceeds from the sale of agricultural produce that should have been sold to the state (Wegren 1994a, 200).

In 1993 the Yeltsin administration began to reduce the required deliveries from farmers. At the same time, however, the state price for grain moved higher than the market price, which caused farmers to sell much more grain to the state in 1993 than officials had planned, leaving the procurement system 60 percent over budget by September 1993. The state then stopped indexing procurement prices to inflation, but it remained the single largest buyer of farm output (Wegren 1994a, 202–3).

At the end of 1993 the government began to privatize large pieces of Roskhleboprodukt, and it officially eliminated mandatory grain deliveries from farms (Khramova and Verkhaim 1999, 2; Desai 1995, 56, 67; Wegren 1998a, 270n122; Serova 1999, 419). A presidential decree in December of that year began the sale of regional and local branches of the procurement agency, a process that continued for much of 1994. On its face, the new policy appeared to turn grain supply over to the market and give farmers a range of options in selling their produce. In practice, however, privatization and fragmentation of the procurement system did not always provide farmers with a choice of local outlets for their goods, since the former Roskhleboprodukt branches simply became regional monopsonies. In addition, while approximately twenty-eight hundred independent enterprises were privatized under the plan, about seven hundred remained with the state. Finally, the government retained a system of grain reserves, or "food funds" as they were called, and the privatized branches of Roskhleboprodukt often contracted with the government to deliver produce to the reserves (Serova, Khramova, and Nichols 2002, 26; Khramova and Verkhaim 1999, 2). Thus the reforms of agrarian suppliers and buyers in the early 1990s significantly restructured ownership of the major assets in the sector, largely by breaking down the state's mechanisms of control. Simply limiting the influence of the state, however, did not determine which actor or actors would take over at the newly released enterprise, a question that remained open for several years.

Strategies of Survival and Growth

The enormous changes in agriculture in the early 1990s produced different reactions from participants in the sector. Some of the responses were defensive, as farms and citizens simply tried to survive in a convulsive time. Other strategies saw actors exploiting the new environment to develop trading companies that would later play defining roles in the sector. Each of these trends would become more apparent after mass privatization and farm reorganization came to a close, but they were already underway while the large-scale reforms were in progress.

One type of defensive response came from former collective and state farm managers after the insider privatization of food processors with which they traditionally did business. Some of the directors reacted by building small processing facilities on their farms' land. In Novosibirsk oblast, for example, twenty-one small-scale meat and sausage facilities were constructed (Stadnik and Aleksanova 1997, 51). Similarly, milk producers in the region expanded their own processing capacities and sold to their own retailers when possible (Schastlivtseva and Gubanova 1995, 11). This strategy was not sufficiently widespread to have a significant effect on the agrarian sector in 1992–94, but it signaled a process that would continue to shape ownership and operation of the sector for many years.

A second defensive strategy had a more immediate, obvious, and far-reaching effect on the structure of agriculture in Russia. That is, while the land reform program failed to tempt large numbers of rural residents to strike out on their own as private farmers, it cleared the way for a rapid rise in subsistence farming by both urbanites and rural dwellers. Whereas the number of private family farms increased by less than 140,000 in 1992, the number of small-scale personal plots jumped by more than one million; the amount of land they cultivated expanded almost as quickly as that of private farms; and their contribution to total agricultural output far outstripped that of private farms (see Tables 4.3 and 4.4). In addition, as price liberalization and the virtual evaporation of credit devastated agriculture in 1992 and 1993, a symbiosis began to develop between small-plot farmers and the carcasses of the state and collective farms (Allina-Pisano 2002; Kitching 1998a, 1998b; Humphrey 2002). The owners of the small plots relied heavily on the large farms to provide such production inputs as seed and tools, while the large farms needed the rural residents to keep working the fields. Ironically, although agrarian reform had aimed to reduce the need for these kinds of gardens, the immediate reaction of Russians was to increase their use dramatically.

Some responses to the new environment were more aggressive. For example, well-placed political and economic actors took advantage of arbitrage opportunities that bridged the industrial and agricultural sectors. Price liberalization in 1992 had aimed in part to reduce open-

TABLE 4.4
Proportion of selected agricultural products from different types of farms, 1991–94

	1991	1992	1993	1994
Personal plots				
Grain	0.4	0.5	0.6	0.7
Sugar beets	0.0	0.2	0.3	0.7
Sunflower seeds	1.2	1.2	1.5	1.6
Potatoes	**72.2**	**78.0**	**82.5**	**88.1**
Vegetables	**46.4**	**54.7**	**64.5**	**66.7**
Cattle and poultry for slaughter	**30.5**	**35.3**	**39.5**	**43.2**
Milk	**26.0**	**31.4**	**34.7**	**38.7**
Eggs	**22.2**	**26.0**	**27.1**	**28.8**
Wool	**28.2**	**32.2**	**35.4**	**37.1**
Honey	**70.2**	**76.3**	**78.0**	**81.9**
Private farms				
Grain	**0.2**	**2.1**	**5.2**	5.1
Sugar beets	0.0	**2.0**	3.9	3.5
Sunflower seeds	**0.4**	**5.8**	**9.9**	10.2
Potatoes	**0.2**	0.8	1.0	0.9
Vegetables	**0.2**	0.8	1.0	1.1
Cattle and poultry for slaughter	0.1	0.7	1.1	1.4
Milk	0.1	0.5	1.1	1.3
Eggs	0.0	0.1	0.2	0.3
Wool	0.1	0.8	1.8	2.7
Honey	**0.6**	**1.3**	2.3	2.2

Source: Rossiiskii statisticheskii ezhegodnik 2001, 402.
Note: Goods produced in greater proportion than what would be predicted by a farm type's proportion of agricultural land are in bold.

ings to buy goods at subsidized rates and resell them on open markets for vast profits. Political and social pressure, however, inadvertently left some loopholes unclosed. Oil prices, for example, remained well below world levels (Lane and Seifulmulukov 1999, 19). While that exception may have helped ease the pain that otherwise skyrocketing prices inflicted on consumers and businesses, it also encouraged schemes to buy oil domestically and sell it abroad. One strategy was to exchange the oil for agricultural produce. For example, the Tomsk oblast government received permission to export 1 percent of its oil production, a right it transferred to Tomskneft, which exported its oil to a foreign company in exchange for grain that would be shipped to Tomskkhleboprodukt. The grain, however, was withheld until prices had dropped, so the value of the grain returned was lower than that of the oil received (Pleines 1999, 102).

In some cases, the new opportunities gave rise to new companies, including Razguliai-Ukrros, founded in 1992. The man who headed the firm, Igor Potapenko, graduated from a military school in Kiev, later studied at the Moscow Institute of International Relations, and founded his company with two classmates from military school (Telitsyna, Kuz'menko, and Kovalenko 2002; Vlasova and Kuz'min 2002; Sagdiev 2002). The first, Sergei Fedorenko, later headed the Ukrros group in Ukraine, while the second, Vladimir Satsiuk, went on to become a legislator in Ukraine (Kuz'menko 2002). The group's military ties probably helped them receive permission to export Russian oil, which they exchanged for Ukrainian sugar (Vlasova and Kuz'min 2002; Pleines 1999).

Oil-for-produce schemes were not solely the province of new enterprises, however, as existing trading companies also moved into the arena. The OGO company, for example, was established in 1988, and in 1990 it became a broker on the Russian Commodities and Raw Materials Exchange (RCRME), facilitating trades in a wide variety of goods (Serova, Khramova, and Nichols 2002, 4).[36] In the final months of the Soviet era, after Arkadii Zlochevskii became president of the company, OGO shifted its emphasis from brokerage services to grain trading. Domestically, OGO bought grain from local elevators or regional administrations and sold it to processors in Russia. Internationally, it bartered for grain and other agricultural goods, often in exchange for oil and petroleum prod-

---

36. For more on the exchanges in the late Soviet and early Russian periods, see Frye 2000; Wegren 1994a; Zhurek 1995.

ucts. On the strength of such trades, as well as its 1993 contract for distributing Western grain delivered as humanitarian aid, OGO developed into the largest nonstate grain company in Russia (Serova, Khramova, and Nichols 2002, 4–5). Its influence would only grow as large-scale privatization ended and a new struggle for property began.

NEW STRUCTURES ON SAND

Russian economic policy in the first years of independence aimed to destroy any remnants of the Soviet economic system. In the industrial sector, that meant the rapid privatization of over fourteen thousand enterprises to shear them from ministerial control and dependence. In agriculture the campaign to reorganize state and collective farms sought to break up large enterprises and replace them with private family farms. Although proponents of the reforms often glossed over the limitations of mass privatization and focused too much attention on the nascent private farmers' movement, both programs significantly restructured ownership in Russia.

In different ways, however, both programs failed on their own terms. It might be tempting to blame their problems on flaws in the reform plans, perhaps the fault of weak "reformers" or strong "hardliners" and "rent seekers." To understand the dynamic of property redistribution during and after mass privatization, however, it is important to see that the outcomes in the two sectors resulted from economically rational decisions by managers, given their interests and resources. The industrialists carried out a particular version of privatization that benefited them by taking advantage of the Privatization Program and the macroeconomic environment of the time in ways no one had anticipated. The agrarians, meanwhile, used their distance from Moscow and their proximity to key assets—most notably land—to resist land reform outright. Understanding these different processes shows how policy on paper can mutate when it interacts with power on the ground and reminds observers that managers' claims to property might be challenged under new circumstances.

Whatever the results—astounding success, unmitigated disaster, or something in between—the large-scale privatization programs represented only part of the sweeping transformation of ownership in Russia in 1992–94. Enormous pieces of valuable property were transferred through processes beyond the reach of most Russians. Meanwhile, millions of ordinary citizens made do with a larger plot of land for subsistence farming.

All these developments represented a tremendous change from the Soviet system, but little in the system was stable. The state still held important property that it promised to sell off; managers' positions remained uncertain; multiple types of reintegration among firms were underway; and regional governments had barely stepped into the fray. As mass privatization wound down, the Russian political economy had survived an enormous upheaval, but it stood at the edge of a new phase in the struggle for property.

CHAPTER 5

MANY CURRENTS, ONE TUMULTUOUS RIVER

Redistribution after Privatization, 1994–97

When voucher privatization formally ended on June 30, 1994, with large-scale farm reorganization having wound down shortly before, it was tempting to think that the competition for property in post-Soviet Russia had come to a close. If the essence of property transformation was the transfer of state assets to private hands, then surely these massive reform programs had done the job. Thousands of enterprises had gone through the voucher privatization process. Tens of thousands of small shops had been sold or given away. Almost all the collective and state farms had reregistered and distributed shares to their members. The Soviet system of state ownership was long gone.

The briefest of glances, however, at scholarly and journalistic coverage of Russia's political economy in the years following mass privatization shows that the struggle for property was not over. Indeed, it seemed only to intensify. Russia's leading national-level economic actors, the "oligarchs," pried oil wells and media outlets from the state and fought with other shareholders for control over major pieces of property. Western investors locked horns with enterprise managers who could erase them from shareholder registers or intimidate them physically. The tentacles of organized crime seemed to be wrapped around more and more of the economy each day. The agricultural sector seemed far less dynamic, but even there the occasional plucky private farmer or presidential decree on the sale and purchase of farmland hinted that change might be underway.

The mid-1990s in Russia, however, were not simply a period of disconnected events and sensational images. The stories that attracted observers' attention, and many that did not, were part of a larger process. Implicitly or explicitly, many interpretations of Russian property reform in 1994–97 argued that the broader context was one of "incomplete transition" (Aslund 1995; Blasi, Kroumova, and Kruse 1997; Shleifer and Treisman 2000). According to that view, the mass privatization of 1992–94 had moved Russia a long way down the path toward a market economy, and the goal for the next few years was to finish the journey. When progress seemed stalled, members of the incomplete transition school argued that the Russian state should both decrease its ownership role and resolve a wide range of inadequacies in the institutional structure of the economy. In the realm of legal development, for example, they pointed to the absence of clear laws on bankruptcy, agricultural land sales, or insider share transactions, as well as a poorly designed tax system and pervasive but incoherent regulation of business. In discussing ownership, they argued that it was either too dispersed or concentrated in the wrong hands. Mass privatization had intentionally spread ownership among millions of citizens; mutual funds never played a significant role in corporate governance; and outside ownership (especially foreign) was low. The most common powerful owners of privatized firms were the old managers, who came in for a barrage of criticism as incompetent, unmotivated, or simply corrupt. Meanwhile, despite the privatizations of 1992–94, the state retained significant ownership of many important assets in the country.

Few of the studies of inadequate "corporate governance" and widespread "rent seeking" were wrong. Most, however, were misleading. Like analyses of the early 1990s, "incomplete transition" studies viewed the system in terms of what it might become and therefore relied on voluntaristic arguments explaining their "optimism" or "pessimism," obscuring many of the changes taking place at the time. This chapter argues that it is more useful to see 1994–97 as the next stage in the struggle for property in Russia, a stage that was just as important for understanding the development of ownership in Russia as mass privatization. The conflict of 1994–97, however, was not a free-for-all. Instead, it was shaped by the environment of the period. Most important, staggering amounts of property were still in play. Mass privatization had excluded key assets from its list, and competition over them was bound to be fierce. Even in privatized enterprises, the state usually retained stakes of nearly 30 percent, providing additional tempting morsels. Furthermore, control over many individual enterprises remained unresolved, and multiple private actors fought each other tooth and nail to secure those assets.

The fall of the Soviet Union and the mass privatization of industrial and agricultural property had shaken the tree of state ownership, but many choice pieces of fruit still dangled within reach, while others remained poorly guarded on the ground.

Even as so much property remained available or potentially available, the formal institutions of politics and law in Russia displayed peculiar characteristics. The president (Boris Yeltsin) dominated the legislature in the realm of policy making, although he was not omnipotent, and the requirement that he stand for reelection in 1996 affected the political economy of the time. At least as important, regional governments in the mid-1990s wielded great power in policy making and especially policy implementation. When Yeltsin disbanded the national and regional legislatures at the end of 1993, he left regional governors in dominant positions, and they only grew stronger as they stood for independent election in 1995–97. Courts appeared disturbingly manipulable, as economic actors, regional officials, and organized crime figures bribed, replaced, or threatened judges who ruled the wrong way. Nevertheless, the legal context did affect the strategies of competitors over property. For example, formal economic groups consulted with regional governments as required; food processors issued supplementary shares in themselves, even if the intended buyers declined to purchase them; and enterprise managers often exploited securities-law loopholes instead of resorting to outright criminality. The weak constraint of laws may be cold comfort to those hoping for a Western-style market economy in Russia, but it should remind us both that rules were not wholly unimportant and that, while passing new ones probably would have shaped the strategy of competitors in the struggle for property, they would not have brought it under control.

With so many assets available and the rules of the game still unclear, the motives for acquiring assets ranged widely. In the economic realm, an enterprise could provide not only a chance of future profits, but also opportunities for asset stripping and myriad financial schemes. Furthermore, it still seemed important to many actors to grab something—anything—while it was still available; longer-term strategies could wait. Politically, ownership of enterprises could convey significant power, especially if the firms employed a large number of people or accounted for a significant part of the economy. Meanwhile, regional politicians strengthened their ties to enterprises for purposes ranging from personal enrichment to the maintenance of local economic and social welfare systems.

In this complex setting five types of participants played major roles in the struggle over property. First came the federal government, which mostly provided new property for the struggle. Second, some of the most important competitors for assets were the many economic ownership groups in the country, both the handful of famous national conglomerates, colloquially known as the "oligarchs," and the myriad "second-tier" groups that received much less coverage. Third, regional governments established themselves as major players in property redistribution, as they shaped the development of large and small ownership groups, took sides in conflicts over individual firms, encouraged integration in agriculture, and directly owned shares in enterprises on their territories. Fourth, the clearest beneficiaries of mass privatization were the managers of industrial and agricultural enterprises, many of whom used the post-privatization years to solidify their hold on their firms' assets. Finally, both Russian and foreign outsiders captured some of those assets for themselves. The competition and collaboration among these actors produced many different, sometimes conflicting, trends in property redistribution in the years after large-scale privatization. The end result was a broad array of new owners with control over vital assets in the Russian economy and strong connections to political power.

THE MANY LEVELS OF COMPETITION FOR INDUSTRIAL PROPERTY

Russian privatization vouchers expired in June 1994; and as that deadline approached, politicians, scholars, and other observers argued about what would come next in industrial property reform. Members of the incomplete transition school, including reformers in the Russian government, expected and advocated two major trends: additional privatization, for money rather than vouchers; and the establishment of effective corporate governance at privatized enterprises, usually by replacing old managers with outsiders. While both kinds of change did occur, the assumption that they were the most important forces at work and that they were part of progress toward a regularized market economy clouded understanding of the period.

Instead, those trends represented minor currents in the torrent of conflict over industrial property. At the national level, the conflict included a scandalous, although overhyped, giveaway of key assets, additional sales of state property, and the expansion of the financial-industrial empires of the oligarchs. Just as important for the future of Russia, however, was the establishment of "second-tier" economic groups across the country. Second-tier conglomerates attracted far less attention than the national groups, but they were often major players in regional political economies and controlled assets that helped them survive the financial crash of 1998. At the same time, much of the competition for industrial property took place at the level of individual enterprises, as insiders, outsiders, and regional governments established unstable alliances in pursuit of important assets. Instead of developing corporate governance that would create competitive enterprises, the alliances fueled a raw struggle for real property that remained unresolved throughout the period.

Bright Lights, Big City

National battles over industrial assets attracted a great deal of attention from scholars and other observers of Russia in the years following mass privatization. The infamous loans-for-shares deals of 1995, which transferred a handful of prime assets to well-placed economic actors for far less than their market value, probably received more coverage than any single development in Russian property reform except voucher privatization (e.g., Freeland 2000; Klebnikov 2000; Hoffman 2002). Additional sales of federal property, along with the oligarchs' increased control over some of the assets they had acquired, also attracted investigators' attention, both because they reflected the audacity and decadence of the time and because the greater concentration of ownership represented potential progress toward a functioning market economy. Events at the national level, however, often received more attention than they deserved, were frequently misinterpreted, and certainly did not represent the end of the struggle for property.

The loans-for-shares auctions served as a clear example of these tendencies. The idea for the sales first surfaced in 1994, when budding oligarch Vladimir Potanin of Interros proposed it, hoping that new bankers could use it to acquire additional property after voucher privatization. In principle, the deals would use market forces to transfer assets out of the state's hands in return for the highest possible price. Stakes in the enterprises were first auctioned to bidders who, instead of buying the shares directly, offered the government loans in exchange for management rights. The government then had three years to repay the loans. If it failed, the managers who had won the first stage organized auctions to sell the shares. The organizers of the sales received 30 percent of the proceeds, and the remaining 70 percent went to the state.

To make any sense economically, the process had to include competition among participants in both rounds of auctions. In practice, however, no such competition occurred. According to one of the players, Leonid Nevzlin of the group Rosprom/Menatep, the participants agreed from the beginning "not to get in each others' way," and they lived up to that agreement (Freeland 2000, 174). For example, when the Menatep banking group organized the auction of a 45-percent stake in Yukos, the second-largest oil company in Russia, the only "competitor" allowed to bid was also financed by Menatep (Gurushina 1995). Similarly, when Oneksimbank ran the auction for a 38-percent stake in the metals giant Norilsk Nickel, it excluded a $350 million bid by Rossiiskii Kredit and declared itself the winner with a bid of $170.1 million, just $100,000 over the minimum (Johnson 1997; Blasi, Kroumova, and Kruse 1997, 75; Kokh 1998). The financial oligarchs, however, were not the only ones rigging auctions. In several other cases, the investment arms of the firms on the block excluded competitors and won the auctions with minimal bids (see Table 5.1). The biggest winner in the auctions was Potanin's Interros group, which acquired stakes in an oil company, two metals enterprises, and a shipping firm. Mikhail Khodorkovskii's Menatep and Boris Berezovskii's LogoVAZ also won pieces of valuable property, while insider groups at Surgutneftegaz, LUKoil, Mechel, and Novorossiiskoe Shipping used the process to increase control over their enterprises.

Before the loans-for-shares auctions occurred, the optimistic interpretation held that they would move Russia a step closer to a functioning market economy. When they proved corrupt, the disappointment they created and the high profile of some of the players and the assets they acquired prompted some analysts to ascribe more influence to the deals than they deserved (e.g., Freeland 2000). It was easy to overstate both the size of the deals and their implications for the Russian political economy.

Certainly the auctions included important assets, but those assets were relatively small compared to the rest of the economy and even to the original loans-for-shares plan. The initial formal proposal, made in March 1995, called on the state to sell shares in twenty-nine different companies, including the electricity monopoly UES and the long-distance carrier Rostelekom (Freeland 2000, 175–76; Blasi, Kroumova, and Kruse 1997, 74). Over the next several months, however, enterprises and their patrons lobbied to have themselves excluded from the process,

TABLE 5.1
Loans-for-shares auctions, 1995

Date	Prize	Winner	Winning bid	Minimum price
Oil companies 11/3/95	40% stake in Surgutneftegaz	Surgutneftegaz's pension fund (an opposing bid was disqualified)	$65 million + promise to pay off $300 million in debt OR $88.3 million + promised investments of $193 million	
12/7/95	5% stake in LUKoil	LUKoil with Bank Imperial (Foreigners and companies cooperating with foreigners were excluded)	$43 million OR $35 million + promised investments of $70 million	
12/7/95	51% stake in Sidanko	Oneksimbank via MFK (Alfa, Inkombank, and RK were disqualified)	Approximately $130 million + promised investments of $160 million	Approximately $130 million
12/8/95	78% stake in Yukos	Menatep via Laguna (Consortium of Rossiiskii Kredit, Alfa, and Inkombank was excluded "for technical reasons")	Approximately $159 million + promised investments of $150–200 million	$150 million + investments
12/28/95	51% stake in Sibneft	Logo VAZ and SBS-Agro via Finance Oil Company (FNK) (Inkombank's bid was exluded)	Approximately $100 million + promise of investments	$100 million

(TABLE 5.1—*cont.*)

Date	Prize	Winner	Winning bid	Minimum price
Oil-trading company				
12/28/95	15% stake in Nafta-Moskva	UNI-BEST OR Oneksim (via Nafta)	Just over $20 million	$20 million
Metals companies				
11/17/95	38% stake in Norilsk Nickel	Oneksimbank (a) (Rossiiskii Kredit's $350 million bid was excluded)	$170.1 million	$170 million
12/7/95	15% stake in NLMK	Oneksimbank via MFK	$31 million	$30 million
11/17/95	15% Stake in Mechel	Management of Mechel OR Bank Imperial	$13 million	
Shipping companies				
11/17/95	49% stake in Murmansk Shipping Company	Menatep	$4.13 million	
	25.5% stake in Northwest Shipping Company	Oneksim via MFK	$6.05 million	$6 million
	45% stake in Novorossiiskoe Shipping Company	Novorossiiskoe Shipping Company	$22.65 million	

Sources: Blasi, Kroumova, and Kruse 1997, 75; Deliagin 1996; Feifer and Semenenko 2000; Popova 1998; Schröder 1999; Johnson 1997; Kohl 1998; Freeland 2000; Rutland 1997; *RRR*, June 19, 1997; Burtin, 2001; "Predpriiatiia i bankovskaia sistema" 1998; Johnson 2000, 187.
Note: An entry that includes "OR" indicates conflicting reports.

and the final list included only seventeen enterprises (see, e.g., Radygin 1996).[1] In practice, five of the auctions attracted no bids at all, so in the end the auctions sold off shares in only twelve enterprises: five oil companies, an oil trader, three metals factories, and three shipping companies (Radygin 1996; "Predpriiatiia i bankovskaia sistema" 1998). Even that list overstates the size of the deals, since several of the stakes were too small to convey operational power (see Table 5.1).

The auctions ended in December 1995, shortly before Yeltsin began to run for reelection. Several bankers, including Potanin and Khodorkovskii, poured tens of millions of dollars, countless hours of favorable media coverage, and invaluable organizational resources into his campaign, firmly embedding the term "oligarch" in the public discourse. The deals themselves, however, neither created the oligarchs nor bought their support for the reelection run. The oligarchs got their starts in the late 1980s and early 1990s, usually in the financial sector, as they took advantage of lax banking laws, rapid inflation, and other aberrations in the economic system (Johnson 2000). Loans-for-shares were simply one way that some of them tried to expand their empires into real assets. As for buying support for Yeltsin, several of the beneficiaries of loans-for-shares were not leading contributors to the campaign. More important, the deals excluded some of the most important bankers in the country, including Most Bank's Vladimir Gusinskii, Rossiiskii Kredit's Vitalii Malkin, and Alfa Bank's Mikhail Fridman and Petr Aven, all of whom contributed mightily to the reelection effort. Furthermore, the oligarchs did not decide to go all out for Yeltsin until the world economic meetings in Davos, Switzerland, in February 1996 (Johnson 2000, 181–82; McFaul 1996, 327; Freeland 2000, 190–95). That meeting took place two months after the last loans-for-shares auction, almost a year after the initial list of enterprises was published, and more than a year after the first discussions of loans-for-shares.

Nonetheless, the deals did affect Russian politics and economics. Most visibly, they raised a great public outcry and represented the first major property scandal to stick to the Yeltsin administration. Communists in the legislature appointed a "Committee to Investigate Privatization and Punish the Guilty," and opponents of privatization argued that the auctions showed the entire transfer of state property to private hands had been corrupt. None of the accusations or prosecutions was pursued

1. Yeltsin, who by then was leading an expensive and embarrassing war in Chechnya, approved the list of seventeen by decree in late August 1995 (Sigel 1995).

far enough to produce substantive results, however, so the most important effect of the auctions was simply their transfer of assets to new hands. Those resources were smaller than sometimes suggested, but they strengthened groups like Interros, Menatep, and Surgutneftegaz while simultaneously weakening the state.

Despite their notoriety, the loans-for-shares deals were far from the only transfers of federal property to new owners in 1994–97. At least 40 percent of Soviet-era enterprises, as well as large stakes in privatized enterprises, remained in state hands after voucher privatization (Rutland 1995, 15). Privatization Committee Chairman Anatolii Chubais and his supporters argued that this proportion was too high for a market economy, so the government should sell off significant pieces of its holdings—for cash rather than vouchers, so they would bring real revenue to the budget or the companies. To pass its proposal, the government introduced a bill to the legislature on July 13, waited for the parliament to reject it, and asked Yeltsin to sign a decree enacting its "Basic Provisions" (Nelson and Kuzes 1995, 161; Vinton 1994; Barnes 2001).

In many ways, however, the implementation of the program disappointed those who hoped it would help Russia complete its transition to a market economy. For example, while the program planned to sell stakes in seven thousand enterprises and raise $2 billion in 1995, through the first ten months of that year it auctioned off shares in only about thirty-five hundred enterprises for a total of $500 million (Blasi, Kroumova, and Kruse 1997, 73). In addition, privatizers received a terrible shock during the two months that Vladimir Polevanov served as chairman of the Russian State Property Committee. Chubais stepped down from that post in 1994, and Polevanov, a regional politician who had supported Yeltsin in his October 1993 confrontation with the parliament, took over. Shortly after taking the position, however, he announced that privatization had been carried out too quickly, had damaged Russia's national security, and in some cases should be reversed (Polevanov 1995, 12). Chubais orchestrated Polevanov's dismissal in January 1995, but not before Polevanov had chilled the enthusiasm of some potential investors.

The most spectacular setback in federal cash auctions came in the first attempted sale of telecom giant Sviazinvest in December 1995, while the loans-for-shares auctions were still underway. A massive holding company, Sviazinvest owned a 38-percent stake (i.e., 51 percent of the voting shares) in Rostelekom, Russia's long-distance and international telecommunications carrier, and in each of Russia's eighty-five regional telecommunications companies (Blasi, Kroumova, and Kruse 1997, 74; *RRR* April 2, 1998). The Russian government planned to sell a 25-percent stake in the company, hoping both to raise about $1 billion from this single sale and to showcase Russia as a market in which large-scale investors could participate (Blasi, Kroumova, and Kruse 1997, 74). The auction seemed to achieve at least some of its goals when the Italian phone company, Stet, won with a bid of $639 million plus a promise to invest $764 million (Blasi, Kroumova, and Kruse 1997, 74; Tagliabue 1995). At the end of December, however, Stet pulled out of the agreement, as it could not finalize details of the sale with the Russian government (Reuters 1995).

Nevertheless, cash auctions of federal shares in 1995–97 did take place and included many significant pieces of federal property. For example, in 1995 the government auctioned off a 38-percent share in the television company ORT (Schröder 1999, 967). As a result, Menatep, SBS, Alfa, National Credit Bank, Gazprom, and Mikrodin each received 5-percent stakes (Schröder 1999, 985n41). Boris Berezovskii's LogoVAZ group received an 8-percent stake, and Berezovskii himself took de facto control of the company.

In addition, while the loans-for-shares scheme privatized some important oil assets, several key pieces of the petroleum sector were transferred in other ways. For example, when Potanin entered the government in 1996, he arranged to sell an additional 34 percent of Sidanko to his own group (Kranz 1996). In addition, the government had organized some of its oil assets into new companies in 1994–95, including Eastern Oil Company (VNK) and Tiumen Oil Company (TNK), and it later sold off pieces of these holdings (Sagers 1998, 298–99). Specifically, it sold a 40-percent stake in TNK for $810 million to Novyi Holding (a creation of the Alfa/Renova group) in July 1997 and a controlling stake in VNK for about $800 million to the Menatep group in December (Feifer and Semenenko 2000; *RRR* October 23, 1997).

Even the Sviazinvest sale was revived after the first disappointment. In 1996 the newly reelected Yeltsin administration gave the Moscow banker and oligarch Vladimir Gusinskii the task of organizing the auction for 25 percent plus one share of the company (Freeland 2000, 274). Many assumed Gusinskii would therefore win the auction, but when Potanin left the government in a cabinet reshuffle in March 1997, he announced that he would participate, and Gusinskii failed in his bid to have him excluded (Freeland 2000, 276–81). In July 1997 the Potanin group, which included foreign investors Boris Jordan and George Soros, won the auction with a $1.875 billion bid, defeating Gusinskii's $1.71 billion offer (Freeland 2000, 284).

Optimists and pessimists could argue about how far such sales moved Russia toward a market economy. On one hand, the auctions were more competitive and brought in more revenue than loans-for-shares, while on the other, the receipts were still lower than planned, and the Sviazinvest auction launched months of political mudslinging that diverted effort from additional reforms. Such arguments have distracted attention from the effects of the sales on the continuing struggle for property. Most obviously, the victorious groups added to their power and prestige in Russian politics and economics. More important, however, the sales themselves did not end competition over assets. Privatization per se was only one part of the struggle over property, as private actors fought bitterly over assets no longer in state hands.

Even for the major national economic groups—which were in better position than anyone else to take advantage of federal-level privatizations in 1994–97—the sale of state property did not mark the end of conflicts over assets. Sometimes the conflicts bred outright violence, as when the director of a chocolate factory who was resisting takeover by Inkombank was murdered (Mellow 1997, 53, 56). More often, however, strategies simply represented creative reactions to the economic and legal environment of the period. An opaque secondary share market, individualized support from the federal government, collaboration with regional administrations, and the persistent use of transfer pricing all shaped the evolution of the leading economic empires in 1994–97.

In theory, the secondary market for shares serves as the chief mechanism for expansion and consolidation of ownership in a market economy. Economic actors who believe they can improve an enterprise's operation buy shares from their current owners, and property thus flows toward its most competent users. One major goal of Chubais and his assistants after mass privatization was therefore to develop Russia's secondary share market, and aggregate statistics suggest they were successful. For example, as foreign capital began to enter the Russian stock market in the second half of 1994, the market capitalization of the top two hundred firms doubled in just two months, reaching $36 billion by September (Brady 1999, 108).[2] Those who bought and sold the shares stood to make a great deal of money, especially if they entered the

---

2. On the growth of the stock market, see especially Frye 2000; Blasi, Kroumova, and Kruse 1997.

market early. Credit Suisse First Boston (CSFB), for example, in the persons of Stephen Jennings and Boris Jordan, helped the Russian government design voucher privatization. That gave them insight into the opportunity for below-market acquisitions and dominance of the share and voucher markets, and they controlled as much as 80 percent of the secondary share market in 1994. Troika Dialog and Brunswick International likewise established themselves as important brokers early in the process (Brady 1999, 108). As capital continued to flow into the country from 1994 to 1997, they and the investors who bought into the most prominent stocks saw their fortunes rise dramatically.

The formal stock market, however, played a fairly small role in the transfer and consolidation of ownership in Russia during that period. Instead, most of the stock trading in the country took place outside the centralized markets, and most stocks had few sellers or buyers, making most transactions spot purchases. Such exchanges were individual phenomena, rather than part of a trend toward more transactions, more participants, or more transparency.

One of the most common methods for gaining control over an enterprise, therefore, was to buy shares from individual workers, who had received them during the initial phases of mass privatization. For example, when Leonard Blavatnik, Joseph Bakaleinik, and Alfa Kapital failed to parlay the 15-percent stake they had acquired in the Vladimir Tractor Factory during voucher privatization into managerial control in 1993, they began to buy shares from workers, while the factory continued to lose money. By the following year, Blavatnik had acquired 40 percent of the factory, and the old manager had resigned in disgrace. Bakaleinik was elected general director with 98 percent of the vote in May 1994 (Brady 1999, 117–20). While Blavatnik's expectation that he could someday sell for $75 the shares he had bought for $1.50 illustrates the advantage big capital had at this early stage of property accumulation, the process in many ways represented a perfectly ordinary capitalist takeover (Galuszka 1994).

A potentially more nefarious outcome lay in the possibility that the secondary market in Russia could enable beneficiaries of questionable privatization deals to "launder" their shares. In 1996, for example, the Russian Federal Property Fund (RFFI) sold a 40-percent stake in the Volzhskii Pipe Factory (VTZ) to a firm called Malakhit without following all the rules to ensure transparency and competition in the auction (*RRR* June 4, 1998). Malakhit was part of Khodorkovskii's Rosprom group, and it soon resold those shares to three other firms in Rosprom.

Several times thereafter, RFFI tried to recover the shares, but a Federal Arbitration Court ruled that, while the sale to Malakhit was illegal, the resale to the other companies was legal, so renationalization could not occur.

Regardless of how it was acquired, ownership was only one part of establishing control over assets. Even for the largest, most powerful groups, political assistance was an invaluable tool in the struggle for property. For example, after Vladimir Potanin won ownership rights at Norilsk Nickel in a loans-for-shares deal, the directors of the company fiercely resisted his restructuring efforts (Galuszka and Brady 1996). After several months of conflict, it took the assistance of Prime Minister Viktor Chernomyrdin to remove general director Anatolii Filatov and replace him with Potanin's supporter, Aleksandr Khloponin, who finally took up his position in May 1996 (Johnson 1997, 357).

Regional governments could also play a role in restructuring large-scale holdings, as in the case of creating the Siberian-Urals Aluminum Company. That company was based on the aluminum holdings of two prominent economic groups, Trastkonsalt and Renova, together with those of the Sverdlovsk oblast government. Vasilii Anisimov traded non-ferrous metals in the early 1990s, created Trastkonsalt during that period, and in 1994 became vice president of Rossiiskii Kredit Bank. From there, he helped Trastkonsalt acquire a controlling stake in the Bogoslovskii Aluminum Factory (BAZ), as well as shares in the Urals Aluminum Factory (UAZ) (Mukhin 2001, 104, 106, 113). On a parallel track, Viktor Vekselberg's Renova company purchased shares in UAZ and acquired a 20-percent stake in the Irkutsk Aluminum Factory (IrkAZ) in exchange for a promise of $37 million in investments (Mukhin 2001, 111). Finally, the Sverdlovsk oblast government created a holding company called the Aluminum Company of the Urals (AlKUr) in 1995 to manage its shares in the aluminum sector, including stakes in UAZ, BAZ, and the Bogoslovskii Aluminum Oxide Plant (BGK). In 1996 these three groups created the Siberian-Urals Aluminum Company (SUAl) by pooling the groups' stakes in UAZ, IrkAZ, and the bauxite mines that supplied BGK. At the time of its creation, 14 percent of SUAl went to AlKUr, with the remaining shares divided evenly between IrkAZ and UAZ (Mukhin 2001, 105, 113).

Dominant players in large economic groups did not have to establish complete ownership over enterprises in their networks. Instead, they could use transfer pricing within the group to realize profits in parts of the conglomerate where other shareholders had little influence. For example, Khodorkovskii's Menatep empire included not only Yukos but also several subsidiary oil producers that did not own shares in the main company. In 1996 Yukos forced some of its subsidiaries to sell oil to the main company at well below the domestic price, which itself was considerably below world levels. Profits were thus realized at Yukos, rather than the subsidiaries, whose stockholders did not share in Yukos's wealth (Black, Kraakman, and Tarassova 2000, 1769; Kahn and O'Brien 1998). According to legal consultants for minority shareholders in the subsidiaries, Yukos's pricing scheme dropped the profits of the subsidiaries from approximately $1 billion to near zero in just one year (Black, Kraakman, and Tarassova 2000, 1769). A similar arrangement benefited the owners of Sibneft, including Boris Berezovskii and Roman Abramovich, at the expense of its main production subsidiary, Noiabrskneftegaz. In 1996, before Berezovskii acquired control of Noiabrskneftegaz, the company earned approximately $600 million. In 1997 earnings fell to zero, while Sibneft's profits rose (Black, Kraakman, and Tarassova 2000, 1772).

Using access to power to exploit federal privatization deals, and employing a range of methods outside the privatization process, the largest economic conglomerates in Russia acquired extraordinary holdings in 1994–97 (see Table 5.2). Their strategies help explain the popular antipathy for the oligarchs, and they provided ample fodder for complaints that Russia had failed to complete its transition to a market economy. It is imperative to recognize, however, that the strategies were part of a struggle for property that grew out of the seemingly limitless array of assets available after mass privatization and the multiple reasons for acquiring them, rather than the presence or absence of any particular law.

Second-Tier Groups in Russian Industry

National-level groups received the lion's share of attention in discussions of Russian property reform in 1994–97. No less important, however, were the much quieter development and transformation of smaller ownership groups, which often wielded regionally concentrated power. Such groups were often not very dynamic, but they formed a "second tier" of conglomerates with the potential to achieve national dominance over time. One such group, the national electricity monopoly Unified Energy System, actually held assets throughout the country and had obvious potential political influence, but it did not take full advantage of its position until 1997 or 1998; I look at it in more depth in the next

TABLE 5.2
Top-200 firms incorporated into leading conglomerates by late 1997

	Enterprises		
Group	Name	Sector	Position in top 200
Gazprom	Gazprom	Gas	2
	Cherepovetskii azot	Chemical and petrochemical	193
LUKoil	LUKoil	Oil	3
Interros-Oneksim	Sidanko	Oil	4
	Norilsk Nickel	Nonferrous metallurgy	8
	NLMK	Ferrous metallurgy	18
	Stinol	Machine building	82
Menatep-Rosprom	Yukos	Oil	6
	Apatit	Chemical and petrochemical	57
	VTZ	Ferrous metallurgy	83
	Voskresenskie mineralnye udobreniia	Chemical and petrochemical	121
	Omskshina	Chemical and petrochemical	134
Inkombank	MMK	Ferrous metallurgy	19
	Sameko	Nonferrous metallurgy	130
	Babaevskii	Food	147
	Rot-Front	Food	176
Berezovskii-Smolenskii	Sibneft	Oil	8
Rossiiskii Kredit	KrAZ	Nonferrous metallurgy	24
	Lebedinskii GOK	Ferrous metallurgy	42
	Mikhailovskii GOK	Ferrous metallurgy	58
	Stoilenskii GOK	Ferrous metallurgy	163
	Tulachermet	Ferrous metallurgy	77
Alfa	ZSMK	Ferrous metallurgy	14
	TNK	Oil	17
	AGK	Ferrous metallurgy	94
Renova-Trastkonsalt	SUAl	Nonferrous metallurgy	41
	BAZ	Nonferrous metallurgy	50

Source: Pappe 2000, 60–65.

chapter. Most other second-tier groups were concentrated in one or a small handful of Russian administrative subunits. Because they controlled significant assets in their regions and enjoyed strong ties to their local administrations, some second-tier groups were better positioned to survive the 1998 financial crash than their better-known brethren of national scope.

One strategy for creating such an organization was to establish a formally registered financial-industrial group (FIG) (see Table 5.3). As early as 1993, the federal government argued that alliances among enterprises from the productive and financial spheres could provide reliable suppliers of inputs and buyers for outputs, so it promised investment assistance and other benefits to groups that formally declared themselves (Johnson 1997). In practice, the government often failed to deliver on its long-term promises, but it frequently provided start-up support for registered FIGs, often in the form of special privileges. For example, a presidential decree (no. 1089, May 27, 1994) allowed Magnitogorskaia Steel to retain its hard-currency earnings from 1994 to 1996 to finance the construction of facilities for making rolled steel. Similarly, a decree in May 1995 (no. 496) freed Rossiiskii Aviation Consortium from federal taxes, allowed it to divert the federal government's dividends to investment for three years, and supported the incorporation of Aeroflot into the FIG. In yet another example, governmental decisions in 1996 directly incorporated Soiuzagroprom and Kamenskaia Agro-Industrial Financial Group into the system of federal food funds, guaranteeing them markets and subsidized credits (Dement'ev 1997, 40–41).

In other instances, the federal government turned over shares in enterprises to the FIGs to manage (Dement'ev 1997, 39, 41). For example, in 1994, the State Property Committee transferred stakes in two plants, Korund and Orgsteklo, to the Ruskhim chemicals group in Nizhnii Novgorod oblast (Larin 1997). A Ruskhim partner also acquired additional stakes in the plants through investment auctions in March 1995. The importance of such transfers should not, however, be exaggerated. As of the summer of 1997, only three FIGs—Ruskhim, Nosta-Truby-Gaz, and Tiazhenergomash—had actually received federal shares to manage, and the Federal Property Fund was pressuring Ruskhim to return them (Dement'ev, 1997, 41; Johnson 1997). More common than a formal transfer of ownership or voting rights was for the government to grant de facto control by passively managing its shares in the main enterprises of a FIG (see, e.g., Utkin and Eskindarov 1998, 65).

Despite the potential for state assistance, many important economic groups decided not to register officially, fearing that the promised benefits would never materialize and formalization would elicit too much attention. Table 5.4 lists ten industrial groups not typically mentioned in discussions of the "oligarchs" in 1994–97 that nevertheless controlled significant real assets in the Russian economy during this period. Like the registered FIGs, these groups included sectors ranging from energy

TABLE 5.3
Registered FIGs in Russia as of April 10, 1997

Name of FIG	Location of HQ	Date of registration	Main sector
1. Uralskie zavody	Izhevsk (Udmurtia)	December 21, 1993	Defense, ferrous metallurgy, and machine building
2. Sokol	Voronezh	March 31, 1994	Aircraft construction
3. Dragotsennosti Urala	Ekaterinburg	May 20, 1994	Gold mining
4. Ruskhim	Moscow	June 2, 1994	Chemicals
5. Sibir	Novosibirsk	August 23, 1994	Electronics
6. Obedinennaia gorno-metallurgicheskaia kompaniia	Moscow	November 21, 1994	Metallurgy
7. Skorostnoi flot	Moscow	December 30, 1994	Ship building (defense)
8. Obedinennaia promyshlenno-stroitelnaia kompaniia	Riazan	March 1, 1995	Construction industry
9. Nosta-Truby-Gaz	Novotroitsk (Orenburg oblast)	March 1, 1995	Metallurgy
10. Vostochno-Sibirskaia gruppa	Irkutsk	March 23, 1995	Chemicals
11. Nizhegorodskie avtomobili	Nizhnii Novgorod	April 4, 1995	Automobiles
12. Sviatogor	Cheliabinsk	June 2, 1995	Machine building
13. Primore	Vladivostok	June 7, 1995	Construction industry
14. Magnitogorskaia Steel	Magnitogorsk	June 7, 1995	Metallurgy
15. Eksokhim	Moscow	June 14, 1995	Chemicals
16. AtomRudMet	Moscow	July 14, 1995	Atomic energy, ore, metallurgy
17. Volzhsko-Kamskaia FPG	Moscow	July 27, 1995	Automobiles
18. Evrozoloto	Moscow	August 11, 1995	Gold mining and trade
19. Tulskii promyshlennik	Tula	August 30, 1995	Machine building (defense)
20. Edinstvo	Perm	October 6, 1995	Food processing
21. Doninvest	Rostov-on-Don	November 10, 1995	Automobiles
22. Mezhgosudar-stvennaia FPG "Interros"	Moscow	September 1, 1995	Metals, oil
23. Zhilishche	Moscow	September 8, 1995	Construction
24. Rossiiskii Aviation Consortium	Moscow	October 12, 1995	Aircraft construction (defense)

(TABLE 5.3—cont.)

Name of FIG	Location of HQ	Date of registration	Main sector
25. Prompribor	Moscow	November 15, 1995	Industrial instruments
26. Metalloindustriia	Voronezh	November 24, 1995	Metallurgy, mining
27. Soiuzagroprom	Voronezh	November 24, 1995	Food processing
28. Gormashinvest	St. Petersburg	December 14, 1995	Metallurgy
29. Morskaia tekhnika	St. Petersburg	January 30, 1996	Defense (for non-nuclear ships)
30. Sibagromash	Rubtsovsk (Altai krai)	March 1, 1996	Agro-industrial complex
31. Belovskaia	Belovo (Kemerovo oblast)	March 1, 1996	Agro-industrial complex, coal mining
32. Trekhgorka	Moscow	April 17, 1996	Agro-industrial complex, light industry
33. Zerno-Muka-Khleb	Moscow	September 6, 1996	Food processing
34. Kamenskaia Agro-Industrial Financial Group	Kamenka (Penza oblast)	May 7, 1996	Agro-industrial complex
35. ROSSA-PRiM	Riazan	May 29, 1996	Electronics (defense)
36. Konsortsium "Russkii tekstil"	Moscow	July 16, 1996	Light industry
37. Transnatsionalnaia aliuminievaia kompaniia (TaNAKo)	Krasnoiarsk	August 21, 1996	Metallurgy
38. Russkaia mekhovaia korporatsiia	Moscow	September 2, 1996	Light industry
39. Tiazhenergomash	Moscow	September 4, 1996	Machine building
40. Transnatsionalnaia promyshlenno-finansovaia gruppa "Tochnost"	Moscow	September 5, 1996	Defense
41. Spetsialnoe transportnoe mashinostroenie	Moscow	October 8, 1996	Defense, machine building
42. Viatka-Les-Invest	Kirov	October 9, 1996	Timber
43. Tsentr-Region	Riazan	October 9, 1996	Agro-industrial complex, machine building, construction
44. Interkhimprom	Moscow	November 8, 1996	Chemicals
45. Tekstilnyi kholding "Iakovlevskii"	Ivanovo	November 15, 1996	Light industry (textiles)

(TABLE 5.3—cont.)

Name of FIG	Location of HQ	Date of registration	Main sector
46. Volzhskaia kompaniia	Nizhnii Novgorod	November 29, 1996	Chemicals
47. Transnationalnaia finansovo-promyshlennaia gruppa "Slavianskaia bumaga"	Moscow	January 1, 1997	Chemicals, paper
48. Aramidy i tekhnologii	Moscow	January 27, 1997	Chemicals
49. Avangard	Moscow	January 27, 1997	Defense
50. Transnatsionalnaia finansovo promyshlennaia gruppa "Aerofin"	Moscow	February 21, 1997	Defense
51. Vtormetinvest	Moscow	March 17, 1997	Defense
52. Aviko-M	Moscow	March 20, 1997	Aircraft construction (defense)
53. Rosstro	St. Petersburg	March 20, 1997	Construction industry
54. Dvigateli NK (Nikolaia Kuznetsova)	Samara	March 20, 1997	Aircraft construction (defense)
55. Oboronitelnye sistemy	Moscow	March 21, 1997	Electronics (defense)
56. Dalnyi Vostok	Vladivostok	March 28, 1997	Ship building
57. Niva Chernozemia	Novgorod	March 28, 1997	Fertilizers
58. Demidovskii stil	Tula	April 2, 1997	Chemicals and much else
59. Korporatsiia "Glavsreduralprodukt"	Moscow	April 2, 1997	Food processing
60. Kuzbass	Kemerovo	April 8, 1997	Coal
61. Transnatsionalnaia finansovo-promyshlennaia gruppa "Optotronika"	Moscow	April 9, 1997	Electronics (defense)
62. Kompaniia "Elbrus"	Moscow	April 10, 1997	Mining

Source: Dement'ev 1997, 19–22; Association of Financial–Industrial Groups 1997.

to metals to finished goods, were spread out across the country, and served as key players in their regional political economies.

The ties between regional governments and second-tier groups began with the groups' foundation and could extend into all facets of operation. For example, registering a FIG required permission from the executives in all the regions where the FIG had members. Even after a FIG had been established, regional governments could place representatives on the boards of companies that were important to the region, an

TABLE 5.4
Second-tier industrial groups, 1997

| Group | Major Enterprises | | |
	Name	Sector	Position in top 200
UES	UES	Electricity	1
Surgutneftegaz	Surgutneftegaz	Oil	5
Volgopromgaz	Sintezkauchuk	Chemical and petrochemical	141
Severstal	Severstal	Ferrous metallurgy	13
	Cherepovetsk Steel-Rolling Plant	Ferrous metallurgy	109
MIKOM	Novokuznetsk Aluminum Factory	Nonferrous metallurgy	93
SibAl	Saianogorsk Aluminum Factory	Nonferrous metallurgy	84
Bioprotsess-NIPEK	Uralmash	Machine building	128
Energomash- korporatsiia	Belenergomash	Machine building	144
	Leningrad Metals Factory	Machine building	159
TVEL	Electrostalskii Machine Building Plant	Machine building	52
Kontinetal-invest	Bratsk Timber Processing Combine	Timber/paper	100

Source: Pappe 2000, 60–65.

approach that was particularly popular in Moscow (Dement'ev 1997, 44, 47). In addition to direct governance approaches, regional administrations could also influence registered FIGs by granting them rights to serve as a region's "authorized bank," thereby ensuring their liquidity, as occurred in Rostov with the FIG Doninvest (Orttung 2002, 3). Such links meant that many formal FIGs were regionally based. Of the sixty-two FIGs registered by April 1997, thirty-three were headquartered outside Moscow, and many of the remainder were also regional groups, either based in the Moscow area itself or registered in Moscow for convenience.

Unregistered groups likewise developed close ties to regional governments, whose support was not a formal requirement, but nonetheless a virtual necessity. For example, Surgutneftegaz won its own loans-for-shares auction in part because the regional government closed the airport on the day of the auction to keep potential outside bidders away. Siberian Aluminum, established in 1995 and based on the Saianogorsk Aluminum Factory, grew in influence as its relationship with the regional government grew stronger, as will be discussed below. Likewise, Severstal, MIKOM, and Bioprotsess-NIPEK developed close relationships with their respective regional governments, and a similar story could be told about each of the other groups in the list in Table 5.4.

Indeed, the list of "second-tier" undeclared FIGs could be extended, and the same pattern of relations with regional governments would continue. In the region of Samara, government officials helped create Metallkhim from the remnants of a Soviet-era network (Hanson 1997, 414). Likewise, the rise of the Primorskii Manufacturers Shareholders Corporation (PAKT) in Primore owed much to the patronage of Evgenii Nazdratenko, who served as governor of the region from May 1993 to February 2001 (Vacroux 1995; Orttung 2002; *RRR* April 24, 1997; *RRR* November 20, 1996). In yet another example, when Verkhniaia Salda Metallurgical Production Organization (VSMPO), which represented leading titanium exporters and over half the world's titanium production capacity, faced a takeover attempt from Russian outsiders in 1997, Sverdlovsk governor Eduard Rossel intervened, citing national security concerns (Startsev 1999, 341).

In some cases, assistance to second-tier unofficial FIGs went hand in hand with nepotism. For example, Aleksandr Rutskoi, former vice president of Russia and a leader of the parliamentary resistance to Yeltsin in 1993, was elected governor of Kursk oblast in 1996 and began handing over significant assets to members of his family (*RRR* December 18, 1997). He made one of his brothers, Mikhail, a chief in the oblast police force and placed another, Vladimir, in charge of a state-owned agricultural conglomerate called Faktor. His youngest son, Aleksandr, began working at the Kurskneftekhim petrochemical enterprise shortly before Rutskoi directed a federal subsidy of 20 billion rubles ($3.4 million) to the firm. Finally, Dmitrii, the governor's son from his first marriage, served first as his father's economic advisor and then as chief executive of the private pharmaceutical company Kurskfarmatsiia, for which he quickly secured government contracts (*RRR* December 18, 1997).

Even when a regional government did not play a direct role in the operation of an economic group, its benign neglect could facilitate the group's development. That kind of blind eye, for example, proved invaluable for managers who created "trading companies" affiliated with the central enterprise of a group. Such companies could serve laudable goals, such as simplifying sales and billing, but they also allowed directors to shift assets to the trading company and leave debts with the original enterprise. For example, the Magnitogorsk Metallurgical Combine (MMK) created a trading company called Profit, from which it bought scrap steel (Goldman 2003, 138). The brother of MMK's director managed Profit, which unsurprisingly overcharged MMK for the scrap. MMK also overpaid for coal and undercharged for steel via barter arrangements with other subsidiaries. In a similar scheme, the commercial director of the Yaroslavl Tire Factory created the Verkhnevolzhsk-shina company in 1994. Officially, the new enterprise aimed to regularize barter and sales among the enterprises that were part of the tire-production process. In practice, it began to bleed the tire factory dry (Goldman 2003, 136–37).

The development of second-tier economic groups depended in part on their connections with regional governments. All else being equal, regional administrators were more likely to favor a regionally concentrated group over one with enterprises scattered throughout the country. Interregional groups might bring economic and social benefits, but they could also take profits, jobs, and technology out of the region. In addition, governors feared that interregional FIGs would squeeze local bidders out of the privatization process, thus bringing in unknown owners and displacing more familiar quantities (Dement'ev 1997, 45–46; Vacroux 1995). Regional concentration, in turn, affected the kinds of assets second-tier groups were likely to include. Soviet industrial planning often linked enterprises by sector, but it spread them out geographically when possible, so production chains frequently crossed regional boundaries. A survey of registered FIGs showed that, although their major holdings tended to focus on one segment of industry, they rarely included enterprises from each stage of a production chain (Savin 1997, 46).

Ownership and Control at Individual Firms

Notwithstanding the importance of national and second-tier economic groups, most of the Russian struggle for industrial property in 1994–97 took place at the level of individual enterprises. The mass privatization program intentionally separated firms from one another and sold them as independent entities. That approach successfully undermined the power of the ministries, as it was designed to do, but it did not resolve competition over the enterprises. Rather, in many ways it simply made such competition possible.

Thanks to mass privatization, especially Option 2, incumbent factory managers had a head start in the race to control their own enterprises. The privatization program did not hand direct control of the firms to

management, however, so many directors spent the years after privatization trying to acquire additional shares in their factories. They enjoyed
considerable advantages in their efforts, including an inside track to buy
shares from employees, as well as a legal structure that did not prohibit
insider share issues, but they were not the only competitors for property.
Regional governments, which were growing increasingly independent
of Moscow, also entered the fray, both as providers of financial support
and as shareholders. In addition, both Russian and foreign outsiders
played significant roles in the struggles over prominent firms. All these
actors clashed repeatedly, employing the resources available to them in
myriad ingenious ways.

During and after mass privatization, enterprise managers openly
stated their desire to retain control of their enterprises. Critics suspected
avarice, while insiders argued that they could best operate the firms, but
no one doubted that managers wanted to keep their positions. Indeed,
survey data showed that about 60 percent of managers would resist
"unexpected accumulation of shares" by outsiders or employees, while
fewer than 22 percent would hand over control to an outside strategic
investor (Filatotchev, Wright, and Bleaney 1999, 495). In practice, they
usually did not have to, since they began the post-privatization era with
significant stakes in their enterprises, along with multiple resources for
strengthening their positions.

The simplest short-term approach was to secure the right to vote the
state's remaining shares in an enterprise (Makarevich 1999c, 233).
Gazprom was a clear example, where the federal government explicitly
turned over voting rights of its approximately 40-percent stake to management of the company. In many other cases, particularly those con-
cerning shares of regional governments, deals were less formal, but they
offered a first step toward greater managerial control.

Quickly, however, enterprise directors supplemented the voting
strategy with several others that were designed to convey actual ownership. One common approach was to buy shares from employees, whose
average ownership in privatized firms dropped from 53 percent to 40
percent from 1994 to 1996 (Randall 2001, 75, 77). By the mid-1990s real
wages had fallen, many firms paid workers late or not at all, and poverty
threatened more and more of the population (Silverman and Yanowitch
2000; Desai and Idson 2000; Javeline 2003). For workers, selling the few
shares they had received during privatization was one way to get the cash
they needed, and since the secondary market for most stocks was
illiquid, the easiest buyer to find was management (Randall 2001, 77;

Edwards, Polonsky, and Polonsky 2000, 67). Furthermore, many workers still trusted their managers to retain jobs, pay some wages, and maintain part of the social safety net, including subsidized housing, day care, and food (Sil 2001, 225n58–226n60). Not only had that been the traditional role of the enterprise director in Soviet times, but union representatives in the factory often worked with management to convey an image of paternalism to workers and to portray the state and outsiders as threats.[3] Whether such impressions were accurate or not, they were enough to encourage employees to sell their ownership stakes to their bosses.

Even as they were buying shares from workers, managers actively tried to prevent outsiders from buying up stock. For example, in July 1995, when Koloss, a food conglomerate owned by Alliance-Menatep, tried to take over the Red October Chocolate Company by advertising it would pay $7.50 a share, management at Red October used the factory public address system to warn that Menatep would fire all the workers if it took over (Blasi, Kroumova, and Kruse 1997, 153–54). Even when Menatep raised its bid to $9.50 a share, it could not accumulate a majority stake: it was easier for workers to sell to their bosses. In this way, shares owned by management rose from 9 percent to 16 percent between 1994 and 1996, and one conservative estimate found that managers had bought shares from employees at more than 31 percent of enterprises (Randall 2001, 75, 77; Filatotchev et al. 1999, 495).

Even those numbers, however, probably underestimate the ability of managers to buy shares from employees. The average stake of outsiders in privatized Russian enterprises rose from 21 percent to 32 percent from 1994 to 1996, but many "outsiders" were actually shell companies set up by managers (Blasi, Kroumova, and Kruse 1997, 55, 66, 193, Table 4; Randall 2001, 77). For instance, the general director and two top managers of a beverage factory in Penza oblast created an outside company that bought up all the shares of the enterprise. In a similar example, the manager of an automotive plant set up a "trading company" to purchase shares from employees, and by 1996, it had bought about 12 percent (Blasi, Kroumova, and Kruse 1997, 59, 62). Finally, at the huge Cherepovetskii Metallurgical Combine, insiders created external companies to buy up vouchers and shares in the main factory and affiliated companies, thus establishing Severstal, a regional economic group with stakes in nearly a hundred companies (Mukhin 2001, 173).

3. See, e.g., Christensen 1999, 136–38. Javeline (2003, esp. chap. 2) provides an especially detailed account of how complex the sources of wage arrears were, making it easier for managers to direct workers' fears and frustrations outward.

Another important set of strategies exploited the fact that Russia in the mid-1990s had no laws preventing the sale of shares to insiders and their allies on preferential terms (Blasi, Kroumova, and Kruse 1997, 94). The most common such scheme issued new shares in the enterprise and made them available only to selected buyers, thereby diluting the stakes of other owners (Makarevich 1999c, 233–35). The first such supplemental emission at a prominent enterprise seems to have taken place in 1994 at Komineft, an oil company. The new issue was approved at a meeting held without adequate notice to outside shareholders, and it diluted their holdings by about a third. Similarly, the Primorskii Sea Shipping Line sold shares for $43,000 that should have fetched about $22 million at market prices, thereby reducing Credit Suisse First Boston's stake by approximately 50 percent (Blasi Kroumova, and Kruse 1997, 93–94). In yet another example, the management of the enormous Surgutneftegaz oil company in 1996 issued new shares in one of its subsidiaries (AO Surneftegaz) and bought many of them "at a price deemed 30 percent below market levels" (Feifer and Semenenko 2000).

Insider share dealings extended beyond rigged supplemental emissions. For example, rather than issuing new shares, directors of a firm could use enterprise funds to buy back existing shares on the secondary market and sell them to managers at a steep discount. Alternatively, a firm could sell off shares still held by the state, making sure management won the "auction," often with a discounted bid. Finally, not only were the auctions fixed and the bids low, but payment was often not in cash. Instead, it was in money borrowed from the firm or a related bank, which allowed insiders to delay payment indefinitely (Blasi, Kroumova, and Kruse 1997, 55, 73, 93).

Managers' success at consolidating control, however, was not simply a function of unclear or nonexistent laws. Erasing other owners from shareholder registers, for example, was illegal, but it happened. In many cases, Russian shareholder registers were not kept electronically, stored centrally, or notarized independently, leaving them wide open to manipulation by management. Owners of stock could, and did, arrive at shareholder meetings only to find they had been removed from the list. Perhaps most famously, the foreign company Trans World Group found two of its representatives excised from the register at the Krasnoiarsk Aluminum Factory in late 1994, part of a struggle that will be examined in greater detail below. That case, however, was not an isolated incident. Most of the time, managers seemed to hold all the cards in competition over their firms.

In reality, however, they did not. After managers, regional governments represented the most powerful actors in struggles over individual enterprises. A combination of factors steadily weakened central control over regional governments in the mid-1990s, giving them almost free rein in dealing with firms on their territories. As discussed above, they helped create and maintain second-tier economic groups, and their role in the development of particular firms was no less important.

Their motives for such involvement were complex. Surely some bureaucrats were driven by bribes, a desire to wield power over the economy, or lack of imagination in facing the new world. Others, however, yielded to structural pressures. Most obviously, the Soviet system had woven the social fabric of regions directly into the operation of enterprises. Not only did they employ thousands or tens of thousands of people, but they provided services ranging from housing and subsidized food to child care, and no government was likely to let such organizations collapse. In addition, with barter playing an increasingly prominent role in Russian economic activity in 1994–97, regional administrators needed predictable access to the real goods enterprises produced, goods that could be provided at a fixed price or as a tax payment and then bartered with other regional governments (Lallemand 1999, 325; Woodruff 1999). Finally, political parties were very weak in the regions, so regional politicians needed the resources of the enterprises on their territories to support their political campaigns.

Under such conditions, the simplest link between regional governments and firms was one of financial assistance, aimed at keeping the enterprises out of bankruptcy. In April 1995, for example, when the federal government tried to force Rybinsk Motor Works to declare bankruptcy and reorganize, Yaroslavl oblast leaders refused to acknowledge the decision and used local police to keep federal officials out of the factory (Slider 1997b, 110). Similarly, the federal government launched bankruptcy proceedings against the AvtoVAZ auto factory in late 1996. The firm owed 11 trillion rubles ($2 billion) in debts, including 2.9 trillion rubles in federal taxes, but Governor Konstantin Titov of Samara oblast negotiated a deal with the center to ease its demands (*RRR* December 4, 1996).[4] In yet another instance, the government of Tatarstan prevented the bankruptcy of the giant KamAZ truck manufacturer. After Yeltsin was reelected in 1996, he revoked KamAZ's five-year tax holiday,

4. The arrangement called for AvtoVAZ to acquire capital by selling a 50-percent stake to a foreign car company, but the sale never materialized. Regional government protection and a dearth of outside buyers made the proposal a dead letter.

opening the door to federal bankruptcy proceedings. The regional government, however, refused to implement the order and on October 19, 1996, agreed to pay 51 billion rubles ($9 million) in back taxes on behalf of KamAZ (*RRR* October 20, 1996; *RRR* February 5, 1997).

In some cases, the relationship between regional governments and enterprises extended beyond mere financial support to include direct ownership. Sometimes the links came about as a quid pro quo for protecting an enterprise from bankruptcy. For example, when the Moscow city government intervened to keep the ZiL auto plant out of bankruptcy in 1996, the price of its assistance was a 60-percent stake in the plant (*RRR* November 13, 1996; *RRR* May 15, 1997).

The more important impetus for regional ownership in 1994–97, however, came from federal property rules. Mass privatization, for example, left significant shares of privatized enterprises in state hands, both federal and regional. Once mass privatization was over, the federal government began to transfer additional shares to the regions (Slider 1997a, 263). The shares often found their way into holding companies, such as Volgograd oblast's Sfera, established in 1994 by the oblast administration, representatives of LUKoil, and some smaller partners. Partly because of transfers from the center, by 1998 Sfera held shares in twenty-eight enterprises, including Vtorchermet, Bioden, and Volgogradbiosintez (Bazyl'chik 1998).

The final direct connection between business and politics in Russia's regions in 1994–97 came in the form of electoral politics, as owners and managers of important businesses won an increasing number of seats in regional governments. In the first years after the fall of the Soviet Union, Boris Yeltsin appointed most of the chief executives directly, but when over fifty regions held direct gubernatorial elections in 1996–97, businesspeople won several of the races (see Table 5.5). For example, the incumbents Leonid Roketskii and Yurii Neelov, board members at Tiumen Oil Company and Gazprom, respectively, were both reelected to their posts (Orttung 2002, 3; Banerjee 1999; Tsentr politicheskoi informatsii 2001, 285). Even without the advantage of incumbency, a number of business leaders, including Yurii Evdokimov in Murmansk oblast and Leonid Gorbenko in Kaliningrad oblast, successfully competed for governors' seats. In still other cases, businesspeople who did not run for office directly nevertheless played key roles in political campaigns. For instance, the support of the Saianogorsk Aluminum Factory helped Aleksei Lebed win the presidency of the Republic of Khakassia (Orttung 2002, 3; *RRR* December 4, 1996).

TABLE 5.5
Regional executives with close ties to business elected in 1996–97

Name	Region	Economic group or company
Yurii Evdokimov	Murmansk oblast	Sistema
Leonid Gorbenko	Kaliningrad oblast	local
Vladimir Butov	Nenets autonomous okrug	local
Aleksei Lebed	Republic of Khakassiia	SibAl (SaAZ)
Leonid Roketskii (incumbent)	Tiumen oblast	TNK
Yurii Neelov (incumbent)	Yamalo-Nenets autonomous okrug	Gazprom
Valerii Maleev	Ust-Orda Buryat autonomous okrug	Sovkhoz "Kamenskii"

Sources: Kryshtanovskaia 2002; Olcott 2002; Tsentr politicheskoi informatsii 2001, 2002; *RRR* January 8, 1997.

A similar phenomenon occurred in regional legislatures. Indeed, economic actors were even more successful in winning election as deputies than in reaching the governor's chair. According to the Russian Central Electoral Commission, 45 percent of the deputies chosen in the 1996 regional legislative elections were from banks, private businesses, or local enterprises (*RRR* February 27, 1997). When the survey is broadened to include elections from 1995 to 1997, nearly 65 percent of deputies had clear economic ties. With political parties so weak in the regions—fewer than 20 percent of deputies elected between 1995 and 1997 professed a local or national party affiliation—candidates developed direct ties to business instead (Stoner-Weiss 2001, 395, 408).[5] While legislatures wielded less power than executives, parliamentary seats could be useful in the struggle for property. In Sverdlovsk oblast, for example, Pavel Fedulev—who owned significant stakes in several metallurgical enterprises—held a seat in the oblast legislature until April 1998. As long as he was in office, his economic activities flourished, but when he lost his seat he also lost his political protection and was arrested on charges of "unlawful privatizations and large-scale fraud" (Startsev 1999, 356).

Russia's post-privatization ownership regime therefore deserved its label of "insider-dominated." Enterprise managers and regional politicians could muster resources—including physical control of assets, relations with the workforce, and the powers of local government—that were

5. Even when winners were nominally affiliated with a party, that party was unlikely to have much influence over them after the election (Stoner-Weiss 2001, 398–99).

unavailable to outside investors, whether Russian or foreign. Outsiders, however, did have access to many of the most desirable assets in the system, and it would be a mistake to assume they played no role in the struggle for property in 1994–97.

While insiders clearly dominated the ownership of privatized enterprises in general, their supremacy was hardly complete. By mid-1996 insiders held majority stakes in only 65 percent of privatized enterprises, while outsiders were majority owners in nearly 20 percent (Russian Federal Securities Commission, cited in Goldman 2003, 95; Blasi, Kroumova, and Kruse 1997, 67, 148, 205, Table 11). In addition, managers were not always able to retain operational control over enterprises, regardless of who held the majority stake. By 1997 over 23 percent of privatized enterprises had replaced their management, and at large and mid-sized enterprises 33 percent of general managers turned over between 1992 and 1996 (Randall 2001, 77; Blasi, Kroumova, and Kruse 1997, 135). Even though a company insider replaced the general director in 80 percent of cases, this kind of turnover belies claims that Soviet-era managers and mentalities controlled Russian firms in the mid-1990s.[6]

Most of the outside owners were Russian, but even foreigners expanded their role in firms after mass privatization. At the aggregate level, their influence seemed quite small, as foreigners' overall stake in privatized enterprises grew from near zero in 1994 to only 1.6 percent in 1996. Their holdings, however, were highly concentrated, and foreign owners held majority stakes in one of every hundred privatized companies by 1996 (Blasi, Kroumova, and Kruse 1997, 56, 193, Table 4).

More important for understanding the struggle for property, however, is the fact that in many firms, particularly the largest ones, no category of owner dominated. In over half of the fifty leading firms in 1996, neither insiders nor outsiders controlled a majority of shares, while the state's average holding stood at about 38 percent (Blasi, Kroumova, and Kruse 1997, 72).[7] Furthermore, even when aggregate statistics showed that "insiders" or "outsiders" held a majority of shares, that majority

6. Moreover, "Soviet-era managers" were perfectly capable of following aggressive, new, if not always desirable, strategies when the opportunity arose. Tarring them all with the brush of poor imagination is misguided. See also Solnick 1998; Kotz and Weir 1997; Hendley 1992, 1998; Hough 2001.

7. If a firm had privatized according to Option 1, which gave insiders a nonvoting 25-percent stake for free, a 38-percent bloc would represent a majority of voting shares. Since this figure was an average, however, and not all firms chose Option 1, the state was frequently a minority shareholder.

could be divided up among several individual shareholders. For example, of the 20 percent of privatized enterprises in which outsiders held majority stakes, only about a quarter (6 percent of the total) were majority-owned by a single shareholder, and another quarter (5 percent of the total) were majority-owned by a small group of shareholders (Blasi, Kroumova, and Kruse 1997, 148, 205, Table 11). Similarly, "insider control" of an enterprise did not mean that one person, or even a small group of people, had a tight grip on the firm. Option 2 technically sold shares not only to managers but to employees as well; and although many enterprise directors spent the mid-1990s trying to gather those shares to themselves, their task was a difficult one. Their troubles created space for outsiders to play a significant role in redistributing assets after mass privatization.

With the ownership question unresolved at many enterprises after mass privatization, competition ensued among all the major players: insiders, regional governments, and foreign and Russian outsiders. In theory, such conflicts could take place at any firm, but they were more likely and more heated at large firms, where managers' control after mass privatization was weak. Victory, which could be tenuous, often required an alliance of two or more major players, none of whom was particularly more inclined than the others to abide by high ethical standards. Instead, the participants all used such tactics as simple purchases, political machinations, and threats of violence to gain the upper hand; and their partnerships did not outlast their immediate shared interests.

One example of this kind of struggle comes from Belgorod oblast's Lebedinskii Ore Enrichment Combine (Lebedinskii GOK), which by the end of the Soviet period was the world's largest supplier of iron ore (Sagers 1993a, 457; Pappe 2000, 159). After mass privatization, the general director, Anatolii Kalashnikov, used regional political connections to undercut the influence of a Russian outsider at the factory. In particular, when Rossiiskii Kredit group tried to expand its 23-percent holding in Lebedinskii GOK to more than 25 percent, Kalashnikov fired workers who sold their shares to the outside group and called in local police to remove its representatives from the grounds (Pappe 2000, 159; *RRR* November 6, 1997). In addition, he convinced the Belgorod regional arbitration court to sequester the shares of Rossiiskii Kredit and its partners just long enough to ram through a supplemental share emission that dropped Rossiiskii Kredit's holding below 5 percent (*RRR* November 6, 1997; Blasi, Kroumova, and Kruse 1997, 146).

Management's victory was incomplete, and in 1997 outsiders worked with the regional administration to turn the tables. In April the oblast governor, Evgenii Savchenko, turned the local police on Kalashnikov, while the arbitration court ruled the share dilution illegal and ordered Kalashnikov to turn over his personal 15-percent stake in the enterprise to the oblast administration. By the end of the conflict, Rossiiskii Kredit's share in Lebedinskii GOK stood at 36 percent, and by voting with the oblast administration it was able to remove Kalashnikov and replace him with Deputy Governor Nikolai Kalinin (*RRR* November 6, 1997).

At another large enterprise (Novolipetsk Metallurgical Combine [NLMK]), a foreign investor conspired with enterprise management to weaken a group of other outsiders but finally lost its position when management switched sides in the struggle. Trans World Group (TWG), a metals-trading company based in Europe, acquired shares in NLMK during mass privatization, building a stake of approximately 38 percent by 1997 (*RRR* October 2, 1997). The general manager, Vladimir Lisin, owned more than 10 percent, and most of the remaining shares lay with a coalition known as Reforma. Reforma consisted of three outsider groups—MFK Bank and Renaissance Capital, both associated with Vladimir Potanin's Interros, and Cambridge Capital Management, representing the interests of unidentified foreign investors. By June 1997 they held a slim majority of shares. In July Reforma called for a vote on the board of directors, which would have removed TWG from power. MFK, however, had acquired its stake in the loans-for-shares deals discussed earlier in this chapter, which helped Lisin convince the Lipetsk arbitration court that approximately 5 percent of MFK's shares should not carry voting rights, dropping Reforma's voting stake below 50 percent (*RRR* August 21, 1997).

Later that year Lisin turned against TWG, complaining that the firm owed NLMK about $100 million for goods already delivered (*RRR* October 2, 1997). Lisin stopped further shipments to TWG and, more important for ownership of the enterprise, voted with Reforma at a December 9 shareholders' meeting. His shift gave Reforma five of the nine seats on the board, while plant directors took three, and TWG received only one. Fissures were clear in the new alliance as well, as Cambridge Capital immediately opposed a charter amendment that would have converted MFK's nonvoting stake into voting shares (*RRR* December 18, 1997).

The variety of ways in which ownership conflicts could be settled is also clear from the experiences of four Siberian aluminum factories in

which TWG developed significant stakes during and after mass privatization: Bratsk (BrAZ), Novokuznetsk (NkAZ), Saianogorsk (SaAZ), and
Krasnoiarsk (KrAZ). Taken together, they show both that outsiders could
be significant players in Russian enterprises and that they did not necessarily exhibit higher ethical or business standards than insiders. At BrAZ,
which produced more aluminum than any other Russian factory in 1992,
TWG purchased shares through intermediaries and lent money to managers to buy additional stocks (Sagers 1992, 594; Behar 2000). TWG
controlled a large majority of the voting shares by the mid-1990s, and it
did not face a serious challenge to its ownership until the end of the
decade. At NkAZ, by contrast, TWG acquired more than 20 percent of
the shares during mass privatization but soon lost control to another
outsider, a Russian company called MIKOM, which received at least tacit
approval from Governor Mikhail Kisliuk of Kemerovo oblast in its takeover bid (Mukhin 2001, 91, 158).

The conflicts at SaAZ and KrAZ were more complicated. TWG was
able to retain control of SaAZ through the mid-1990s but only in conjunction with another outsider and the regional government. During
mass privatization TWG teamed up with Oleg Deripaska, a Moscow State
University graduate who began playing the international metals-trading
market in the early 1990s.[8] When SaAZ was privatized, Deripaska bought
shares for TWG and himself, at least in part by using a bank loan he and
his partner, Arkadii Sarkisian, never repaid. Through this process, TWG
and its intermediaries acquired 37.5 percent of SaAZ by 1994, and by
voting with Deripaska at a shareholders' meeting the group elected him
general director of the aluminum company (Mukhin 2001, 94–97). Two
years later, Deripaska helped elect Aleksei Lebed to the presidency of
Khakassia, and that relationship quickly paid off for SaAZ and TWG. In
particular, Lebed named Sarkisian to his cabinet and lowered taxes on
both SaAZ and its electrical supplier (*RRR* June 19, 1997; *RRR* May 8,
1997). When Saianogorsk mayor Sergei Bondarenko protested the
changes, Lebed launched an armed audit of Saianogorsk in March 1997,
shutting down regional media during the raid (*RRR* May 8, 1997). The
TWG-Deripaska relationship began to lose strength near the end of
1997, but it had already served to establish outside control over a key
firm in the Siberian aluminum industry.

---

8. TWG's partners also reportedly included alleged organized crime figure Vladimir Tatarenkov (Latynina 2002a).

At KrAZ, the struggle involved tactics ranging from deceit to blood-shed, as insiders, Russian outsiders, and foreigners competed for control of the firm. As usual, TWG acquired a significant stake in KrAZ through intermediaries during mass privatization. In November 1994, however, the managing director of KrAZ, Yurii Kolpakov, erased two of those intermediaries, holding over 17 percent of the company, from the shareholder register (Mukhin 2001, 90–91; Freeland 1994).[9] TWG was left with a stake of approximately 11 percent and set about trying to recover the other 17 percent. As part of its efforts, TWG allied itself with the real muscle at the plant, Anatolii Bykov, a former boxer who had run protection rackets and a private "security service" in the 1980s and joined KrAZ in the early 1990s (Volkov 2002, 107). Soon after the alliance was formed, the struggle at KrAZ turned horribly violent, and none of the main actors appears entirely blameless. Within a year, the dead included a state inspector for the metals sector, a codefendant of a TWG representative in a separate criminal probe, and an employee of TWG's most significant foreign competitor at KrAZ (Behar 2000).

Between July and October 1997 the competition for KrAZ moved back to the boardroom. Under pressure from an embezzlement scandal, Kolpakov resigned on July 14, 1997, and Igor Vishnevskii, representing the Swiss company Glencore International, replaced him (*RRR* July 17, 1997). Dominance of the firm, however, was far from settled. Rossiiskii Kredit surprised the investment world by announcing in October that it owned 27 percent of KrAZ and that Bykov was now a vice president of the bank (Yorke 2003, 243; Mukhin 2001, 108). At the same time, Vasilii Anisimov's Trastkonsalt also held KrAZ shares, and Anisimov himself was a vice president of Rossiiskii Kredit. Together Rossiiskii Kredit and Trastkonsalt were able to make Bykov the vice chairman of the board of directors at KrAZ (Yorke 2003, 243; Mukhin 2001, 108). At the October board meeting an uneasy alliance of TWG, Rossiiskii Kredit, Trastkon-salt, and Bykov appointed the plant's fifth director in four months, Yurii Ushenin, former deputy director of Krasnoiarskenergo, the main electri-cal supplier for KrAZ (*RRR* October 16, 1997). The fault lines in the

---

9. It later turned out that Kolpakov was also stripping assets from KrAZ and ship-ping them abroad. As he acknowledged during a criminal investigation, Kolpakov sent $20 million to Leo Trust, an offshore company, allegedly as advanced payment for bauxite, but the bauxite never arrived (*RRR* June 12, 1997; *RRR* July 3, 1997). This was a classic strategy for exporting capital from Russia (see, for example, Tikhomirov 1997).

coalition were too numerous to count, but as in the case of SaAZ, the original insiders had clearly lost out.

The struggle for control at all these firms was thus a complex mess of actors, goals, and strategies. Casting it as a simple conflict between proponents and opponents of marketization—or even of "good corporate governance"—is misleading, since few of the competitors were thinking in such systemic terms. Instead, the goal was to take control of property because of the economic and political power it could bring in the environment of the time. A similar conflict was underway in the agrarian sector, although the peculiar characteristics of agricultural production and agrarian reform legislation pushed the struggle in somewhat different directions.

AGRARIAN PROPERTY REDISTRIBUTION IN THE MID-1990S

It is tempting to see the post-privatization era in Russian agricultural production and ownership as a period of stagnation or worse. On questions of output and profitability, the sector was in dire straits by almost any measure. Grain production, for example, the most politically popular single indicator of the performance of Russian agriculture, had shrunk by historic proportions: in 1995, less land was cultivated for grain than in 1950, while grain yields were in line with performances from the early 1960s (Wegren 1998a, 268n86). Agricultural production as a whole continued to drop in 1995 and 1996, finally leveling off in 1997 at 89 percent of the 1994 level, itself only about 75 percent of the 1991 figure (See Table 5.6).

Meanwhile, the food-processing industry had shrunk even further. By 1997 it was operating at less than 25-percent capacity (Kurtsev 1999, 90). Processors in the relatively fertile Povolzhe region in the south of Russia had better access to raw materials than comparable enterprises elsewhere, but even they operated well below their potential. In Volgograd oblast, for example, the Volgogradskii Milk Factory could theoretically produce up to 60,000 tons of milk per year, but in 1994 it processed only

TABLE 5.6
Physical output of Russian agriculture as percentage of 1991 output

Year	1991	1992	1993	1994	1995	1996	1997	1998	1999	2000
Output	100	91	87	76	70	67	68	59	61	66

Source: Calculated from *Rossiiskii statisticheskii ezhegodnik* 2001, 396.

42,400 tons, and in 1995 only 30,600 ("AOOT 'Molochnyi zavod "Vol-gogradskii"'" 1996, 5). Similarly, livestock processors in the Povolzhe region operated at 25–30 percent of capacity in 1997, while meat pro-duction in the region in 1996–97 was 44 percent lower than the average for 1986–90 (Belokopytova, Alekseeva, and Trifonova 1998, 5; Cherniaev and Belokopytova 1999, 26).

Not surprisingly in such a context, the balance sheets of the farms themselves bled increasing volumes of red ink in the 1990s. Fewer than 5 percent of large agricultural enterprises were officially unprofitable in 1990, but the number had jumped to 59 percent by the end of 1994 and rose to 82 percent in 1997 (see Table 5.7). Again, enterprises in the Povolzhe region performed somewhat better, but even in that favorable environment more than 70 percent of agricultural producers were offi-cially unprofitable (Belokopytova, Alekseeva, and Trifonova 1998, 5).

As the productivity of Russian agriculture was mired in a depression, the struggles over property in the sector could also seem underwhelming, lacking even the guilty fascination provoked by the decadence of conflicts in industry. There were no loans-for-shares auctions in agriculture. Private farmers did not drive around Moscow in Mercedes cars or pull rolls of hundred-dollar bills from their pockets in casinos. Newspapers did not brim with stories of upstart speculators battling corrupt managers and organized crime bosses for control over agricultural production. Instead, the sector often seemed interesting only for its pity value.

Upon closer examination, however, ownership changes in agriculture in this period bore some resemblance to the process in industry. As in the industrial sector, for example, agricultural assets in 1994 were emerg-ing from a period of rapid privatization, farms via the reorganization drive and other pieces of the sector via the mass privatization program. Control over agricultural assets, as in industry, was still in flux, and com-petition for them was often heated. Participants in the struggle could also parallel those in the industrial sector, as regional governments and economic groups of various stripes played leading roles in the redistribu-tion of property.

TABLE 5.7
Percentage of large farms formally "unprofitable"

Year	1990	1991	1992	1993	1994	1995	1996	1997	1998	1999	2000
Percentage of farms	3	5	5	10	59	57	79	82	88	54	51

Source: Rossiiskii statisticheskii ezhegodnik 2001, 402.

In terms of scholarly interpretation, the Russian agricultural sector found itself under the same "incomplete transition" lens observers applied to the changes in industrial ownership. According to that understanding, large-scale farm reorganization and the privatization of food processors in 1992–94 had laid the foundation for a market, and the task for the next period was to establish an environment in which market forces could restructure production in the sector. Similar to outside owners in industry, new private farmers were to drive that transformation—either directly, by creating new farms with assets from the old ones, or indirectly, by forcing large farms to restructure in order to compete. The sine qua non for creating this environment was therefore a property law that would allow an unrestricted market in agricultural land.

Despite similarities, however, industry and agriculture in Russia did not follow identical trajectories after rapid privatization, and a focus on the struggle for property can help explain the differences better than a search for the obstacles to a complete market transition. The issue was not, for example, that private farms were stymied by hardline opposition to an adequate legal structure. Instead, it was that agriculture developed in a different political and economic context than industry. At the bottom of the system, the shock to the agricultural sector continued to foster a pattern of individual survival that undermined the viability of many of the large farms and some food processors. At the top, the federal government played a less direct role in the struggle over agrarian property than it had in industry, since it had few major assets left to privatize. The role of official policy, especially from regional governments, was instead to encourage integration of assets in agriculture more actively than in industry. At the same time, the economic actors that controlled bottlenecks in the agrarian sector began to expand beyond the reach of individual regional governments, although they never gained the prominence of the industrial and financial oligarchs. The agrarian sector was thus the site of its own struggle for property, broadly similar to the conflict in industry, but with idiosyncrasies that created its own cluster of actors pursuing their own particular strategies of redistribution.

Private Farms as Red Herrings

As discussed in the preceding chapter, private farms were to serve as the main engine for pulling Russian agriculture out of its Soviet-era doldrums. With agriculture in worse shape by the mid-1990s than it had been in the 1980s, arguments about the efficacy of such farms grew louder. Supporters of the private farm movement argued that its limited influence stemmed mostly from its small size. When large-scale farm reorganization and subsidies for private farmers came to an end in 1994, the number of private farms virtually stopped growing, leveling off at a number far below the one million mark originally called for. Likewise, private farms accounted for a negligible proportion of farmland in the country (see Table 5.8). Conversely, the growth of the private farm sector had no effect on the number of large farms, which held steady from 1993 to 1996 and actually grew in 1997 (Wegren 1998b, 88). If only the legislature would create a new Land Code, the argument went, the private farmers' movement could grow and reshape Russian agriculture.

That view, however, is misleading. Most obviously, it misrepresents the nature of the agricultural land market in Russia in the mid-1990s and misstates the politics of land-reform legislation that affected that market. While outright sales of agricultural land were rare, for example, two Russian sociologists documented the existence of a significant market for lease rights to farmland (Kliamkin and Timofeev 2000). The growth of some private farms in Volgograd oblast, for example, from an initial allotment of fewer than twenty hectares to more than two hundred was possible only because of lease markets. Furthermore, several legal supports for at least a restricted market in land did exist, including the 1990–91 land laws, the 1993 Constitution, Yeltsin's decree of 1993, and similar decrees in 1996 and beyond. Finally, to the extent that the absence of a coherent Land Code undermined the private farmers' movement, those responsible were not "hardliners" in the legislature but Yeltsin, who abolished the Code after his victory over parliament in October 1993.

More broadly, suggesting that more and bigger private farms would resurrect Russian agriculture was an act of faith rather than an argument from evidence. First, except for a few products, the private farms that did exist in the mid-1990s produced an even smaller proportion of Russia's agricultural output than their share of land would have predicted. In particular, while they produced 13–15 percent of Russia's sunflower seeds in 1995 and 1996, they produced less (usually far less) than 5 percent of the grain, sugar beets, potatoes, vegetables, meat and poultry, milk, or eggs (see Table 5.9).

Second, even the much-touted Nizhnii Novgorod model of farm privatization had mixed results at best. The first round of restructuring

TABLE 5.8
Number of farms and size of landholdings

	1991	1992	1993	1994	1995	1996	1997	1998
Large farms								
Number (thousands)	25.5	26.6	26.9	26.9	26.9	26.9	27.0	27.3
Land farmed (million hectares)	186.3	162.8	157.9	155.8	154.1	152.4	149.2	154.8
Avg. size (hectares)	7,306	6,120	5,870	5,792	5,729	5,665	5,526	5,670
% of total ag. land	**97.2**	**93.9**	**91.1**	**89.0**	**88.8**	**88.6**	**88.2**	**87.9**
Personal plots								
Total								
Number (millions)	39.4	40.7	39.1	38.9	38.7	38.4	38.2	35.6
Land (million hectares)	5.253	8.510	7.646	7.892	7.655	7.648	7.732	8.170
% of total ag. land	**2.7**	**4.9**	**4.4**	**4.5**	**4.4**	**4.4**	**4.6**	**4.7**
Subsidiary farming plots								
Number (millions)	17.6	19.3	16.6	16.6	16.3	16.3	16.4	16.0
Land (million hectares)	3.654	6.826	5.825	6.062	5.810	5.805	5.923	6.433
Avg. size (hectares)	0.21	0.35	0.35	0.37	0.36	0.36	0.36	0.40
Gardens or orchards (*sady*)								
Number (millions)	12.2	13.5	14.3	14.7	15.0	15.1	15.1	14.5
Land (million hectares)	0.930	1.083	1.167	1.209	1.242	1.267	1.264	1.260
Avg. size (hectares)	0.08	0.08	0.08	0.08	0.08	0.08	0.08	0.09
Vegetable gardens (*ogorody*)								
Number (millions)	9.6	7.9	8.2	7.6	7.4	7.0	6.6	5.1
Land (million hectares)	0.669	0.601	0.654	0.621	0.603	0.576	0.545	0.477
Avg. size (hectares)	0.07	0.08	0.08	0.08	0.08	0.08	0.08	0.09
Peasant farms								
Number (thousands)	4.4	49	182.8	270.0	279.2	280.1	278.6	274.3
Land (million hectares)	0.181	2.068	7.804	11.342	11.870	12.011	12.237	13.045
Avg. size (hectares)	41.1	42.2	42.7	42.0	42.5	42.9	43.9	47.6
% of total ag. land	**0.1**	**1.2**	**4.5**	**6.5**	**6.8**	**7.0**	**7.2**	**7.4**

Sources: Rossiiskii statisticheskii ezhegodnik 2001, 402–4, except for the following: data on personal plots in 1991 are from Shaw 1992, 554, and those in 1992–94 are from Rudnev and Borobov 2000, 106–7. When direct comparison with the official statistics of Rudnev and Borobov was possible, Shaw's data overstated the number of personal plots, which suggests that the jump in microfarming between 1991 and 1992 is probably understated in this table.

TABLE 5.9
Proportion of selected agricultural products from different types of farms, 1991–98

	1991	1992	1993	1994	1995	1996	1997	1998
Large Farms								
Grain	**99.4**	**97.4**	**94.2**	**94.2**	**94.4**	**94.6**	**93.0**	**92.3**
Sugar beets	**100.0**	**97.8**	**95.8**	**95.8**	**95.9**	**96.0**	**95.7**	**95.2**
Sunflower seeds	**98.4**	**93.0**	**88.6**	**88.2**	**86.3**	**87.0**	**87.8**	**87.6**
Potatoes	27.6	21.2	16.5	11.0	9.2	8.9	7.7	7.8
Vegetables	53.4	44.5	34.5	32.2	25.3	22.1	22.2	18.6
Cattle and poultry for slaughter	69.4	64.0	59.4	55.4	49.9	46.7	42.5	41.5
Milk	73.9	68.1	64.2	60.0	57.1	53.1	51.3	50.1
Eggs	77.8	73.9	72.7	70.9	69.4	68.4	69.2	69.5
Wool	71.7	67.0	62.8	60.2	53.0	49.8	44.3	40.0
Honey	29.2	22.4	19.7	15.9	14.2	13.2	10.9	9.9
Personal Plots								
Grain	0.4	0.5	0.6	0.7	0.9	0.8	0.8	0.9
Sugar beets	0.0	0.2	0.3	0.7	0.6	0.7	0.8	0.8
Sunflower seeds	1.2	1.2	1.5	1.6	1.4	1.6	1.4	1.5
Potatoes	**72.2**	**78.0**	**82.5**	**88.1**	**89.9**	**90.2**	**91.3**	**91.2**
Vegetables	**46.4**	**54.7**	**64.5**	**66.7**	**73.4**	**76.8**	**76.3**	**79.6**
Cattle and poultry for slaughter	**30.5**	**35.3**	**39.5**	**43.2**	**48.6**	**51.6**	**55.9**	**56.9**
Milk	**26.0**	**31.4**	**34.7**	**38.7**	**41.4**	**45.4**	**47.2**	**48.3**
Eggs	**22.2**	**26.0**	**27.1**	**28.8**	**30.2**	**31.2**	**30.4**	**30.1**
Wool	**28.2**	**32.2**	**35.4**	**37.1**	**42.5**	**45.9**	**51.3**	**55.0**
Honey	**70.2**	**76.3**	**78.0**	**81.9**	**83.7**	**84.7**	**87.0**	**88.1**
Private Farms								
Grain	**0.2**	**2.1**	**5.2**	5.1	4.7	4.6	6.2	6.8
Sugar beets	0.0	**2.0**	3.9	3.5	3.5	3.3	3.5	4.0
Sunflower seeds	**0.4**	**5.8**	**9.9**	10.2	12.3	11.4	10.8	10.9
Potatoes	**0.2**	0.8	1.0	0.9	0.9	0.9	1.0	1.0
Vegetables	**0.2**	0.8	1.0	1.1	1.3	1.1	1.5	1.8
Cattle and poultry for slaughter	0.1	0.7	1.1	1.4	1.5	1.7	1.6	1.6
Milk	0.1	0.5	1.1	1.3	1.5	1.5	1.5	1.6
Eggs	0.0	0.1	0.2	0.3	0.4	0.4	0.4	0.4
Wool	0.1	0.8	1.8	2.7	4.5	4.3	4.4	5.0
Honey	**0.6**	**1.3**	2.3	2.2	2.1	2.1	2.1	2.0

Source: *Rossiiskii statisticheskii ezhegodnik* 2001, 402.
Note: Goods produced in greater proportion than would be predicted by a farm type's proportion of agricultural land are in bold.

in the oblast, which took place in 1993–94, created a handful of farms that seemed to outperform others in the oblast, although their success came at a cost of significant subsidies to the new farms. When the project was expanded in 1994–96, however, the new farms were actually *less* profitable than those that had not reorganized, and they paid wages that were at best no higher than those at other farms in the oblast (Wegren 1998b, 90). Furthermore, the reforms did not improve overall agricultural performance in Nizhnii Novgorod oblast. According to the Russian Academy of Agricultural Science, from 1993 to 1996 the area of land in the oblast cultivated for grain dropped by a third and the number of cattle by 10 percent, while overall agricultural productivity in the oblast fell farther than in Kirov oblast, which borders Nizhnii Novgorod (*RRR* April 17, 1997).

Third, and perhaps most important, Russian agriculture in the mid-1990s was at the mercy of myriad forces entirely unrelated to landowner-ship rules in general or the private farmers' movement in particular. The most common complaint of agricultural producers in the 1990s, for example, was that the prices they paid for inputs rose dramatically faster than the prices they received for outputs. Statistics generally bear out their claims. Figures from the Povolzhe region, for example, show that the price gap between industrial and agricultural goods rose fivefold between the beginning of reforms and 1997 (Belokopytova, Alekseeva, and Trifonova 1998, 5). In Siberia, the proportion of agricultural pro-ducers' expenses going toward industrial inputs rose from 11.5 percent in 1990 to 37.3 percent in 1997, and the rise in costs of production was about twice the rate of the rise in prices of output (Kurtsev 1999, 89, Table 1). In Volgograd oblast, the price of milk rose by seventeen times from 1992 to 1995, and the price of milk products rose by thirty-five times, but the price of energy increased by nearly a thousand times ("AOOT 'Molochnyi zavod "Volgogradskii"'" 1996, 4).

Another major problem facing agriculture was the flood of imported foods. As trade liberalization made imports available, and price liberal-ization made domestic goods more expensive, Russians shifted from domestic to foreign products in large numbers. By late 1995 food imports made up about 40 percent of food consumption in Russia, and by 1997 the proportion had reached nearly 50 percent (Wegren 1998a, 116; Lysenko 1998, 80). The 1997 figures included about 18 percent of milk and milk products, 37 percent of fish and fish products, 42 percent of vegetable oil, and 73 percent of sugar (Wegren 2000, 266n29).

The turn to imports hit meat and poultry production especially hard. In 1992 Russia imported 45.7 tons of poultry meat and in 1993, 73.9 tons. In 1994, however, the number jumped to 500 tons, and in 1995 it stood at 825.4 tons, 75 percent of which came from the United States (Denin et al. 1999, 13). Imports accounted for 50 percent of poultry in Russia in 1996. Meanwhile, although meat consumption per capita dropped by more than 30 percent from 1992 to 1997, meat imports tripled between 1992 and 1996 and stood at about 36 percent of total meat supply in 1997. The phenomenon was even more pronounced in the cities, as about 70 percent of meat and poultry products in Moscow and St. Petersburg were imported (Wegren 2000, 243).

Meanwhile, agriculture's external sources of investment disappeared overnight, as inflation and dramatic cuts in federal funding all but eliminated federal support for agriculture. For example, total capital investments in the agro-industrial complex of Novgorod oblast in 1995 were a mere 4 percent of their 1991 levels in real terms. The federal government's contribution dropped 98.6 percent over the same period (El'diev 1998, 48). Similar patterns appeared around the country, as agriculture's share of federal budget expenditures dropped from about 12 percent in 1991 to 1 percent in 1998, even as the budget itself shrank dramatically. Federal investment in rural Russia likewise fell from about 11 percent of all federal capital investment in 1992 to about 2.5 percent in 1997, the largest percentage drop of any sector in the economy (Wegren 2000, 244–45, Table 1). Furthermore, the funds that were allocated often did not appear in practice because of anemic tax collection and the drive to reduce the budget deficit. In fact, nearly half of the Ministry of Agriculture's budget for enterprises in 1997 was sequestered because of low tax revenues (Shcherbak 1998, 8).

Even when farmers could produce outputs and find buyers for them, they could not get paid in cash. Like most of the economy, agriculture was caught in a web of nonpayments, debts, and barter. For example, as of October 1995, the Volgograd Milk Factory owed its milk suppliers 3.8 billion rubles, more than half the value of the milk it had received ("AOOT 'Molochnyi zavod "Volgogradskii"'" 1996, 6). While some producers simply failed to pay their debts, others covered them with bartered goods. For instance, the Semias Meat Combine (Seminkarakorskii miasokombinat) paid its suppliers in petroleum products and auto parts, while the Telets Meat Combine (Kamenskii miasokombinat) paid in electricity and other items (Lysenko 1998, 83). Indeed, according to some observers, virtually all transactions in the agrarian sector were for barter by 1998 (*Sel'skaia zhizn'* June 9, 1998, cited in Wegren 2000, 242). Even government assistance to the sector, embodied in the "commodity credit" system, amounted to a state-mandated system of inter-enterprise barter.

In the face of such powerful external forces, individual private farms were unlikely to affect Russian agriculture radically, and some of them sought refuge in alliances with one another. In many cases, for example, they formed credit cooperatives, hoping to improve their chances of securing financing. Their efforts created multi-tiered structures extending from raion-level organizations to the All-Russian Confederation of Credit Cooperatives, designed to participate in the international credit market (Glushchenko 1998). Those organizations tried to aggregate the borrowing power of their members to leverage better terms from lenders, but they met with limited success at best.

Even more common were producers' cooperatives. Agricultural equipment was usually too expensive to be a sensible purchase for a single peasant farmer, but the combined resources of several private farms could put it within reach. In addition, by pooling output farmers could increase their bargaining power with processors. Perhaps most important, each individual farm could reduce its risk of disaster in the event of a bad year. The Morozovka cooperative in the Nikolaevskii raion of Volgograd oblast was a typical example of such an association. Pooling the resources of thirty-seven peasant farms, the members of the cooperative used their six thousand hectares of land to grow grain and other products, which they processed in their own mill, and they used the flour to bake 1.5 tons of bread a day, which were sold in town (Melikhov 1998, 17–24). In a similar case, the Melnik cooperative in the Ilovlinskii raion of Volgograd oblast combined the assets of twenty-three peasant farms covering twenty-four hundred hectares (Melikhov 1998, 23). They grew, cleaned, and processed their own grain, dividing 60 percent of the profits among the farms in proportion to the grain each contributed, and sharing the other 40 percent as dividends.

As players in Russian agriculture, however, associations of peasant farms were hardly dominant, and their numbers actually declined from 1994 to 1997. On January 1, 1994, the 270,000 peasant farms in Russia had created about 900 associations (Wegren 1998a, 77). By 1997, even though the number of farms had risen slightly, the number of associations had dropped to near 750 (Lysenko 1998, 80). Associations of peasant farms could be important potential sources of property in the future, since they accounted for significant swaths of agricultural land in Russia, as well as some processing facilities and financial assets. Their role in 1994–97, however, was very limited.

Indeed, private farms in general became even less significant actors in the competition for property than they had been in 1992–94. Their weakness, however, did not result from a lack of laws, and a few legal changes were unlikely to create a fundamentally different system in Russian agriculture. Private farming is a highly risky endeavor at the best of times, and even offering land to would-be private farmers for free would not likely have enticed many into the sector under the conditions of 1994–97. Resistance from large farm managers and local politicians slowed the growth of private farms in 1992–94, but market forces were not any more supportive; and when special subsidies for private farms disappeared, the movement stalled.

Autarchy, Dacha Plots, and Microfarming

While the private farmers' movement never had a very large impact on the agrarian sector, other moves in the direction of small-scale production became increasingly influential, as none of the trends discussed previously reversed direction. Their combined effect was to produce a strange kind of decay, which allowed both the large farm and its residents to survive in a new form. One part of this process might have seemed like dynamism and entrepreneurship, but in practice it was a shift toward inefficient autarchy. That is, while food-processing plants in Russia often operated well below capacity in the mid-1990s, they also often failed to pay their suppliers on time, if at all, so many farms began building their own small processing facilities (Miloserdov and Frolov 1998, 87). In 1994–96, farms constructed about three thousand meat-processing, sausage, and curing shops (*tsekhi*), along with approximately two thousand small-scale dairy factories and innumerable mills and bakeries (Lysenko 1998, 83). By 1996 about 25 percent of large farms had built processors, and even as overall investment in agriculture plummeted, 21 percent of the investment in the construction of processing facilities in 1991–95 went into building small-scale, on-site processors (Wandel 2000, 371; Shcherbak 1997, 6). The result was an enormous shift in food production in Russia: whereas large plants had produced 67 percent of Russia's meat and 66 percent of its milk in 1990, by 1997 these figures had dropped to 28 percent and 35 percent, respectively (Shcherbak 1997, 6; Shchetnina 1999, 50–51).

A second type of decay was more obvious, as some failed collective and state farms, especially around cities, were broken into small plots that were sold or rented for dacha construction. This process became legal in 1992 and continued in the mid-1990s (Kliamkin and Timofeev 2000). The construction of more and less ritzy dacha neighborhoods outside Russian towns is likely to be part of the socioeconomic stratification of society, although its effect on ownership in agriculture itself was minimal. It did not, for example, significantly reduce the number of large farms in the country (see Table 5.8).

Finally, Russian agriculture in 1994–97 continued its slide toward farming on plots barely large enough for subsistence. The number and size of the personal plots of rural and urban residents increased very little in 1994–97, but the level of activity on those plots escalated (Allina-Pisano 2002; Kitching 1998a). Formally or informally, rural residents who remained in the area continued to siphon inputs and time from the former collective farms and devote them to their personal plots (see Table 5.9). Thus, between 1994 and 1997 the proportion of vegetables grown on personal plots grew from 67 percent to 77 percent, of cattle and poultry from 43 percent to 52 percent, of milk from 39 percent to 45 percent, and so on. Furthermore, farm workers received more income in 1997 from their personal plots than from any other single source. Similarly, the personal plot was the second most important source of income for pensioners in farming communities (Wegren 2000, 250).

This shift in control over assets at many farms was not particularly dynamic, and it was not likely to increase productivity even in the long run, but it represented a significant change from the old system, and it was stable in important ways. In particular, as the large farms provided de facto infrastructural support for personal-plot farmers, those farmers gave the large farms a reason to exist as a political entity that could at least request assistance from the local, regional, or federal government (Kitching 1998a; Humphrey 2002). The arrangement was a low-level economic equilibrium at best, but it did represent a new de facto system of ownership rights, and it provided the context for future developments on a majority of farms in Russia.

The Sea Change in Agrarian Ownership, 1994–97

Beyond the stagnation of the private farm movement and the various forms of large-farm decay, significant property redistribution was underway in the agrarian sector in the mid-1990s. In particular, whether because of direct state coordination or independent reactions to a changing environment, agrarian enterprises across Russia began to develop integrated groups of various sorts. Some regional governments created networks in their agricultural sectors that nearly reproduced the structures of the Soviet period. They also encouraged farms to buy shares in food processors, hoping to reestablish links broken by privatization. In practice, however, agricultural producers rarely played leading roles in the integration process. Instead, players with significant advantages from the Soviet era or the first years of Russian reforms became the dominant players in the new system. On occasion, a particularly large collective farm, or a successor to a Raion Agro-Industrial Association (RAPO), could play a leading role. More often, however, food processors and traders used their control of bottlenecks in the system to create the most important economic groups in the sector. In 1994–97 none of those groups climbed into the first tier of economic conglomerates in the country, but like their brethren in the second tier of industrial groups, they controlled real assets in important segments of the Russian political economy.

State-led Integration

The move toward integration partly reflected a shift in official policy. As in industry, reform in Russian agriculture in 1992–94 sought to privatize individual farms, processors, and suppliers independently, hoping to lay the groundwork for market-based relations among participants in the sector. By the end of 1994, however, many scholars and policy makers in Russia argued that the reformers' approach to privatization had created one of the main problems in the agrarian sector. As discussed previously, farms in Russia were privatized separately from processors, which generally chose Option 2 in the Privatization Program, handing control of the processors to insiders. In particular, several scholars, politicians, and journalists argued that privatizing food processors and large farms separately created independent entities with conflicting interests, specifically producers who wanted high prices for their outputs and processors who wanted low prices for their inputs (Shcherbak 1997, 6). The solution to this problem, an increasing number of observers argued, lay in reintegrating some of the enterprises that had been split from one another in 1992–94.[10] In particular, they argued that vertical integration between producers and processors would serve the interests of both groups and benefit agricultural production in general, since an integrated group could set internal prices at levels that would benefit all participants (Kurtsev 1999, 90–91; Maksimov 1998, 79–80; Aleshin 1998, 4).

Economically, this interpretation was questionable at best. For example, the price gap between farms' input and output prices, which naturally widened after the state stopped trying to close it through price controls in 1992, actually stopped growing after 1994. In 1995 and 1996

---

10. For examples of works arguing for reintegration, see Belokopytova, Alekseeva, and Trifonova 1998; Kamyshanov 1994; Maksimov 1998; Rutskoi 1998, 5; Samofalova 1998, 72; Shcherbak 1997.

agricultural output prices rose slightly faster than input prices, and subsequent inflation rates were similar in the two sectors (see Table 5.10). Furthermore, while most processors technically enjoyed monopsony positions vis-à-vis their suppliers, most operated well below capacity, so their market power over producers was minimal in practice. In the early 1990s, processors lost their federal and local subsidies, struggled to find credit, suffered customers who could not pay cash, and faced rapidly increasing costs, including transport costs that rose about twelve times faster than output prices in 1990–95. Thus, although it is true that 57 percent of agricultural producers in Russia were unprofitable in 1994, so were about 21 percent of agricultural processors (Wegren 1996, 156, 178n44).

Nevertheless, arguments in favor of integration won the day, and several regional governments either facilitated or mandated the creation of ownership groups in agriculture. For example, ten of the first sixty-two officially registered FIGs focused directly on the agro-industrial sector (see Table 5.11). The Kamenskaia Agro-Industrial Financial Group (Kamenskaia agropromyshlennaia finansovaia gruppa) in Penza oblast, for instance, included twenty-five agricultural enterprises and the Penza branch of Agroprombank (Lysenko 1998, 84). In Novgorod oblast Governor Mikhail Prusak helped establish the Niva Chernozemia holding in March 1997 (*RRR* January 22, 1998). The FIG was concentrated in the fertilizer industry and included the leading fertilizer plant in the region, Akron, which Viacheslav Kantor reportedly controlled, having bought it at a "bargain price" (*RRR* April 30, 1997).

Not all instances of regional government-led integration resulted in officially registered FIGs, however. In other cases, the role of the state in the management of the enterprises was even more direct. In Saratov oblast, for example, the Balakovskii Milk Processing Plant and the raion administration created the Balakovskaia Association in 1994. The group

TABLE 5.10
Price increases by sector (as multiples of preceding year)

	1992	1993	1994	1995	1996	1997	1998
Consumer prices	26.1	9.4	3.2	2.3	1.2	1.1	1.8
Prices paid to ind. producers	33.8	10.0	3.3	2.7	1.3	1.1	1.2
Prices paid to ag. producers	9.4	8.1	3.0	3.3	1.4	1.1	1.1
Ratio: ind. rise/ag. rise	3.6	1.2	1.1	0.8	0.9	1.0	1.1

Source: Rudnev and Borobov 2000, 57.

TABLE 5.11
Registered FIGs in agrarian sector by mid-1997

Name of FIG	Location of HQ	Date of registration
Edinstvo	Perm	October 6, 1995
Soiuzagroprom	Voronezh	November 24, 1995
Sibagromash	Rubtsovsk (Altai krai)	March 1, 1996
Belovskaia	Belovo (Kemerovo oblast)	March 1, 1996
Trekhgorka	Moscow	April 17, 1996
Grain-Flour-Bread	Moscow	September 6, 1996
Kamenskaia agro-industrial financial group	Kamenka (Penza oblast)	May 7, 1996
Center-Region	Riazan	October 9, 1996
Niva Chernozemia	Novgorod	March 28, 1997
Glavsreduralprodukt	Moscow	April 2, 1997

Source: Dement'ev 1997, 19–22.

united the plant and twenty-three milk producers under the joint leadership of the head of the raion-level ministry of agriculture and the manager of the processing plant ("AOZT molochnyi zavod 'Balakovskii'" 1995, 5; Iakovlev 1995, 52, 55–57; Cherniaev 1996). Similarly, in June 1994 in Yaroslavl oblast, twenty-seven production enterprises, eighty retail outlets, and a central milk-processing factory united under the banner of the Sodeistviia Association, where raion and city officials sat on the board of directors together with the head of the milk factory and representatives from the producers and stores (Schastlivtseva and Gubanova 1995, 11).

Some regional governments not only helped operate the new associations but also owned parts of them. For instance, in Tula and Ulianovsk oblasts, agricultural producers turned their shares in food processors over to funds managed by the regional administrations (Shcherbak 1997, 7; Cherniaev 1996). Likewise, the founders of the Opole-Vladimir Agro-industrial Group included four producers, two dairy processors, the Vladimir regional branch of the Moscow Industrial Bank, and the city committee for property management (Shchetnina 1999, 52; Schastlivtseva and Gubanova 1995, 12). Along the same lines, in Volgograd oblast, the regional government worked with the oil giant LUKoil, which had a large presence in Volgograd, as well as some smaller investors, to create the Volgograd Agro-Industrial Financial Corporation (VAPFK) in June 1994 (Inshakov 1995, 448). The chair of the Volgograd oblast committee on agriculture headed VAPFK, and the regional government held a 51-percent stake in the entity, which included thirty-three producers, processors, retail outlets, and financial institutions (Somov 1998, 1; Inshakov 1995, 237). These arrangements did not strikingly affect agricultural production in the mid-1990s, but they represented another redistribution of assets, and they formed part of the context for the struggle over property in 1998 and beyond.

A major effort to reintegrate virtually the entire agro-industrial sector under the direction of the state came from Kursk oblast and its governor, former Russian vice president Aleksandr Rutskoi. Begun in 1997, the project mimicked the old RAPO structure, uniting agricultural enterprises within subsectors, such as the poultry, meat, dairy, and fruit and vegetable sectors in Kursk raion. The raion-level institutions, in turn, belonged to an oblastwide corporation—OAO Kurskaia—51 percent of whose shares the oblast property committee owned, with the remainder divided among member enterprises (Rukavitsyn and Khalina 1998). In addition, funding for the sector was to come from an oblast banking network under the administration (Rutskoi 1998, 9–11).

Perhaps the best-known such experiment, however, comes from Orel oblast, where the regional and district governments helped create and run several integrated agricultural groups. At the oblast level, the administration founded Orlovskaia niva in 1994 (Miloserdov and Frolov 1998, 88; Stroev, Zlobin, and Mikhalev 1998, 46). Anatolii Sudorgin, who had served as a district secretary for the Communist Party in the Soviet era and as the chief agricultural procurements officer for the oblast in 1993, became general director of Orlovskaia niva when it was founded in May 1994 (Kulefeeva, Trushin, and Khodyrev 2001). The company served as a middleman for agricultural producers in the oblast, buying their outputs (including about 200,000 tons of grain a year) and supplying them with such inputs as fuel and fertilizer. In addition, it assisted in creating distribution networks and provided investment capital and seasonal loans (Miloserdov and Frolov 1998, 88, 90). In other words, it was set up to perform the same organizational and support functions as the old agricultural administration.

With Orlovskaia niva directing inter-enterprise trade, the oblast administration began to establish several integrated groups that focused on production. The first was Orlovshchina, founded in 1997 (Zlobin 2000, 115–18). The main enterprise in the group was the broiler plant Naryshkinskaia, which produced six million broilers a year. The organization also included two grain-producing enterprises, a machine-technological station, a grain-receiving enterprise, a mixed-feed factory, and thirteen stores (Shcherbak 1998, 13). In a similar fashion, the integrated firm Niva-Verkhove, in Verkhovskii raion, was formed with special permission from the governor. The leader of the board of directors was Iu. A. Grishin, who was also the head of the executive branch of the raion government (Grishin et al. 1998, 5). Among the privileges the governor granted were free land on which to grow feed crops, an exemption from local taxes, a 50-percent discount on electricity, subsidies from the oblast budget, and a release from obligations to pay for workers' housing (Frolov 1998, 4). In addition, Niva-Verkhove received a 1.9 billion-ruble credit to invest in a project called "Miaso" (Meat) and additional credit for a project called "Korma" (Feed) (Grishin et al. 1998, 7). In yet another instance, the ZAO Mtsenskoe was created in 1997–98 in the Mtsenskii raion, bringing together two processing plants (one for meat and one for sugar-beet products), a small number of producers, and a repair shop for farm equipment (Miloserdov and Frolov 1998, 89; Zlobin 2000, 23).

Opponents of this approach, of course, saw it as a cynical attempt to reestablish Soviet-era controls over the agro-industrial sector. Given the devastated state of Russian agriculture at the time, however, it is not hard to see why some hoped this arrangement would allow the regional administration to assist the sector in a more sensible and coordinated fashion than earlier in the decade. More important for this book, some regional governments in the mid-1990s were clearly expanding their control over agro-industrial assets in a more direct way than in the industrial sector. In addition, because official policy favored vertical integration and because most regions included enterprises at each stage of the food-production process, the groups created by regional governments were more likely to encompass entire production chains than their counterparts in industry. The structure of such regional groups would help shape conflicts over their assets in future rounds of competition.

Independent Integration

In addition to such direct intervention in the ownership and control of agrarian assets, federal and regional governments encouraged other participants in the sector to integrate. Most notably, they required food processors to sell shares in themselves to the farms that supplied their raw inputs. Most producers, however, were not in a position to build strong ownership groups. Instead, both food processors and actors from outside the production process were more likely to establish the kind of conglomerates that could significantly influence economics and politics.

The rhetoric and laws encouraging producer-led integration were legion. For example, a December 20, 1994, decree called on the Russian government to seek ways to "overcome local monopolism," which referred to the presumed monopsony power of processors over their suppliers (Shcherbak 1997, 7).[11] The resulting governmental decision recommended measures to regional governments, including the transfer of controlling stakes in processors to producers.[12] At about the same time, the government referred positively to regional experiments, such as those in Chuvashia, which included producers in the initial distribution of shares in processors. In addition, the Ministry of Agriculture made celebratory videos with titles such as "New Types of Relationships among Goods Producers and the Rybinskii Milk Factory of Yaroslavl Oblast," "The Cheboksary Meat Combine's Experience with Incorporation," and "The Ulianovsk Variant," praising efforts to transfer ownership of processing plants to farms (Shcherbak 1997, 7). In 1996 the government further advocated agro-industrial integration in its law "On the Development of Agricultural Cooperation" (Pakhomchik 1998, 4). Finally, on October 24, 1996, the Ministry of Agriculture officially recommended the creation of FIGs in agriculture (Iugai and Petrov 1998).

More directly, regional governments sometimes gave incentives to processors to encourage the transfer of some ownership to producers. For example, the administration in Belgorod oblast forgave some of processors' debt to the budget on the promise that the processors would use the increase in enterprise value to issue new shares, which would go to producers. Similarly, the administration of Stupinskii raion of Moscow oblast persuaded the Stupinskii Milk Factory to issue new shares to the point that producers held a 78.6 percent stake in the enterprise (Shcherbak 1997, 7).

The Russian agricultural press carried a number of examples of reportedly successful integration along those lines. For example, when the Permmoloko milk-processing plant carried out a supplemental emission in 1995, it helped raise milk producers' stake in the company to 57 percent (Shcherbak 1997, 7). Similarly, a transfer of shares from sugar factories to sugar-beet growers reportedly helped guarantee a supply of raw materials to the processors in Altai krai (Lysenko 1998, 83–84).

---

11. Decree of the Russian President no. 2205.
12. Decision of the Government of the Russian Federation no. 195 (February 28, 1995).

Likewise, supplemental share emissions in a meat-packing plant in Zolo-tukhinskii raion of Kursk oblast gave agricultural producers as a whole a 51-percent stake in the plant (Maksimov 1998, 80).

In some cases, the resulting structures seemed to reintegrate farms with their surrounding environment as intended. One example of such integration is Agrofirma Nikolaevskaia, located in the Saratov raion of Saratov oblast and focusing on livestock and related products (Andreev, Chapanova, and Brel' 2000). Built on the basis of the former Leninskii Put Collective Farm, the enterprise included production, processing, and distribution assets by 1998. Another illustration of this kind of expansion comes from Promkor, an enterprise in the Ramonskii raion of Voronezh oblast (Konovalova and Averin 1998). The holdings of the former Rossiia Collective Farm formed the basis of the new enterprise, which by 1996 included production, processing, and distribution capabilities.

Some of these groups also managed to incorporate providers of equipment services into their networks. Although the large farms retained their own equipment from the Soviet era, that machinery broke down over time, and the local branches of the former state supply system (Agrosnab) emerged as monopoly providers of repair services and rentals of farm machinery. In many ways, then, they served functions similar to those of the Soviet-era machine-tractor stations, and they even used the same acronym, although MTS now stood for "machine-technological station." By 1998 over 280 MTSs had sprouted up across the country, with 200 more under development ("MTS zavoevyvaiut" 1998). The response of the growing conglomerates, unsurprisingly, was to try to incorporate such entities into their organizations (Shcherbak 1998, 13).

Stories of producer-led integration, however, often exaggerated the extent to which the organizations were really new. Many of the supposed success stories came from enterprises that were already enormous and included assets beyond the bare necessities for production. For example, the Novo-Raevskii State Farm, in the Alsheevskii raion, Bashkortostan, included twelve thousand hectares of land, ten thousand head of cattle, a fattening complex, a slaughterhouse, meat processors, a machine-tractor park, and much more ("Sovkhoz 'Novo-Raevskii'" 1998, 2). Such an enterprise could respond to changes in its external environment by internalizing parts of the production process relatively easily. For example, in the face of rising prices for feed, Novo-Raevskii in 1997 simply expanded the land it devoted to grain from about twenty-seven hundred hectares to about thirty-seven hundred, in part by acquiring land from a neighboring unprofitable enterprise.

Even more significant for the drive to create producer-based agro-industrial groups, most farms either could not afford to buy shares in processors or were not interested in acquiring them. Thus, despite the supplementary emissions, farms held a controlling stake in only 14 percent of processors by the end of 1996. In the meat industry, the figure stood at 9 percent; in milk, 16 percent; and in milling, 14 percent (Wandel 2000, 370). Furthermore, even in cases where farms in general owned a large percentage of shares in a processor, those shares were dispersed among several different owners, who faced significant collective action problems in coordinating their activities. Overall, then, the policies on secondary share emissions from processors did not produce the expected results, even on the question of asset ownership, to say nothing of real output from the sector.

Most of the initiatives for vertical integration in Russian agriculture therefore came from processors. Some instances of such integration were relatively small in scale and did not have much immediate impact on the sector, although they did create part of the context of the struggle for property in agriculture after 1998. For instance, in Saratov oblast the Sixty-second Army poultry factory created a joint-stock company called Volgogradagrokompaniia in 1993. By 1995 it included twenty enterprises, including grain producers, feed processors, breeding facilities, and meat-packaging enterprises (Cherniaev 1996). Likewise, the Ramoz dairy factory in Yaroslavl oblast created an association that included several producers and retail outlets (Shchetnina 1999, 53). In a similar case, workers at the Volgogradskii Milk Factory in Volgograd oblast owned 51 percent of the factory, while twenty-four raw materials suppliers (twenty-one producers and three primary processors) held the remaining 49 percent. The factory tried to mitigate the problem of deadbeat customers by building or buying its own retail outlets, although by 1996 it operated only five stores and two kiosks, selling about 8 percent of its output through that network ("AOOT 'Molochnyi zavod "Volgogradskii"'" 1996, 1, 7).

Other cases of processor-led integration, however, had both short-term and long-term implications for the sector, as some firms acquired important assets in 1994–97 (see Table 5.12). Probably the most famous such group for visitors to Russia is Wimm-Bill-Dann, a juice- and milk-packaging company whose brand can be found in every grocery store in Moscow, as well as elsewhere in the country. It began when a handful of

TABLE 5.12
Major independent agricultural groups, 1994–97

Name of group	Leader	Important notes for 1994–97
Based on processors:		
Wimm-Bill-Dann	David Iakobachvili (president)	Established majority control at Lianozovo Dairy Plant in 1995 1996–97: acquired Moscow Baby Food Plant, Tsaritsino Dairy Plant, and Ramenskii Dairy Plant
APK Cherkizovskii	Igor Erzolovich Babaev	Located in Moscow Included Ostankinskii Meat-Processing Plant
Omskii bekon	Aleksandr Kivich	Purchased controlling stakes in Kirovskii Meat-Processing Plant and Luzinskii Fodder-Production Plant
Snezhka		Based on a poultry factory By 1996 controlled over 5,000 hectares of land for grain and 5,000 head of cattle
Iug Rusi	Sergei Kislov	Initially specialized in flour processing Built a river terminal in Rostov in 1995 By 1997 was Russia's largest sunflower exporter
Based on traders:		
OGO	Aleksei Diumulen	1994–95: Purchased elevators and grain-products combines 1996: Established a bank 1997: Leased two broiler farms
Razguliai-Ukrros	Igor Potapenko	Purchased sugar plants Purchased grain processors
Roskhleboprodukt	Leonid Cheshinskii	Main agent of state in food fund program
Rusagro	Vadim Moshkovich	Founded in 1995 Moved into sugar processing only in 1997

people leased a production line at the Lianozovo Dairy Plant in Moscow in 1992, formed a partnership with juice-concentrate supplier Cargill, and began selling juice under the intentionally Western-sounding name of Wimm-Bill-Dann (Wimbledon) (www.wbd.com, accessed October 31, 2003). During and after mass privatization, the founders bought up shares of the Lianozovo plant, establishing majority ownership in 1995. Over the next two years, they bought majority stakes in three more Moscow factories: the Moscow Baby Food Plant, the Tsaritsino Dairy Plant, and the Ramenskii Dairy Plant.

Another important group that grew out of a processor was APK Cherkizovskii, based on the Cherkizovskii Meat-Processing Plant in Moscow (IRG 2003, 88). The plant itself was among the top seventy-five firms in the country, and by 1997 it had acquired another top–two hundred enterprise, the Ostankinskii Meat-Processing Plant, also in Moscow (Pappe 2000, 60–65). Similarly, workers at the Omskii bekon meat processor, in Omsk oblast, bought controlling stakes in the Kirov Meat Combine and the Luzinskii Combined Feed Plant (Shchetnina 1999, 53). The conglomerate thus created was a major economic and political force in Omsk oblast.

The poultry and meat conglomerate Snezhka in the Briansk raion of Briansk oblast demonstrated even more impressive expansion ("Aktsion-ernoe obshchestvo 'Snezhka'" 1997; Denin et al. 1999). The central entity of the group was the Snezhka Poultry Factory, constructed in the Soviet period. In 1993 the enterprise began to expand its feed-production capacity in a joint effort with Koudais, a Dutch company, and by 1995 Snezhka could provide for its own feed needs. After mass privatization, Snezhka moved to acquire neighboring enterprises, including the former Leninets Collective Farm. On the strength of its acquisi-tions, Snezhka by 1996 controlled over five thousand hectares of land for grain production, as well as five thousand head of cattle. At the retail end of the production chain, Snezhka bought or leased ten stores and operated a network of drivers to take produce to markets all around the oblast. On the question of machinery provision, Snezhka's machine-technological park doubled in size between 1995 and 1997, because of the acquisition of other enterprises and new machinery. In 1997 Snezhka even acquired the energy supplier "Agropromenergo" by paying off its debts.

Finally, Iug Rusi, one of the groups that came to dominate the pro-duction and export of Russian sunflower-seed oil, also developed on the basis of a food processor. Founded in 1993 in Rostov-on-Don, Iug Rusi processed Russian grain into flour for domestic companies, rather than importing raw materials or exporting processed flour. Sergei Kislov became director of Iug Rusi in 1995 and rapidly expanded its activities. In terms of the group's physical assets, Kislov used the connections he had developed as manager of the subsidiary agricultural enterprise of the main Rostov port from 1988 to 1991 to negotiate the construction of a transportation terminal for Iug Rusi in 1995 (Kulefeeva, Trushin, and Khodyrev 2001, 5–6; IRG 2003, 84). In terms of business profile, Iug Rusi entered all phases of the sunflower industry and by 1997 had become the largest exporter of sunflower oil in Russia (IRG 2003, 84; Bezmenov 2002). Like other groups of this type, Iug Rusi aggressively built on its control of bottlenecks in the agricultural production process to become a prominent player in the sector.

While regional governments and food processors were leading actors in the integration of agrarian enterprises in 1994–97, various outsiders also took advantage of the post-privatization environment to acquire stakes in the sector. In some cases, the most famous "oligarchs" from finance and industry entered the fray, acquiring potentially significant agrarian assets. Menatep/Rosprom, for example, through Alliance-Menatep, owned shares in the food processor Koloss and the fertilizer producer Apatit (Blasi, Kroumova, and Kruse 1997, 156). Likewise, Alfa Group branched into food processing, especially sugar refinement in the Kuban region (Johnson 1997, 346–47; Kulefeeva, Trushin, and Khodyrev 2001, 1). SBS-Agro, Inkombank, and LUKoil also controlled farms, processors, or trade outlets (Johnson 1997, 346–47; Khramova and Verkhaim 1999; Kulefeeva, Trushin, and Khodyrev 2001, 9). The attention of such groups, however, was not focused on the agricultural sector in 1994–97, and they played largely peripheral roles until after the 1998 financial crash.

Rather than deriving their influence from financial-industrial oligarchs, the most important integrated ownership groups in Russian agriculture in the mid-1990s grew out of former trading companies (see Table 5.12). The OGO group, for example, which had become a major trader of Russian grain by 1992, began to expand in 1994 by buying shares in storage facilities (Serova, Khramova, and Nichols 2002). In particular, it acquired controlling stakes in two elevators in Saratov oblast. Soon thereafter, it began to buy shares in processing facilities, aided by the supplementary share emissions encouraged by the government. In 1994, for example, it bought the Schadrin Grain-Product Combine in Kurgan oblast, a collection of assets that included both elevators and processing facilities, for a little under $700,000. The company followed that acquisition by purchasing a grain-product combine in Vologda oblast and one in Astrakhan oblast. The acquisition of those grain processors allowed OGO to turn some of its attention to producing mixed feed for poultry, which proved important in the further development of the group. After establishing its own bank in 1996, OGO in 1997 leased two major broiler farms, Niandomskaia in Arkhangelsk oblast and Rassvet in Tula oblast. OGO thus took advantage of new laws, a general acceptance of integration, and the absence of strong competitors to develop a collection of assets with the potential to be every bit as politically and economically important as the financial-industrial "oligarchs" with whom we are more familiar.

Razguliai-Ukrros was a second agricultural trading group that began to expand and diversify its holdings after the end of mass privatization and farm reorganization. Created in 1992 as a trader of Ukrainian sugar and Russian oil, Razguliai-Ukrros first moved into processing in late 1995, when it bought the Bolshevik Sugar Factory in Belgorod oblast (IRG 2003, 86; Telitsyna, Kuz'menko, and Kovalenko 2002). In 1996 Razguliai-Ukrros bought another sugar factory, this one in Kursk oblast, and began to enter the grain-processing sector as well (Kuz'menko 2002).

If OGO and Razguliai-Ukrros built on their successes in 1992–94 to acquire new assets in 1994–97, Roskhleboprodukt, the successor of the Soviet grain distributor, entered the post-privatization property struggle as an entity in danger of losing key assets. It was privatized in 1993–94, with many of its regional branches made officially independent of the central organization (Serova 1999, 419). Roskhleboprodukt itself, however, remained an important player in grain distribution in Russia. While state procurements of grain dropped significantly in the 1990s, the government still retained a grain reserve system, and Roskhleboprodukt remained the central agent in that system, working together with its regional units to collect grain for the state food funds (Wegren 1998a, 135).

The final important group based on a trading company in this period was called Rusagro. Compared to the others, Rusagro was a latecomer to the game, established only 1996 (Telitsyna, Kuz'menko, and Kovalenko 2002). Its founder, Vadim Moshkovich, was a trader on the Moscow Commodities Exchange in 1991–92, much as several players in the struggle over the Russian metals sector had been (Kulefeeva, Trushin, and Khodyrev 2001, 6). After working at two other enterprises, Moshkovich created the sugar-trading company Rusagro, which imported processed sugar from Ukraine in exchange for fuel oil, becoming the leading supplier of such major Russian confectionery plants as Red October, Babaevskii, and Rot Front (IRG 2003, 91). In 1997, after tariffs increased on Ukrainian sugar, Rusagro began to process its own sugar, purchasing a plant in Belgorod oblast (Telitsyna, Kuz'menko, and Kovalenko 2002).

Even these trade-and-production groups in Russian agriculture could not wrest the journalistic and scholarly spotlight from the financial and industrial oligarchs in the mid-1990s, perhaps because farms, pigs, and fertilizer never attract the attention of oil, diamonds, and cash. Even so, the assets they controlled clearly placed them in the category of second-tier groups, similar in importance to their counterparts in industry. As such, some of them stood well positioned to take advantage of changes in the Russian political economy beginning in 1998.

A GATHERING STORM IN AN UNSTABLE LAND

The struggle for property in Russia after mass privatization represented more than an attempt by reformers to complete a market transition or opponents to block it. It was a multifaceted conflict in the wake of a massive drop in state control over assets and in the context of unresolved disputes over the shape of formal government institutions. That environment produced a dizzying array of clashes among a wide range of actors: the federal government, economic ownership groups, regional administrations, enterprise managers, and various outsiders.

By late 1997 those conflicts had produced several ownership groups with control over important assets in the economy and access to political power. In industry the famed "oligarchs" stood at the top of the hill and used their economic and political power to expand and consolidate their holdings. Not far below them, however, second-tier groups with connections to regional politicians controlled resources that could profoundly influence the development of regional political economies. In agriculture, meanwhile, groups based on processors and traders acquired assets at multiple stages of the production process, again often with the support of regional administrations.

Throughout the system, then, economic groups looked increasingly powerful. At the same time, great swaths of property were still only weakly claimed, and multiple competitors still sought to bring those assets under their control. It seemed that the struggle for property could persist in this form for years. In reality, neither the groups nor the struggle were as stable as they appeared. Even the most prominent conglomerates were vulnerable to debt pressures, changes in political leadership, and attacks from the outside. Some less visible groups were in a position to benefit from an oligarch's fall, although they, too, faced risks if the context of the struggle changed. That is exactly what began to happen as 1997 drew to a close. As the clouds of financial crisis began to gather, the tools and goals of competition for property began to shift.

CHAPTER 6

THE EARTH MOVES

Finance, Politics, and a New Era of Redistribution, 1997–2002

The post-privatization phase of the struggle for property did not end as clearly as the mass privatization programs. Instead, two sets of shocks affected the system over time and worked together to create a new era of property redistribution, one in which control over cash, inputs, and regional politics grew increasingly important. The shocks toppled some national economic groups, reshaped others, and brought some erstwhile second-tier groups to the fore. The new environment even made agricultural assets attractive in new ways, both to groups already active in the sector and to large industrial groups that had paid little attention to the countryside in the mid-1990s.

The first set of forces that changed the Russian struggle for property in the late 1990s centered on the precarious financial position of most enterprises in the system. In 1997, under fiscal and political pressure, the energy monopolies Gazprom and Unified Energy System (UES) began to call in debts from their customers, sometimes accepting stock as payment. Around the same time, regional governments likewise began to accept ownership stakes in lieu of tax arrears. Both of these trends helped initiate a new round of property redistribution, but the floodgates truly opened in 1998 with the passage of a new bankruptcy law and the onset of the August financial crash. Together, those events changed the opportunities and strategies of competitors for property throughout the system.

As the financial shocks continued to work their way through the system, a second seismic shift hit the Russian political economy in the person of Vladimir Putin. Elected president in 2000 partly on his pledge to reestablish order in the economic arena, he stepped boldly into the struggle for property and promised to bring it under control. While he did not stop the conflict, his effect on it was profound. In the realm of real ownership, he drove two oligarchs out of the country, and he reasserted the state's position at Gazprom, strengthening control over several assets that had begun to slip away in the mid-1990s. Meanwhile, in the political world, Putin changed the way competitors for property interacted with the state, making their federal actions less blatant and pushing them to focus more on regional political networks.

The two sets of shocks altered the conduct of the struggle for property in 1997–2002. Competitors did not completely abandon their old strategies or motives, but new ones became more important. The financial changes, for example, made debt and the manipulation of new laws—a phenomenon I call "political bankruptcy"—the tool of choice for taking over key assets in the system. The new environment, in turn, forced economic actors to focus even more intensely on controlling pieces of real property, especially those that could provide inputs to a production process or access to cash and therefore protection against debt. Access to political power, especially at the regional level, also proved invaluable for actors employing or defending themselves against the weapon of bankruptcy. At the same time, as Putin tried to limit the influence of major players in Moscow and gain greater control over regional politicians, the strategy for many economic actors was to enter regional politics more directly. The most successful competitors for property in this era, therefore, were the economic groups that best reshaped themselves to survive or take advantage of the debt maelstrom and those that best developed their political influence in the regions.

The financial and political changes in Russia at the end of the century not only reshaped the struggle for property, but they also cleared the way for a new popular interpretation of post-Soviet Russia. Especially after the August 1998 crash, which sent stocks and the ruble into tailspins, observers switched from asking which reforms Russia most needed to complete its transition to wondering where the transition had gone wrong. Two related answers, in circulation before 1998 but not widely accepted until then, challenged the conventional view of likely impediments to marketization. Whereas the orthodoxy of the late 1980s and early 1990s feared an impoverished population and an intrusive bureaucracy, the new wisdom saw obstacles in an enriched oligarchy and a captured state. Those who benefited from initial liberalization would protect their new positions by preventing the government from allowing real competition to flourish (Hellman 1998; Ericson 2000; McFaul 1998; Holmes 1997; Verdery 1996, 204–28).

Such correctives were invaluable, but they remained limited for understanding the fate of real assets in Russia. An emphasis on first-round winners, for example, rightly focused attention on some of the most powerful actors in the country, but it could overstate the stability of a situation like the one that existed in Russia by 1997. In practice, the positions of national economic groups were more precarious than they appeared, and groups and sectors that seemed to have been left behind in the initial asset grab could roar to prominence later. In a similar fashion, focusing on state capacity highlighted the importance of government action in creating and sustaining a market economy, but it could produce broad characterizations that proved misleading in practice. Under Yeltsin, for example, while economic interests had clearly penetrated the state, and while legal changes such as regional laws on land purchases in 1998 had little effect on the distribution of property, the new bankruptcy law made an enormous impact.[1] Conversely, while Putin spoke firmly about the need for a stronger Russian state and in practice changed state-business relations in the country, he did not end the struggle for property or the influence of economic groups on the government.

More fundamentally, however, the new wisdom did not step outside the "transition" model of post-Soviet change. Instead, it remained locked into a view of Russia on a path to a particular end—a path blocked by oligarchs and corruption, but a path nonetheless. That vision, in turn, produced a new round of arguments between "optimists" and "pessimists." The positive thinkers believed the oligarchs would reform themselves or that Putin would reinvigorate the reform process and enforce the rule of law, while the doomsayers did not. More useful than a return to that hopelessly rancorous debate is to view the period of 1997–2002 simply as another stage in the struggle for property, one that unleashed a new wave of redistribution with a new set of dominant actors, strategies, and goals.

---

1. Saratov oblast was the first region to pass a law clearly allowing the purchase and sale of agricultural land with few restrictions, and more than twenty regions followed soon thereafter ("Russian Regions" 1998). Nevertheless, while various administrations held land auctions based on the new laws, the major land transactions noted in this chapter still relied on leases.

NEW CONTEXT, NEW TACTICS

By 1997 an extraordinary amount of debt had built up among enterprises in the Russian system.[2] In addition, uncertainty about Boris Yeltsin's state of mind and body seemed to increase by the day. Over the next several years, the resolution of both pathologies—first in myriad processes of converting debt into ownership and then in the rise of Vladimir Putin—fundamentally reshaped the Russian struggle for property.

The Debt Roll-up

The issue of debt and nonmonetary exchange in the Russian system cropped up in a wide range of policy discussions in late 1996 and early 1997. Natural-monopolies reform, tax collection, and bankruptcy legislation were all connected in some way to government efforts to monetize economic transactions and thus tax receipts. In less obvious ways, however, all these issues were also tied to ownership, and the process of dealing with debt began a redistribution of assets that eventually reshaped the Russian political economy.

The energy monopolies Gazprom and UES were both born with control over the central assets in their sectors, but not over regional and local distribution networks. The original Gazprom, for example, received the main gas fields, associated equipment, and large-scale pipelines and compressors to move gas from extraction points to smaller-scale distributors in regions and cities.[3] Small-gauge pipes and compressors, however, which supplied gas directly to industrial, governmental, agricultural, or residential consumers, usually fell under the control of regional or local administrations.[4] Likewise, while UES owned the largest power plants, the main electrical transmission lines, and stakes in many regional power generators, regional governments also owned shares in the generators and controlled distribution and pricing of electricity for most final consumers (Woodruff 1999, 195; Kramer 2003). These arrangements meant

2. For more on the process of debt accumulation, see Woodruff 1999; Johnson 2000; Treisman 2000; Ickes, Murrell, and Ryterman 1997; and the contributions in Seabright 2000.

3. See Presidential Decree no. 1333, November 5, 1992; OECD 2002, 107.

4. In addition, two regional systems, Norilskgazprom and Yakutskgazprom, which could operate independently of the main system, were not included in Gazprom (OECD 2002, 107).

regional governments could effectively prevent cash payments by insisting that local enterprises and government offices be allowed to pay for electricity and gas in kind or with IOUs. Furthermore, they had every incentive to act in just that way to sustain economic activity in their jurisdictions.

Over the course of 1997, in the context of natural-monopolies reform, both Gazprom and UES tried to modify this setup, albeit in slightly different ways and with different results. Both companies lobbied for the right to lower their prices for consumers who paid in cash and to negotiate directly with large customers, rather than working through regional governments, and in the first half of 1997 the government granted them these concessions.[5] Gazprom created a payment-collection subsidiary, Mezhregiongaz (MRG), that successfully combined negotiation and confrontation to monetize receipts and take over important property more effectively than UES. MRG, for example, made deals regarding supply and payment arrangements with sixty-two regional governments by the end of 1997, and it continued to add regions in the following years (Woodruff 1999, 193; www.gazprom.ru/articles/article4395.shtml, accessed June 19, 2004). The company also cut supplies to nonpaying customers, many of whom were regional and local gas distributors that eventually paid off those debts with shares in themselves. In the first such confrontation to go to court, an arbitration judge forced Uralgazservis to pay MRG over 100 million rubles in January 1998 (Kozlov 1998).[6] Using such tactics, Gazprom/MRG established direct or indirect control over about 90 percent of the oblast distribution networks and fifty-two of the two hundred major local distribution networks by 2002 (OECD 2002, 108, 109, Figure 22). In addition to taking over regional and local gas distributors, however, Gazprom also used its new powers to pursue other key assets in Russia. The largest debtors to the company, for example, were the electricity generators, which owed about 44 billion rubles for gas by mid-1998. Beginning in July 1998, Gazprom took advantage of its new powers and began to demand 100-percent

5. See, for example, presidential decrees no. 426 (April 28, 1997), which legalized payments clearing houses for natural monopolies, and no. 628 (June 19, 1997), which gave Gazprom the right to offer 40-percent discounts to cash-paying customers. (A year later, decree no. 697 [June 11, 1998] lowered the discount to 30 percent.) In addition, by August 1998 MRG had signed about two hundred contracts with large customers to sell them gas directly (*RRR* August 6, 1998).

6. Uralgazservis temporarily won an appeal later in the year, but MRG eventually prevailed.

cash payments from those generators, threatening to cut off gas supplies if they failed to comply (Klasson 1998).[7] In the short run, the power plants sought to use coal and oil as fuels, but their vulnerability to debt pressures was now clear.

The electricity giant UES, under its new CEO Boris Brevnov, likewise revised its approach to debt collection in 1997, but it clashed more directly with regional generators and administrations than did Gazprom. In particular, while UES allowed large final consumers to purchase electricity directly at a 30-percent cash discount, it took a tougher approach to regional generators and distributors, demanding that they pay at least 30 percent of their bills to UES in cash (Woodruff 1999, 196). Furthermore, the April 1997 decree on natural monopoly reform (no. 426, April 28, 1997) contained the outlines of a plan to separate the regional generation and distribution systems from UES entirely, allowing the bigger company to deal directly with the most solvent consumers in the country. In response, regional governors and heads of the regional generators combined forces to push Brevnov out of UES in early 1998, bringing former privatization minister Anatolii Chubais to the CEO's chair (Woodruff 1999, 197–98). As will be discussed later, Chubais began to negotiate more earnestly with regional leaders, formed alliances with large industrialists, and used debts to take over productive assets, although he was never able to copy the Gazprom/MRG strategy of taking over regional distribution networks. Instead, UES continued to try to jettison the regional generators and distributors, much to the chagrin of several minority shareholders.

At about the same time that Gazprom and UES began to tug on the chains of enterprise arrears in the Russian system, regional governments also intensified their efforts to convert debt into ownership. Although such exchanges had taken place in the mid-1990s as well, they became increasingly widespread as time passed. Most commonly, the deals amounted to accepting shares as payment for tax debts, usually overvaluing the stock in comparison to the price it would fetch in an open exchange. In December 1996, for example, the president of Bashkortostan signed a decree clearing the way for several subsidiaries of his republic's oil-processing conglomerate to repay tax debt with new shares (*RRR* December 18, 1996; *RRR* April 24, 1997). That story was repeated

7. At the same time, UES claimed that consumers of electricity owed it about 100 billion rubles and owed regional generators another 87 billion rubles (Klasson 1998).

throughout the country, as KamAZ transferred shares to Tatarstan, AvtoVAZ exchanged stock for tax relief from federal and Samara oblast administrations, Norilsk Nickel handed the Krasnoiarsk Nonferrous Metals Factory to the Krasnoiarsk krai government, at least temporarily, and innumerable firms made similar deals.[8]

In other cases, regional governments convinced federal authorities to transfer additional shares to the regional level as a way of either paying off debts or shifting responsibility for them. In March 1997, for example, Yeltsin transferred the federal government's 29-percent stake in the St. Petersburg port to the city administration as partial payment of Russia's debt to St. Petersburg (*RRR* March 13, 1997). In a slightly different deal in April 1998, acting Prime Minister Sergei Kirienko transferred a stake in the Moskvich auto plant to the Moscow city government in exchange for 56 million rubles ($9.3 million) and a promise to pay the factory's 1.38 billion rubles in federal debt and fines (*RRR* April 23, 1998).

Natural-monopolies reform and tax concerns thus ushered in the use of debt as a tool of acquisition on a fairly large scale. A quantum leap, however, occurred in early 1998, when a new law allowed a creditor to launch bankruptcy proceedings against a company that was more than ninety days in arrears on a loan of minimal size.[9] The new law made popular a strategy of "political bankruptcy." The target company might be fundamentally healthy, but a well-connected rival could nonetheless force it under the control of a court-appointed manager, who would loot the company or hand it over to the challenger. In the wake of the new law, the number of bankruptcy suits in Russia jumped dramatically, from forty-three hundred in 1997 to eleven thousand in 1999. At the same time, a study by the Russian economist Ekaterina Zhuravskaia found no evidence that companies placed into bankruptcy were any worse at servicing their debts than those that escaped such proceedings (Tavernise 2000). International observers had long called for a Russian bankruptcy law with teeth, but this one was quickly used to bite off chunks of property that almost certainly could have survived with less radical restructuring.

8. On KamAZ, see *RRR* (February 5, 1997, and October 22, 1998); on Norilsk Nickel, *RRR* (November 20, 1997); and on AvtoVAZ, *RRR* (September 4, 1997, and October 23, 1997).

9. Zakon "O nesostoiatel'nosti (bankrotstve)," which passed both houses of the legislature in December 1997 and was signed into law January 8, 1998.

The final important financial shock to the Russian distribution of property in the late 1990s came with the August 1998 crash. When the government defaulted on its treasury obligations, it started a chain of events that restructured ownership groups throughout the system. Most immediately, the collapse of the ruble pushed banks with assets tied up in government bonds and dollar-forward contracts to the brink of bankruptcy. In general, they employed three interlocking strategies to survive: they froze deposits (and payments on other debts); they requested (and received) short-term capital from the Central Bank; and they transferred assets to new banks ("bridge banks") or other holdings, leaving their obligations with the old institutions.[10] The large banks that failed in those efforts were Vladimir Vinogradov's Inkombank and Aleksandr Smolenskii's SBS-Agro, and many of their industrial assets were left up for grabs.

Some banks did successfully transform themselves, most notably Vladimir Potanin's Oneksimbank, which became Rosbank, and Mikhail Khodorkovskii's Menatep, which became Menatep–St. Petersburg. Even these institutions, however, lost some of their industrial assets and no longer stood at the head of Russia's leading conglomerates, because the financial crash closed the last easy channel to cash through the banking sector. There was no more high inflation, no more rigged foreign exchange market, no more directed credits from the Central Bank, and no more runaway treasury-bill market. The sources of money and power became exports, energy, debts, and control over inputs and outputs. The most powerful economic groups after the crash, therefore, did not seek to build (or rebuild) dominant positions in the banking sector but instead focused on the "real" sector.

At the same time that the August 1998 events brought down some conglomerates, wresting valuable assets from their hands, it handsomely rewarded others. For example, players who had guessed right on state treasury bills and dollar-forward contracts had money to spend, as did companies with large oil holdings. In addition, regional governments took advantage of the new conditions to pry assets away from Moscow-based, bank-centered economic groups that had been beyond their reach for several years. The enormous changes in Russian finance had thus pulled the rug from under the dominant economic groups in the system.

10. For much more on this process, see Johnson 2000.

The Rise of Putin

In the midst of crash-induced chaos in the world of Russian property, Vladimir Putin ascended from obscurity to the office of president. Having been appointed prime minister in August 1999, he enjoyed the advantages of virtual incumbency when Yeltsin stepped down on December 31, 1999, triggering early presidential elections in March 2000. At the same time, his campaign platform was also genuinely popular, if vaguely articulated.[11] He promised get-tough policies toward Chechnya and, more important for the conflict over assets, toward the economic groups that had succeeded so ostentatiously in the Yeltsin era and the regional leaders who had worked hand-in-hand with them. He pledged to strengthen the state and institute a "dictatorship of law," taming the struggle for property and creating a more productive and equitable economy. While he did not bring the conflict to a close, he changed its contours, both by influencing the assets available in the system and by altering the relationship between economic groups and the state.

Putin's most direct impact on the Russian struggle for property was simply to change the assets up for grabs. Shortly after coming to power, he pushed two oligarchs, Vladimir Gusinskii and Boris Berezovskii, out of the country, thereby putting some important industrial property back in play, and both the state and private actors grabbed it up. In addition, he reasserted control over the state's shares in Gazprom and tightened that company's grip on some assets that had begun to slip away in the Yeltsin era.

Although he denied it, Putin's moves against the holdings of Gusinskii and Berezovskii had clearly political goals. Gusinskii, through Media-Most, controlled Independent Television (NTV), while Berezovskii wielded great editorial influence at the Public Television (ORT) and TV-6 networks. The two oligarchs had begun to use their holdings to make trouble for the administration even before Putin came to power, and Yeltsin's team had taken its share of swipes at them (Rutland 2000; Belin 2002). After Putin became acting president at the end of 1999, the conflict intensified.

In February 2000, for example, the Supreme Arbitration Court revoked NTV's discounted access to public airwaves (Raff 2001). In April and May, Putin blocked Gusinskii's attempt to sell Most Bank to the Central Bank for cash in order to pay off a loan that Gazprom had

11. On Putin's path to power, see Rutland 2000; McFaul 2000; Huskey 2001.

guaranteed back in 1998 (Belin 2002, 149). On May 11, four days after Putin's inauguration, tax and security police raided the offices of Media-Most, and on June 13 Gusinskii himself was arrested on charges he had defrauded the government of at least $10 million in the privatization of the St. Petersburg firm Russkoe Video (Rutland 2000, 339; Saradzhyan 2000; Shchedrov 2000). In exchange for his freedom, he agreed to sell his assets to Gazprom; although he later backed out of that deal, he never regained full control of NTV. Instead, raids, lawsuits, and criminal charges continued, and Gazprom insisted its loan guarantee be compensated (Thornhill and Jack 2000; Karush and Zolotov 2000; Belin 2002, 150, 158–59n59). Gusinskii left the country in July and did not return, eventually transferring 16 percent of NTV to Gazprom to retire some of his debt, bringing Gazprom's stake in the network to 46 percent (Raff 2001). An NTV shareholders' meeting held in Gazprom headquarters in April 2001 appointed a new board of directors, including Boris Jordan, who had led Credit Suisse First Boston's charge into the voucher-privatization arena in the early 1990s (Higgins and Cullison 2001; Raff 2001). When Jordan crossed the picket lines of striking NTV employees on April 14, the conflict was effectively over and Gusinskii stricken from the scene (Baker 2001).

The removal of Berezovskii from ORT also superficially involved the collection of a debt, but the conflict as a whole played out differently from the one at NTV. Although the state already owned 51 percent of ORT's stock, Berezovskii owned most or all of the remaining shares through intermediaries, and more important, his allies were effectively in charge of day-to-day decision making at the network. During 2000, Berezovskii made a habit of loudly criticizing Putin: he protested the president's federal reforms, tried to launch a political opposition, used ORT to disparage Putin's handling of the *Kursk* submarine disaster, and in September published an open letter accusing the state of trying to throw him in jail if he did not give up his stake in ORT.[12] Each time, the government retaliated—whether by pressuring state-owned Vneshekonombank to call in a $100 million loan; reopening an investigation of the foreign currency accounts at Aeroflot, where Berezovskii was a major shareholder; or having the general director of ORT pull Berezovskii's news commentator, Sergei Dorenko, from the air and fire two of

---

12. Feifer 2000; Rutland 2000, 340; Belin 2002, 150. For an overview of the federal reforms, see Hyde 2001; Gel'man 2001. On the *Kursk*, see Kramer 2000. The open letter appeared in the newspaper *Novye Izvestiia*, September 5, 2000.

Berezovskii's supporters in the news department.[13] In an attempt to circumvent Putin, Berezovskii tried to create a trust that would be run by a group of famous journalists and intellectuals and to which he would transfer his shares in ORT, but the effort never bore fruit (Interfax 2000; Belin 2002, 150). Investigations into Berezovskii's business dealings continued, and Berezovskii finally left the country in November 2000. In January 2001 he sold his stake in ORT to his partner, Roman Abramovich, reportedly for $80 million (Belin 2002, 150; *Jamestown Monitor* 2001). Abramovich then effectively transferred the shares back to the state in a deal whose details were never clear.

Berezovskii retained his controlling stake at a smaller network, TV-6, and initially tried to make a stand there. For example, he attracted some former NTV journalists to the station. The pension fund of oil giant LUKoil, however, which held 15 percent of TV-6, filed suit in May 2001, arguing that the network was poorly run and should be liquidated (Belin 2002, 151). In the NTV case, Gazprom could find a fig leaf of business logic to explain its takeover of the network, but LUKoil had no such cover—if the oil company truly objected to operations at TV-6, it should have sold its shares at a reasonable price, rather than calling for a fire sale (Belin 2001). After a series of lawsuits and appeals, the Supreme Arbitration Court ordered the liquidation of TV-6 in January 2002 and transferred its broadcast rights to another network (Zolotov 2002). A consortium of former TV-6 journalists eventually reacquired the frequency in a tender competition, but Berezovskii had lost his media influence (Abdullaev 2002).

The attacks on Gusinskii and Berezovskii—who were themselves far from blameless—significantly undermined media freedom, especially in television, as several important analyses have clearly demonstrated. To understand the Russian political economy more broadly, however, it is important to remember that the two oligarchs also lost control over other assets, such as Aeroflot and Sibneft, and other actors swooped in to capture them. In addition, not all of Putin's early interventions in the world of ownership were directed at political opponents. Like other economic actors at the time, his government sought to strengthen control over its assets and protect them from outside takeover. The clearest example of this process came in the reorganization of Gazprom's management and assets. The Russian state retained a little over 38 percent of the shares of Gazprom during the Yeltsin administration but

13. Rutland 2000, 340; Starobin and Belton 2000; Belin 2002, 150.

did little to enforce its ownership rights. Putin, by contrast, made an explicit decision to reassert control over some of the operations of the company. In the summer of 2001 he installed his ally Aleksei Miller as CEO of Gazprom, ousting Yeltsin-era executive Rem Viakhirev from the post. As discussed below, the new management team quickly set about regaining lost assets and clarifying and strengthening ownership rights, a process that reshaped Gazprom and affected the struggle for property more broadly.

In shaking property loose or helping a group recover it, Putin's actions affected only the objects over which competitors for property clashed. During his first few years in office, however, he also began to change the overall nature of the struggle by altering the way businesses interacted with the state. At the federal level he forced business people to change their strategies for influencing government decisions. Economic groups did not lose their status, but they became far less visible in Moscow politics. At the same time, intentionally or not, Putin encouraged businesses to turn toward the regions.

In his campaign to transform national politics, Putin employed both stick and carrot to discourage large business groups from pressuring the state for special breaks. For example, Gusinskii and Berezovskii were not the only oligarchs to feel the heat of official investigations in the summer of 2000. LUKoil, AvtoVAZ, Gazprom, and Sibneft all received visits from the tax inspectors, and UES, TNK, and Interros each faced accusations of privatization abuses (Rutland 2000, 340). Although no arrests or charges followed most of the investigations, they served to put the business groups on notice—the lawsuit challenging Potanin's acquisition of Norilsk Nickel in the 1995 loans-for-shares auctions, for instance, was filed just after Gusinskii's arrest and release (Shukshin 2000). If any prominent economic leader somehow failed to understand the meaning of the raids, Putin made it explicit in a July 28 meeting with heads of most of the largest economic groups in the country: business people should remain "equidistant" from politics, rather than seeking individual advantage (Rutland 2000, 340–41).

Even as he threatened them with arrest or harassment if they pursued special influence on their own, Putin offered business leaders another avenue into the policy-making arena. Shortly after his election, he helped create the governmental Council on Entrepreneurship and revitalize the Russian Union of Industrialists and Entrepreneurs as a lobbying group (Bunin 2002a). In principle, these organizations created opportunities for regular, formal, and relatively transparent discussions between the president and economic leaders, in contrast to the person-alistic system of the Yeltsin era.

Most of the leading economic actors of the time joined the groups, and the new system seemed to produce tangible benefits for them. Most notably, in mid-2002 it led to a new tax code that Russian business leaders and foreign advisors lauded for simplifying the rules, standard-izing practices across regions, and decreasing the tax burden on busi-nesses (Aslund and Boone 2002). From Putin's perspective, confining economic elites within well-defined institutions would increase his lever-age in negotiations with business, and the arrangement seemed to give him the upper hand early in his first term. For example, instead of doling out additional favors, Putin was able to extract $1.5 billion from business leaders to fund social programs for military personnel (Kolesnichenko, Pivovarova, and Tseplyaev 2002).

Beyond attempts to transform political competition at the national level, Putin also tried to establish greater control over regional politics, which had grown so important in economic actors' pursuit of property in the 1990s. Soon after his inauguration, he signed a decree creating seven federal districts, or "super-regions," headed by close associates of Putin and meant to give him greater control over regional develop-ments. For example, the new system reorganized such agencies as the Ministry of Internal Affairs and the Tax Police along the lines of the federal districts and moved decisions about appointing and dismissing regional chiefs of police away from governors and back to Moscow (Taylor 2002, 3–4). Additional legislation changed the rules of choosing representation to the upper house (Federation Council) of Russia's legislature, changes that again aimed to limit regional leaders' influ-ence. Since 1995, governors and speakers of regional legislatures had personally represented their regions in the upper house. Beginning January 1, 2002, however, governors began to *appoint* representatives with approval from their legislatures. At the very least, the new rule would strip governors of the immunity from prosecution that a seat in the Federation Council conveyed, and it held out the possibility of weak-ening their influence on national legislation.

All these reforms affected state-business relations in Russia, but none of them drove competitors for property from politics. At the national level, some of the changes seemed more symbolic than substantive, as even the relative success of group lobbying did not stop powerful eco-nomic actors from pursuing individual strategies to influence policy. Oleg Deripaska, for example, continued to seek and obtain direct access to the president, as he had under Yeltsin. Likewise, staff members connected to Alfa Group served directly in the presidential administration, another arrangement reminiscent of the Yeltsin era (Treisman 2002, 60). Meanwhile, within the RUIE itself, leading members clashed over the group's proposal on banking reform in 2001, as they suspected each other of shaping the recommendations to suit their own selfish ends (Zudin 2002). Overall, the influence of large economic groups on legislation had become less direct, but they retained access to the administration and worked closely with it on such reforms as lowering taxes and limiting currency repatriation requirements.

Furthermore, Putin's efforts to limit major economic actors' access to power at the national level encouraged them to increase their presence in regional politics. Second-tier groups had been active at the regional level for many years, and they continued to expand their efforts. By 2001, for example, a majority of members of the Vologda oblast legislature were from the "metallurgic party," which is to say they were connected to Severstal (Mereu 2002). Similarly, the largest faction in the legislature of Perm oblast represented leading local industrialists, and a full thirteen of the twenty-five deputies in Stavropol krai's legislature were directors or managers of regional enterprises (Chirkov 2002; Porshakov 2002).[14] Ironically, the reforms of the Federation Council enabled business groups with a strong regional presence to parlay that influence into access to the federal legislature. By the middle of 2002, almost a third of representatives to the upper house came from private enterprises, and that number stood only to grow as governors appointed powerful regional business people as deputies (Paszyc and Wisniewska 2002).

Even more striking, however, was the jump in the number of nationally prominent economic leaders who won direct election to office, especially as regional executives. The first to do so had been the flamboyant Kirsan Iliumzhinov, who essentially bought himself the presidency of the republic of Kalmykia in 1993 (Kryshtanovskaia 2002). In the 1996 elections, three more figures from business won elections in their regions. In 2000–2002, however, after Putin promised to move the oligarchs out of power in Moscow, Russia saw a veritable deluge of such

---

14. In 1998, Governor Mikhail Prusak of Novgorod oblast publicly opposed parties, since "parties cause problems." He liked to see the legislature itself—whose members were all listed as independents—as "the party of business" (quoted in Stoner-Weiss 2001, 408).

figures, leaving more than 10 percent of Russia's eighty-nine regions under the direct control of national or regional oligarchs (see Table 6.1).[15] The creation of federal districts was supposed to give the Kremlin a significant means of influencing gubernatorial elections, but it failed, as independent political and business actors defeated Moscow's preferred candidates at an embarrassing pace (Taylor 2002, 4; Gel'man 2001, 2).

The relationship between business and the state thus changed significantly in the first years of Putin's administration. The new government attacked some of the most perverse aspects of that relationship as it had developed under Yeltsin and demonstrated a willingness to tread on some principles of democracy to do so. Despite real changes, however, access to political power, especially at the regional level, remained both a central motive and a key tool in the struggle for property in Russia.

TABLE 6.1
Business people as heads of regional administrations in Russia

Year of election	Name	Region	Economic group
1993	Iliumzhinov	Kalmykia	local
1996	Evdokimov	Murmansk oblast	Sistema
	Gorbenko[a]	Kaliningrad oblast	local
	Butov	Nenets autonomous okrug	local
2000–2001	Abramovich	Chukotka autonomous okrug	Millhouse/RusAl/Sibneft
	Khloponin	Taimyr autonomous okrug	Interros
	Zolotarev	Evenk autonomous okrug	Menatep/Rosprom
	Tkachev	Krasnodar krai	local
	Loginov	Koriak autonomous okrug	local
	Darkin	Primore	local
2002	Shtyrov	Sakha (Yakutia)	Alrosa
	Sovmen	Adygeia	local
	Khloponin	Krasnoiarsk krai	Interros

Sources: Kryshtanovskaia 2002; Olcott 2002.
[a]Voted out in 2000.

15. For another analysis of why businesspeople may run directly for office instead of trying to influence politicians in other ways, see Gelbach and Sonin (2004). Their argument is compatible with the one here.

THE NEW WINNERS

The seismic shifts of 1997–2002 brought down some of the most famous economic actors in Russia, but new ones quickly rose to take their place. The changed environment gave some of the benefits of controlling property a new urgency, which in turn affected which players emerged victorious. Most important, productive assets offered a form of defense against rivals. In an economy characterized by cash shortages and ubiquitous debt, economic actors sought resources that would bring them cash, such as retail outlets or exportable goods, which in turn could help lower their exposure to bankruptcy takeovers. Similarly, producers in Russia often sought to control sources of inputs or outlets for finished goods, lest their opponents withhold materials, raise prices to the breaking point, or accumulate debts to use in a takeover attempt.[16] Conversely, access to cash or inputs also served as an effective offensive tool in the struggle for property in Russia. Coal, for example, served as a battering ram for knocking down barriers in the steel sector when Yuzhnyi Kuzbass leveraged its position as a supplier of coking coal into significant ownership in the Mechel metals factory in 2001 (Deriabina 2001).

In addition to their utility as direct sources of strength in the struggle for property, assets also provided access to political power, which could be less reliable than other resources but was nonetheless useful. Control over resources, especially when they made up a large part of a regional political economy, enabled groups to influence political leaders, whether through direct bribes or by predicting economic collapse if a certain policy was not adopted. That influence was enhanced when holdings crossed regional boundaries, as happened increasingly in the latter part of the 1990s (see Table 6.2). While a strong Moscow presence was the key to success earlier in the decade, over time the big groups spread their influence across the country. Similarly, a number of groups that were never very influential in Moscow began to break out of their original geographic boundaries in the late 1990s. For example, the steel conglomerate Severstal expanded well beyond its original home in Vologda oblast, and the oil group Surgutneftegaz grew from its birth-

---

16. For example, even though the Russian coal sector had been an economic black hole for most of the post-Soviet period, the Severstal steel conglomerate and the Magnitogorsk Metallurgical Combine purchased stakes in the Kuzbassugol coal mine in September 2001, thereby securing vital inputs and protecting themselves against takeover (Latynina 2001; Vin'kov and Sivakov 2001, 34).

TABLE 6.2
Regional expansion of selected integrated industrial groups,
1993–2000

	Number of regions with active participation by enterprises in the group			
Name of group	1993	1995	1997	2000
National groups				
LUKoil	5	15	23	22
Interros	1	11	15	25
Alfa/Renova	3	8	8	38
Yukos	10	15	22	28
Sistema	1	13	21	43
Regional groups				
Surgutneftegaz	3	no data	7	10
Severstal	—	3	5	8

Source: Dynkin and Sokolov 2001.

place in Tiumen oblast to have holdings in nine other regions by 2000. Several other groups had similar experiences (Kryshtanovskaia 2002). The new incentives in the system played out differently in industry and agriculture, but economic actors in both sectors created a new set of dominant holdings.

The Transformation of Industrial Ownership Groups

In that environment, the leading economic actors in industry proved to be large, integrated ownership groups, since they were best positioned to develop political assets, maintain a reliable supply of inputs, and therefore expand or defend themselves against attacks. Unfortunately, the most common methods of categorizing such groups—by market capitalization, sector, type of owner (state or private), or transparency of ownership—focus on ancillary characteristics that do not help observers understand the behavior of competitors for property. More useful for making sense of the asset redistribution of 1997–2002 is to see economic actors in terms of their vulnerability to takeover. That, in turn, means considering the depth and breadth of their holdings (Table 6.3). A "deep" holding in this context means that the group has control over several stages in the production chain and therefore is less vulnerable. Breadth—significant holdings across sectors—allows a group to carry on after losing part of its empire.

TABLE 6.3
Leading industrial groups in Russia, 2002

Type of holding	Name of group	Name of leader(s)	Major assets
Deep			
Gas	Gazprom	Miller (replaced Viakhirev)	Assets of former Soviet Ministry of Natural Gas
Electricity	UES	Chubais	Assets of former Soviet electrical monopoly
Oil	LUKoil	Alekperov	Oil fields, processors, and pipelines
	Menatep/Rosprom	Khodorkovskii	Yukos (oil)
			Rospan (gas)
			Regional power stations (electricity)
	Surgutneftegaz	Bogdanov	Surgut oil fields and affiliated enterprises
Metals	Interros	Potanin	Norilsk Nickel (metals)
			Perm Motors, Siloye Mashiny (machine-building)
			Agros (agriculture)
	Severstal	Mordashov	Cherepovets Metallurgical Combine, its suppliers, and several customers
	Metalloinvest	Kiselev	Rossiiskii Kredit's metallurgical holdings
Broad	Alfa/Renova	Fridman, Aven/Vekselberg	Oil (TNK, Onako, Sidanko)
			Aluminum (SUAl)
			Cement (Alfa Cement)
			Telecommunications (Golden Telecom, Vympelcom, Vympelcom-R)
			Food products (United Food Company)
			Banking (AlfaBank)

(TABLE 6.3—cont.)

Type of holding	Name of group	Name of leader(s)	Major assets
Deep and broad			
	Bolshaia MADAM:		
	Millhouse Group	Abramovich	Sibneft (oil)
			KrAZ, BrAZ (aluminum)
			Aeroflot (airlines)
	Base Element (formerly *SibAl*)	Deripaska	SaAZ (aluminum)
			GAZ, PAZ (automobiles)
	UGMK/Evrazkholding	Makhmudov/Abramov	Urals Mining and Metallurgical Combine (metals)
			Magnitogorsk Metallurgical Combine (metals)
			Coal mines
	MDM Group	Melnichenko	MDM Bank (banking)
			Coal
			Steel
			Pipes
			Fertilizer
Narrow and shallow			
	Sistema	Evtushenkov	Telecom companies
	Second-tier groups		Often based on a single firm and/or concentrated within a single region.

Sources: Mukhin 2001; Dynkin and Sokolov 2001; Pappe 2000, 2002; Paszyc and Wisniewski 2002; press accounts.
Note: Other than the second-tier groups, this list represents an informal consensus among Russian and other scholars regarding the eleven most economically and politically important integrated business groups in Russia by 2002. See the sources listed above and Boone and Rodionov 2001.

Emphasizing depth and breadth of holdings assists analysts in two key respects. First, it opens our eyes to the fact that state-owned and privately held groups in 1997–2002 faced similar incentives and therefore behaved in comparable ways. Contrasting public and private groups distracts attention from the similar actions of, say, state-controlled Gazprom and privately owned Yukos, while recognizing that both groups faced incentives to deepen their holdings allows observers to see and explain those groups' actions. Second, it alerts us to potential competitors and conflicts beyond the most eye-catching. An emphasis on current revenue or profits calls attention to the most prominent ownership groups in the country, which by 2002 accounted for the vast majority of value added in the Russian economy. These narrow statistics, however, ignore much of the value that Russian economic actors found in assets. Focusing on them may therefore blind analysts to the possibility of a conflict over a historically unprofitable resource like coal or the rise of a new economic group to prominence. By contrast, an analysis that highlights relative vulnerability to takeover and points out narrow and shallow groups that nonetheless have the potential to expand allows observers to see potential sources of instability in the system.

At the same time, it is important to recognize what this categorization system does *not* imply. It does not suggest that observers should concern themselves with the long-term profitability of a concentrated versus a diverse portfolio. Nor should it draw attention to which groups have sectoral competitors and which ones do not, since takeover attempts can and do come from other sectors of the economy. Finally, it does not imply that groups fit perfectly into any of the categories, that they could not shift from one category to another, or even that their structures resulted from conscious, long-term decisions. All economic groups in Russia had elements of the "deep" and "broad" strategies, and the mix depended as much on historical legacies and short-term Darwinism as anything else. For example, acquiring assets up and down a production chain (i.e., "deepening") was usually easier than diversifying across sectors, since it involved acquiring suppliers and customers with which a business already had established relationships. Only groups originally based on financial institutions were likely to develop broad portfolios, as cash was their most important asset. Shallow groups, meanwhile, had to deepen or be absorbed by other conglomerates. This section enumerates groups' dominant features in 1997–2002, shows how they developed those characteristics, and highlights their main strengths and vulnerabilities.

The *deep* holding was the most common in Russia for several reasons. The Soviet industrial structure bequeathed deep holdings to all the groups formed on the basis of Soviet ministries or parts of them. Acquiring assets up and down a production chain was also easier than diversifying across sectors, and, perhaps most important, it offered an effective defense against piling up debt to suppliers, who could then use the bankruptcy process in a takeover bid.

Arguably the most important deep groups in Russia from 1997 to 2002 were the gas and electricity behemoths Gazprom and UES. Gazprom, which already controlled most of the infrastructure for extracting, processing, and delivering natural gas within Russia and beyond, used the financial and legal environment after the 1998 crash both to expand further and to reassert control over straying assets. In terms of expansion down the production chain, Gazprom intensified efforts to create a petrochemical holding company, including the production of tires. In particular, it tried to pluck some of the largest tire factories in the country from the conglomerate Rosshina, which was suffering from the effects of the crash. A combination of cash, political negotiations, and an agreement to retain the old director brought the Yaroslavl Tire Factory into the fold and partially severed its ties to Verkhnevolzhkshina. Taking over the Omsk factory was even easier (Drankina 1999b, esp. 16–17).

Efforts to tighten the ownership links within the conglomerate began in earnest after Putin was elected and replaced Yeltsin-era manager Rem Viakhirev with his own man, Aleksei Miller, whom he instructed to change the mode of operation at the company. First, Gazprom exercised a buyback option for a controlling stake in gas producer Purgaz, which under Viakhirev had been transferred to Itera, a gas-trading company with murky origins but widely believed to be connected to the Viakhirev clan (Jack 2002). Next, in January 2002, Gazprom gave federal investigators information that led to a raid of petrochemical subsidiary Sibur's headquarters. It was on Viakhirev's watch that Gazprom had lost its hegemony over Sibur, and Gazprom's new management wanted to reassert control.[17] After the raid, three Sibur executives were arrested, two of whom were charged with "abuse of authority" for alleged asset stripping (Raff 2002b; Whalen 2002). Pursuing yet another avenue to regain control over Sibur, Gazprom took it to bankruptcy court, and by March 2002 the court had agreed with Gazprom to appoint an outside manager

17. Even though Gazprom retained a 51-percent stake in Sibur, it was unable to change the management through a shareholders' meeting, because Sibur's charter required a 75-percent majority for such a decision.

at Sibur and to cancel a stock emission that would have diluted Gazprom's stake (Cottrell 2002b; Miller and Vasilieva 2003, 59). By April 2003 Gazprom had raised its stake in Sibur to 75.7 percent by acquiring several affiliated enterprises (Miller and Vasilieva 2003, 63).

Gazprom did not win every fight it entered, and its most notable loss was an indirect subsidiary, Rospan. Gazprom had sold Rospan in August 1998 to the loosely affiliated Itera, but Itera was unable to retain control when two major oil companies, Tiumen Oil (TNK) and Yukos, began acquiring Rospan's debt and shares. By 2002 Yukos had acquired 100 percent of Rospan after agreeing to resell 44 percent to TNK (Doronin 2002; Whalen 2000; Starobin and Belton 2002). Gazprom's holdings were so enormous that this loss did not threaten its stature, but the event demonstrated that even a giant like Gazprom could be vulnerable to takeovers in postcrash Russia.

UES was likewise the successor to a Soviet monopoly, controlling major power generators, the main electricity grid, and large shares of most regional power stations, although other actors also held stakes in them. Like Gazprom, UES was already concentrated in a sector, controlled most (although not all) assets it needed to operate, and wielded tremendous political power, at least at the federal level. Despite its size, however, it was still vulnerable to attacks on its assets at both ends of the production chain.

On the input side, Gazprom pressured UES by calling in debts, especially those of regional power generators, as discussed earlier. Similarly, coal suppliers began to accumulate IOUs from the generators in order to pursue ownership. In late 1998, for example, Primorskugol and other creditors filed bankruptcy charges against Dalenergo in the Far East (*RRR* December 8, 1998). Other coal companies, especially those acquired by outside actors after the crash, likewise pressured generators to pay back loans or face bankruptcy (Deriabina 2001; Vin'kov and Sivakov 2001). Perhaps most ominously for UES, the rival MDM group purchased a 40-percent share in Dalvostugol in early 2002, giving MDM control over more than 60 percent of the coal used for electricity production in Russia's Far East (Vin'kov 2002a). In many cases, regional leaders supported the local generators and helped settle bankruptcy claims without a complete transfer of assets, as in the case of Dalenergo in September 1999, but the potential for takeovers was clear.[18]

18. On Dalenergo, see *RRR* (December 8, 1998); www.ifs.ru/body/memo/2000/jan/e170100.doc, accessed July 22, 2004.

On the output side, UES's problems were more explicitly political. Regional administrators clashed with UES over prices policies, interfered with efforts to collect debts, and in May 1998 persuaded Yeltsin to sign off on a redistribution of ownership in the company (Law no. 74-F3, May 7, 1998). The legislature had approved the restructuring long before, and Yeltsin's approval may have been the only way he could convince regional leaders to accept Anatolii Chubais as a replacement CEO for the ousted Boris Brevnov in April 1998 (*RRR* May 14, 1998). In any case, the new plan would keep federal ownership in UES at at least 51 percent, allow regional governments to vote one-third of the federal government's share, and limit foreign ownership to 25 percent, even though in practice it already stood at about 30 percent.

Chubais pursued two political strategies to combat the influence of regional governors, but neither proved entirely effective. On one hand, he periodically cut off electricity to important enterprises that had not paid their bills. On the other, he tried to reorganize the holding according to a plan first codified in the 1997 law on natural monopolies and revised periodically thereafter. That restructuring plan envisioned bundling together clusters of regional generators and selling them off, preferably to friendly economic groups but certainly in a way that would diminish regional leaders' control over them. In practice, shutting off electricity to local enterprises won few political points, and the restructuring plan remained bogged down until well into Putin's first term, so UES remained vulnerable throughout the period.

Oil served as another sector that sustained major economic groups after the crash. The largest was LUKoil, whose assets spanned much of the Commonwealth of Independent States (CIS) and Southeastern Europe, as well as several regions within Russia. Like Gazprom and UES, LUKoil avoided the destructive force of the 1998 financial crisis, since it relied little on the banking sector for its success. The rise in oil prices, however, was important for LUKoil, allowing the company to continue expanding both at home and abroad. For example, it acquired the number-twelve Russian oil producer KomiTEK in 1999 and the American company Getty Petroleum in 2000 (Feifer and Semenenko 2000; Jack 2001).

Not all of LUKoil's moves worked out as planned, of course. In the international arena, foreign observers derided its lack of transparency and the apparent absence of a business plan. More practically, the oil company Severnaia neft, in the north of Russia, frustrated LUKoil's attempts to take over Komineft by diluting KomiTEK's 25-percent stake in the company in 1999 (Feifer and Semenenko 2000). Severnaia neft also used its political connections in Nenets autonomous okrug to fend off a full-fledged takeover attempt from LUKoil and beat out the larger company in an effort to acquire another oil property in the region (Feifer and Semenenko 2000; Corwin 2001; Drankina 2001). Despite such annoyances, LUKoil managed to avoid significant outside attacks on its holdings.

Another major player with a large, integrated holding in the oil sector by the late 1990s was led by Mikhail Khodorkovskii and centered on the oil company Yukos. Menatep's bank went under in the wake of the financial crisis, but Khodorkovskii was able to move its assets to a bank he creatively called Menatep–St. Petersburg. The bank was no longer the center of the group, however, and the experience of Yukos may provide the best example of using oil money to pay off debts, buy out minority shareholders, and then expand. As discussed previously, Yukos used transfer pricing in 1996–97 to realize profits in the main company, rather than production subsidiaries in which outside owners held stakes. The largest of those shareholders was billionaire Kenneth Dart, who protested the arrangement. After much public feuding and an attempt to dilute minority owners' stakes in the subsidiaries, Khodorkovskii decided to use some of the new money available from higher oil prices to reach a settlement with Dart in 1999, consolidating his control over Yukos (Feifer and Semenenko 2000; Criscione and Jack 2001).

Khodorkovskii's next step was expansion, first within the oil sector itself. His acquisitions in this area included the purchase of 22 percent of Norway's Kaevner in November 2001, as well as an oil field in Kazakhstan, 49 percent of Slovakia's oil pipeline, and a refinery in Lithuania in 2002 (Jack 2001; Binyon 2002; Zhdannikov 2002). Closely related to oil drilling is natural gas extraction, and Yukos also moved into the gas sector. It used the bankruptcy process to gain 100-percent ownership of Rospan, which had 550 million cubic meters of gas reserves, with a market value of $9 billion—Yukos paid $121 million (Starobin and Belton 2002). It also signed a deal to purchase a 68-percent stake in Artikgaz, with 200 billion cubic meters of proven reserves and possibly 400 billion more, for $190 million ("Yukos" 2002). Finally, Yukos also entered the electricity sector, having purchased large shares in a number of regional power stations (Starobin and Belton 2002). Thus, while Khodorkovskii's group continued to deepen its holding structure, it began to broaden itself as well.

Surgutneftegaz was a relatively new independent player in the Russian oil sector, but it successfully expanded by acquiring enterprises connected to the original production chain it inherited. Its management and owners purchased about 80 percent of the shares of the main enterprise during the mass privatization program of 1992–94, but for much of the 1990s Surgut was part of a strategic alliance with Vladimir Potanin's Interros. The financial crisis freed Surgutneftegaz from that arrangement, and rising oil profits allowed it to expand its holdings regionally (Pappe 2002, 39).

In addition to gas, electricity, and oil, the metallurgical sector attracted a great deal of attention from participants in the struggle over property in Russia after 1998. Like oil and gas, metals offered the possibility of export profits, but unlike those sectors, metallurgy was a complex production process running from energy and raw-materials extraction through processing to the production of finished goods. That meant there were multiple points at which debts could accumulate, supplies be cut off, and rivals attack. As a result, the list of dominant players in metallurgy after the fall of the Soviet Union proved far less stable than in energy or natural resources.

Three of the most powerful economic groups in Russia by 2002 had major holdings at several stages in the metallurgical sector. The most prominent was Vladimir Potanin's Interros, although the 1998 financial crisis damaged it severely. Even before the crisis came to a head in August, Interros was forced to sell its stake in the Baltiiskii zavod shipbuilding company to raise cash and pay off debts (Pappe 2002, 35). The crash itself stimulated additional sell-offs and shook up the partnership of Potanin and Boris Jordan, which further weakened Interros. These blows undermined Interros's position in several important enterprises. Most notably, Potanin essentially lost control over the Sidanko oil company to an external rival. The Alfa/Renova group, through its oil company TNK, took over two of Sidanko's main production subsidiaries, Kondpetroleum and Chernogorneft, through bankruptcy (Feifer and Semenenko 2000). It also slowly moved to take over the rest of the company, although BP-Amoco, which owned 10 percent of Sidanko at the time of the crash, used political pressure, including blocking a loan guarantee from the U.S. Import-Export Bank, to force TNK to include it in the process.[19]

Sidanko was not the only company at which Interros lost influence after the crash. At the Novolipetsk Metallurgical Combine (NLMK), the

---

19. While Potanin lost control of Sidanko itself, he seems to have moved most of its liquid assets to offshore companies after the crash (Corwin 1999a).

general director, Vladimir Lisin, built on his success in 1997 to dominate ownership at the firm: his Rumelko company controlled a 60-percent stake by 2001 (Mukhin 2001, 147; Pappe 2002, 38). Finally, Potanin was forced to sell off his shares in the telecommunications holding Sviazinvest to his partner, George Soros (Korchagina, Koriukin, and Startseva 2001).[20]

Nonetheless, Interros remained a strong player in the Russian political economy, and it did so by focusing on the metals sector, particularly the Norilsk Nickel complex. With the cash it received from selling off other assets, Interros acquired additional shares in Perm Motors and Silovye Mashiny, both of which made jet engines and related goods (Korchagina, Koriukin, and Startseva 2001). Perhaps more important, it solidified control over the suppliers of raw materials to the Norilsk factory (Mukhin 2001, 177–79).

A second significant metallurgical holding emerged from the Rossiiskii Kredit group, which was led by a high-flying, pre-1998 bank of the same name that the financial meltdown almost destroyed. The bank's president, Vitalii Malkin, lost his position; and the bank itself folded, replaced by a weaker one called Impeksbank (Pappe 2002, 38). In addition, Rossiiskii Kredit lost its stake in Lebedinskii GOK, a supplier of about 25 percent of Russia's iron-ore concentrate and iron pellets, to the Oskolskii Electro-Metallurgical Combine and, eventually, Gazprominvestkholding (*RRR* August 13, 1998; *RRR* December 3, 1998; Mukhin 2001, 147). The group's remaining metals assets, however, including large stakes in Mikhailovskii GOK, Stoilenskii GOK, and the ferrous-metals plant Tulachermet, remained under the control of Oleg Kiselev's Metalloinvest holding company (Mukhin 2001, 148). The conglomerate therefore continued to dominate a significant part of the production chain within the metals sector.

Severstal, a third major metals group, was a relative newcomer to the national stage, having begun life as the Cherepovetskii Metallurgical Combine in Vologda oblast. During the 1990s the combine's management gained control over its raw materials suppliers in the oblast, and

20. In the end, that sale may have been fortuitous for Potanin, since Sviazinvest suffered weaknesses similar to those of UES, in that it controlled a central network but faced challenges over ownership of regional distributors (see, e.g., *RRR* May 7, 1998). Soros himself, who famously called his original purchase of Sviazinvest "the worst investment of my life," sold the entire stake of 25 percent plus one share to Leonid Blavatnik of Access/Renova in 2004 (Jack, Ostrovsky, and Pretzlik 2004; MosNews 2004a; Svyazinvest 2004).

in 2000 it began to expand further down the production chain and into new regions. In particular, Severstal purchased controlling stakes in plants making engines, pipes, and diesel locomotives (Pappe 2002, 39). It was still exposed to the whims of its energy suppliers, but it had established firm control over several outlets for its product.

Even the deepest groups, however, could not completely insulate themselves from reliance on others, who could then use debts, blackmail, or political connections to take over property. An alternative strategy was to develop *broad* holdings—a collection of important assets in several sectors but without dominance of any single production chain. At the very least, such a strategy would allow a group to continue to exist as an entity even if it lost a significant enterprise to a rival. In a world of widespread debt and bankruptcy, however, the broad strategy was risky one, and Alfa/Renova was the only major player to make it work well in the years after the crash. That group centered on Alfa Bank, which was not caught in the treasury-bill collapse and had always aimed at controlling parts of profitable enterprises (and perhaps reselling them), rather than the whole production process. It therefore entered 1998 with holdings in several sectors, and it continued to acquire widely. In metals, for example, Alfa/Renova established control over the SUAl group, which had bought out the Sverdlovsk oblast administration's AlKUr holding in 1999 and grown to include the Timan Bauxite deposit in Komi republic (Mukhin 2001, 105, 107; Starobin and Belton 2002). It also began to buy up pieces of regional electric companies, which provided a key input into the aluminum production process (Starobin and Belton 2002). Meanwhile, in the telecommunications sector, the group purchased 43.8 percent of Golden Telecom in April 2001 and a large part of mobile operator Vympelcom in May 2001 (Korchagina, Koriukin, and Startseva 2001).

Alfa/Renova also began to develop characteristics of a deep holding after the crash, especially in the oil sector. The group was an influential shareholder of the Tiumen Oil Company (TNK) even before 1998, and it used its strengthened economic position to expand its holdings in TNK in 1999. In particular, it bought an additional 49-percent stake in the company from the state in December 1999 for $200 million, far less than the $810 million it paid for a 40-percent stake in July 1997 (Feifer and Semenenko 2000). After that move, Alfa/Renova owned essentially 100 percent of TNK. As noted above, Alfa/Renova also used TNK to pry additional assets from Sidanko. In September 2000 Alfa/Renova purchased an 85-percent stake in yet another oil company (Onako) from the state for $1.08 billion, more than twice the $425 million starting price (A. Ostrovsky 2000).

Finally, in a struggle that revealed that individualistic lobbying by major business groups was alive and well even under Putin, Alfa/Renova captured an enormous piece of the oil company Slavneft in 2002. The Russian government had originally planned to sell off 20 percent of Slavneft in late 2002, and that decision sparked heated confrontations among major economic actors, especially Sibneft and Rosneft. Lawsuits, political pressure, and a physical confrontation that included security forces and a bomb threat swirled around the company as the two groups sought to install their preferred candidates for company president (Raff 2002a).

Unable to bring the competitors into line, Putin's government elected to put its entire 75-percent stake up for sale, promising a clean, transparent auction that would end the struggles once and for all. In practice, the only real bidder at the auction was a secret partnership between Sibneft and TNK, which paid only $16 million more than the $1.7 billion minimum the government had set. Potential competitors Yukos, LUKoil, and Surgutneftegaz largely avoided the process, arguing that Sibneft's political ties would carry it to victory, and that its control of some important Slavneft assets would make running the company difficult for an outsider (Belton 2002; Glasser 2002). The Chinese National Oil Corporation—which many had hoped would give the auction the prestige of an international participant—pulled out less than twenty-four hours before the bidding because of political pressure, including a request from the Duma that Slavneft remain in Russian hands (Jack and Stern 2002). Rosneft, the only significant Russian competitor that did not bow out early, was excluded from the auction by a court decision two days before the sale (Belton 2002).

Alfa/Renova thus acquired impressive extraction and refining capacity after the crash, but its most effective defenses lay elsewhere. Most important, it had enviable access to cash (through its bank, exports of oil and metal, and retail sales of telecommunications services) and a long history of connections to political leaders. In addition, the conglomerate established a significant presence in enough sectors that the loss of assets in one area would probably not bring down the whole group.

A combination of both of these strategies—depth and breadth—should have been attractive for industrial groups in Russia trying to protect themselves from takeover. Indeed, such deep groups as Interros and Yukos appeared to be broadening. By 2002, however, only one industrial group could be called both *deep and broad*, and it was the result of an alliance among several groups that gained control over complete production chains in a number of sectors after the 1998 crisis. The political scientist Iakov Pappe (2002, 39) has dubbed the alliance "Bolshaia MADAM" (loosely, "Big Mama") after the initials of its most famous figures—Makhmudov, Abramovich, Deripaska, Abramov, and Melnichenko. Each of these men emerged from the financial crash in a position to expand their holdings aggressively, both because they were not encumbered with portfolios of worthless state treasury bills and because they controlled real assets that were vital in other production processes.

The two most famous members of that group were Oleg Deripaska, who was building a second-tier group around the Saianogorsk Aluminum Factory (SaAZ) in the mid-1990s, and Roman Abramovich, who was the rarely visible partner of oligarch Boris Berezovskii. Deripaska had developed an alliance with Trans-World Group (TWG) that gave him the manager's seat at SaAZ. In 1998, however, he began to strike out on his own, both by pushing TWG out and by expanding from his base at SaAZ. In the spring of 1998, SaAZ carried out a supplemental share emission that dropped TWG's stake in the firm below the level needed to block decisions (Radygin 1999, 62). The emission also dropped the federal government's share from 15 percent to 6.15 percent, but Deripaska avoided prosecution from the Federal Property Fund by donating shares back to the state—he made no such concession to TWG (*RRR* June 25, 1998). At the same time that he was securing his position at SaAZ, Deripaska began to acquire additional firms, building a nationally prominent ownership group, which he called "Siberian Aluminum" (SibAl). In 1998, for example, SibAl acquired a controlling block of shares in Sameko, an aluminum and aluminum products factory in Samara oblast, from a declining Inkombank (Mikhailov 1998). He expanded his holdings in several other areas, as well, including large stakes in the automakers GAZ and PAZ in 2000 (AFP 2001).

Central to the success of Deripaska's group, as both a defense against takeover and a tool for expansion, was control over electricity, and he was most successful in pursuing it politically. In particular, his alliance with Anatolii Chubais, the CEO of UES since 1998, proved invaluable. In 1999, for example, Chubais, through Kuzbassenergo, initiated bankruptcy proceedings against the Novokuznetsk Aluminum Factory (NkAZ), which was then under the control of the MIKOM group

(Mukhin 2001, 99–100). Because of support from Governor Aman Tuleev of Kemerovo oblast, the bankruptcy court appointed Sergei Chernyshev, Deripaska's choice, as the receiver at NkAZ, and SibAl took over the factory in 2000 (Pirani 2001). Also in 1999, Chubais supported Deripaska's proposal to unite SaAZ and the Saiano-Shushenskaia Hydroelectric Power Plant in a venture in which SaAZ would own 60 percent and UES 40 percent (Mukhin 2001, 99). Even when Deripaska and Chubais fell out, Deripaska turned for protection to Governor Aleksei Lebed of Khakassia, whose campaign he had supported. Through that relationship, SibAl sustained its preferential links to Saiano-Shushenskaia, thus creating a chain of enterprises that extended from energy inputs to aluminum manufacturing to finished goods.

In contrast to Deripaska, Abramovich had little to do with the metals sector for most of the 1990s. He had joined Boris Berezovskii in creating and acquiring the Sibneft oil company in 1995–96; and as Berezovskii turned his attention toward his media holdings, Abramovich strengthened his control over Sibneft (Mukhin 2001, 118–22). Meanwhile, nasty ownership disputes enveloped the metals assets he would eventually take over—the Bratsk and Krasnoiarsk Aluminum Factories (BrAZ and KrAZ) and the Achinsk Aluminum Oxide Combine (AGK). TWG had played a role in all three enterprises, but it was under pressure from all quarters as a carpetbagger, and its influence weakened steadily. At BrAZ, for example, where TWG actually held more than 50 percent of the shares, it feared mutinous managers enough to postpone a shareholders' meeting in May 1998 (*RRR* May 21, 1998).

At KrAZ, the complications were much more significant. Anatolii Bykov, the former wrestler who had established himself as the leading figure at the factory by the end of 1997, also won a seat in the Krasnoiarsk regional legislature in December of that year. He then supported the former presidential candidate General Aleksandr Lebed in his run for governor in 1998, hoping he would help solidify KrAZ's connections to the Krasnoiarsk regional power generator (Yorke 2003, 243–44; *RRR* June 25, 1998; Orttung 2002, 3; *RRR* October 15, 1998). When the two men fell out soon thereafter, their public feud landed Bykov in jail in Hungary from 1999 to 2000 and in Moscow from 2000 to 2002, leaving him unable to defend most of his metals holdings.[21] In February 2000 TWG sold its shares in both BrAZ and KrAZ to Abramovich (Yorke 2003,

21. The charges included ordering a contract murder that never actually happened (Cottrell 2002a).

245–50). At about the same time, Abramovich pried AGK away from Alfa/Renova through bankruptcy proceedings (Pappe 2002, 35). Over the next two years, with the help of the regional administration, KrAZ pushed Bykov's financial house into bankruptcy; and Abramovich carried out supplemental share emissions at KrAZ and AGK, pushing Bykov almost completely out of those factories (Yorke 2003, 249–50).

With Deripaska (supported by Chubais) and Abramovich sweeping through the aluminum sector so rapidly, the question by mid-2000 was how to stop them before they turned on each other. The immediate solution in May 2000 was to pool the two groups' aluminum holdings into Russian Aluminum (RusAl) (Pirani 2001). Abramovich and Deripaska each owned 50 percent of the holding company, which controlled over 75 percent of Russian aluminum production (Mukhin 2001, 66).

As enormous as it was, RusAl represented only part of the Bolshaia MADAM alliance. Iskander Makhmudov and Aleksandr Abramov developed their second-tier groups into increasingly deep holdings in the ferrous metals sector by the late 1990s. Makhmudov began his career in the early 1990s as the director of the Gaiskii Mining and Enrichment Combine (Gaiskii GOK), from which he expanded his holdings into the copper sector. By 1998 he had created the Urals Mining and Metallurgical Combine (UGMK), which included coal suppliers, as well as raw-materials and production facilities (Mukhin 2001, 149–50).

Abramov, for his part, turned Soviet-era contacts from his time at the Institute of High Temperatures in Moscow into business dealings with steel mills and political relationships with Aman Tuleev, governor of the coal-rich Kemerovo oblast. He joined the board of directors at the Nizhnii Tagil Metallurgical Combine (NTMK) in the mid-1990s and began to pursue significant ownership in several enterprises in 1997. He exchanged debt for equity at NTMK, orchestrated a supplementary share emission to shrink Kakha Bendukidze's stake in the company to 13 percent, and used his influence in the coal sector and with Tuleev to take over two other steel plants through the bankruptcy process (A. Ostrovsky 2003c; Mukhin 2001, 172). He eventually consolidated his metals assets into Evrazkholding and allied with Makhmudov's UGMK, which had taken over NTMK's chief supplier of iron ore, Kachkanarskii GOK (Mukhin 2001, 149–50, 155; Pappe 2002, 39).

The final member of this loose alliance was Andrei Melnichenko's MDM group, a holding that grew out of MDM Bank. The bank had provided financial services to the other figures discussed here, and when it emerged on the right side of the treasury-bill fiasco, it used its post-crisis cash to expand into coal, steel, pipes, and fertilizer (Cottrell and Wagstyl 2002). All told, then, the Bolshaia MADAM group brought together large parts of production chains in a number of different sectors, thus combining aspects of the deep and broad strategies more fully than any other group in Russia and making it the most insulated group in the country from outside attack. Because it was an alliance of independent partners, however, the group was more vulnerable than others to pressures from within.

The *narrow and shallow* structure seemed inauspicious. Groups without control over input and output chains or a major presence in a wide variety of sectors were at a real disadvantage in the struggle for property in 1998–2002. Indeed, they were at risk of being swallowed by competitors. They tended to be geographically concentrated and relied even more heavily than others on direct political patronage for survival.

With so many disadvantages, only one nationally prominent group, Sistema, seemed to fit into the narrow and shallow category by 2002, and even Sistema showed signs of significant breadth. A creation of Moscow mayor Yurii Luzhkov and led by Vladimir Evtushenkov, it began as a very diverse holding, and by 2002 still held stakes in as many as two hundred different enterprises, including a small presence in the oil sector (Boreiko 2002). Soon after its conception, however, the group began to concentrate on the telecommunications sector. It briefly held a stake in the mobile phone provider Beeline, next gained a controlling interest in Mobile TeleSystems (MTS), and in 1998 acquired a controlling stake in the Moscow telephone company MGTS (Freeland 2000, 254–55; Pappe 2000, 184–85). Its telecom holdings gave Sistema a presence in over forty regions and access to a significant source of cash, but it did not give the group depth, leaving it vulnerable to the same kinds of pressures from the suppliers and maintainers of its telecommunications infrastructure as industrial groups received from their input providers. At least as important as its physical holdings were Sistema's political ties. Its strength lay not in its ability to defend its assets on its own, but in its advantageous relationship with the Moscow city government. Even as the group tried to spread its influence across the country, it was hard to imagine that it could long survive a serious blow to its direct political patron, Luzhkov.

Because of Sistema's unique position, the more important narrow and shallow groups may have been the second-tier conglomerates that had not yet appeared on lists of the most important integrated business groups in Russia. Earlier chapters have noted the growth of second-tier groups in different periods, and some of the national groups discussed in this chapter—such as Severstal, Surgutneftegaz, SibAl, and Evrazkholding—would have been considered second-tier before the crash. Such groups continued to play significant roles in their regional political economies, and conditions after the 1998 crash brought a new wave of them to the fore.

In some cases, as financially strapped national groups came unglued, regional governments took over pieces of the old empires and created regional conglomerates (Kryshtanovskaia 2002). In Pskov oblast, for example, Governor Evgenii Mikhailov used the bankruptcy process to take over enterprises in such industries as alcoholic beverages and timber. Like other regional leaders at the time, he combined those firms into "state unitary enterprises" (GUPs), which he hoped would provide a more stable revenue stream than their private, tax-evading predecessors (Kryshtanovskaia 2002).

Such direct state intervention, however, was hardly essential for small-group expansion after the crash. Perhaps unsurprisingly, retail and commodities served as two of the most important sources of newly energetic second-tier groups. On a small scale, for example, Aleksei Tupolov's ROSbilding group used the bankruptcy process after the crash to acquire several of the largest supermarkets in Moscow (Drankina 2000). In the oil sector relatively small companies like Tatneft, which specialized in oil extraction and in which the Tatarstan administration held only a 30-percent stake, continued to try to deepen their holdings up and down the production chain (Feifer and Semenenko 2000).

Another commodity, timber, produced two important second-tier groups—Ilim Pulp Enterprise and Titan. Ilim Pulp proved especially adept at using newfound cash together with political influence to expand after the crash. Created as an export company in 1992, and having acquired Kotlass Pulp and Paper Combine (Arkhangelsk oblast) in an investment tender in the mid-1990s, Ilim Pulp in 1999 built up a 75-percent stake in the Bratsk Timber Processing Combine (LPK) (Butrin 2002). Then, in late 2001, Ilim Pulp faced down Oleg Deripaska and SibAl to buy a majority stake in the Ust-Ilim LPK (Butrin 2002; Clark 2003; Latynina 2002b). Ilim Pulp had not yet reached national prominence—nor fully escaped the sights of Deripaska—but it was developing the offensive and defensive capacity to do so.

Even outside the realm of easily tradable goods, second-tier groups grew in size and stature after the crash. United Machine Works (OMZ) was the clearest example of this phenomenon. Based on second-tier oligarch Kakha Bendukidze's Uralmash machine-building works in Sverdlovsk, the group's main strengths initially lay in its close ties to the regional government, its intimidation of potential competitors, and the fact that it was not adversely affected by the financial crisis. As financial conditions deteriorated, it maintained those advantages and expanded beyond its regional borders and into supply chains that would give it leverage over other groups. In 1998, for example, Uralmash merged with the St. Petersburg machine-building complex Izhorskie zavody, giving Bendukidze control over 45 percent of the country's assets in building equipment for metallurgy, mining, petrochemicals, and ship building (Miloslavskaia 2001; Mukhin 2001, 170–71). The new conglomerate went on to acquire both a Russian and an American designer of offshore oil-rig platforms, helping the group become a monopoly supplier for oil companies drilling offshore (Vin'kov 2002b; Reuters and AP 2002). It remained heavily reliant on outsiders for inputs, but its control over others' supplies made it a potentially vital player in the system.

Renewed Interest in Agriculture

The financial crash of 1998 did something extraordinary to Russian agriculture: it made it profitable, or at least solvent. Agriculture was the first sector in which the import-substitution effect of a fourfold currency devaluation took hold, as citizens switched from hopelessly expensive imported foods to acceptable Russian substitutes. The shift significantly increased the number of profitable farms in the country, and the output of Russian agriculture as a whole rose every year from 1999 to 2001.[22] Small private farms also benefited from the new environment, although their contribution to overall production remained relatively tiny. Likewise, with the growth of output from large farms, the proportion of Russian food grown on tiny personal plots finally declined marginally, although it still far outweighed the percentage of farmland in those plots.

Devaluation or no devaluation, however, growing food was still a tough way to make a living. Perhaps more important than its effect on farm profitability, therefore, was how the 1998 shock changed the characteristics of the struggle over agrarian assets, as economic actors recog-

---

22. For output data from 1999 and 2000, see *Rossiiskii statisticheskii ezhegodnik* 2001, 396; for 2001, see *Statisticheskoe obozrenie* 2002, 34.

nized agriculture as a potential source of cash, takeover defense, and political influence. As in industry, the postcrash environment rewarded players that could control bottlenecks in production chains. From those positions, they could use cash, debt, or other mechanisms to deepen their holdings or expand into related areas.

To be sure, the new environment provoked some defensive reactions, especially by regional governments as they sought to stabilize their local economies in the wake of a crushing financial blow. The most common response in areas with large agrarian sectors was to forbid cross-regional trade in agricultural goods and used administrative measures to slow price increases, as governments sought to maintain regional food supplies. In a complementary approach, regions that had established large agrarian conglomerates in 1994–97 tried to sustain or even expand them, which made it easier to influence the price and supply of food in the region. In Orel oblast, for example, the administration continued to add enterprises to the network it had developed in the mid-1990s.

Overall, however, the new pressure and opportunities in the sector produced a kind of dynamism and intensity in the struggle for agrarian property not seen before the crash. Within individual regions, new second-tier groups developed as a result of the new financial conditions. Heliopax, for example, began as a tiny trading company in Volgograd oblast (Chazan 2001). Four agronomists in the region had created the firm back in 1993, and it had slowly acquired a few grain elevators, but it was the crash that allowed Heliopax to become a significant agricultural player in the region. Using leases, which the firm arranged with individual rural residents or directly with large farms, and applying pressure through built-up debt, Heliopax took over about thirty-six thousand hectares of farmland from four different enterprises by 2001 (Chazan 2001). In a similar fashion, the Iuzhnyi Put group in Krasnodar krai leased approximately fifty-seven thousand hectares from former collective farms, and the pattern was repeated elsewhere in the country.

At the same time, the crash also fueled the growth of enormous, cross-regional groups that began to look a great deal like their industrial counterparts. Several of the groups in the sector from the mid-1990s used the new environment to expand significantly; and newcomers also entered the field, as its potential as a source of cash became apparent.

As in earlier periods, however, the nature of the agrarian sector and its previous reforms gave the struggle for property in agriculture a different dynamic from the conflict in industry. For example, while integrated groups developed in the sector before 1998, it remained uncrowded relative to the strongest, most active players, so old and new groups could expand without coming into direct conflict in 1998–2002.[23] To be sure, the fields were not truly empty, as multiple actors had staked claims to agricultural assets before 1998. Some claimants—rural citizens operating their personal plots in symbiosis with large farms—quite literally depended on those assets for their survival, so the radical transformation of asset control in agriculture after the crash had potentially even greater social implications than changes in industry. In general, however, agriculture did not witness the kind of violent conflicts that took place in, say, the "metals wars" in industry.

More important for understanding the contours of the conglomerates, the relative openness of the field affected the depth and breadth of groups in the sectors. Virtually none of the major groups in agriculture in 1998–2002 began as a farm. Unlike in industry, raw-materials producers were simply too numerous, too debt-ridden, and too cash-poor to provide leverage over other players in the system. Therefore, the agrarian groups that fared best after the crash were those that had built up control over food-processing or commodities-trading bottlenecks earlier, which gave them great advantages in the new system (see Table 6.4). After the crash, they tended to expand up and down a production chain, perhaps branching into related products, as when companies moved from grain to chicken feed to poultry production.

Newcomers to the sector from industry, by contrast, grew differently. Flush with cash but lacking useful network ties in agriculture, the new groups made eye-popping but unfocused acquisitions. They leased hundreds of thousands of hectares of land, bought famous pieces of the Soviet agrarian system, and developed such large holdings that they sometimes encompassed significant parts of production chains almost inadvertently. Their assets, however, tended to be less focused and less integrated than those of groups that had been in the sector before the crash. If agriculture ever became crowded, and the struggle for property intensified, their holdings were likely to shift significantly.

Among the agricultural processing groups that built on their pre-1998 successes to take their place on the national stage after the crash was the drink-packaging company Wimm-Bill-Dann, which grew from a handful of processing facilities to more than twenty. In 1998 it began to

---

23. Some of the new large players in the agricultural sector cited the absence of competition as one of its appeals.

TABLE 6.4
Significant integrated groups in Russian agriculture, 2002

	Name	Origin (subsector or industrial group)	Notes
With pre-1998 origins			
As processors	Wimm-Bill-Dann	Milk processing	Assets throughout Russia and beyond; remained focused on processing
	APK Cherkizovskii	Meat processing	Controlled 11% of Russian meat market
	Iug Rusi	Grain processing	Included vast land holdings; large player in Russian sunflower oil market
	EFKO	Edible-oils processing	Branched into dairy and other areas; included about 100,000 hectares of land
As traders	OGO	Grain trading	Expanded into sunflower oil
	Razguliai-Ukrros	Sugar trading	Acquired processors in sugar, grain, meat, and poultry
	Rusagro	Sugar trading	Supplied major confectionary plants in Russia; branched into grain, edible oils
	Rusagrokapital	Grain trading	Broke out of Roskhleboprodukt
Formed by industrial groups since 1998			
	Agriko	LUKoil	Leased about 100,000 ha of land
	Stoilenskaia niva	Metalloinvest	Included more than 300,000 ha of land
	Agros	Interros	Included Roskhleboprodukt
	Planeta Management	Sibneft/Millhouse	Included Omskii bekon

move outside the Moscow area, acquiring dairy plants in Novosibirsk, Nizhnii Novgorod, and Vladivostok oblasts. In 2000, it spread beyond Russia's borders to include factories in Ukraine and Kyrgyzstan (*RRR* November 5, 1998; www.wbd.com, accessed October 31, 2003). With over two thousand outlets in Moscow alone, distribution centers throughout Russia and beyond, and more than eighteen thousand employees, the company had become a significant player in the Russian political economy, and it even went public on the New York Stock Exchange in January 2002 (Tolkacheva 2002). Generally, Wimm-Bill-Dann relied on contracts with domestic and foreign milk producers for raw inputs, although it also began to develop its own herd (Kostina 2002a).

APK Cherkizovskii, a budding meat-processing group in late 1997, did not fare well in the immediate aftermath of the financial crash, but it recovered quickly. The group found itself about $200 million in debt at the end of 1998, but it used some of its own shares to reduce that figure and then began to expand again (IRG 2003, 88). In particular, it acquired meat and broiler plants in the regions of Penza, Rostov, Belgorod, Krasnodar, and Moscow, and its share of the Russian meat market shot up to 11 percent, more than double that of its next competitor (Kostina 2002c).

The grain and seed processor Iug Rusi also grew rapidly after the crash. Having already established itself as the largest exporter of industrial sunflower oil in Russia, the company brought another large plant online in 1999–2000, and its brand "Zolotaia Semechka" quickly cornered the largest single share of the Russian market for edible oil (Kostina 2001b; IRG 2003, 85). In addition, Iug Rusi reached down the production chain to bring over twenty farms and their 200,000 hectares of land into the group (Khramova 2002; IRG 2003, 85). The key to its power lay in its control over processing and export facilities, but it sought additional predictability by taking over raw-materials producers, as well.

The company EFKO, a final major agricultural group based on a food processor, had been even less prominent before the crash than the groups already mentioned, but it also took advantage of increased cash receipts to grab property after 1998. Growing out of the Efirnoe edible oils plant in Belgorod oblast, the group acquired five elevators in 1999, two dairy plants in 2000, and by the end of 2001 had taken control of thirty farms with approximately 100,000 hectares of farmland. Despite the fact that it remained concentrated in Belgorod and nearby regions, EFKO thus became an enormous company in the oil and condiments market (IRG 2003, 41–43).

Processing, however, was not the only source of strength in the competition for agrarian assets in Russia in 1998–2002—several of the biggest groups in that period took advantage of their roots in the trading business instead. The OGO group, for instance, continued to expand throughout the agricultural sector. Having already acquired storage and processing facilities for grain, OGO began to establish equipment-repair parks ("machine-technological stations") in 1999, leased about eight thousand hectares to grow grain, and began to procure sunflower seeds (Serova, Khramova, and Nichols 2002, 16). It also expanded its holdings in the grain sector by purchasing shares in the Petrokhleb holding in

St. Petersburg, and it became a major player in the industrial sunflower-oil market by purchasing an oil-extraction factory (Kostina 2002b, 2001b).

Razguliai-Ukrros, a former sugar-for-oil trader, captured assets in several subsectors of agriculture after 1998, although it remained focused on the processing phase of production. By 2002 the group included six sugar plants, six grain processors, three meat-processing plants, three poultry factories, and more (IRG 2003, 87). All those acquisitions made Razguliai-Ukrros the second-largest agricultural company in Russia by annual turnover, which stood at more than $400 million (Kuz'menko 2002).

Another sugar trader, Rusagro, took advantage of its postcrash position to become the largest agricultural group in the country (Telitsyna, Kuz'menko, and Kovalenko 2002; Kuz'menko 2002). From a holding of only one sugar processor in Belgorod oblast, Rusagro grew to control five such plants, thirteen trading houses, and assets in the grain and edible-oils subsectors (Telitsyna, Kuz'menko, and Kovalenko 2002; IRG 2003, 91). At the same time, it continued to supply some of the leading confectionary plants in Russia, ensuring it continued access to cash.

Finally, the group Rusagrokapital split from the grain-trading network Roskhleboprodukt in 1999. From that position, the group expanded into production by acquiring a mill and feed complex in Smolensk oblast (www.rusagrocapital.ru, accessed July 24, 2004). By 2003 it included over twenty enterprises for processing and storing grain, flour, and feed, as well as poultry- and meat-processing facilities ("Rusagrocapital" 2003). Like the other groups, Rusagrokapital thus used its newly increasing supply of cash to capture assets that could serve defensive and offensive purposes as the struggle for property in agriculture continued.

The growth of existing groups in agriculture stood to reshape political, economic, and social patterns throughout the sector. Even more striking at the time, however, was the appearance after 1998 of new major players in the struggle for assets in agriculture—the national-level industrial groups. In the Soviet system, large industrial enterprises often operated significant auxiliary farms to feed their workers, and financial-industrial groups had dabbled in agriculture in the mid-1990s, but this was different. The organizations discussed below represented the oligarchs' turn to agriculture as a new source of cash and political support.

The first major industrial group to set up a large-scale agricultural holding after 1998 was LUKoil, which founded Agriko. Vladimir Bovin, a man with military education and marketing experience but little formal knowledge of agriculture, headed the company (Kulefeeva, Trushin, and Khodyrev 2001, 9). Showing off LUKoil's might, and demonstrating that the absence of a clear law on purchasing land was not an insurmountable obstacle to investment in agriculture, Agriko leased about 100,000 hectares from large farms and their members, quickly becoming one of the biggest farm operators in the country (Kostina 2002a).

On an even larger scale, the Metalloinvest group of Oleg Kiselev entered the agricultural sector in the form of the Stoilenskaia niva holding in Belgorod oblast in the year 2000. Fedor Kliuka, who headed the group, was a metallurgist by training, and he brought most of his management team from Stoilenskii GOK (Kulefeeva, Trushin, and Khodyrev 2001, 3). Creating the new entity was part of a plan the oblast governor launched in 1999 to restructure insolvent farms. Debts were transferred to a newly established regional company, and the administration sought outside investors to take over the assets of the farms at no up-front cost (Ryl'ko 2002, 62). Through that process, Metalloinvest acquired agricultural assets of staggering size, including sixty-four farms, fifteen processors, six elevators, trade enterprises, and over 300,000 hectares of agricultural land (IRG 2003, 93; Kostina 2002a).

The following year, Vladimir Potanin's Interros group entered the agricultural sector with great fanfare. In October 2001 Potanin established the Agros holding company with $100 million of start-up capital and a promise of $200 million in operating funds (Kostina 2001a). In an even more eye-catching move, Agros moved quickly to acquire the remaining assets of Roskhleboprodukt, the old Soviet grain distribution network. Although it was a cumbersome asset at risk of losing some of its individual pieces to outside takeovers, Roskhleboprodukt gave Agros control over an important link in the agricultural production chain, providing a strong base for further expansion. In less than two years, the group included Kontrakt Holding, which controlled pig-breeding and grain-trading assets, and dozens of other enterprises (Kotova 2001; "Konflikt vokrug" 2003).

Finally, Roman Abramovich's newly renamed Millhouse Capital, which was still based on the Sibneft oil holding, staked its claim to part of the agricultural sector at about the same time. Planeta Management, established by former Sibneft chair Andrei Blokh, quickly developed a large presence in the meat, dairy, and retail sectors. Most notably, at the end of 2001 it acquired the Omskii bekon Meat-processing Complex (IRG 2003, 25).

Thus the behemoths had come to the countryside. Both the arrival of industrial giants and the expansion of existing agricultural groups signaled that the struggle for agrarian property had heated up. Cash-based takeovers, threats of bankruptcy, and political deals all appeared with increasing frequency, as the pursuit of assets in agriculture looked more and more like the process in industry. Still, the kind of holdings that would afford the greatest defensive and offensive capabilities remained less clear in the agrarian than the industrial sector, and several groups showed signs of potential instability. The oligarchs, in particular, seemed inclined to acquire vast landholdings—rather than focus on processing and trading assets that were easier to control—and to branch into several sectors very quickly, without first establishing firm control over complete production chains. At the same time, the new entrants to the sector brought with them capital and national political resources far beyond those of the major integrated groups with a history in agriculture. The division and redivision of property in Russian agriculture seemed certain to continue, but it was impossible to say which kinds of groups would be victors in the struggle.

THE NEW UNSTABLE EQUILIBRIUM

The Russian political economy in 2002 was not the same as it had been in 1995, or even in 1998. Some of the business conglomerates that seemed to dominate the system in the mid-1990s had disappeared, and those that survived did so through significant restructuring. Several of the new giants bestriding the country were barely discussed in the heyday of the oligarchs. At the same time, a new second tier of economic groups developed, influencing regional politics and economics and ready to step onto the national stage if the opportunity arose. Even agriculture, long deemed a hopeless morass of abysmal productivity, attracted widespread attention, although not for the reasons many observers expected. Finally, a new president had come to power and disrupted the links between the big groups and policy makers that had developed in the Yeltsin era.

Some analysts at the time began to argue that the new groups and activity represented the culmination of a phase of transformation. According to this view, the best pieces of state property had been sold off, the most desirable assets in the Russian economy were concentrated in a few hands, and the next step, which was already underway, was for the new private owners to invest in production and lobby for the rule of law (Aslund and Boone 2002; Cottrell 2002c; Boone and Rodionov 2001). Whether because of principled economic reformers or blind luck, Russia had finally turned the corner and reached a new stage of normal, market-based economic development.

The consolidation thesis held intuitive appeal. If most state property had indeed been sold off, then economic actors might be in a position to focus on developing their businesses, rather than prying additional assets from the state. Similarly, if the group of major economic players in a system was relatively small, as in Russia in 2001–2, those actors might be able to overcome barriers to collective action and press for universal rules of the game, rather than seeking preferential legal treatment. The argument also seemed to enjoy some empirical support. In particular, industrial investment in 2000 and 2001 rose by 17 percent and 9 percent, respectively, and Russian business leaders helped pass market-friendly laws like a new tax code and a reduction of hard-currency repatriation requirements (Gaddy and Ickes 2002, 199; Aslund and Boone 2002; Cottrell 2001b).

The significance of those trends, however, should not be overstated. For example, on the question of investment, real expenditures on new construction and equipment were lower in 2000 than they had been in 1996 (Gaddy and Ickes 2002, 199). Furthermore, the rise in export revenues after the devaluation left Russian exporters with surplus cash that they needed to put somewhere. Meanwhile, the Central Bank forced companies to convert at least some of their hard-currency earnings into rubles, and the global economic slowdown made external investment less attractive than it once was. All these factors increased the likelihood that Russian businesses would plow their windfall profits into domestic projects, but none of them was the result of a consolidation of ownership.

In a similar fashion, while several legal changes in 2002 promised to regularize competition for property, first in the sale and purchase of land and then in the sordid world of business litigation, in practice they seemed as likely to open a new round of clashes as to bring the struggle under control. On July 24, 2002, Putin signed the Law on Turnover of Agricultural Land, which once again tried to set guidelines for the purchase and sale of farmland.[24] For optimists in the transition school, the passage of the new law again raised hopes that a land market would

---

24. "Ob oborote zemel' sel'skokhoziaistvennogo naznacheniia." The law was amended on July 7, 2003, and June 29, 2004, but with little substantive effect. For more detail on the original law, see Wegren 2002.

develop and improve the performance of the agrarian sector, although even they found shortcomings in the law. First and foremost, while it allowed foreigners to lease farmland for up to forty-nine years, it prohibited them from owning it (Article 3). In addition, regional governments and large farms enjoyed the right of first refusal in land sales, making such exchanges cumbersome even on paper. Independent farmers could sell their land on the open market only after granting their regional or local government a month to consider buying it first. Landholders within a large farm faced yet another hurdle, as they had to offer their shares both to the other members of the collective and to the government before appealing to outsiders. In all cases, the final sale price had to reach at least the level of that offered to coworkers or the government (Articles 8 and 12). Nevertheless, despite such imperfections, if Russia were fundamentally on a path to a market economy, this new law would have represented a major step in that direction.

Understanding the Russian political economy as a struggle for property, however, leads to more modest expectations. Instead of creating a flourishing land market that would fundamentally reshape ownership in the countryside, the new law would more likely alter some of the strategies for capturing agricultural land. Early entrants into the sector, for example, who may have acquired ownership rights through informal transactions, stood to make a financial killing if they could sell out of their holdings under the new law. Similarly, major players in the sector who had considerable access to cash could purchase the land they were renting without competing against foreigners or other large investors. For medium-sized farms, however, and others without significant cash flow, the new law raised the fear of rising lease prices (LaFraniere 2002). The rules changes were real, but in light of all that had come before, they stood little chance of creating a simple and transparent market for agricultural land.

By 2002 most observers had lowered their expectations for a new policy on land sales and were far more concerned with the widespread manipulation of the court system in pursuit of property. Two reforms aimed to limit that abuse. First, a new version of the Arbitration Procedure Code came into effect on September 1, 2002, requiring minority shareholders to sue companies in the region where the enterprise was located, rather than where the shareholder lived.[25] The intent was to

---

25. See Zakon "O vvedenii v deistvie arbitrazhnogo protsessual'nogo kodeksa Rossiiskoi Federatsii," July 24, 2002.

make it more difficult for outsiders, especially large economic actors, to file suits in regions where they were politically strong (Andreev 2002, cited in Woodruff 2004, 101n44). Second, the innumerable calls to amend the 1998 bankruptcy code finally produced a new version of the law, which was signed on October 26, 2002, and came into force on December 3.[26] An imposing tome of more than forty-eight thousand words (compared to twenty-three thousand in the 1998 version), the new law introduced several changes to the bankruptcy process. For example, it raised the level of debt at which bankruptcy proceedings could begin, albeit only to 100,000 rubles, which was less than $4,000 at the time (Article 6). Potentially more significant, the law gave debtors a voice in choosing the receiver that would take over their firm (Article 45). Furthermore, it required creditors to try other methods of debt recovery before launching bankruptcy proceedings, and it specified that debtors could end the process by paying off their debts (Woodruff 2004, 101).

Official sources suggested that the new laws had some positive effects. Tatiana Trefilova, head of the Russian Federal Bankruptcy Commission, went so far as to claim in December 2003 that political bankruptcies were a thing of the past, since taking over property through the bankruptcy process had become so difficult. Even officialdom, however, recognized that the law did not close all loopholes related to ownership. In particular, Trefilova admitted that many enterprises continued to move assets to new firms and declare the old ones bankrupt to avoid paying debts or to oust minority shareholders (Panina 2003). Other observers remained even more skeptical that such a complex law could close all the loopholes in the bankruptcy process. According to one analyst writing in September 2003, "Bankruptcy remains the preferred mechanism for redistributing property, and the much ballyhooed adoption of a new bankruptcy law did little to change this" (Delyagin 2003).

Each new rule thus filled a hole left by earlier legislation, but none of them prevented actors from finding creative ways to capture resources. At best, they channeled the activity in different directions, and in some cases they failed to do even that. Certainly they, and business lobbying in general, did not represent a spontaneous decision on the part of economic leaders to work together in pursuit of a "dictatorship of law." First, the main business lobbying organization in Russia—the Russian Union of Industrialists and Entrepreneurs—was rejuvenated at Putin's

26. "O nesostoiatel'nosti (bankrotstve)."

suggestion. Furthermore, even if the contemporary RUIE were a real attempt on the part of Russian economic elites to pool their political resources, observers should have withheld judgment of its significance, since all previous such efforts in Russia—including the original incarnation of the RUIE—broke down after a brief heyday.[27] Finally, and more important for the Russian political economy as a whole, oligarchical support for a particular new law is not the same as submission to the rule of law more generally. Economic groups in Russia in 2001–2 were still powerful enough to manipulate governmental decisions to their advantage, use selective legal enforcement in pursuit of assets, or simply ignore laws when it suited them.

Most fundamentally, then, the underlying dynamic of the system had not changed—a multifaceted struggle for property continued to rage, even as the debt crisis and Putin's election changed some of the motives and strategies involved. Large pieces of property still dangled enticingly in front of contenders throughout the system. The state itself still controlled plenty of desirable assets, with the most obvious being shares in the gas giant Gazprom, the electricity monopoly UES, oil companies like LUKoil and Rosneft, and the holdings of the Railways Ministry. Furthermore, the prospect of continued conflict among major private actors loomed large, as industrial groups sorted out their strategies in the agrarian sector, national conglomerates sought an international presence, and second-tier groups nipped at the heels of larger ones.

Meanwhile, the range of motives driving competitors remained wide. Cash was still short, debt still pervasive, and political influence still a must for economic actors. For a few select firms, access to international capital markets could mitigate the first two problems, but that was not an option for many participants in the Russian economy, even if they had the wherewithal to employ Western accounting standards. The acquisition of strategic assets, by contrast, was a potential solution to all three of the problems, and companies could pursue it whether they had international economic reputations or not. In addition, the fact that even companies as large as Gazprom and Interros had proven vulnerable to takeovers simply emphasized to other players in the Russian political economy the benefits of developing closed production cycles so as to avoid exposing themselves to rivals. The struggle would continue, although outside forces would continue to reshape it.

27. On the early rise and fall of the RUIE and the Civic Union of which it was a part, see McFaul 1993.

CHAPTER 7

A NEW WORLD, BUT HOW NEW?

The Yukos Affair and Beyond, 2002–2005

Any sense that the distribution of property in Russia was stable evaporated with a police raid on a hospital in July 2003. The resulting arrest of Mikhail Khodorkovskii's associate, Platon Lebedev, marked the beginning of what would be called the "Yukos affair," in which Putin's government dismantled the most famous private company in the country and captured its main asset for the state. The outcome of the attack remained uncertain in the first half of 2005, but clearly the rules for redistributing property had undergone another transformation.

Once again, however, many analysts tried to force the Yukos events into a bipolar view of the world. Optimists hoped the prosecution of Yukos for tax evasion meant that laws would be applied equally to all actors in the system, regardless of wealth, while pessimists worried that the action represented backsliding toward state control of economic assets. Both interpretations failed to account for a number of other trends in ownership at the time. Focusing on property and strategies for pursuing it provides a different view of this era. The tumultuous Russian struggle for property simply continued, but the grounds for competition changed again, as one actor in the system—the central state—established itself as the most important player in the competition. Old defenses, including deep and broad structures, were not as effective in a world where the government was such a strong competitor for assets, so the remaining groups began to develop new methods for protecting and expanding their holdings.

REMAKING THE CONTEXT OF OWNERSHIP

The state takeover of Yuganskneftegaz, the main production subsidiary of the oil giant Yukos, was far from straightforward.[1] Some of the problems came from the sheer scale of the project of taking over a multibillion-dollar company. Such deals frequently hit roadblocks even in established capitalist systems and when both parties are amenable to the merger—neither of which held in this case. Moreover, internal Russian politics repeatedly gummed up the works, especially when the heads of Rosneft and Gazprom quarreled about details of the transaction. Furthermore, the global reach of some of the participants in the deal nearly made it possible for an unexpected international event to derail the process.

Because of the deal's audacity, complexity, and occasional surreality, observers' initial reactions tended toward shock and disbelief. The opening salvoes against Yukos surprised nearly everyone watching Russia, but most quickly assumed it was simply another chance for Putin to rattle an oligarch's cage, remind economic actors to stay out of formal politics, and perhaps retrieve some unpaid taxes for the treasury. Even as the conflict spun out of control and the state ended up with Yugansk, it was easy to see the events simply as a game of chicken where no one had given in. In reality, however, the move against Yukos was part of a broader trend toward redefining the rules of the ownership game.

The Bumbling Takeover of Yukos

Mikhail Khodorkovskii is hardly a hero. The former Komsomol bureaucrat took over the giant oil company Yukos by taking advantage of the loans-for-shares auctions in 1995 and undermining minority shareholders through transfer pricing in the latter part of the 1990s (Johnson 1997, 2000; Freeland 2000; Black, Kraakman, and Tarassova 2000). Likewise, his Menatep financial-industrial group exploited almost all of the strategies—legal and less so—for acquiring property in post-Soviet Russia. Still, most observers in 2003 believed that those actions represented water under the bridge, interpreting Putin's repeated assurances he would not reconsider old privatizations to mean he would not chal-

---

1. Yuganskneftegaz, often shortened to "Yugansk," accounted for about 1 million barrels a day, or 60 percent of Yukos's oil.

lenge the oligarchs. In addition, analysts pointed out that Yukos had recently become the poster child for improved corporate governance in Russia. Khodorkovskii had released his company's accounting records for investor scrutiny, and Yukos seemed poised to attract the kind of foreign investment that Putin claimed to want.

In July 2003, however, police arrested Menatep's CEO Platon Lebedev from his hospital bed and put him in jail to await trial on charges of failing to pay about $300 million for shares of the Apatit fertilizer plant in 1994 (Dow Jones 2003). At about the same time, another Menatep executive, security chief Aleksei Pichugin, was arrested and charged with two murders (Glasser 2003a). While observers were shocked that even Menatep and Yukos were not immune from such investigations, many investors, including Exxon-Mobil and Chevron-Texaco, nevertheless decided the flap would probably blow over (A. Ostrovsky 2003d). Putin could not afford to damage a flagship company, the argument ran, and at worst he probably wanted to remind leading business figures to stay out of politics in the run-up to elections in late 2003 and 2004. In reality, however, the initial arrests were only the beginning. After putting Lebedev and Pichugin in jail, the authorities questioned Khodorkovskii and other company executives, raided Yukos's headquarters, and expanded their investigation (Glasser 2003b; Tavernise 2003; Lipman 2003; A. Ostrovsky 2003b). On October 25 prosecutors arrested Khodor-kovskii himself and held him without bail on several counts of embezzle-ment, tax fraud, and other economic violations (Glasser 2003a).[2] Soon thereafter, with Moscow's encouragement and assistance, Roman Abramovich's Sibneft oil company backed out of a merger with Yukos (Glasser and Baker 2003b).[3]

Even after the government had hit Yukos with several back tax charges and announced that it would auction off Yuganskneftegaz to pay the fines, the future of the company remained uncertain, in no small part because the state's actions against it seemed so confused. Shortly after announcing the planned auction, the government began

2. Although most observers remained uncertain as to the endgame in the Yukos conflict, the arrest of Khodorkovskii was enough to convince both Exxon-Mobil and Chevron-Texaco to suspend talks on acquiring a large stake in the company (Jack, Ostrovsky, and Saigol 2003).

3. The merger had Yukos paying about $3 billion for a 92-percent stake in Sibneft, leaving Abramovich with a little more than 25 percent of the new entity—Yukos-Sibneft, or Yuksi (Belton 2003). The share exchange actually took place in October, but Sibneft was able to break the deal in November.

making arrangements to create a state-owned energy behemoth. Igor Sechin, deputy chief of Putin's administration, joined the board at the 100-percent state-owned Rosneft in June 2004, and on July 27 he became its chair (A. Ostrovsky 2004a; Koptev 2004). In the past Sechin had called for combining Rosneft and the natural gas giant Gazprom into a single holding company that could operate oil and gas resources in the interests of the state (Koptev 2004). In September the government announced that Gazprom would acquire Rosneft in exchange for the 13-percent stake in Gazprom that its subsidiaries owned, a move that would increase the state's direct share in Gazprom from about 38 percent to over 50 percent (Baker 2004b).[4] Despite some objections from Rosneft's Sergei Bogdanchikov (AFP 2004d), it appeared that the state had its vehicle for taking over Yugansk.

Yukos, however, launched a creative defense on December 14, 2004, less than a week before the scheduled auction of Yugansk, by filing for Chapter 11 bankruptcy protection in the United States (Nicholson 2004c; Zhdannikov and Busvine 2004). The company argued that it deserved protection under American law because Yukos's chief financial officer, Bruce Misamore, had moved back to Houston not long before and opened some bank accounts in the name of "Yukos USA" (Zhdannikov and Busviné 2004). When the Houston court ordered a ten-day delay in the auction, the international banking consortium that had planned to lend Gazprom the money to buy Yugansk pulled out of the deal, fearing legal action in U.S. or international courts (AFP 2004f; White and Bahree 2004; Tolkacheva 2004; Zhdannikov and Busvine 2004).

The auction itself went forward on December 19, but it was much more complicated than originally planned, and it left many issues unresolved. The most important change from the initial script was that Gazprom—which had significant private ownership and therefore risked exposure to the U.S. court decision—did not buy Yugansk. Gazprom had created Gazpromneft not long before specifically to take over Rosneft and, presumably, to buy and operate Yugansk, but the Houston suit had forced it to scramble for new options. On December 21 Gazprom

4. At the same time, the government pledged to allow foreign investors to buy stocks in Gazprom directly after the state had acquired a majority stake (Baker 2004a). That announcement caused great excitement in the Western investment community.

announced it had sold Gazpromneft on December 17 (i.e., before the auction) and therefore was not in violation of the court order prohibiting it from participating in the auction (Kaban 2004; MosNews 2004b). In the end, rather than having Gazprom acquire Yugansk, even indirectly, the government had a shell company, Baikal Finance Group (BFG), purchase Yugansk at the auction and then allowed Rosneft to purchase BFG.

That change in plans created major headaches for the Russian government, Gazprom, and Rosneft. Most immediately, they made it difficult to finance the purchase of Yugansk without exposing important players to foreign legal action. According to official sources, the $9.37 billion purchase price was transferred properly on December 30, 2004; and when representatives of Rosneft arrived at Yugansk headquarters on December 31 (supported by court officers), the Yukos team turned over operations (White and Pottinger 2005). The sources of financing for the alleged purchase, however, were not clear at all; and every move the state made seemed to expose Rosneft, Russian state banks, foreign governments, or others to legal action.[5]

Eventually, Deutsche Bank won a countersuit arguing that the U.S. court did not have jurisdiction in the case, but the unexpected turmoil had already caused problems inside Russia, throwing a wrench into the plans to merge Rosneft with Gazprom. Most directly, the acquisition of Yugansk and the financial shenanigans associated with the takeover muddied the book value of Rosneft, whose management argued it should have a more prominent role in any new entity (Faulconbridge 2005a, b). In addition, officials argued about what should happen to Yugansk itself. While most observers expected it to be folded into Gazprom as part of a Rosneft merger, the government announced soon after the auction that Yugansk would be spun off into a 100-percent state-owned company and held separately (Zhdannikov 2004; A. Ostrovsky 2004b; White and Bahree 2004).

As the merger saga continued, including roles for the Chinese and Indian governments, the trial of Khodorkovskii ground on (Zhdannikov 2004; Faulconbridge 2005c). The spectacle finally concluded in May 2005 with a twelve-day reading of the verdict by multiple judges. Khodorkovskii and his partner Lebedev received nine-year sentences for fraud and tax evasion (Lowe and Zhdannikov 2005). Despite promises to

---

5. See A. Ostrovsky 2005; Nicholson 2005; Kaban 2005; Belton 2005; Buckley 2005; Yenukov 2005; Zhdannikov 2004; RIA Novosti 2005; Faulconbridge 2005c.

appeal, one of the most powerful early winners in the struggle for property seemed to have met his match in Putin.

Method in the Madness

This was not the first time Putin had gone after an oligarch, of course. Shortly after coming to power, he sent state forces after both Vladimir Gusinskii and Boris Berezovskii, separating them from their property and eventually forcing them into exile. When the Yukos affair began, it was common to think it would be resolved in a similar fashion. When it was not, some analysts speculated that Khodorkovskii had made a mistake in standing up to the Kremlin. That is, if Khodorkovskii had simply given up, like Gusinskii or Berezovskii, the conflict could have been resolved without outright nationalization of the company, but when Khodorkovskii called Putin's bluff (repeatedly), total victory for the state became necessary. In this view, the eventual nationalization of Yuganskneftegaz seems almost accidental. The Kremlin had hoped to remind Khodorkovskii who was boss, perhaps even redistribute some of his assets to other would-be oligarchs, but the fight had gotten out of hand. Neither the direct evidence from the Yukos affair, however, nor the circumstantial evidence from other state actions at the time supports such a generous interpretation.

The state's behavior from very early in the conflict suggests that an outright takeover was in the plan from the beginning. The key weapons in the attack proved to be a series of tax assessments that gave no indication Yukos would be allowed to escape. On December 30, 2003, the tax ministry announced it would file a claim for about $3.3–3.5 billion against Yukos for the year 2000 to cover underpaid taxes and concomitant fines (Arvedlund 2003; AFP 2004a). On July 1, 2004, the same day the courts insisted Yukos pay the claim for 2000, the Tax Ministry announced an additional claim of about $3.4 billion, this one for back taxes and associated fees from 2001 (AFP 2004c). On November 1, 2004, tax authorities announced still more charges against Yukos. They filed a claim for about $6.7 billion in underpaid taxes for 2002 against Yukos itself, demanded that Yuganskneftegaz repay about $1 billion for 2002, and announced that Yugansk had probably underpaid its taxes in 2001 by another $2.25 billion (AFP 2004e). Not long after, claims for 2003 appeared. The deluge was inescapable.

The state, of course, argued that the tax assessments were simply deserved, and the world was witnessing the application of the rule of law in Russia. In practice, however, the government directly impeded any possible resolution of the disagreement by freezing assets, blocking payment avenues, and announcing the sale of Yuganskneftegaz as Yukos managed to repay some of the early demands. The first asset freeze took place just after Khodorkovskii's arrest, when the state quarantined the 44-percent stake in Yukos that Khodorkovskii and his partners owned (Baker and Glasser 2003). Then, in April 2004, the tax administration won a court ruling to prevent Yukos itself from selling assets (White and Chazan 2004). Ostensibly, the freezes were to prevent Yukos from moving its assets abroad during the conflict with the government, but they also had the effect of making it harder to pay the tax assessment.

Once it lost a court appeal of the original $3.4 billion charge, Yukos began to offer payment plans for settling it, including offering its 35-percent stake in Sibneft as collateral (Bloomberg News 2004a; Titova 2004; Reuters 2004; Nicholson 2004a). The state, however, showed no interest in being repaid. In a strategy reminiscent of private actors' use of the bankruptcy laws to take over rivals in 1998–2002, the government made unreasonable demands, tried to prevent Yukos from meeting them, and used the courts to justify an asset grab regardless of progress toward repayment. For instance, when the state won its final court case on the 2000 tax bill (in July 2004), it gave Yukos only a month to pay, and it froze the company's bank accounts, making even partial repayment very difficult (Yenukov 2004; Bloomberg News 2004a).[6] Soon thereafter, although the deadline for paying the 2000 tax bill had not yet passed, and the 2002 and 2003 assessments had not even been filed, the Justice Ministry announced that the subsidiary Yuganskneftegaz would be sold off to pay some of Yukos's tax debts (Ayton 2004; A. Ostrovsky 2004a).[7] The decision seemed less like frustrated reaction to Khodorkovskii's defiance than an attempt to prevent Yukos from paying off its taxes and fines any other way.

In addition to the incessant attempts to force Yukos to sell Yugansk, the state also appeared to reassess the status of several other important economic groups. While Yukos was the largest and most famous company to face renewed tax investigations in 2003 and 2004, it was hardly the

6. Despite obstacles, Yukos had paid about $2.6 billion in back taxes and fines by early October (Nicholson 2004b).

7. The sale would actually be of a 76.8-percent stake in Yugansk, which would represent 100 percent of the voting rights, since the remaining 23.2 percent of the company was divided among thirteen preferred shares (Faulconbridge, Korchagina, and Belton 2004).

only one. In July 2003, for example, soon after arresting Lebedev, prosecutors reopened an investigation into Oleg Deripaska's acquisition of several properties, including Avtobank and the Nosta steel plant (Bloomberg News 2003). They had closed the investigation in June for lack of evidence, but it was reopened because, in the words of a spokesperson, the original investigation had been conducted in a "nonobjective way" (A. Ostrovsky 2003a). Similarly, the government launched a tax investigation into Sibneft in November 2003, and in March of the following year it announced the company owed $1 billion in back taxes (Munter 2003; Baker 2004a). In yet another example, a tiny customer of the telecommunications giant Vympelcom sued the company in late 2003, arguing that he did not have to pay his $800 phone bill because Vympelcom did not actually hold the license for the cellular frequencies it used. Lending credence to charges that the customer was a front for a rival company founded by Putin's telecommunications minister, the government agreed with the customer in January 2004, essentially ruling that Vympelcom could not bill its subscribers (S. Ostrovsky 2004; Fraser 2004). Later in the year, it also denied Vympelcom an expected increase in the number of phone numbers available for new customers (Bloomberg News 2004b). Each of these conflicts developed along different paths, and they each produced a wide range of speculation about causes and implications, but they clearly demonstrated that pieces of the federal government were reasserting themselves as major and aggressive arbiters in disputes over property.

Even more ominous for those who were concerned about an increasing state role in property redistribution, in late 2004 the Russian Audit Chamber issued a report on privatization from 1993 to 2003, claiming that the process was significantly flawed (Yurova 2004). Broadly speaking, the report stated that early legislation and enforcement mechanisms had been so poorly designed and monitored that privatization had frequently been carried out incorrectly. In a preliminary report, the Russian Audit Chamber found that some kind of violation had occurred in 56 of the first 140 cases examined (Goldman 2004, 323). The final version pointed to problems in several specific cases, including the insurance company Rosgosstrakh; the oil majors Sidanko, TNK, and Surgutneftegaz; Vnukovo Airlines; the Rybinsk Motor Plant; and the Baltic shipyards (Yurova 2004).

Foreigners were not exempt from criticism either. In January 2004, for example, the government decided to invalidate Exxon-Mobil and Chevron-Texaco's 1993 victory in an auction for rights to develop the oil fields at Sakhalin–3 and put those rights up for re-auction (Hill 2004, 31; White 2005). In early 2005 an Audit Chamber report claimed Royal Dutch/Shell (and its partners, including Japan's Mitsui and Mitsubishi) had deprived the Russian state of up to $2.5 billion by buying inputs from expensive suppliers (Reuters 2005). The next day, the Russian Ministry of Natural Resources announced that majority foreign-owned companies would not be allowed to bid for the rights to develop a number of large oil fields (or some gold and copper deposits) expected to be auctioned off in 2005 (White 2005).[8] The rules of ownership were being rewritten once again.

INTERNAL AND EXTERNAL LIMITS ON THE STATE

Recognizing that the conflict between the Russian government and Yukos represented more than a one-time attack on Khodorkovskii that got out of hand, however, should not mean succumbing to the opposite view: that it signaled a return to state control over property throughout the system. Instead, two other sets of forces help explain developments in 2002–5 better than such an either-or interpretation. First, the central state's own actions were not unambiguously self-aggrandizing, as Putin's vision of Russia's future seems to have valued private economic actors under the right circumstances. Second, and more important, regardless of how strong the central state became under Putin, it was not the only competitor for property. Even as the Yukos storm clouds were gathering, leading economic conglomerates experimented with a range of new approaches, and smaller groups took advantage of the new political and economic conditions to assert themselves against their larger brethren. Just as private actors had not ended their squabbles voluntarily in the first post-Soviet decade, so Putin could not eliminate them by force in the second.

Putin's Vision of the State's Role in the Economy

One of the greatest difficulties in arguing that the attack on Yukos and other actors represented the end of state support for private property is

---

8. The official justification was that Western companies might be content just to hold the assets as reserves, while the Russian government was interested in seeing the fields developed, which it argued Russian companies would be more likely to do (White 2005).

that even as Putin's government launched those attacks, it was privatizing other major assets. Putin oversaw the privatization of the oil company Slavneft in late 2002 and allowed a private consortium (TNK and Sibneft) to win. Indeed, the state-owned company Rosneft was excluded from the auction by a court decision two days before the sale. In addition, he allowed an unprecedented merger between TNK and British Petroleum (BP) in 2003. After years of antagonistic relations followed by a series of complicated negotiations, including direct meetings with Putin, TNK and BP agreed in June 2003 to pool their Russian oil assets into a 50–50 joint venture called TNK-BP ("BP Seals Historic TNK Tie-Up" 2003; Fridman, Jack, and Ostrovsky 2003). Finally, Putin's government sold its remaining stake in the oil giant LUKoil (about 7.6 percent) to ConocoPhillips for about $2 billion in September 2004, and the foreign company then expanded its holding to approximately 10 percent through stock-market purchases (Cameron, Ostrovsky, and Wagstyl 2004; Bloomberg News 2004c).

Maybe none of those decisions will win Putin great praise from supporters of private property in light of the Yukos affair, but they do need to be explained. One frequent approach is to argue that antimarket forces (usually in the form of the "siloviki"—men from the former KGB and other power ministries) had not entirely captured the Russian state by 2005 and therefore had to make concessions to economic liberals. Clearly, insider politics is important in Russia, and it will only become more so as the system grows less and less accountable to society, but the murky science of Kremlinology has a spotty history at best. Events may be easier to understand if we view Putin as a consistent Russian statist.

There is considerable evidence that Putin saw himself this way both before and after coming to office. The tax allegations against Yukos and other companies, for example, frequently did not charge that the companies violated laws directly. Instead, they complained that by using loopholes, particularly internal tax havens intended to foster regional economic development, the companies had failed in their duties to society (White and Chazan 2004; AFP 2004b; Hanson 2004). At a meeting of the Russian Union of Industrialists and Entrepreneurs on July 1, 2004, Putin himself appears to have said as much. According to Aleksei Mordashov, head of the steel company Severstal: "Putin didn't mention Yukos. *He talked about the social responsibility of Russia's businesses*" (Bloomberg News 2004a, emphasis added).

In addition to arguing that private businesses should assist the state in overall economic development plans regardless of the precise wording of laws, Putin also seemed to see natural resources as a logical source of international influence. He argued even before he became president that the Russian government should use the oil and gas sectors as tools to reassert itself in the world (Balzer 2005). That vision seemed to drive his political choices when, in the same week that he stated Russian foreign policy should "serve the cause of the overall development and modernization of the country," he appointed Energy Minister Viktor Khristenko as his envoy to the Commonwealth of Independent States (Hill 2004, 20).

Putin thus consistently presented himself as a patriot, one who wanted to redevelop the country domestically and internationally, and there has been no reason not to believe him. Furthermore, his actions seemed to derive from an understanding of the political and economic world that consisted of three important parts. First, while private economic activity is a powerful engine of growth, the state can and should foster economic development, especially when a country is far behind the economic leaders of the world. Second, the international economy is one in which states, not firms, are the main competitors and in which relative gains are important. And third, control over natural resources can be an effective lever for gaining international influence, and the realities of the early twenty-first century probably meant it would be Russia's best option. Those premises may turn out to be misguided, but they are not entirely without intellectual and political pedigree. State-led development, economic nationalism, and economic statecraft have guided regimes throughout history and have met with some success in the past.[9]

In terms of understanding the conflict over property in Russia in 2002–5, this interpretation of Putin's goals can help explain otherwise perplexing actions of his government. Khodorkovskii, for example, interfered with virtually every aspect of this vision of state-business relations. His lobbying against oil tax increases and his "aggressive minimization" of Yukos's tax liabilities undermined the state's ability to direct revenues where it thought they were needed, and his moves to build an oil pipeline to China outside the direction of the state hampered

9. Gerschenkron (1962) is a classic investigation of the virtues of state involvement in the economy in a country that needs to "catch up" with others. Economic nationalism has had its supporters in the United States at least since Alexander Hamilton, who wrote in 1791 that "Every nation . . . ought to endeavor to possess within itself, all the essentials of national supply" (cited in Gilpin 1987, 180) Baldwin (1985) is a landmark study of the use of economic tools in pursuit of foreign-policy goals.

Putin's ability to use energy as a foreign policy tool. Other major players, by contrast, were more than ready to play the new game. LUKoil spokesperson Dmitrii Dolgov, for example, said, "We understand that we have obligations to shareholders. But they are no more important than our obligations to society" (Raff 2004). Meanwhile, several companies began to publicize how much they were paying in taxes. LUKoil broadcast that its tax payments rose by 24 percent, while Sibneft said its effective tax rate in 2004 would be 20 percent, up from 15 percent (and even 12 percent in earlier years). The Novolipetsk Iron and Steel Works claimed it had paid more in taxes in the first eight months of 2004 than in all of 2003, and Andrei Braginskii of Mobile TeleSystems noted that MTS's effective tax rate in 2003 was 29 percent (Raff 2004). These statements were not complaints about high tax rates, as one might expect, but advertisements of companies' commitment to the state and to society.

A general worldview, of course, may offer only a weak constraint on governments in practice, since it can be extremely flexible under the right circumstances. Soviet governments supported NEP, extreme centralization, and eventually some privatization, all under the banner of one official ideology. The Russian government could certainly reclassify more and more property as of central importance to state development over time. Still, understanding Putin's particular vision of statist economic development helps explain the pattern of government involvement in Russian property in 2002–5 better than an interpretation that can differentiate only between a larger or smaller state role in the economy.

Other Players

Whatever their practical effects, Putin's self-imposed constraints were not alone in shaping the new role of the state in Russian property redistribution. To make sense of the period, analysts also need to remember the other competitors for assets in the system and examine how the environment of the time affected their resources, limitations, and strategies for dealing with the central state and with one another. The biggest economic groups often seemed most rattled by early moves against Yukos, and they scrambled to react to their new circumstances. Even among these groups, however, some took advantage of their rivals' misfortune or faintheartedness to expand. Second-tier groups, meanwhile, seemed in better position to benefit from the changing context, and some of them proved especially adept at using the new environ–ment of center-regional relations to challenge their larger antagonists successfully.

For the leading conglomerates, the new approaches ranged from exit to new forms of aggression against rivals. Vladimir Potanin and Roman Abramovich seemed most eager to follow the path of simply quitting the game by converting property to cash, although Potanin's efforts were not nearly as pronounced as Abramovich's. Indeed, Potanin's Agros holding continued to grow, acquiring the Ekstra-M and Pervaia peterburgskaia makaronnaia factories to become the largest pasta producer in the country ("Konflikt vokrug" 2003). At the same time, Potanin moved out of the defense sector, where the state's inter-ests were likely to be more intense than in, say, food processing. He sold his 50-percent stake in Oboronitelnye sistemy (Defense Systems) to a company affiliated with the state firm Rosoboroneksport ("Interros" 2003).

Abramovich, for his part, made increasingly obvious moves toward the door beginning in 2002. At the end of that year, the oil giant Sibneft paid him a secret $1 billion dividend on profits and planned to pay him another $1 billion in late 2003, thus allowing him to pull cash out of the enterprise without having to sell it (Jack 2003). In several other cases, Abramovich went even farther by parting with actual property. In the spring of 2003, he sold his 26-percent stake in Aeroflot to National Reserve Bank for about $135 million; in September his 50 percent of RusAl went to his partner Oleg Deripaska for $2.5 to $3 billion; and in November he sold his 37.5-percent stake in Ruspromavto to Deripaska for an undisclosed amount ("Deripaska Buys" 2003; "Oligarch Sells" 2003). He also tried to sell out of Sibneft, as noted above, although he reconsidered in light of the political pressure surrounding the Yukos affair. In still further evidence of his plans to exit Russia, Abramovich purchased the Chelsea football (soccer) club in July 2003 for £150 million and began to make his home in London ("Deripaska Buys" 2003; Jack 2003; "Russian Oil Tycoon" 2004).

Other actors, by contrast, took advantage of opportunities to expand, although they seemed more cognizant of the need to work with the Kremlin in doing so. At Gazprom, where the state had restored firm control, the management continued to bring wandering enterprises back into the fold and sought out new pieces to add to its empire (Gazprom 2002). Much more aggressively, Oleg Deripaska's group snapped up several of the assets Roman Abramovich sold off. In addition, Deripaska chased new prizes, especially in collaboration with Alisher Usmanov of Gazprominvest, who had avoided the wrath of Aleksei Miller during the house cleaning at Gazprom in 2001–2. In 2003 Usmanov and Deripaska founded Urals Steel, into which they poured their shares in the Nosta Iron and Steel Works (Helmer 2004). Deripaska's Base Element, along with Millhouse Capital and Nafta-Moskva, had sued Nosta for bankruptcy in 2001–2, forcing Andrei Andreev to sell out to them. Millhouse and Nafta-Moskva later sold their shares to Usmanov, allowing the creation of Urals Steel, which Deripaska soon sold to Usmanov. In another joint effort, Deripaska and Usmanov bought a 31-percent stake in the iron ore factory Olkon, which supplied the steel giant Severstal (AKSnews.ru 2003). Severstal yielded no ground in the face of litigation threats or rival shareholders' meetings, but Deripaska had clearly decided to remain aggressive in the new political and economic environment.

In an expansion strategy that looked beyond Russian borders, the oil company TNK and its owner, Alfa Group, forged an unprecedented deal with British Petroleum in 2003, but not before making certain that Putin approved of the agreement. As discussed earlier, TNK had used the bankruptcy process to grab Sidanko's two most productive oil fields in 1998, not long after BP had bought 10 percent of Sidanko from Vladimir Potanin. British Petroleum, however, fought TNK in the courts and in the capitals of several countries, and TNK eventually returned the fields to Sidanko in 2001 and bought out all shareholders in Sidanko except BP, which retained its 10-percent stake. In 2002 BP bought an additional 15 percent of Sidanko from TNK, demonstrating a continuing strong interest in Russian oil reserves (Whalen and Bahree 2003). The 2003 merger that created TNK-BP cost BP $2.4 billion in cash up front and $3.75 billion in BP stock transferred to TNK in three yearly payments from 2005 to 2007 (Hoyos, Jack, and Ostrovsky 2004). Alfa Group thus aggressively pursued the financial resources of an international investor but also recognized the need for explicit permission from Putin in the new environment.[10]

While the Yukos affair marked the most obvious change in the methods of property redistribution under Putin, other reforms altered

10. In a separate transaction that also suggested approval from the Kremlin, Leonard Blavatnik, founder of Access Industries and a shareholder in TNK-BP, bought George Soros's 25-percent plus one share of the telecommunications giant Sviazinvest in early 2004 (Jack, Ostrovsky, and Pretzlik 2004).

the process as well. Center-regional relations represented one part of the system on which Putin had focused particular attention, and by late 2002 two second-tier groups took advantage of the new atmosphere to defend themselves in court against assaults from two previously dominant players, Oleg Deripaska and Vladimir Potanin. Ilim Pulp Enterprise controlled three major firms in the Russian timber sector at the beginning of 2002: Kotlas Pulp and Paper Combine in Arkhangelsk oblast, Ust-Ilim Timber Processing Combine (LPK) in Irkutsk oblast, and Bratsk LPK. After a few months, however, Oleg Deripaska's Base Element once again tried to pry Kotlas and BLPK away from Ilim Pulp. In both cases, a micro-shareholder that most observers believed was connected to Deripaska filed suit against Ilim Pulp in Kemerovo oblast, which was not home to any of the plants in question. The shareholder did not sue any of the factories directly, but instead charged that Ilim Pulp had not lived up to its obligations to invest in either Kotlas or BLPK (Chazan 2002; Clark 2002b). In the case of Kotlas, the Kemerovo court awarded 3 billion rubles in damages to the plaintiff, and a share registrar close to Deripaska determined that Ilim Pulp's 61 percent stake in Kotlas should be turned over to the Russian Federal Property Fund to cover the award (Chazan 2002; Smith 2002). The Fund, in turn, sold the shares to the St. Petersburg banker Vladimir Kogan, who was an ally of Deripaska, along with others (Clark 2002a, b). Similarly, the court transferred Ilim Pulp's shares in Bratsk LPK to the Property Fund, which sold them to Continental Invest, at the time at least 30-percent owned by Deripaska (Clark 2003).

In the Russia of 2000, that would have been the end of the story. By the middle of 2002, however, Ilim Pulp did not have to crawl away and lick its wounds. Instead, the company convinced Putin to send the Ministry of Economic Development and Trade, the Ministry of Justice, and the office of the Prosecutor General to investigate (Clark 2002a). In addition, when Deripaska and his team elected a new board of directors at Kotlas and tried to enter the grounds, they and their armed guards were turned back by gunmen supporting the original Kotlas leadership (Chazan 2002). Finally, in a clear change from earlier practice, the presidium of the Kemerovo court overturned the court's original decision. It argued that the micro-shareholders had neither given Ilim Pulp enough warning to mount a legal defense nor shown injury to themselves, which would have been necessary for an award of damages (Clark 2002b). Over the next several months, which included another round of armed standoffs, Ilim Pulp eventually regained ownership of the plants it had held before the suits began and seemed to have chastened Deripaska, at least for the moment (berkon.com.ua/novosti_e.htm, accessed July 14, 2004). Whether the possibly temporary victory represented the triumph of law or the strength of Ilim Pulp's political connections was for optimists and pessimists to discuss, but it certainly indicated that some of the rules of the struggle for property had changed.

A similar conflict occurred in 2003 between Vladimir Potanin's Agros Group and the Taganskii Meat Processing Plant (TAMP), which controlled about 7 percent of Moscow's market for processed meat (Borisova 2003). In January 2003, through mechanisms never fully disclosed, Nikolai Kolosov acquired about 14 percent of TAMP-kholding, which owned TAMP ("Konflikt vokrug" 2003). Over the next several weeks, he launched a series of lawsuits designed to help take over the plant for Agros. The new arbitration code did not seem to constrain him at all, since his filings all took place outside Moscow. In Volgograd oblast, he won a claim to freeze about 75 percent of TAMP's stock, while a court in Khakassia removed the other sixteen managers of TAMP-kholding, arguing their failure to pay dividends at TAMP had undermined the holding's financial position ("Konflikt vokrug" 2003). Kolosov then transferred a controlling stake in TAMP to a new company; and by February 11, 2003, Agros had bought almost 60 percent of TAMP from MDM-Bank, which claimed to have bought it from investors "who are not well known in Russia" ("Konflikt vokrug" 2003; Borisova 2003).

As in the case of Ilim Pulp, however, the original management team at TAMP fought back and won. Although the Agros team took over TAMP by force in March 2003, the Moscow oblast arbitration court ruled on July 7 that Agros needed to return the factory to the old management. The court reversed itself two days later, but the TAMP team brought its own armed guards on July 10 and took the plant back (Borisova 2003). Agros appealed to the federal prosecutor's office, but in September the Moscow oblast court reiterated its demand that Agros return the shares in TAMP to TAMP-kholding ("Konflikt vokrug" 2003). Finally, in February 2004 Agros seemed to give up, hiring Halic Investment to sell off its stake in TAMP (Vysshii arbitrazhnyi sud 2004). The scuffle was hardly an unambiguous demonstration of the rule of law, but it again indicated that second-tier groups had found another weapon to add to their arsenals.

NEW SCENE, SAME PLAY

Russian voucher privatization, agricultural de-collectivization, and loans-for-shares auctions were long over by 2005, but the struggle for property was not. Not even the positive macroeconomic performance after 1998, the election of Vladimir Putin in 2000, or the president's crack-down in the middle of his first term signaled an end to the process, because they altered the context in which it took place rather than the underlying forces that drove it. A diverse cast of industrial and agricultural business groups still perceived incentives to acquire property for reasons beyond its likely impact on profit. Even if some groups were ready to end the struggle, they could not be sure that the state or other competitors would acquiesce.

The most important "lurkers"—groups that lay just at the edge of observers' field of view—were the second-tier groups that stood ready to make the leap to national prominence if the circumstances were right. Most obviously, Ilim Pulp, which had defeated Deripaska twice, controlled a large part of the timber industry and clearly enjoyed enough administrative support to make the courts work in its favor. The group hovered just outside the upper echelon of political and economic power. Its competitor in the timber sector, Titan, also seemed capable of major activity (Butrin 2002). Elsewhere in the economy, Mezhprombank owned shares in a wide range of firms, including coal enterprises, the Belye Nochi and Aki-Otyr oil companies, the St. Petersburg shipbuilder Severnaia verf, and the holding company New Programs and Concepts (Pronina 2004). In addition, Mezhprombank seemed to enjoy close ties to the Putin administration (Kolesnichenko, Pivovarova, and Tseplyaev 2002). Other groups were in similar positions, and they were poised to seize property when it became available.

In addition, after well over a decade of ownership reform, the state still owned enormous chunks of desirable property, including a significant stake in Magnitogorsk Metallurgical Combine (MMK), a large share of Sviazinvest, and the assets of the Railways Ministry; and planned sales of those resources promised to shake up the Russian world of ownership yet again. One company whose reorganization seemed likely to have a great effect on the political economy of the country was Unified Energy System. The sprawling electricity generator and distributor affected virtually every household and business in the country, and arguments over the theory and practice of restructuring it continued to rage under Putin. In September 2002 Chubais had finally offered three pledges with enough sincerity to satisfy many investors. First, he would not sell any UES assets for less than market value; second, no property would be exchanged for loans; and third, existing UES shareholders would receive pro-rated stakes in any companies spun out of UES. Given Chubais's role in earlier backroom privatization deals, and given the rumor at the time that RusAl stood to receive a large stake in a hydropower plant in Siberia for about 1 percent of what UES had invested in it, the assurance was essential for discussions of reorganization to proceed (Startseva 2002). Based on those discussions, a new law on the electricity industry and a new version of the UES restructuring plan received government approval in 2003 (Kramer 2003). Under the plan, UES would spin off its genera-tors into about ten separate companies and distribute stakes in them among its current shareholders. The federal government would admin-ister UES's large-scale transmission capacity, while low-voltage transmis-sion systems would remain under the control of the smaller-scale regional generators. The state would eventually sell off its shares in the new, large generating companies and begin to deregulate the electricity industry.

Even as participants debated and prepared for the reorganization, however, well-placed actors tried to grab what assets they could. Regional governments sought to pry large-scale generators out of UES before they were incorporated into the spin-off companies. In Khakassia, where the Saiano-Shushinskaia Hydroelectric Plant played such a large role in sus-taining the aluminum company SaAZ, the governor pursued several legal gambits to take over the generator (Kramer 2003, 3). In addition, several leading economic groups—including Gazprom, MDM, Interros, and Evrazkholding—won seats on the UES board of directors in 2004 ("Gazprom" 2004). Long before issues of how best to regulate an elec-tricity market could be decided, the Russian state and major economic actors would fight over the pieces of the system itself.

Property in Russia thus continued to offer offensive and defensive muscle in conflicts with other economic players, as well as potential access to political assistance. In this context even major legislative reforms, financial shocks, or leadership changes were unlikely to change the fundamental dynamic of the system. Early in Putin's second term, the economic groups at the top of the system struggled to regain their footing, while a varied collection of second-tier groups lay spread out across the country. The Russian economy continued to grow, but the fundamental question was still whether entrepreneurs could shift their attention from a struggle for property to a competition for customers. In 2005, despite all the changes, it was far from clear that they could.

CHAPTER 8

FACE FORWARD

Lessons for Understanding Change

In analyzing political events, most people have a tendency to see today in terms of what they expect tomorrow. How significant are Putin's moves to arrogate even more power to himself? What do individual acts of violence mean for future developments in Iraq or Afghanistan? How should we interpret any particular law on economic reform in postcommunist states? Our answers often depend on what we expect to come next: whether more power grabs or a resolution of real problems in Russia; rising or declining unrest in U.S.-occupied territories; or a coherent or perverted market economy in a developing country. That tendency, in turn, may foster a search for "silver bullet" solutions to problems. If we are already incorporating the outcome into our analysis, then there must be a straightforward path to that outcome, and disappointments along the way must be due to ill-conceived strategies or ill-motivated resistance.

The central lesson of this study, however, is that today's conflicts produce tomorrow's resolutions, not the other way around. Furthermore, in Russia those resolutions are likely to be a long time coming, given the complexity of the current situation. Major reforms are possible, but they are unlikely to resolve the problem rapidly, and they will certainly bring unexpected—and often undesired—results.

These insights are derived from a particular theoretical and methodological approach to the study of property redistribution. The theoretical framework emphasizes the possibility of a wide variety of outcomes from any particular starting point. It also encourages the analyst to look inside the distribution of power and opportunity at any given time for sources of change, while remaining attentive to differences in the political and economic environment over time and across sectors.[1] Methodologically, I have relied on a detailed examination of leading actors and their resources and constraints in order to make claims about the broader processes at work.[2] This concluding chapter highlights several areas where this approach might shed light on complex and evolving processes of political and economic development.

PROPERTY IN RUSSIA

The wrenching changes of the late twentieth and early twenty-first centuries were not simply part of a necessary transition that laid a foundation for growth and then ceased to affect Russian development. Rather, they represented an unbridled competition over real assets that continued to shape the Russian political and economic landscape well into the Putin era. In each period of its development after the fall of the Soviet Union, the Russian system continued to change, and each new transformation carried implications for the ongoing redistribution of assets in the country. Recently, the most obvious changes have concentrated more and more formal power in the hands of Vladimir Putin. Legislative elections at the end of 2003 returned a parliament even more deferential to Putin's wishes than before, and no one seriously considered the possibility that he would lose reelection in March 2004. Indeed, he appointed his new prime minister and cabinet before the elections. In September of that year, in the wake of the horrifying terrorist attack on a school in southern Russia, he further strengthened his position by acquiring the power to appoint and dismiss governors and by changing electoral rules for the lower house in ways likely to benefit parties affiliated with him.[3] As these and future reforms work their way through the

1. This approach draws heavily on the historical-institutional school of political analysis. In addition to the works cited earlier, see Krasner's (1984) concept of "punctuated equilibrium," although I place greater emphasis on the conflict that can occur even during periods of "equilibrium."

2. In this way, the book shares characteristics with an expanding group of focused, empirically driven investigations of post-Soviet Russia. See, among others, Stoner-Weiss 1997 on regional political economies; Sperling 1999 on women; Christensen 1999 and Crowley 1997 on workers; Woodruff 1999 on monetary consolidation; Johnson 2000 on banks; Wegren 1998a and Allina-Pisano 2002 on rural change; and Volkov 2002 on organized crime.

3. The glaring exception to Putin's string of victories in gathering power to himself is Chechnya, where his "get tough" policy has so far proved singularly unsuccessful.

system, and as events like the 2008 presidential election come and go, they are likely to produce new rules governing ownership and control of property.

Analysts should not seek in any of these changes, however, a final hardening of property rights that would produce the constant but unspectacular redistribution of assets characteristic of developed capitalist economies. Indeed, the concept of "strengthening property rights" seems weak when applied to the real world. In general, it is almost impossible to measure the strength of property rights outside of the results they are supposed to produce, making discussions of the security of property rights highly speculative. If ownership remains unchallenged for a period of time, observers begin to assume that the rules of the game are stable, but when a prominent company is attacked, the structure of the system as a whole comes into question.

More concretely, such analyses often overemphasize the role of the state in establishing and maintaining the new rules. While there are multiple reasons why competitors may not seek each other's assets— including shared interests, network ties, or lack of opportunity[4]—talk of "strengthening property rights" tends to focus almost exclusively on the state's ability to enforce those rights. Furthermore, in practice such investigations frequently highlight state challenges to ownership while ignoring private competition over resources, which makes their analyses unnecessarily narrow. In the Russian case, even if Putin were to transform the central government into an effective tool of impartial law enforcement—itself a task of Herculean proportions—using it to bring all the participants in the conflict over assets to heel at the same time would be an extraordinary feat.

A more fruitful approach, therefore, is to understand the multiple important actors in the system and their motives and resources for action. Doing so helps explain the persistent nature of the struggle for property and offers a better way of thinking about how it might evolve in the future. Players in an uncertain environment will be unlikely to pursue or submit to universal enforcement of rules unless none of them believes that he or she would have an advantage over rivals in a one-on-one conflict. With so many actors, however, at so many levels of the system, and with such fluid circumstances for each, such a "balance of fear" seems unlikely to develop all on its own. Too many decisions could disrupt the equilibrium.

4. See also Woodruff 2004.

If stability is unlikely to emerge without some sort of guiding hand, then perhaps the market's invisible one could provide it. The idea of "mobsters going legit" appeals to some part of our imagination. If corrupt business leaders realize they can make more money, or dramatically reduce risks to themselves and those they care about, by operating under established rules of the game, then maybe they will do so. For example, perhaps the appeal of gaining access to foreign capital will pressure oligarchs to become more trustworthy business partners. In practice, however, such pressures are often at work on only a handful of actors at any particular time, and the incentives to cheat when the market is the only enforcer remain high.

The developments most likely to attenuate the struggle, therefore, may be those that foster a piecemeal resolution, beginning with explicit agreements among two or three players in the game. If, for example, second-tier oligarchs and regional governments could agree on general shared interests or even stumble into a fortuitous distribution of power, they could conceivably commit to universal rules governing future conflicts over property. From such a starting point, the agreement might expand to include other players over time. Even in that case, however, there would be no guarantee that such smaller truces would be expanded, and players outside the agreement would almost certainly continue to uncover methods of takeover that went well beyond the normal mergers and acquisitions practices of developed capitalism. Furthermore, if one of the participants in the agreement were the central state, which in Russia faces few limitations on its policy-making authority, the other parties would simply have to hope it did not use its power arbitrarily.

Perhaps the best observers can hope for, then, is an analysis that helps explain why the Russian struggle for property moves from phase to phase rather than to a stable system of regularized capitalist competition. Recognizing the range of key players chasing property in post-Soviet Russia, as well as the environment in which they operate, sheds light on how this or that player can appear dominant in one period but nonetheless be unseated in future rounds of asset redistribution. In particular, it shows that participants who control bottlenecks or political resources in one stage of the struggle for property have a decided advantage over those who do not, but they are still vulnerable to takeover attempts from opponents who exploit the system's pressure points. Eliminating or regularizing access to such areas will require a great deal of time and no small amount of good fortune.

POLITICAL ECONOMIES UNDER CONSTRUCTION

The questions of political and economic transformation that periodically motivate analysts and policy makers have been on the front burner since the fall of the Soviet bloc, and recent events in the Middle East have only raised interest levels further. The lessons of this study therefore have relevance beyond Russia's borders. In general, they speak to the danger of offering explanations or prescriptions based on expectations for the future, rather than a nuanced understanding of the past and present. Similarly, they warn against interpretations that see societies moving only forward or backward along a clear path toward that expected future.

That a unidimensional picture of economic transformation clouds understanding should be clear by now. The problem may be compounded, however, if we conflate economic and political change. First, that decision leads us to see political reform only as moving toward or away from an idealized democracy, rather than creating a new regime that incorporates long-standing institutions and practices from society. Whether past characteristics are largely democratic or authoritarian, analysts must be prepared to study them for what they are, rather than for what they might become. Second, and potentially even more significant for analysis and advice, equating marketization with democratization simply confuses two separate processes, one allowing the free flow of goods and the other allowing the open competition of ideas. Pursuing one goal may facilitate achieving the other, but it may not. To insist on a particular set of economic policies from the outset is to risk undercutting democratic institutions before they are firmly established. To be sure, in today's world most opposition groups in authoritarian states demand some form of economic liberalization along with political opening, so the two processes need not always conflict with each other. Even in the best of circumstances, however, competing political groups' images of "more open" economies may vary widely, and the countries that have most successfully liberalized their politics and economies simultaneously are those that have allowed the democratic process to shape and reshape economic reform policies.[5]

Regardless of the particular goal of the transformation project, advisors and policy makers are bound to be surprised and frustrated if they are guided largely by their expectations about the future. Whether the

5. See, for example, Kitschelt 1992; Fish 1998; Orenstein 2001; Bunce 2001.

goal is to create a new political system, transform the institutions of tax collection, establish new rules for allocating housing, or something else, the myriad actors affected by the change and the range of strategies they employ to survive it will almost invariably prevent the reforms from producing their expected results. Some of the deviations may themselves represent acceptable outcomes, but even when they do not, observers should beware the temptation to blame them on malicious resistance from defenders of the old ways. Some unintended outcomes may not even stem from conscious resistance at all. In the complex environment of a functioning society, policies change dramatically from inception to passage to implementation, as government officials and their citizens simply adapt them to reality with little thought of defiance.[6] Furthermore, even direct challenges to new rules can result from more than simple opposition to the long-term vision of the reformer. Rational self-preservation or even a different picture of a better society could just as easily distort reforms in practice.

Rather than simply labeling all opposition "hardline" and all opponents "holdovers," therefore, thoughtful analysis requires that we pay attention to the structural attributes of the system that affect the motives and strategies of participants in the conflict. Who are the most important players in the system, and what resources do they have at their disposal? Resistance is a certainty. The only question is what form it will take, and that depends on the incentives and opportunities the environment provides.

---

6. Scott (1998) explores the disastrous outcomes that can result when governments do *not* adapt their reforms to the realities of daily life.

REFERENCES

Common abbreviations in citations or references:

AFP   Agence France Presse
EBRD   European Bank for Reconstruction and Development
IEWS   Institute for East-West Studies
JRL   *Johnson's Russia List* (www.cdi.org/russia/johnson)
OMRI   Open Media Research Institute
RFE/RL   Radio Free Europe/Radio Liberty
RRR   *Russian Regional Report* (www.isn.ethz.ch/news/rrr)

Sources

Abalkin, Leonid, *Neispol'zovannyi shans: poltora goda v pravitel'stve* (Moscow: Politizdat, 1991).

Abdullaev, Nabi, "TV6 Team Says It's 'Return of the Jedi,'" *Moscow Times* (June 3, 2002), via www.internews.ru/article/tv6/tv6return.html, accessed July 21, 2004.

Abramovich, N., "Nyneshnee pokolenie budet zhit'. Pri chastnoi sobstvennosti?" *MIG* (March 15, 1993).

AFP, "Russia's Oligarchs Put Business before Politics," (January 10, 2001) via *JRL*, no. 5018.

——, "Russia's Beleaguered Yukos Cuts Last Ties with Core Shareholders" (February 2, 2004a), via *JRL* no. 8045.

——, "Spectre of Bankruptcy as Yukos Told to Pay $3.5 Billion Tax Bill" (May 26, 2004b), via *JRL* no. 8225.

——, "Russia's Yukos Left Reeling after New Multi-billion Tax Claim" (July 1, 2004c), via *JRL* no. 8278.

——, "Russia Energy Merger Hits Snag amid Kremlin Bickering" (October 4, 2004d), via *JRL* no. 8394.

——, "Russia Slaps Yukos with Fresh, Potentially Fatal, Tax Claims" (November 1, 2004e), via *JRL* no. 8436.

——, "Russia Shrugs Off U.S. Court Freeze on Oil Giant Yukos Auction" (December 17, 2004f), via *JRL* no. 8504.

Ageev, Sergei, and Anastasiia Matveeva, "Smertel'nyi poluraspad," *Ekspert* (March 8, 1999): 47–51.

Agurbash, N., "Razvitie agropromyshlennykh kombinatov i ob"edinenii v RSFSR," *APK: ekonomika, upravlenie*, no. 3 (1990): 26–31.

AKSnews.ru, "OAO 'Olenegorskii gorno-obagatitel'nyi kombinat,'" Agenstvo konfliktnykh situatsii (February 17, 2003), via www.aksnews.ru/industry/25/3700.html, accessed July 15, 2004.

"Aktsionernoe obshchestvo 'Snezhka,'" *Ekonomika sel'skokhoziaistvennykh i pererabatyvaiushchikh predpriiatii*, no. 11 (1997): 2–9.

Aleshin, Aleksei, "Kooperatsiia na Orlovshchine," *Ekonomika sel'skogo khoziaistva Rossii*, no. 4 (1998): 4.

Allina-Pisano, Jessica, "Reorganization and Its Discontents: A Case Study in Voronezh Oblast'," in *Rural Reform in Post-Soviet Russia*, ed. Stephen K. Wegren and David J. O'Brien (Washington, DC, and Baltimore: Woodrow Wilson Center and Johns Hopkins University Press, 2002).

Andreev, Anatolii, "Prezident kak klassnyi rukovoditel'," *Russkii predprinimatel'* (October 3, 2002), via www.ruspred.ru/arh/06/6.htm, accessed August 9, 2004.

Andreev, V., N. Chapanova, and V. Brel', "Effektivnost' raboty mnogoprofil'nogo predpriiatiia," *APK: ekonomika, upravlenie*, no. 3 (2000): 57–61.

"AOOT 'Molochnyi zavod "Volgogradskii,"'" *Ekonomika sel'skokhoziaistvennykh i pererabatyvaiushchikh predpriiatii*, no. 7 (1996): 1–8.

"AOOT 'Volgogradskaia agropromyshlennaia finansovaia korporatsiia,'" *Ekonomika sel'skokhoziaistvennykh i pererabatyvaiushchikh predpriiatii*, no. 8 (1996): 40–45.

"AOZT molochnyi zavod 'Balakovskii,'" *Ekonomika sel'skokhoziaistvennykh i pererabatyvaiushchikh predpriiatii*, no. 8 (1995): 2–11.

Aris, Ben, "Picking Up and Passing On the Pieces of Privatization," *Moscow Times* (November 25, 2002).

Arkhangel'skaia, Natal'ia, Mikhail Kozyrev, Tat'iana Lysova, and Anatolii Sautin, "Utruska oligarkhov," *Ekpert* (February 8, 1999), via ISI Emerging Markets (www.securities.com).

Arvedlund, Erin E., "Yukos Faces Tax Charge As Merger Rift Widens," *New York Times* (December 31, 2003).

Aslund, Anders, *Gorbachev's Struggle for Economic Reform: The Soviet Reform Process, 1985–88* (Ithaca, NY: Cornell University Press, 1989).

——, *How Russia Became a Market Economy* (Washington, DC: Brookings Institution, 1995).

——, *Building Capitalism: The Transformation of the Former Soviet Bloc* (Cambridge: Cambridge University Press, 2002).

Aslund, Anders, and Peter Boone, "Russia's Surprise Economic Success," *Financial Times* (October 9, 2002): 19.

Association of Financial–Industrial Groups, "Svedeniia o finansovo–promyshlennykk gruppakh, vnesennykh v reestr FPG RF," Moscow, mimeo (1997).

Ayton, Richard, "YUKOS Production Unit Heads for Fire Sale," *Reuters* (July 20, 2004), via *JRL* no. 8299.

Baker, Peter, "To Russia, With Capital," *Washington Post* (May 14, 2001), via *JRL* no. 3255.

——, "Russia Targets Another Mogul," *Washington Post* (March 4, 2004a).

——, "Russia State Gas, Oil Firms Merge," *Washington Post* (September 15, 2004b).

Baker, Peter, and Susan B. Glasser, "Russia Freezes Stock of Oil Giant," *Washington Post* (October 31, 2003).

Balcerowicz, Leszek, *Socialism, Capitalism, Transformation* (Budapest: Central European University Press, 1995).

Baldwin, David A., *Economic Statecraft* (Princeton, NJ: Princeton University Press, 1985).

Ball, Alan, *Russia's Last Capitalists: The Nepmen, 1921–1929* (Berkeley: University of California Press, 1987).

Balzer, Harley, "The Putin Thesis and Russian Energy Policy," *Post-Soviet Affairs* 21 (July–September 2005): 210–25.

Banerjee, Neela, "Another Setback for BP Amoco in Its Investment in Russia," *New York Times* (October 23, 1999).

Barnes, Andrew, "What's the Difference? Industrial Privatisation and Agricultural Land Reform in Russia, 1990–1996," *Europe-Asia Studies* 50 (July 1998): 843–57.

———, "Property, Power, and the Presidency: Property-rights Reform and Russian Executive-Legislative Relations, 1990–1999," *Communist and Post-Communist Studies* 34 (March 2001): 39–61.

———, "Comparative Theft: Context and Choice in the Hungarian, Czech, and Russian Transformations, 1989–2000," *East European Politics and Societies* 17 (Summer 2003): 533–65.

"BasEl Tries To Enter Ilim Mill," *Moscow Times* (December 19, 2002).

Bazyl'chik, Svetlana, "V novoi partii 'Sfera' stavit na kupnuiu mast'," *Delovoe Povolzh'e*, no. 10 (1998): 3.

Behar, Richard, "Capitalism in a Cold Climate," *Fortune* (June 12, 2000).

Beissinger, Mark R., *Nationalist Mobilization and the Collapse of the Soviet State* (Cambridge: Cambridge University Press, 2002).

Beissinger, Mark R., and Crawford Young, eds., *Beyond State Crisis? Postcolonial Africa and Post-Soviet Eurasia in Comparative Perspective* (Washington, DC, and Baltimore: Woodrow Wilson Center Press and Johns Hopkins University Press, 2002).

Belin, Laura, "Will TV-6 Go Out with a Bang or a Whimper?" *RFE/RL Russian Political Weekly* 1 (December 10, 2001).

———, "The Russian Media in the 1990s," in *Russia after Communism*, ed. Rick Fawn and Stehen White (London: Frank Cass, 2002).

Belokopytova, Liubov', Natal'ia Alekseeva, and Valentina Trifonova, "Integratsionnye sviazi v molochnom podkomplekse APK Povolzh'ia," *Ekonomika sel'skogo khoziaistva Rossii*, no. 8 (1998): 5.

Belton, Catherine, "Sibneft, TNK Snap Up Slavneft for $1.8 Billion," *Moscow Times* (December 19, 2002).

———, "Khodorkovsky Armed With $1.3 Billion," *Moscow Times* (September 10, 2003).

———, "Menatep Sues Russia for $28 Billion," *Moscow Times* (February 9, 2005).

Belousov, N., and A. Golovin, "Fermerskoe khoziaistvo—dostoinyi konkurent krupnogo proizvodstva," *APK: ekonomika, upravlenie*, no. 1 (1998): 61–66.

Berger, Mikhail, "Goskomimushchestvo gotovitsia k peredache imushchestva," *Izvestiia* (March 27, 1992).

Berliner, Joseph S., *Factory and Manager in the USSR* (Cambridge, MA: Harvard University Press, 1957).

Bezmenov, Aleksandr, "Formula Kislova," *Rossiiskaia gazeta* (December 25, 2002), via www.rg.ru/prilog/agrar/02-12-25/5.shtm, accessed February 20, 2004.

Bialer, Seweryn, *Stalin's Successors: Leadership, Stability, and Change in the Soviet Union* (Cambridge: Cambridge University Press, 1980).

Binyon, Michael, "Russian in a Hurry Ignites Oil Revolution," *The Times (London)* (February 2, 2002).

Black, Bernard, Reinier Kraakman, and Anna Tarassova, "Russian Privatization and Corporate Governance: What Went Wrong?" *Stanford Law Review* 52 (2000): 1731–1808.

Blanchard, Olivier, Maxim Boycko, Marek Dobrowski, Rudiger Dornbusch, Richard Layard, and Andrei Shleifer, *Post-Communist Reform: Pain and Progress* (Cambridge, MA: MIT Press, 1993).

Blasi, Joseph R., Maya Kroumova, and Douglas Kruse, *Kremlin Capitalism: Privatizing the Russian Economy* (Ithaca, NY: Cornell University Press, 1997).

Block, Kevin P., "Depoliticizing Ownership: An Examination of the Property Reform Debate and the New Law on Ownership in the USSR," *Berkeley-Duke Occasional Papers on the Second Economy in the USSR* no. 26 (March 1991).

Bloomberg News, "Probe into Dealings of Aluminum Baron Reopened in Russia," *Washington Post* (July 16, 2003).

——, "Yukos Says Oil Output May Stop, Bank Accounts Frozen" (July 1, 2004a), via *JRL* no. 8278.

——, "VimpelCom Shares Retreat," *International Herald Tribune* (July 13, 2004b), via www.iht.com/articles/529121.htm, accessed August 8, 2004.

——, "Russia: ConocoPhillips Raises Lukoil Stake," *New York Times* (December 24, 2004c).

Bochkarev, Andrei, and Vera Krasnova, "Razumnyi korporativnyi egoizm," *Ekspert* (November 16, 1998), via ISI Emerging Markets (www.securities.com).

Bogatykh, Mariia, Tat'iana Gurova, Tigran Oganesian, and Dmitrii Sivakov, "Aliuminievaia kost'," *Ekspert* (April 10, 2000): 10–14.

Bondarenko, Vladimir, " 'Chuzhie zdes' ne khodiat,' " interview with Vladimir Polevanov, *Zavtra* (August 3, 1999), via www.zavtra.ru/cgi/veil/data/zavtra/99/296/31.html, accessed November 25, 2003.

Boone, Peter, and Denis Rodionov, "Rent Seeking in Russia and the CIS," paper prepared for EBRD tenth anniversary conference (December 2001).

Boreiko, Alexander, "There Is a New Billionaire in Town," *Moscow Times* (July 16, 2002).

Borisova, Yevgenia, "Investigators Wrap Up Inquiry Into Meat Plant," *Moscow Times* (August 12, 2003).

Boulton, Leyla, "Volga Car Sell-Off Reveals $30M Abuse," *Financial Times* (February 23, 1994).

Boycko, Maxim, Andrei Shleifer, and Robert Vishny, *Privatizing Russia* (Cambridge, MA: MIT Press, 1995).

"BP Seals Historic TNK Tie-Up, Minus $600M," *Moscow Times* (June 27, 2003).

Brady, Rose, *Kapitalizm: Russia's Struggle to Free its Economy* (New Haven: Yale University Press, 1999).

Breslauer, George W., *Khrushchev and Brezhnev as Leaders: Building Authority in Soviet Politics* (London: Allen and Unwin, 1982).

Brom, Karla, and Mitchell Orenstein, "The Privatised Sector in the Czech Republic: Government and Bank Control in a Transitional Economy," *Europe-Asia Studies* 46 (1994): 893–928.

Brooks, Karen M., "Soviet Agriculture's Halting Reform," *Problems of Communism* 39 (March–April 1990): 29–41.

Brooks, Karen M., and Zvi Lerman, *Land Reform and Farm Restructuring in Russia* (Washington, DC: World Bank, 1994).

Buckley, Cynthia J., "Back to the Collective: Production and Consumption on a Siberian Collective Farm," in *Rediscovering Russia in Asia: Siberia and the Russian Far East*, ed. Stephen Kotkin and David Wolff (Armonk, NY: M. E. Sharpe, 1995).

Buckley, Neil, "Questions Remain over Russian Oil Giant," *Financial Times* (February 4, 2005), via *JRL* no. 9048.

Builov, Maksim, and Petr Rushailo, "Strazha so vzlomom," *Den'gi* (October 13, 1999): 13–16.

Bunce, Valerie, *Do New Leaders Make a Difference? Executive Succession and Public Policy under Capitalism and Socialism* (Princeton, NJ: Princeton University Press, 1981).

——, *Subversive Institutions: The Design and the Destruction of Socialism and the State* (Cambridge: Cambridge University Press, 1999).

——, "Democratization and Economic Reform," *Annual Review of Political Science* 4 (2001): 43–65.

Bunich, Pavel, "'Chernye spiski' predprinimatelei," *Literaturnaia gazeta* (February 27, 1991).

Bunin, Igor', "Vlast' i biznes: etapy bol'shogo puti," www.politcom.ru/2002/aaa_c_b3.php (2002a).

——, "Oligarkhi idut v regiony," *Delovoe Povolzh'e* (February 13–19, 2002b).

Burawoy, Michael, and Kathryn Hendley, "Between *Perestroika* and Privatisation: Divided Strategies and Political Crisis in a Soviet Enterprise," *Soviet Studies* 44 (1992): 371–402.

Burawoy, Michael, and Pavel Krotov, "The Soviet Transition from Socialism to Capitalism: Worker Control and Economic Bargaining in the Wood Industry," *American Sociological Review* 57 (February 1992): 16–38.

Butrin, Dmitrii, "Komu prinadlezhit Rossia: Chernaia metallurgiia-2001," *Kommersant-Vlast'* (September 19, 2001), via subscribe.ru/archive/people.severstal/200109/26010616.text or www.compromat.ru/main/top50/chernmet01.htm, accessed December 22, 2003.

——, "Komu prinadlezhit Rossiia–lesnaia promyshlennost'," *Kommersant-Vlast'* (January 29, 2002), via www.kommersant.com/page.asp?id=307741 and www.compromat.ru/main/top50/les01.htm; accessed July 14, 2004.

Butterfield, Jim, "Raion Agroindustrial Associations in Soviet Agriculture," in *Communist Agriculture: Farming in the Soviet Union and Eastern Europe*, ed. Karl-Eugen Wädekin (London: Routledge, 1990).

Cai, Hongbin and Daniel Treisman, "State-Corroding Federalism," *Journal of Public Economics* 88 (March 2004): 819–43.

Cameron, Doug, Arkady Ostrovsky, and Stefan Wagstyl, "Conoco to Acquire Minority Stake in Lukoil for $2 Billion," *Financial Times* (September 30, 2004).

Chazan, Guy, "Companies Turn Collectives into Profitable Businesses," *Wall Street Journal* (February 15, 2001), via *JRL* no. 5096.

——, "Pulp-and-Paper Mill Shows Flaws of Russia's Capitalism," *Wall Street Journal* (August 12, 2002), via *JRL* no. 6397.

Chekmareva, E. N., "Rol' bankov v integratsii bankovskogo i promyshlennogo kapitala," *Den'gi i kredit*, no. 7 (1999): 17–22.

Cherniaev, A. A., "Sovershenstvovanie strukturnykh preobrazovanii v sel'skom khoziaistve Povolzh'ia," Doctoral dissertation, Vserossiiskii nauchno-issledovatel'skii institut ekonomiki, truda i upravleniia v sel'skom khoziastve (Moscow, 1994).

——, "Razvitie vertikal'noi integratsii v Povolzh'e," in *Problemy koopiratsii i integratsii v APK Rossiiskoi Federatsii (Tezisy dokladov vserossiiskoi konferentsii 20–22 avgusta 1996 goda)*, ed. Anatolii Antonovich Shut'kov, Vladimir Vasil'evich Kuznetsov, and Aleksandr Nikolaevich Tarasov (Rostov-on-Don: Poligraf, 1996): 24–28.

Cherniaev, A. A., and Liubov' Belokopytova, "Miasoproduktovyi podkompleks Povolzh'ia," *APK: ekonomika, upravlenie*, no. 6 (1999): 26–30.

Chirkov, Leonid, "Novye strasti: FPG stremiatsia k vlasti," *Parlamentskaia gazeta* (March 21, 2002).

Chotiner, Barbara Ann, "The Agricultural Ministries," in *Executive Power and Soviet Politics: The Rise and Decline of the Soviet State*, ed. Eugene Huskey (Armonk, NY: M. E. Sharpe, 1992).

Christensen, Paul T., "Industrial Russia under the New Regimes: Labor Relations and Democratization, 1985–1993" (Ph.D. dissertation, Princeton University, 1993).

———, *Russia's Workers in Transition: Labor, Management, and the State under Gorbachev and Yeltsin* (Dekalb: Northern Illinois University Press, 1999).

Chubais, Anatolii, "Plan restrukturizatsii RAO 'EES Rossii,'" *Rynok tsennykh bumag*, no. 9 (2000): 36–39 (from his presentation at a meeting of the company's board of directors at the Kremlin, April 4, 2000).

Clark, Torrey, "Chips Fly in Fight Over Paper Mill," *Moscow Times* (August 6, 2002a).

———, "Ilim Pulp: Court Overturns $95M Decision," *Moscow Times* (November 5, 2002b).

———, "Ilim Pulp Sues Tycoons in Top London Court," *Moscow Times* (January 15, 2003).

Clarke, Simon, "Privatisation and the Development of Capitalism in Russia," in *What about the Workers? Workers and the Transition to Capitalism in Russia*, ed. Simon Clarke, Peter Fairbrother, Michael Burawoy, and Pavel Krotov (London: Verso, 1993).

———, ed., *The Russian Enterprise in Transition: Case Studies* (Cheltenham, UK: Edward Elgar, 1996).

Clarke, Simon, Peter Fairbrother, Vadim Borisov, and Petr Bizyukov, "The Privatisation of Industrial Enterprises in Russia: Four Case-studies," *Europe-Asia Studies* 46 (1994): 179–214.

Cohen, Stephen F., *Bukharin and the Bolshevik Revolution: A Political Biography, 1888–1938* (New York: Knopf, 1973).

———, *Rethinking the Soviet Experience: Politics and History since 1917* (New York: Oxford University Press, 1985).

Colton, Timothy J., *The Dilemma of Reform in the Soviet Union* (New York: Council on Foreign Relations, 1984).

Conquest, Robert, ed., *Agricultural Workers in the USSR* (New York: Praeger, 1968).

———, *The Harvest of Sorrow: Soviet Collectivization and the Terror-Famine* (New York: Oxford University Press, 1986).

Cook, Edward C., "Uncertainties over Reform: Decentralization or Recentralization?" in *Communist Agriculture: Farming in the Soviet Union and Eastern Europe*, ed. Karl-Eugen Wädekin (London: Routledge, 1990).

Cook, Linda J., "Workers in the Russian Federation: Responses to the Postcommunist Transition, 1989–1993," *Communist and Post-Communist Studies* 28 (March 1995): 13–42.

Corwin, Julie A., "Government Poised to Nationalize SBS-Agro Bank," *RFE/RL Newsline* 2 (31 August 1998a).

———, "Government Offers Farmers Assistance," *RFE/RL Newsline* 2 (5 October 1998b).

———, "Central Bank to Save SBS-Agro," *RFE/RL Newsline* 2 (14 October 1998c), Part 1.

———, "Yeltsin Cancels Purneftegaz Sale," *RFE/RL Newsline* 2 (October 15, 1998d).

———, "Menatep, Most, SBS-Agro Make Bail-Out List," *RFE/RL Newsline* 2 (16 November 1998e).

———, "Rosneft Becoming Whole Again?" *RFE/RL Newsline* 2 (November 29, 1998f).

———, "Sidanko on Verge of Bankruptcy," *RFE/RL Newsline* 3 (February 2, 1999a).

———, "Sibneft Raided . . . after Berezovskii Expresses Concern about Future Government Repression," *RFE/RL Newsline* 3 (February 3, 1999b).

———, "Oil Companies Grumble about Tender in Far North," *RFE/RL Newsline* 5 (March 15, 2001).

Cottrell, Robert, "The Oligarchs Take Over Yet Again," *Financial Times* (September 11, 2001a).

———, "Russia Plans to Ease Foreign Currency Rules for Exporters," *Financial Times* (July 3, 2001b).

———, "Fuelled by the Frontier Spirit," *Financial Times* (March 12, 2002a).

———, "Gazprom Slides after Tax Threat," *Financial Times* (March 13, 2002b).

———, "Russia's Rising Tycoons," *Financial Times* (August 6, 2002c).

Cottrell, Robert, and Stefan Wagstyl, "Introducing a New Kind of Russian Oligarch," *Financial Times* (April 17, 2002).

Craumer, Peter R., "Regional Patterns of Agricultural Reforms in Russia," *Post-Soviet Geography* 35 (1994): 329–51.

Criscione, Valeria, and Andrew Jack, "Yukos Chief Tries to Show He Is No Wolf in Sheep's Clothing," *Financial Times* (October 25, 2001).

Crowley, Stephen, *Hot Coal, Cold Steel: Russian and Ukrainian Workers from the End of the Soviet Union to the Post-Communist Transformations* (Ann Arbor: University of Michigan Press, 1997).

Csaki, Csaba, John Nash, Vera Matusevich, and Holger Kray, *Food and Agricultural Policy in Russia: Progress to Date and the Road Forward* (Washington, DC: World Bank, 2002).

Daniels, Robert V., *The Stalin Revolution: Foundations of Soviet Totalitarianism*, 2d ed. (Lexington, MA: Heath, 1972).

Daniszewski, John, "Struggling Collective Leases Fields in Return for Capital, Technology," *Los Angeles Times* (May 2, 2001), via *JRL* no. 5235.

Davies, R. W., *The Industrialisation of Soviet Russia*, 3 vols. (Cambridge, MA: Harvard University Press, 1980–89).

Deliagin, Mikhail, "Zakon na vyrost," *Rossiiskaia gazeta* (January 17, 1991): 2.

———, "Zalogovye auktsiony: tseli i dostizheniia uchastnikov," *Ekspert* (April 15, 1996).

Delyagin [Deliagin], Mikhail, "Beating the Sword of Bankruptcy," *Moscow Times* (September 24, 2003), via *JRL* no. 7334.

Dement'ev, V., "Aktivizatsiia strukturno-investitsionnoi politiki i FPG," *Ekonomist*, no. 9 (1996): 44–51.

———, "Ofitsial'nye FPG: kontseptual'nye orientiry i real'nye tendentsii," in *Finansovo-promyshlennye gruppy i konglomeraty v ekonomike i politike sovremennoi Rossii*, ed. Ia. Sh. Pappe (Moscow: Tsentr politicheskikh tekhnologii, 1997).

Denin, N. V., E. P. Chirkov, N. A. Sokolov, and A. S. Parfenova, "Vertikal'naia integratsiia v ptitsevodstve v ramkakh AO," *Ekonomika sel'skokhoziaistvennykh i pererabatyvaiushchikh predpriiatii*, no. 1 (1999): 13–15.

Denisova, Natal'ia, "... A biudzhet tozhe rozit sudom," *Delovoe Povolzh'e*, no. 1 (1998): 4.

Deriabina, M., "Restrukturizatsiia rossiiskoi ekonomiki cherez peredel sobstvennosti i kontrolia," *Voprosy ekonomiki*, no. 10 (2001): 55–69.

"Deripaska Buys Up Other Half of RusAl," *Moscow Times* (September 25, 2003).

Desai, Padma, "Russian Privatization: A Comparative Perspective," *The Harriman Review* (August 1995) via www.columbia.edu/~pd5/privatization.pdf, accessed August 20, 2003.

Desai, Padma, and Todd Idson, *Work without Wages: Russia's Nonpayment Crisis* (Cambridge, MA: MIT Press, 2000).

Doronin, Semen, "Bankrot po sobstvennomu zhelaniiu," *Ekspert* (April 29, 2002): 22–23.

Dow Jones/Associated Press, "Russian Tycoon Is Suspect in Stock Theft," *Washington Post* (July 3, 2003).

Drankina, Ekaterina, "Agressora berut na ispug," *Ekspert* (July 26, 1999a): 14–15.

——, "'Rezinovyi' krug zamknulsia," *Ekspert* (August 23, 1999b): 16–17.

——, "Otkryt' kingstony!" *Ekspert* (November 1, 1999c): 16–19.

——, "Nu, zdravstvui, eto ia," *Ekspert* (May 8, 2000): 34–35.

——, "Val Vavilova," *Ekspert* (March 19, 2001): 26–27.

Dynkin, A., and A. Sokolov, *Integrirovannye biznes-gruppy—proryv k modernizatsii strany* (Moscow: VShB MGU, IMEMO RAN, and ISKI RAN, 2001).

Edwards, Vincent, Gennady Polonsky, and Avgust Polonsky, *The Russian Province after Communism: Enterprise Continuity and Change* (New York: St. Martin's, 2000).

Ekiert, Grzegorz, and Stephen E. Hanson, eds., *Capitalism and Democracy in Central and Eastern Europe: Assessing the Legacy of Communist Rule* (Cambridge: Cambridge University Press, 2003).

El'diev, M., "Ekonomicheskoe regulirovanie prodovol'stvennogo obespecheniia v regione," *APK: ekonomika, upravlenie,* no. 2 (1998): 47–52.

Ericson, Richard E., "Is Russia in Transition to a Market Economy?" *Post-Soviet Affairs* 16 (January–March 2000): 18–25.

——, "Does Russia Have a 'Market Economy'?" *East European Politics and Societies* 15 (Summer 2001): 291–319.

Erlich, Alexander, *The Soviet Industrialization Debate, 1924–1928* (Cambridge, MA: Harvard University Press, 1960).

Esliamova, T., "Vaucher—na aktsiiu—vash luchshii vybor," *Volgogradskaia pravda* (February 9, 1993).

Fainsod, Merle, *How Russia Is Ruled* (Cambridge, MA: Harvard University Press, 1957).

Faulconbridge, Guy, "Rosneft Merger Hangs in Balance," *Moscow Times* (February 8, 2005a).

——, "Yukos Targets Gazprom in $20 Billion Suit," *Moscow Times* (February 14, 2005b).

——, "Indians Arrive Seeking Landmark Energy Deals," *Moscow Times* (February 22, 2005c).

Faulconbridge, Guy, Valeria Korchagina, and Catherine Belton, "Report: Yukos Value Slashed for Fire Sale," *Moscow Times* (October 15, 2004), via *JRL* no. 8411.

Feifer, Gregory, "Berezovsky's Letter Dominates News," *Moscow Times* (June 1, 2000), via *JRL* no. 4339.

Feifer, Gregory, and Igor Semenenko, "A Guide to the Oil Majors," *Moscow Times* supplement (June 20, 2000).

Filatotchev, Igor, Trevor Buck, and Mike Wright, "Privatisation and Buy-outs in the USSR," *Soviet Studies* 44 (1992): 265–82.

Filatotchev, Igor, Mike Wright, and Michael Bleaney, "Privatization, Insider Control and Managerial Entrenchment in Russia," *Economics of Transition* 7 (1999): 481–504.

Filippov, Petr, "Privatizatsiia: poisk kompromissov," *Rossiiskaia gazeta* (March 20, 1991a).

——, "Kazhdyi budet imet' to, chto okhraniaet?" *Rossiiskaia gazeta* (July 2, 1991b).

Filippov, P. A., and L. G. Dubovskaia, "Opyt preobrazovaniia miasokonservnogo kombinata v aktsionernoe obshchestvo," *Ekonomika sel'skokhoziaistvennykh i pererabatyvaiushchikh predpriiatii,* no. 4 (1994): 10–12.

"Finansovye supermarkety," interview with Nikolai Tsvetkov (president of NIKoil group) and Vladimir Sodorov (deputy chair of the board of directors for investment banking activity), *Ekspert* (April 5, 1999), via ISI Emerging Markets (www.securities.com).

Fish, M. Steven, *Democracy from Scratch: Opposition and Regime in the New Russian Revolution* (Princeton, NJ: Princeton University Press, 1995).

——, "The Determinants of Economic Reform in the Post-Communist World," *East European Politics and Societies* 12 (Winter 1998): 31–78.

Fitzpatrick, Sheila, *The Cultural Front: Power and Culture in Revolutionary Russia* (Ithaca, NY: Cornell University Press, 1992).

Fomin, D., "Formy agropromyshlennogo vzaimodeistviia," *APK: ekonomika, upravlenie*, no. 11 (1999): 50–57.

Fortescue, Stephen, "The Industrial Ministries," in *Executive Power and Soviet Politics*, ed. Eugene Huskey (Armonk, NY: M.E. Sharpe, 1992).

——, "Organization in Russian Industry: Beyond Decentralization," *RFE/RL Research Report* 50 (December 17, 1993): 35–39.

——, *Policy-Making for Russian Industry* (New York: St. Martin's, 1997).

Fraser, Hugh, "Vimpelcom: The New Yukos?" *BBC News* (March 10, 2004), via news.bbc.co.uk/1/hi/business/3533711.stm, accessed August 8, 2004.

Freeland, Chrystia, "Fears over Share Security Deter Investors in Russia," *Financial Times* (November 16, 1994).

——, *Sale of the Century: Russia's Wild Ride from Communism to Capitalism* (New York: Crown Business, 2000).

Fridman, Mikhail, Andrew Jack, and Arkady Ostrovsky, "Power Broker in Russia's Shifting Scene," *Financial Times* (August 29, 2003).

Frolov, Valentin, "Agrofirma 'Niva-Verkhov'e,'" *Ekonomika sel'skogo khoziaistva Rossii*, no. 6 (1998): 4.

Frydman, Roman, Andrzej Rapaczynski, and John S. Earle, *The Privatization Process in Russia, Ukraine, and the Baltic States* (Budapest: Central European University Press, 1993).

Frye, Timothy, *Brokers and Bureaucrats: Building Market Institutions in Russia* (Ann Arbor: University of Michigan Press, 2000).

——, "Private Protection in Russia and Poland," *American Journal of Political Science* 46 (July 2002a): 572–84.

——, "Capture or Exchange? Business Lobbying in Russia," *Europe-Asia Studies* 54 (November 2002b): 1017–36.

Frye, Timothy, and Ekaterina Zhuravskaya, "Rackets, Regulation, and the Rule of Law," *Journal of Law, Economics, and Organization* 16 (October 2000): 478–502.

Gaddy, Clifford G., and Barry W. Ickes, *Russia's Virtual Economy* (Washington, DC: Brookings Institution, 2002).

Gaidar, Egor, *Gosudarstvo i evoliutsiia* (Moscow: Evraziia, 1995).

Galuszka, Peter, "It's Like Climbing the Himalayas," *Business Week* (May 2, 1994): 106.

Galuszka, Peter, and Rose Brady, "The Battle For Russia's Wealth," *Business Week* (April 1, 1996): 50.

Gazprom, "History of the Company" (2002), via www.gazprom.com/eng/articles/article8517.shtml, accessed August 9, 2004.

"'Gazprom' beret naturoi," *Ekspert* (October 5, 1998).

"Gazprom, ESN Energy, Interros, EvrazHolding Have One Rep on RAO UES BOD Each," via www.gateway2russia.com/art.php?artid=245081andrubid=andparent=andgrandparent= (June 30, 2004), accessed July 14, 2004.

Gelbach, Scott, and Konstantin Sonin, "Businessmen Candidates: Special-Interest Politics in Weakly Institutionalized Environments," William Davidson Institute Working Papers Series, no. 733 (December 2004).

Gel'man, Vladimir, "The Rise and Fall of Federal Reform in Russia," PONARS Policy Memo no. 238, December 2001.

Gerschenkron, Alexander, *Economic Backwardness in Historical Perspective* (Cambridge, MA: Harvard University Press, 1962).

Gibson, Edward L., ed., *Federalism and Democracy in Latin America* (Baltimore: Johns Hopkins University Press, 2004).

Gill, Graeme, *The Collapse of a Single-Party System: The Disintegration of the Communist Party of the Soviet Union* (Cambridge: Cambridge University Press, 1994).

Gilpin, Robert, *The Political Economy of International Relations* (Princeton, NJ: Princeton University Press, 1987).

Glasser, Susan B., "Russia Disappointed in Sale of State Oil Company," *Washington Post* (December 19, 2002).

——, "Probe Widens to Include Russia's Richest Man," *Washington Post* (July 4, 2003a).

——, "Russian Billionaire Questioned in Stock Fraud," *Washington Post* (July 5, 2003b).

——, "Russia Says Imprisoned Tycoon's Swiss Assets Are Frozen," *Washington Post* (March 12, 2004).

Glasser, Susan B., and Peter Baker, "Russian Tycoon and Putin Critic Arrested in Raid," *Washington Post* (October 26, 2003a).

——, "Merger Unravels between Russian Oil Companies," *Washington Post* (November 29, 2003b).

Glaz'ev, S. Yu., "Privatisation of State Property in the USSR: Possible Ways and Implications, *Communist Economies and Economic Transformation*, 3 (1991).

Glushchenko, A., "Kreditnaia kooperatsiia v Volgogradskoi oblasti," *APK: ekonomika, upravlenie*, no. 4 (1998): 24–27.

Goldman, Marshall I., *The Piratization of Russia: Russian Reform Goes Awry* (New York: Routledge, 2003).

——, "The Yukos Affair," *Current History* 103 (October 2004): 319–23.

Gorbachev, Mikhail, *Memoirs* (New York: Doubleday, 1996).

Gorbatova, Larisa, "Formation of Connections between Finance and Industry in Russia: Basic Stages and Forms," *Communist Economies and Economic Transformation* 7 (1995): 21–34.

Gorbunov, S., "Ne oskudeet povolzhskaia zhitnitsa," *APK: ekonomika, upravlenie*, no. 12 (1999): 10–17.

Gorlin, Alice C., "The Power of Soviet Industrial Ministries in the 1980s," *Soviet Studies* 37 (July 1985): 353–70.

Grechaniuk, S., and N. Dunaeva, "Vsesoiuznaia broilernaia sistema 'Bol'shevik,' " *APK: ekonomika, upravlenie*, no. 11 (1991): 73–77.

Griadov, S., and T. Dozorova, "Effektivnost' proizvodstva v fermerskikh khoziaist-vakh," *APK: ekonomika, upravlenie*, no. 6 (1998): 55–61.

Grigor'ev, I., "Kak my stali aktsionerami," *Khoziain*, no. 11 (1991): 7–9.

Grishin, Iu. A., V. I. Frolov, G. A. Baklazhenko, and M. A. Kochanov, "Agrofirma 'Niva-Verkhov'e': Verkhovskaia model' agropromyshlennoi integratsii," *Ekonomika sel'skokhoziaistvennykh i pererabatyvaiushchikh predpriiatii*, no. 4 (1998): 2–7.

Grishin, P., "Agropromyshlennaia integratsiia—osnova povysheniia effektivnosti prodovol'stvennogo kompleksa," *APK: ekonomika, upravlenie*, no. 12 (1999): 71–76.

Grossman, Gregory, "The 'Second Economy' of the USSR," *Problems of Communism* 26 (September–October 1977): 25–40.

Gurushina, Natalia, "Menatep Gains Control of Yukos," *OMRI Daily Digest* (December 11, 1995).

Haggard, Stephan, and Robert R. Kaufman, eds., *The Politics of Economic Adjustment* (Princeton, NJ: Princeton University Press, 1992).

Hahn, Werner, "The Farms' Revolt and Grain Shortages in 1991," in *The "Farmer Threat": The Political Economy of Agrarian Reform in Post-Soviet Russia,* ed. Don Van Atta (Boulder, CO: Westview, 1993).

Hale, Henry E., "Divided We Stand: Institutional Sources of Ethnofederal State Survival and Collapse," *World Politics* 56 (January 2004): 165–93.

——, "The Makeup and Breakup of Ethnofederal States: Why Russia Survives Where the USSR Fell," *Perspectives on Politics* 3 (March 2005): 55–70.

Hanson, Philip, "Ownership Issues in *Perestroika,*" in *Socialism, Perestroika, and the Dilemmas of Soviet Economic Reform,* ed. John E. Tedstrom (Boulder, CO: Westview, 1990).

——, "Samara: A Preliminary Profile of a Russian Region and Its Adaptation to the Market," *Europe-Asia Studies* 49 (1997): 407–29.

——, "Putin and Russia's Economic Transformation," *Eurasian Geography and Economics* 45 (September 2004): 421–28.

Hardt, J. P., and Frankel, T., "The Industrial Managers," in *Interest Groups in Soviet Politics,* ed. H. G. Skilling and F. Griffiths (Princeton, NJ: Princeton University Press 1971).

Hedlund, Stephan, *Crisis in Soviet Agriculture* (New York: St. Martin's, 1984).

Heinzen, James W., *Inventing a Soviet Countryside: State Power and the Transformation of Rural Russia, 1917–1929* (Pittsburgh: University of Pittsburgh Press, 2004).

Hellman, Joel S., "Winners Take All: The Politics of Partial Reform in Postcommunist Transitions," *World Politics* 50 (January 1998): 203–34.

——, "Russia's Transition to a Market Economy: A Permanent Redistribution?" in *Russia after the Fall,* ed. Andrew C. Kuchins (Washington, DC: Carnegie Endowment for International Peace, 2002).

Helmer, John, "Deripaska Cashes Out of Controversial Steelmill," *Russia Journal* (May 22, 2004), via www.russiajournal.com/print/russia_news_43887.html, accessed July 15, 2004.

Hendley, Kathryn, "Legal Development and Privatization in Russia: A Case Study," *Soviet Economy* 8 (April–June 1992): 130–57.

——, "Legal Development in Post-Soviet Russia," *Post-Soviet Affairs* 13 (July–September 1997): 228–51.

——, "Struggling to Survive: A Case Study of Adjustment at a Russian Enterprise," *Europe-Asia Studies* 50 (1998): 91–119.

Herrera, Yoshiko M., *Imagined Economies: The Sources of Russian Regionalism* (Cambridge: Cambridge University Press, 2005).

Hewett, Ed A., *Reforming the Soviet Economy: Equality versus Efficiency* (Washington, DC: Brookings Institutionm 1988).

Heymann, Hans, Jr., "*Perestroika* and Innovation in Soviet Industry," in *Socialism, Perestroika, and the Dilemmas of Soviet Economic Reform,* ed. John E. Tedstrom (Boulder: Westview, 1990).

Higgins, Andrew, and Alan Cullison, "U.S. Financier Sits at Center of Russian Media Tempest," *Wall Street Journal* (April 26, 2001), via *JRL* no. 5224.

Hill, Fiona, *Energy Empire: Oil, Gas, and Russia's Revival* (London: Foreign Policy Centre, 2004), via www.brookings.edu/dybdocroot/views/articles/Fhill/20040930.pdf, accessed February 25, 2005.

Hoffman, David, *The Oligarchs: Wealth and Power in the New Russia* (New York: Public Affairs, 2002).

Holmes, Stephen, "What Russia Teaches Us Now: How Weak States Threaten Freedom," *The American Prospect* (July–August 1997): 30–39.

Hough, Jerry F., *The Soviet Prefects* (Cambridge, MA: Harvard University Press, 1969).

——, *Democratization and Revolution in the USSR, 1985–1991* (Washington, DC: Brookings Institution, 1997).

——, *The Logic of Economic Reform in Russia* (Washington, DC: Brookings Institution, 2001).

Hough, Jerry F., and Merle Fainsod, *How the Soviet Union Is Governed* (Cambridge: Harvard University Press, 1979).

Hoyos, Carola, Andrew Jack, and Arkady Ostrovsky, "Russian Partners Seek to Change BP Deal," *Financial Times* (May 4, 2004).

Humphrey, Caroline, *Marx Went Away—But Karl Stayed Behind* (Ann Arbor: University of Michigan Press, 1998).

——, *The Unmaking of Soviet Life: Everyday Economies after Socialism* (Ithaca, NY: Cornell University Press, 2002).

Huskey, Eugene, "The Rebirth of the Russian State," in *Executive Power and Soviet Politics*, ed. Eugene Huskey (Armonk, NY: M. E. Sharpe, 1992).

——, *Presidential Power in Russia* (Armonk, NY: M. E. Sharpe, 1999).

——, "Overcoming the Yeltsin Legacy: Vladimir Putin and Russian Political Reform," in *Contemporary Russian Politics: A Reader*, ed. Archie Brown (Oxford: Oxford University Press, 2001).

Hyde, Matthew, "Putin's Federal Reforms and the Implications for Presidential Power in Russia," *Europe-Asia Studies* 53 (2001): 719–43.

Iakovlev, A. V., *Agrarnaia reforma na regional'nom urovne* (Saratov: Izdatel'stvo Saratovskogo universiteta, 1995).

Ickes, Barry W., Peter Murrell, and Randi Ryterman, "End of the Tunnel? The Effects of Financial Stabilization in Russia," *Post-Soviet Affairs* 13 (April–June 1997): 105–33.

"Inkombanku nuzhny garantii," *Delovoe povolzh'e*, no. 10 (March 1998): 2.

Inshakov, O. V., *Mekhanizm sotsial'no-rynochnoi transformatsii i ustoichivogo razvitiia APK Rossii* (Volgograd: Izdatel'stvo Volgogradskogo gosudarstvennogo universiteta, 1995).

Interfax News Agency, *Food and Agriculture Report* (May 27–June 3, 1994), via The Russian Agricultural Listserve, www.friends-partners.ru/oldfriends/science/agriculture/rusag.940620.html, accessed August 20, 2003.

——, "Berezovsky Names People to Whom He Hands His ORT Stock" (September 7, 2000), via *JRL* no. 4498.

"Interros Sheds Last of Its Defense Assets," *Moscow Times* (August 13, 2003).

IRG (Interactive Research Group), *The Top 100 Emerging Companies of the Russian Consumer Market* (Moscow: IRG, 2003).

Iugai, A. M., and V. A. Petrov, "O finansovo-promyshlennykh gruppakh v agrarnoi sfere," *Ekonomika sel'skokhoziaistvennykh i pererabatyvaiushchikh predpriiatii*, no. 1 (1998): 30–32; no. 2 (1998): 39–46.

Ivanova, I. L., "Opyt privatizatsii pererabatyvaiushchikh predpriiatii v Chuvashskoi respublike," *Ekonomika sel'skokhoziaistvennykh i pererabatyvaiushchikh predpriiatii*, no. 1 (1995): 17–18, 28–30.

Jack, Andrew, "UES Chairman Chubais Fights to Protect His Job," *Financial Times* (June 7, 2000).

——, "A Better Class of Baron," *Financial Times* (December 1, 2001).

——, "New Broom Brings Change to Gazprom," *Financial Times* (February 18, 2002).

——, "Abramovich Tries to Sell Assets," *Financial Times* (August 9, 2003), via *JRL* no. 7282.

Jack, Andrew, Arkady Ostrovsky, and Charles Pretzlik, "Soros to Sell 'the Worst Investment of My Life,'" *Financial Times* (March 17, 2004).

Jack, Andrew, Arkady Ostrovsky, and Lina Saigol, "Khodorkovsky Arrest Halts Talks with Yukos," *Financial Times* (October 27, 2003).

Jack, Andrew, and David Stern, "Chinese Group 'Pulls Out of Russian Oil Sale,'" *Financial Times* (December 8, 2002).

Jamestown Monitor, "Is Berezovsky's Latest Demarche an Attempt to Take Over NTV?" 7 (February 8, 2001), via www.jamestown.org/publications_details.php?volume_id=24andissue_id=1956andarticle_id=18017, accessed July 21, 2004.

Javeline, Debra, *Protest and the Politics of Blame: The Russian Response to Unpaid Wages* (Ann Arbor: University of Michigan Press, 2003).

Johnson, Juliet Ellen, "The Russian Banking System: Institutional Responses to the Market Transition," *Europe-Asia Studies* 46 (1994): 971–96.

——, "Russia's Emerging Financial-Industrial Groups," *Post-Soviet Affairs* 13 (October–December 1997): 333–65.

——, *A Fistful of Rubles: The Rise and Fall of the Russian Banking System* (Ithaca, NY: Cornell University Press, 2000).

Johnson, Simon, and Heidi Kroll, "Managerial Strategies for Spontaneous Privatization," *Soviet Economy* 7 (October–December 1991): 281–316.

Jones, Anthony, and William Moskoff, *Ko-ops: The Rebirth of Entrepreneurship in the Soviet Union* (Bloomington: Indiana University Press, 1991).

Kaban, Elif, "YUKOS May Seek U.S. Ruling vs. Gazprom," *Reuters* (December 22, 2004), via *JRL* no. 8512.

——, "Yugansk Proves Hard to Digest for Russia's Rosneft," *Reuters* (January 26, 2005), via *JRL* no. 9035.

Kahn, Jeffrey, *Federalism, Democratization, and the Rule of Law in Russia* (Oxford: Oxford University Press, 2002).

Kahn, Joseph, and Timothy L. O'Brien, "For Russia and Its U.S. Bankers, Match Wasn't Made in Heaven," *New York Times* (October 18, 1998).

Kaiser, Robert G., "Oasis Built on Oil," www.washingtonpost.com (September 5, 2001), via *JRL* no. 5427.

Kamyshanov, Ia., "Ob ekonomicheskom mekhanizme v novykh formirovaniiakh APK," *Ekonomist,* no. 1 (1994): 85–87.

Kaplan, Fred, "Russian Army Reels, Posing Risk of Disaster for Economy," *Boston Globe* (January 17, 1995).

Karush, Sarah, and Andrei Zolotov, Jr., "Gusinsky Swapped Assets for Liberty," *Moscow Times* (September 19, 2000), via *JRL* no. 4523.

Kazannik, A. I. (general procurator of the Russian Federation), "Informatsiia po voprosam fermerstva," memo to Prime Minister Viktor Chernomyrdin (December 1993).

Kenway, Peter, and Eva Klvačová, "The Web of Cross-Ownership among Czech Financial Intermediaries: An Assessment," *Europe-Asia Studies* 48 (1996): 797–809.

Khomutov, V., A. Popov, F. Kozlovtsev, and E. Narbekov, "Agropromyshlennaia sistema 'Sareptskaia gorchitsa,'" *APK: ekonomika, upravlenie,* no. 11 (1991): 78–80.

Khramova, I. G. [Irina Grigor'evna], interview with the author, Moscow (May 21, 2002).

Khramova, I. G. and P. Verkhaim, "Rynochnye struktury prodovol'stvennogo kompleksa Rossii v usloviiakh perekhodnoi ekonomiki," Working Paper, Institute for the Economy in Transition (1999), via www.iet.ru/personal/agro/6articl.htm, accessed July 30, 2003.

Kitching, Gavin, "The Development of Agrarian Capitalism in Russia 1991–97: Some Observations from Fieldwork," *Journal of Peasant Studies* 25 (April 1998a): 1–30.

——, "The Revenge of the Peasant? The Collapse of Large-Scale Russian Agriculture and the Role of the Peasant 'Private Plot' in That Collapse, 1991–97," *Journal of Peasant Studies* 26 (October 1998b): 43–81.

Kitschelt, Herbert, "The Formation of Party Systems in East Central Europe," *Politics and Society* 20 (March 1992): 7–50.

Kiva, A. V., "Rossiiskaia oligarkhiia: obshchee i osobennoe," *Obshchestvennye nauki i sovremennost'*, no. 2 (2000): 18–28.

Klasson, Mikhail, "Viakhirev i Chubais torguiutsia," *Vremia MN* (July 1998), via www.oduv.ru/op/1998/07/30, accessed June 2, 2004.

Klebnikov, Paul, *Godfather of the Kremlin: Boris Berezovsky and the Looting of Russia* (New York: Harcourt, 2000).

Kliamkin, Igor', and Lev Timofeev, *Tenevaia Rossiia: Ekonomiko-sotsiologicheskoe issledovanie* (Moscow: Rossiiskii gosudarstvennyi gumanitarnyi universitet, 2000).

Kogut, Bruce, and Andrew Spicer, "Institutional Technology and the Chains of Trust: Capital Markets and Privatization in Russia and the Czech Republic," William Davidson Institute Working Papers Series, no. 291 (March 1999).

Kohli, Atul, "Centralization and Powerlessness: India's Democracy in a Comparative Perspective," in *State Power and Social Forces: Domination and Transformation in the Third World*, ed. Joel S. Migdal, Atul Kohli, and Vivienne Shue (Cambridge: Cambridge University Press, 1994).

Kokh, Alfred, *The Selling of the Soviet Empire: Politics and Economics of Russia's Privatization* (New York: S.P.I. Books, 1998).

Kokorev, V. P., and V. K. Tolstov, *Kontsern: organizatsiia i upravlenie* (Barnaul: Izdatel'stvo Altaiskogo gosuniversiteta, 1995).

Kolesnichenko, Alexander, Ludmilla Pivovarova, and Vitaly Tseplyaev, "Tycoons Flattened," *Argumenty i fakty* (February 6, 2002), via *JRL* no. 6060.

Komitet po sel'skomu khoziaistvu administratsii Volgogradskoi oblasti, "Doklad 'O sostoianii sel'skokhoziaistvennogo proizvodstva i prognoze ego razvitiia v 1994 godu,'" Volgograd, mimeo (n.d.).

"Konflikt vokrug OAO 'Taganskii miasopererabatyvaiushchii zavod,'" via www.aksnews.ru/industry/34/3709.html (December 4, 2003), accessed July 13, 2004.

Konovalova, Svetlana, and Nikolai Averin, "Ot polia do prilavka," *Ekonomika sel'skogo khoziaistva Rossii*, no. 2 (1998): 5.

Koptev, Dmitry, "St. Petersburg Team Building Their Own 'Family,'" Gazeta.ru (July 28, 2004), via *JRL* no. 8305.

Korchagina, Valeria, Kirill Koriukin, and Alla Startseva, "The New Face of the Russian Oligarchy," *Moscow Times* (November 1, 2001).

Korelin, Avenir P., "The Social Problem in Russia, 1906–1914: Stolypin's Agrarian Reform," in *Reform in Modern Russian History: Progress or Cycle?* ed. Theodore Taranovski (Cambridge: Cambridge University Press, 1995).

Koslov, Al'bert, "'Mezhregiongaz' ot obeshchanii primenit' vynuzhdennye zhestkie mery k predpriiatiiam-neplatel'shchikam pereshel k konkretnym deistviiam," *Trud* (July 1998), via www.oduv.ru/op/1998/07/30, accessed June 2, 2004.

Kostina, Galina, "Sel'khozintegratsiia," *Ekspert* (February 8, 1999a): 30–31.

——, "Put' Il'icha k rynku," *Ekspert* (March 15, 1999b): 34–36.

——, "Eto vam ne semechki," *Ekspert* (January 29, 2001a): 20–22.

——, "Sel'skaia nov'," *Ekspert* (October 29, 2001b): 24–26.

——, "Ul'ianovskii forpost," *Ekspert* (March 4, 2002a): 20–21.

——, "Okhota na bulochnikov," *Ekspert* (April 29, 2002b): 20–21.

——, interview with the author, Moscow (May 31, 2002c).

Kotkin, Stephen, *Magnetic Mountain: Stalinism as a Civilization* (Berkeley: University of California Press, 1995).

——, *Armageddon Averted: The Soviet Collapse, 1970–2000* (Oxford: Oxford University Press, 2001).

Kotova, Tatyana, "Interros Group Buys Farm Assets," *RFE/RL Business Watch* 1 (November 6, 2001), via www.rferl.org/businesswatch/2001/11/17–061101.asp, accessed July 12, 2004.

Kotz, David M., and Fred Weir, *Revolution from Above: The Demise of the Soviet System* (New York: Routledge, 1997).

Kozlov, Al'bert, " 'Mezhregiongaz' ot obeshchanii primenit' vynuzhdennye zhestkie mery k predpriiatiiam-neplatel'shchikam pereshel k konkretnym deistviiam," *Trud* (July 1998), via www.oduv.ru/op/1998/07/30, accessed June 23, 2004.

Kramer, Mark, "The Sinking of the Kursk," PONARS Policy Memo no. 145 (September 2000).

——, "Restructuring Russia's Electricity Industry," PONARS Policy Memo no. 304 (November 2003).

Kranz, Patricia, "Entrepreneur in the Kremlin," *Business Week* (September 23, 1996): 22.

Krasner, Stephen, "Approaches to the State: Alternative Conceptions and Historical Dynamics," *Comparative Politics* 16 (January 1984): 223–46.

Krasnikov, V., "Povyshenie konkurentosposobnosti predpriiatiia s pomoshch'iu diversifikatsii," *APK: ekonomika, upravlenie*, no. 1 (1998): 82–86.

Kroll, Heidi, "Monopoly and the Transition to the Market," *Soviet Economy* 7 (April–June 1991).

Kryshtanovskaia, Ol'ga, "Kremlevskie zavsegdatai," *Vremia MN*, no. 874 (February 13, 2002).

Kryshtanovskaya [Kryshtanovskaia], Olga, and Stephen White, "From Soviet Nomenklatura to Russian Elite," *Europe-Asia Studies* 48 (1996): 711–33.

Kto est' kto v Rossii i v blizhnem zarubezh'e: Spravochnik (Moscow: Novoe vremia and Vse dlia vas, 1993).

Kulefeeva, Elena, Aleksandr Trushin, and Aleksei Khodyrev, "Vizhu zemliu," *Kar'era*, no. 10 (October 2001), via www.kariera.orc.ru/10–01/Allst006.html, accessed February 18, 2003.

Kupchinsky, Roman, "U.S. Suit Casts New Light on 'The Little Guy,' " *RFE/RL Crime and Corruption Watch* 2 (May 23, 2002), via www.rferl.org/corruptionwatch/2002/05/20–230502.asp, accessed November 11, 2003.

Kurtsev, I., "Integratsionnye protsessy v APK Sibiri," *Ekonomist*, no. 3 (1999): 88–91.

Kuz'menko, Irina, " 'My sebia k oligarkham ne otnosim,' " interview with Igor' Potapenko, *Kompaniia*, no. 237 (October 28, 2002), via www.ko.ru/document.asp?d_no=5505, accessed September 16, 2003.

Kuz'minskii, Iu., "Kak 'Svoboda' shla k svobode," *Khoziain*, no. 10 (1991): 8–9.

LaFraniere, Sharon, "Russian Lawmakers Grant Right to Sell Farmland," *Washington Post* (June 27, 2002).

Laird, Roy D., and Betty A. Laird, *Soviet Communism and Agrarian Revolution* (Harmondsworth, UK: Penguin, 1970).

Lallemand, Jean-Charles, "Politics for the Few: Élites in Bryansk and Smolensk," *Post-Soviet Affairs* 15 (October–December 1999): 312–35.

Lane, David, and Iskander Seifulmulukov, "Structure and Ownership," in *The Political Economy of Russian Oil*, ed. David Lane (Lanham, MD: Rowman and Littlefield, 1999).

Larin, Mikhail, " 'Ruskhim' mozhet lishit'sia dvukh predpriiatii," *Kommersant''-Daily* (February 14, 1997).

Latsis, Otto, "The Land and the Law," *Russia Journal* (September 28–October 4, 2001), via *JRL* no. 5468.

Latynina, Iuliia [Yulia], "Direktora protiv oligarkhov," *Ekspert* (September 21, 1998).

——, "A Short History of the Russian Coal Industry," *Moscow Times* (October 3, 2001).

——, "Kompromat No Longer Does the Job," *Moscow Times* (January 30, 2002a).

——, "Forestry Industry: Ripe for Carving Up," *Moscow Times* (July 17, 2002b), via *JRL* no. 6357.

Lehmbruch, Barbara, "Managing Uncertainty: Hierarchies, Markets, and 'Networks' in the Russian Timber Industry, 1991–1998," BOFIT Discussion Paper, no. 4 (Helsinki: Bank of Finland, 1999).

Le Huérou, Anne, "Elites in Omsk," *Post-Soviet Affairs* 15 (October–December 1999): 362–86.

Lepekhin, V. A., "Ot administrativno-politicheskoi diktatury k finansovoi oligarkhii," *Obshchestvennye nauki i sovremennost'*, no. 1 (1999): 66–82.

Lerman, Zvi, Csaba Csaki, and Gershon Feder, *Agriculture in Transition: Land Policies and Evolving Farm Structures in Post-Soviet Countries* (Lanham, MD: Lexington Books, 2004).

Lewin, Moshe, *Lenin's Last Struggle* (New York: Pantheon, 1968a).

——, *Russian Peasants and Soviet Power: A Study of Collectivization* (Evanston, IL: North-western University Press, 1968b).

——, *Political Undercurrents in Soviet Economic Debates: From Bukharin to the Modern Reformers* (Princeton, NJ: Princeton University Press, 1974).

——, "The Civil War: Dynamics and Legacy," in *Party, State, and Society in the Russian Civil War: Explorations in Social History*, ed. Diane P. Koenker, William G. Rosenberg, and Ronald Grigor Suny (Bloomington: Indiana University Press, 1989).

Liefert, William M., "The Food Problem in the Republics of the Former USSR," in *The "Farmer Threat,"* ed. Van Atta (1993).

Lih, Lars T., *Bread and Authority in Russia, 1914–1921* (Berkeley: University of California Press, 1990).

Linden, Carl, *Khrushchev and the Soviet Leadership*, 2d ed. (Baltimore: Johns Hopkins University Press, 1990 [1st ed., 1966]).

Lipman, Masha, "The Big Shakedown on Russian Business," *Washington Post* (July 10, 2003).

Lipton, David, and Jeffrey Sachs, "Creating a Market Economy in Eastern Europe: The Case of Poland," *Brookings Papers on Economic Activity*, no. 1 (1990): 75–133.

Litvin, Valentin, *The Soviet Agro-Industrial Complex: Structure and Performance* (Boulder, CO: Westview, 1987).

Lohr, Eric, "Arkadii Volsky's Political Base," *Europe-Asia Studies* 45 (1993): 811–29.

Lowe, Christian, and Dmitry Zhdannikov, "Russia's Khodorkovsky Jailed for 9 Years," *Reuters* (May 31, 2005), via *JRL* no. 9164.

"'LUKoil' idet v glubiny Zavolzh'ia," *Oblastnye vesti* (February 13, 1998): 2.

L'vova, Valeriia, "Kak uderzhat' molodykh na sele? Dat' im sovremennuiu tekhniku!" *Krest'ianskie vedomosti* (October 2, 2002), via www.agronews.ru/newsp. php?NewsId=4846, retrieved November 12, 2002.

Lysenko, E., "Razvitie sel'skokhoziaistvennoi kooperatsii i integratsii," *Ekonomist*, no. 1 (1998): 80–84.

Lysova, Tat'iana, "Khoziain truby," interview with Dmitrii Saval'ev of Transneft', *Ekspert* (August 24, 1998).

Macalister, Terry, and Patrick Collinson, "BP and Shell Fuel Rush to Invest in Russia," *The Guardian* (April 17, 2002), via *JRL* no. 6190.

Macey, David A. J., "Agricultural Reform and Political Change: The Case of Stolypin," in *Reform in Modern Russian History,* ed. Theodore Taranovski (Cambridge: Cambridge University Press, 1995).

Mahoney, James, and Dietrich Rueschemeyer, eds., *Comparative Historical Analysis in the Social Sciences* (Cambridge: Cambridge University Press, 2003).

Makarevich, L. "Rossiiskaia ekonomika—arena bor'by 'bez pravil.' Aktivizatsiia gosudarstva—imperativ 1999 g." *Obshchestvo i ekonomika,* no. 6 (1999a): 182–201.

——. "Finansovo-ekonomicheskaia situatsiia serediny 1999 g.—problemy nakaplivaiutsia, a ne reshaiutsia," *Obshchestvo i ekonomika,* no. 7–8 (1999b): 129–62.

——. "Struktura sobstvennosti i bor'ba za ee peredel v Rossii v 1992–1999 gg.," *Obshchestvo i ekonomika,* no. 10–11 (1999c): 230–53.

Maksimov, N., "Nuzhen effektivnyi mekhanizm khoziaistvovaniia," *APK: ekonomika, upravlenie,* no. 1 (1998): 77–81.

Materialy Plenuma TsK KPSS, 23 aprelia 1985 goda (Moscow: Politizdat, 1985).

Materialy Plenuma Tsentral'nogo Komiteta KPSS, 27–28 ianvaria 1987 goda (Moscow: Izdatel'stvo politicheskoi literatury, 1987).

McDaniel, Tim, *Autocracy, Capitalism, and Revolution in Russia* (Berkeley: University of California Press, 1988).

McDermott, Gerald M., "Institutional Change and Firm Creation in East-Central Europe: An Embedded Politics Approach," *Comparative Political Studies* 37 (March 2004): 188–217.

McFaul, Michael, "Russian Centrism and Revolutionary Transitions," *Post-Soviet Affairs* 9 (July–September 1993): 196–222.

——, "State Power, Institutional Change, and the Politics of Privatization in Russia," *World Politics* 47 (January 1995): 210–43.

——, "Russia's 1996 Presidential Elections," *Post-Soviet Affairs* 12 (October–December 1996): 318–50.

——, "Russia's 'Privatized' State as an Impediment to Democratic Consolidation," Parts I and II, *Security Dialogue* 29 (Spring 1998): 191–99; 29 (Summer 1998): 315–32.

——, "One Step Forward, Two Steps Back," *Journal of Democracy* 11 (2000): 19–33.

McFaul, Michael, and Tova Perlmutter, eds., *Privatization, Conversion, and Enterprise Reform in Russia* (Boulder, CO: Westview, 1995).

McGregor, Caroline, "Gazprom and Itera: A Case Study in Russian Corporate Misgovernance," report on presentation of William F. Browder, CEO, Hermitage Capital Management, Moscow, to the Carnegie Endowment for International Peace (March 18, 2002), via *JRL* no. 6149.

Medvedev, Iurii, chairman of Volgograd oblast property committee, interview with the author, Volgograd (November 1994).

Melikhov, V., "Stabilizirovat' agroproizvodstvo," *APK: ekonomika, upravlenie,* no. 6 (1998): 17–24.

Mellow, Craig, "Russia: Rise of the Banker Clans," *The Banker* (April 1, 1997).

Mereu, Francesca, "Putin Presidency at Two-Year Mark—Do Oligarchs Still Have a Role? (Part I)" *RFE/RL Magazine* (April 19, 2002), via *JRL* no. 6199.

Miasnikov, A., "Perspektivy razvitiia kooperatsii v Sverdlovskoi oblasti," *APK: ekonomika, upravlenia,* no. 5 (1998): 49–55.

Migdal, Joel S., *Strong Societies and Weak States: State-Society Relations and State Capabilities in the Third World* (Princeton, NJ: Princeton University Press, 1988).

Mikhailov, Vladimir, " 'Sibirskii aliuminii' stal otchasti Volzhskim," *Delovoe Povolzh'e,* no. 12 (1998): 13.

Miller, A. B., and E. A. Vasilieva, *Gazprom: Financial Report 2002* (Moscow: Gazprom, May 15, 2003), via www.gazprom.com/documents/fin_eng.pdf, accessed July 21, 2004.

Miller, Robert F., *One Hundred Thousand Tractors: The MTS and the Development of Controls in Soviet Agriculture* (Cambridge, MA: Harvard University Press, 1970).

Miloserdov, V., and V. Frolov, "Formy agropromyshlennoi integratsii (opyt Orlovskoi oblasti)," *Ekonomist*, no. 4 (1998): 87–91.

Miloslavskaia, Ekaterina, "Bendukidze: Kak biolog stal odnim is samykh bogatykh liudei v Rossii," *Kto est' kto*, no. 1 (2001), via www.whoiswho.ru/russian/Curnom/12001/kb.htm; accessed July 17, 2003.

Moskatin'ev, V., "Ch'ia teper' monopoliia, ili kak kolkhozu vyzhit' v usloviiakh rynka," *Khoziain*, no. 9 (1991): 2–4.

MosNews, "Soros Sells Svyazinvest Shares," *Moscow News* (April 20, 2004a), via www.mosnews.com/money/2004/04/20/soros.shtml, accessed July 22, 2004.

——, "Putin's 'Gray Cardinal' Sechin May Be Behind Baikal Finance" (December 22, 2004b), via *JRL* no. 8512.

"MTS: Privlechenie investitsii v selo," *Delovoe Povolzh'e*, no. 10 (1998): 2.

"MTS zavoevyvaiut rossiiskie polia," *Ekonomika sel'skogo khoziaistva Rossii*, no. 3 (1998): 32.

Mukhin, A. A., *Biznes-elita i gosudarstvennaia vlast': Kto vladeet Rossiei na rubezhe vekov?* (Moscow: Tsentr politicheskoi informatsii, 2001).

Munter, Paivi, "Russia Tumbles as Yukos Scandal Widens," *Financial Times* (November 19, 2003).

"My sebia k oligarkham ne otnosim" (interview with Igor' Potapenko), *Kompaniia*, no. 237 (October 28, 2002), via www.ko.ru/document.asp?d_no=5505, accessed September 16, 2003.

Myers, Steven Lee, "Jailed Russian Tycoon Mourns Liberty's Losses," *New York Times* (March 30, 2004).

"Nado pokupat' ne tovar, a zavody," interview with Stanislav Anisimov, president of the federal contract corporation Roskontrakt, *Ekspert* (October 5, 1998), via ISI Emerging Markets (www.securities.com).

Nagibina, I., "Uchastie oblasti v ustavnykh kapitalakh negosudarstvennykh kommercheskikh organizatsii," *APK: ekonomika, upravlenie*, no. 12 (1998): 64–67.

Nelson, Lynn D., and Irina Y. Kuzes, *Property to the People: The Struggle for Radical Economic Reform in Russia* (Armonk, NY: M. E. Sharpe, 1994).

——, *Radical Reform in Yeltsin's Russia: Political, Economic, and Social Dimensions* (Armonk, NY: M. E. Sharpe, 1995).

Nemtsov, B., "Osnova vlasti," *Rossiiskaia gazeta* (November 24, 1990a): 1.

——, "Kogda privatizatsiei pravit ministr," *Rossiiskaia gazeta* (December 8, 1990b): 8.

Nicholson, Alex, "Yukos Offers to Pay Tax Claims in 2 Years," *AP* (July 14, 2004a), via *JRL* no. 8291.

——, "Report: Part of Yukos Tax Debt Recovered, *AP* (October 6, 2004b), via *JRL* no. 8397.

——, "Report: Consortium Freezes Gazprom Credit," *AP* (December 17, 2004c), via *JRL* no. 8504.

——, "Yukos Crisis Blamed for Business Woes," *AP* (February 7, 2005), via *JRL* no. 9052.

"Norilsk Buys Top Gold Firm," *Moscow Times* (October 25, 2002).

Nove, Alec, *Soviet Agriculture: The Brezhnev Legacy and Gorbachev's Cure* (Los Angeles, CA: RAND/UCLA Center for the Study of Soviet International Behavior, 1988).

——, *An Economic History of the USSR*, 2d ed. (London: Penguin, 1989).

Novikov, N., "Institutsional'nye preobrazovaniia v sel'skom khoziaistve," *Ekonomist*, no. 12 (1996): 69–75.

Novikov, V. N., "Opyt reorganizatsii sel'skokhoziaistvennykh predpriiatii," *Ekonomika sel'skokhoziaistvennykh i pererabatyvaiushchikh predpriiatii,* no. 11 (1995): 22–26.

"Ob AO 'Rosagrosnab,'" www.rosagrosnab.ru/Rekl.html, last accessed August 3, 2001.

OECD [Organization for Economic Cooperation and Development], *OECD Economic Surveys: Russian Federation* (Paris: OECD, 2002).

Olcott, Martha Brill, "Reforming Russia's Tycoons," *Foreign Policy* (May–June 2002).

"Oligarch Sells His Last Assets in Russia," *Russia Journal* (November 11, 2003), via www.russiajournal.com/news/cnews-article.shtml?nd=41261, accessed August 9, 2004.

"Opyt i problemy agrarnykh preobrazovanii," *Ekonomika sel'skokhoziaistvennykh i pererabatyvaiushchikh predpriiatii,* no. 5 (1998): 55–60.

Orenstein, Mitchell A., *Out of the Red: Building Capitalism and Democracy in Postcommunist Europe* (Ann Arbor: University of Michigan Press, 2001).

Orttung, Robert W., "Business and Politics in the Russian Regions," paper presented at the Annual Meeting of the American Association for the Advancement of Slavic Studies, Pittsburgh, PA (November 21–24, 2002).

Ostrovsky, Arkady, "Russian Oil Sell-off Raises $1.08 Billion," *Financial Times* (September 20, 2000), via *JRL* no. 4527.

——, "Russian Oligarch in Fresh Buy-up Inquiry," *Financial Times* (July 16, 2003a).

——, "Yukos Inquiry Shifts Focus from Economic to Criminal Offences," *Financial Times* (July 19, 2003b).

——, "The Science of Forging a Steel Empire," *Financial Times* (August 27, 2003c).

——, "Yukos to Expand Beyond Russia," *Financial Times* (September 29, 2003d).

——, "Fresh Yukos Probe Targets Oil Production Site in Siberia," *Financial Times* (November 13, 2003e).

——, "Adrift on the Ob, Yukos Faces Uncertain Fate," *Financial Times* (July 22, 2004a).

——, "Gazprom Merger to Proceed without Yukos Asset," *Financial Times* (December 30, 2004b), via *JRL* no. 8521.

——, "Russian Banks Financed Rosneft's Purchase of Yukos Unit," *Financial Times* (February 7, 2005), via *JRL* no. 9051.

Ostrovsky, Simon, "Vimpelcom under Attack as Speculation Rife," *The St. Petersburg Times* (February 6, 2004), via www.sptimes.ru/archive/times/941/news/b_11599. htm, accessed August 8, 2004.

Pakhomchik, Sergei, "Vertikal'naia sel'skokhoziaistvennaia kooperatsiia," *Ekonomika sel'skogo khoziaistva Rossii,* no. 1 (1998): 4.

Pallot, Judith, "Update on Russian Federation Land Reform," *Post-Soviet Geography* 34 (1993): 211–17.

Panina, Tat'iana, "Vozvrashchenie bludnogo dolga," interview with head of Russia's Federal Bankruptcy Commission, *Rossiiskaia gazeta* (December 24, 2003), via www. rg.ru/2003/12/24/trefilova.html, accessed August 9, 2004.

Paniushkina, Iu., "Teoreticheskie skhemy budut ottorgnuty narodom," *Nezavisimaia gazeta* (June 25, 1991).

Pappe, Ia. Sh., *"Oligarkhi": ekonomicheskaia khronika, 1992–2000* (Moscow: Gosudarstvennyi universitet and Vysshaia shkola ekonomiki, 2000).

——, "Rossiiskii krupnyi biznes kak ekonomicheskii fenomen: osobennosti stanovleniia i sovremennogo etap razvitiia," *Problemy prognozirovaniia,* no. 1 (2002): 29–46.

Paszyc, Ewa, and Iwona Wisniewska, "Big Business in the Russian Economy and Politics under Putin's Rule," Center for Eastern Studies (Warsaw), no. 5.1 (May 2002), translated by Jim Todd, via www.osw.waw.pl/english/earc/2002/05maj/praceNR5/01.htm, accessed June 27, 2002.

Perekhod k rynku, chast' 1: Kontseptsiia i programma (Moscow: Arkhangel'skoe izdatel'stvo, 1990a).

Perekhod k rynku, chast' 2: Proekty zakonodatel'nyk aktov (Moscow: Arkhangel'skoe izdatel'stvo, 1990b).

Perotti, Enrico C., and Stanislav Gelfer, "Investment Financing in Russian Financial-Industrial Groups," *CASE-CEU Working Paper Series*, no. 10 (Warsaw, July 1998).

Petrushkov, M. A., and N. I. Vostrikov, "Sovershenstvovanie ekonomicheskikh otnoshenii v aktsionernykh obshchestvakh zakrytogo tipa," *Ekonomika sel'skokhoziaistvennykh i pererabatyvaiushchikh predpriiatii*, no. 10 (1994): 16, 39–42.

Pipes, Richard, "The Establishment of the Union of Soviet Socialist Republics," in *The Soviet Nationality Reader: The Disintegration in Context*, ed. Rachel Denber (Boulder, CO: Westview, 1992).

Pirani, Simon, "Siberia's Great Smelting Pot," *The Observer (UK)* (February 18, 2001).

Pishchikova, Evgeniia, "O sel'skom khoziaistve zamolvili slovo," *Rossiiskaia gazeta* (January 17, 1992a): 2.

——, "Puty dlia vol'nykh zemledel'tsev," *Rossiiskaia gazeta* (May 12, 1992b).

Pistor, Katharina, and Andrew Spicer, "Investment Funds in Mass Privatization and Beyond: Evidence from the Czech Republic and Russia," Harvard Institute for International Development, Discussion Paper no. 565 (December 1996).

Pleines, Heiko, "Corruption and Crime in the Russian Oil Industry," in *The Political Economy of Russian Oil*, ed. David Lane (Lanham, MD: Rowman and Littlefield, 1999).

Pliskevich, N. M., "Rossiiskaia privatizatsiia: revoliutsiia ili evoliutsionnyi perekhod?" *Obshchestvennye nauki i sovremennost'*, no. 4 (1999): 29–43.

Polanyi, Karl, *The Great Transformation* (New York: Rinehart, 1944).

Polevanov, Vladimir, "Tekhnologiia velikogo obmana," pamphlet (Moscow, 1995).

——, interview in *What the Papers Say* 10 (October 15, 1998), via *JRL* no. 2439.

Political Report of the CPSU Central Committee to 27th Congress of the CPSU (Moscow: Novosti, 1986).

Ponomarev, A., and A. Matushkin, "Krupnye spetsializirovannye kompleksy—osnovnoi postavshchik miasnykh resursov," *APK: ekonomika, upravlenie*, no. 8 (1995): 68–71.

Popova, Tatyana, "Financial-Industrial Groups and Their Roles in the Russian Economy," *Review of Economies in Transition* (December 30, 1998): 5–28.

Porshakov, Sergei, " 'Vrashchaiushchaiasia dver' " ustanovlena," *Izvestiia* (February 17, 2002).

"Pravitel'stvo i 'Gazprom' o chem-to dogovorilis'," *Ekspert* (August 10, 1998).

"Predostavlenie zemel' dlia kollektivnogo sadovodstva i ogorodnichestva v Rossiiskoi Federatsii," *APK: ekonomika, upravlenie*, nos. 11–12 (1993): 26.

"Predpriiatiia i bankovskaia sistema," *Obzor ekonomiki Rossii: osnovnye tendentsii razvitiia*, no. 4 (1998): 131–50, via www.budgetrf.ru/Publications/Magazines/recep/1998/4/rcpb199840000firm/rcpb199840000firm000.htm, accessed December 22, 2003.

"Privatisation in the Soviet Union," *Economist* (May 18, 1991).

"Programma stabilizatsii ekonomiki i perekhoda k rynochnym otnosheniiam v RSFSR (proekt)," *Rossiiskaia gazeta* (March 29, 1991).

Pronina, Lyuba, "IST Dumps Stake in Top St. Pete Shipyard," *Moscow Times* (October 8, 2002).

——, "Mezhprom to Create $2 Billion Conglomerate," *Moscow Times* (June 1, 2004).

Prosterman, Roy L., Robert G. Mitchell, and Bradley J. Rorem, "Prospects for Family Farming in Russia," *Europe-Asia Studies* 49 (1997): 1383–407.

Prosterman, Roy L., Leonard J. Rolfes, Jr., and Robert G. Mitchell, "Russian Agrarian Reform: A Status Report from the Field," Rural Development Institute Reports on Foreign Aid and Development, no. 84, Seattle, WA (August 1994).

Przeworski, Adam, *Democracy and the Market: Political and Economic Reforms in Eastern Europe and Latin America* (Cambridge: Cambridge University Press, 1991).

Radygin, Aleksandr, "Rossiiskaia privatizatsiia v 1993 g.: nekotorye itogi i problemy," *Panorama privatizatsii* 2 (1993): 40–60.

——, *Reforma sobstvennosti v Rossii: na puti iz proshlogo v budushchee* (Moscow: Respublika, 1994).

——, "Residual Divestiture Following Mass Privatization: The Case of Russia," paper for OECD Advisory Group on Privatization Ninth Plenary Meeting, Berlin (May 6–7, 1996), via www.iet.ru/special/oecd/Rad1agp9.htm, accessed December 22, 2003.

——, "Pereraspredelenie prav sobstvennosti v post-privatizatsionnoi Rossii," *Voprosy ekonomiki*, no. 6 (1999): 54–75.

Raff, Anna, "No Happy Ending for NTV," *Moscow Times* (April 23, 2001) via *JRL*, no. 5219.

——, "Top Sibur Executives Hauled in By Feds," *Moscow Times* (January 10, 2002a).

——, "Armed Showdown at Slavneft Office," *Moscow Times* (May 27, 2002b).

——, "Companies Can't Wait To Pay the Tab in Russia," *Wall Street Journal* (September 21, 2004), via *JRL* no. 8377.

Randall, Linda M., *Reluctant Capitalists: Russia's Journey through Market Transition* (New York: Routledge, 2001).

Reshenie Malogo Soveta Oblsoveta narodnykh deputatov (Volgograd oblast), "O khode zemel'noi reformy v oblasti," *Vestnik APK*, no. 6 (1993): 1.

Reuters, "Big Russian Privatization Is Called Off," *New York Times* (December 26, 1995).

——, "Russia's YUKOS Offers Government $7.5 Billion" (July 11, 2004), via *JRL* no. 8287.

——, "Shell's Sakhalin Venture Faces $2.5 Billion Claim," *Moscow Times* (February 10, 2005).

Reuters and AP, "OMZ Eyes Caspian With Purchase of U.S. Rig Firm," *Moscow Times* (May 27, 2002).

RIA Novosti, "India to Buy Yugansk Block" (January 15, 2005), via *JRL* no. 9017.

Roeder, Philip G., "Soviet Federalism and Ethnic Mobilization," *World Politics* 43 (January 1991): 196–232.

——, *Red Sunset: The Failure of Soviet Politics* (Princeton, NJ: Princeton University Press, 1993).

Rosenberg, William G., and Lewis H. Siegelbaum, eds., *Social Dimensions of Soviet Industrialization* (Bloomington: Indiana University Press, 1993).

Rossiiskii statisticheskii ezhegodnik (Moscow: Goskomstat Rossii, 2001).

Rudnev, V. D., and V. N. Borobov, *Gosudarstvennoe i rynochnoe regulirovanie form khoziaistvovaniia v agrarnom sektore ekonomiki* (Moscow: Izdatel'stvo GNOM i D, 2000).

Rukavitsyn, A., and L. Khalina, "Struktura upravleniia APK Kurskogo raiona Kurskoi oblasti," *APK: ekonomika, upravlenie*, no. 1 (1998): 38–46.

"Rusagrocapital Sells Blocking Stock Interest," via www.russiannj.com/eng/AllNews/News/26788 (December 18 2003), accessed July 27, 2004.

"Russian Industry: The Revolution Begins," *Economist* (July 3, 1993).

"Russian Oil Tycoon Is UK's Richest Man," *Russia Journal* (March 9, 2004), via www.russiajournal.com/news/cnews-article.shtml?nd=42842, accessed August 9, 2004.

"Russian Regions 1998: Year in Review," *RRR* special issue (January 5, 1999).

Rutland, Peter, "Privatisation in Russia: One Step Forward, Two Steps Back?" *Europe-Asia Studies* 46 (1994): 1109–31.

——, "A Twisted Path toward a Market Economy," *Transition* special issue: 1994 in Review, Part II (1995).

——, "Lost Opportunities: Energy and Politics in Russia," *NBR Analysis* 8 (December 1997): 5–31.

——, "Putin's Path to Power," *Post-Soviet Affairs* 16 (October–December 2000): 313–54.

Rutskoi, A., "Reformirovanie APK Kurskoi oblasti: problemy i kontseptsiia razvitiia," *APK: ekonomika, upravlenie*, no. 1 (1998): 4–12.

Ryl'ko, Dmitrii N., "New Agricultural Operators, Input Markets, and Vertical Sector Coordination," in *Factor Markets in Russia's Agri-Food Sector: Frameworks of Further Analysis*, ed. Evgeniia Serova and Bruce Gardner (Moscow: Center AFE, USAID, and IRIS, 2002).

Ryzhkov, N. I., *Desiat' let velikikh potriasenii* (Moscow: Kniga, prosveshchenie, miloserdie, 1995).

Safronov, V., "Formy sobstvennosti i vidy khoziaistvennovaniia v usloviiakh reformy," *APK: ekonomika, upravlenie*, no. 1 (1998): 13–16.

Sagdiev, Rinat, "Igor' Potapenko: 'Inogda dazhe posie otkaza gubernatora my priobretaem predpriiatie," *Vedomosti* (December 16, 2002), via raz.ru/rus/group.asp?+id=8&op=view&id=341), accessed October 3, 2005.

Sagers, Matthew J., "The Aluminum Industry in the Former USSR in 1992," *Post-Soviet Geography* 33 (1992): 591–601.

——, "Review of the Iron and Steel Industry in the Former USSR in 1992 and Thereafter," *Post-Soviet Geography* 34 (1993a): 453–76.

——, "The Energy Industries of the Former USSR: A Mid-Year Survey," *Post-Soviet Geography* 34 (1993b): 341–418.

——, "Privatization of Rosneft': A Research Communication," *Post-Soviet Geography and Economics* 39 (1998): 297–308.

Saivetz, Carol R., "Russian Foreign Policy Free-Lancing: The Cases of LUKoil, Gazprom, and Rosvooruzheniye," *Post-Soviet Affairs* 16, no. 1 (2000): 25–32.

Sakwa, Richard, "Russian Regionalism, Policy-Making and State Development," in *Shaping the Economic Space in Russia: Decision Making Processes, Institutions, and Adjustment to Change in the El'tsin Era*, ed. Stefanie Harter and Gerald Easter (Aldershot, UK: Ashgate, 2000).

Samofalova, L., "Partnerstvo—osnova obshchego uspekha," *APK: ekonomika, upravlenie*, no. 1 (1998): 72–77.

Samorukova, G. V., "Voprosy integratsii tovaroproizvoditelei krakhmaloproduktov," *Ekonomika sel'skokhoziaistvennykh i pererabatyvaiushchikh predpriiatii*, no. 4 (1999): 13–14.

Saradzhyan, Simon, "Prosecutors Arrest NTV Boss Gusinsky," *Moscow Times* (June 14, 2000), via *JRL* no. 4366.

Savin, A. Iu., *Finansovo-promyshlennye gruppy v Rossii* (Moscow: FinStatInform, 1997).

Schastlivtseva, L. V., and N. V. Gubanova, "Opyt bor'by s monopolizmom na regional'nykh rynkakh prodovol'stviia," *Ekonomika sel'sko-khoziaistvennykh i pererabatyvaiushchikh predpriiatii*, no. 7 (1995): 11–14.

Schröder, Hans-Henning, "El'tsin and the Oligarchs: The Role of Financial Groups in Russian Politics Between 1993 and July 1998," *Europe-Asia Studies* 51 (September 1999): 957–88.

Schroeder, Gertrude E., "Property Rights Issues in Economic Reforms in Socialist Countries," *Studies in Comparative Communism* 21 (Summer 1988).

Scott, James C., *Seeing Like a State: How Certain Schemes to Improve the Human Condition Have Failed* (New Haven: Yale University Press, 1998).

Seabright, Paul, ed., *The Vanishing Rouble: Barter Networks and Non-Monetary Transactions in Post-Soviet Societies* (Cambridge: Cambridge University Press, 2000).

Selivanova, Valeriia, "Koshelek ili zhizn'," *Ekspert* (July 5, 1999): 28–29.

Semenov, Aleksandr, "Farforovyi zavod na dve persony," *Den'gi* (October 20, 1999): 11–13.

Semenov, S., "K vertikal'noi integratsii pridem obiazatel'no," *Ekonomist*, no. 1 (1999): 43–47.

Serova, E. V., *Agrarnaia ekonomika* (Moscow: TACIS and Gosudarstvennyi universitet Vysshaia shkola ekonomiki, 1999).

Serova, Eugenia, Irina Khramova, and John P. Nichols, "OGO: Vertical Integration in the Agro-Food Industry," paper for the 4th Maple Leaf Conference, Noordwijk, Holland (June 8, 2002), via www.iet.ru/afe/english/projects/ogo-e.pdf, accessed August 20, 2003.

"S"ezd stanovitsia bar'erom na puti reform, pravitel'stvo Rossii ukhodit v otstavku," *Izvestiia* (April 13, 1992).

Shaw, Denis J. B., "Further Progress with Land Reform," *Post-Soviet Geography* 33 (October 1992): 554–56.

Shchedrov, Oleg, "Russian Media Mogul Freed amid Growing Outcry," *Reuters* (June 16, 2000), via *JRL* no. 4371.

Shcherbak, V. N., "O razvitii integratsii v agropromyshlennom komplekse Rossiiskoi Federatsii," *Ekonomika sel'skokhoziaistvennykh i pererabatyvaiushchikh predpriiatii*, no. 10 (1997): 6–10.

——, "Po puti real'nykh preobrazovanii," *APK: ekonomika, upravlenie*, no. 4 (1998): 3–15.

Shchetnina, I., "Integratsiia v APK Rossii," *APK: ekonomika, upravlenie*, no. 6 (1999): 50–53.

Shelepa, A., "Reorganizatsiia sovkhozov na Dal'nem Vostoke," *APK: ekonomika, upravlenie*, no. 11 (1992): 28–32.

Shevtsov, V., "Upravlenie predpriiatiem proizvodstvennoi infrastruktury APK," *APK: ekonomika, upravlenie*, no. 1 (2000): 38–45.

Shleifer, Andrei, and Daniel Treisman, *Without a Map: Political Tactics and Economic Reform in Russia* (Cambridge, MA: MIT Press, 2000).

Shukshin, Andrei, "Russian Press Says Norilsk Suit Threatens Oligarchs," *Reuters* (June 21, 2000), via *JRL* no. 4380.

Shut'kov, A. A., ed., *Mnogoukladnaia ekonomika v APK Rossii: voprosy, teorii, i praktiki* (Moscow: Kolos, 1998).

Sigel, Thomas, "Shares-for-Loans Plan Moves Forward," *OMRI Daily Digest* (September 26, 1995).

Sil, Rudra, "Privatization, Labor Politics, and the Firm in Post-Soviet Russia: Non-market Norms, Market Institutions, and the Soviet Legacy," in *The Politics of Labor in a Global Age: Continuity and Change in Late-industralizing and Post-socialist Economies*, ed. Christopher Candland and Rudra Sil (Oxford: Oxford University Press, 2001).

——, *Managing "Modernity": Work, Community, and Authority in Late-Industrializing Japan and Russia* (Ann Arbor: University of Michigan Press, 2002).

Silverman, Bertram, and Murray Yanowitch, *New Rich, New Poor, New Russia: Winners and Losers on the Russian Road to Capitalism*, second ed. (Armonk, NY: M. E. Sharpe, 2000).

Simis, Konstantin, *USSR: The Corrupt Society* (New York: Simon and Schuster, 1982).

Sivakov, Dmitrii, "Upravnenie s dvum'ia izvestnymi," *Ekspert* (August 2, 1999): 24–25.

——, "Plavka na zhizn'," *Ekspert* (April 8, 2002): 84–88.

Slider, Darrell, "Privatization in Russia's Regions," *Post-Soviet Affairs* 10 (October–December 1994): 367–96.

——, "Elections to Russia's Regional Assemblies," *Post-Soviet Affairs* 12 (July–September 1996): 243–64.

——, "Regional and Local Politics," in *Developments in Russian Politics*, ed. Stephen White, Alex Pravda, and Zvi Gitelman, 4th ed. (Durham, NC: Duke University Press, 1997a).

——, "Regional Aspects of Privatization in Russia," in *Beyond the Monolith: The Emergence of Regionalism in Post-Soviet Russia*, ed. Peter J. Stavrakis, Joan DeBardeleben, and Larry Black (Washington, DC, and Baltimore, MD: Woodrow Wilson Center Press and Johns Hopkins University Press, 1997b).

——, "Politics in the Regions," in *Developments in Russian Politics*, ed. Stephen White, Alex Pravda, and Zvi Gitelman, 5th ed. (Durham, NC: Duke University Press, 2001).

Sluzhakov, Vladimir, "Parol'—privatizatsiia," *Rossiiskaia gazeta* (January 31, 1991): 2.

Smith, Geoffrey T., "Battle For Russian Paper Mills Revives Old Specter," *Dow Jones Newswires* (August 5, 2002), via *JRL* no. 6388.

Smyshliaev, V., "Organizatsionno-pravovoi mekhanizm raionnykh agropromyshlennykh formirovanii," *APK: ekonomika, upravlenie*, no. 9 (1999): 30–36.

Solnick, Steven L., "Federal Bargaining in Russia," *East European Constitutional Review* 4 (Fall 1995): 52–58.

——, *Stealing the State: Control and Collapse in Soviet Institutions* (Cambridge, MA: Harvard University Press, 1998).

——, "Is the Center Too Weak or Too Strong in the Russian Federation?" in *Building the Russian State: Institutional Crisis and the Quest for Democratic Governance*, ed. Valerie Sperling (Boulder: Westview, 2000): 137–56.

Somov, Luk'ian, "Kogo v korporatsii za mal'chikov derzhat," *Oblastnye vesti* (March 27, 1998): 1.

Sonin, Konstantin, "Why the Rich May Favor Poor Protection of Property Rights," *Journal of Comparative Economics* 31 (2003): 715–31.

Sovet Agrarnogo soiuza Volgogradskoi oblasti, "Postanovlenie 'O polozhenii del v agropromyshlennom proizvodstve i merakh po ego stabilizatsii,'" *Vestnik APK*, no. 13 (1993): 1.

"Sovkhoz 'Novo-Raevskii,'" *Ekonomika sel'skokhoziaistvennykh i pererabatyvaiushchikh predpriiatii*, no. 3 (1998): 2–6.

Sperling, Valerie, *Organizing Women in Contemporary Russia: Engendering Transition* (Cambridge: Cambridge University Press, 1999).

Spicer, Andrew, "Institutions and the Social Construction of Organization Form: The Development of Russian Mutual Fund Organizations, 1992–1997," Ph.D. dissertation, University of Pennsylvania (1998).

Stadnik, A. T., and V. V. Aleksanova, "Razvitie agropromyshlennoi integratsii v Sibiri," *Ekonomika sel'skokhoziaistvennykh i pererabatyvaiushchikh predpriiatii*, no. 3 (1997): 51–54.

Stark, David, and László Bruszt, *Postsocialist Pathways: Transforming Politics and Property in East Central Europe* (Cambridge: Cambridge University Press, 1998).

Starobin, Paul, and Catherine Belton, "Open Season on Russia's Oligarchs," *Business Week* (July 10, 2000), via *JRL* no. 4385.

——, "Russia's New Wealth," *Business Week*, International ed. (August 5, 2002).

Startsev, Yaroslav, "Gubernatorial Politics in Sverdlovsk Oblast'," *Post-Soviet Affairs* 15 (October–December 1999): 336–61.

Startseva, Alla, "Chubais Orders Asset Sales Halted," *Moscow Times* (September 26, 2002).

Statisticheskoe obozrenie: Ezhekvartal'nyi zhurnal, no. 1 (40) (2002).

Steinmo, Sven, Kathleen Thelen, and Frank Longstreth, eds., *Structuring Politics: Historical Institutionalism in Comparative Analysis* (Cambridge: Cambridge University Press, 1992).

Stepan, Alfred, "Russian Federalism in Comparative Perspective," *Post-Soviet Affairs* 16 (April-June 2000): 133–76.

Stoner-Weiss, Kathryn, *Local Heroes: The Political Economy of Russian Regional Governance* (Princeton, NJ: Princeton University Press, 1997).

——, "The Limited Reach of Russia's Party System: Underinstitutionalization in Dual Transitions," *Politics and Society* 29 (September 2001): 385–414.

——, "Whither the Central State? The Regional Sources of Russia's Stalled Reforms," in *After the Collapse of Communism: Comparative Lessons of Transition*, ed. Michael McFaul and Kathryn Stoner-Weiss (Cambridge: Cambridge University Press, 2004).

——, *Resisting the State: Reform and Retrenchment in Post- Soviet Russia* (Cambridge: Cambridge University Press, forthcoming).

Stroev, E. S., E. F. Zlobin, and A. A. Mikhalev, *Teoriia i praktika agrarnykh preobrazovanii v Orlovskoi oblasti* (Moscow: AgriPress, 1998).

Suny, Ronald Grigor, *The Revenge of the Past: Nationalism, Revolution, and the Collapse of the Soviet Union* (Stanford, CA: Stanford University Press, 1993).

Sutela, Pekka, "Insider Privatisation in Russia: Speculations on Systemic Change," *Europe-Asia Studies* 46 (1994): 417–35.

"Svodnyi otchet o khode privatizatsii," *Panorama privatizatsii*, no. 18 (45) (September 1994).

Svyazinvest [Sviazinvest], "Yashin Says Soros Rep to Stay on Svyazinvest Board for One Year," JSC Svyazinvest Press Release (July 1, 2004), at eng.svyazinvest.ru/press/?id=1205, accessed July 22, 2004.

Szamuely, Tibor, *The Russian Tradition*, ed. Robert Conquest (New York: McGraw-Hill, 1974).

Taibbi, Matt, "Privatized: Your Guide to Stripping Russia's Assets," *eXile* (October 16, 1999).

Tagliabue, John, "Italy's Stet to Update Russian Phone System," *New York Times* (December 2, 1995).

Tarasov, A., "Formirovanie regional'nykh rynkov sel'skokhoziaistvennoi produktsii," *APK: ekonomika, upravlenie*, no. 4 (1998): 34–40.

Tarasova, Mariia, Director of Information Department, Association of Financial Industrial Groups of Russia, interview with Juliet Johnson, Moscow (July 18, 1997).

Tatu, Michel, *Power in the Kremlin: From Khrushchev to Kosygin* (London: William Collins Sons, 1968).

Tavernise, Sabrina, "Using Bankruptcy as a Takeover Tool," *New York Times* (October 7, 2000).

——, "New Twist in BP Dispute in Russia," *New York Times* (June 1, 2001).

——, "Russian Authorities Search Office of Powerful Oil Tycoon," *New York Times* (July 12, 2003).

Taylor, Brian D., "Strong Men, Weak State: Power Ministry Officials and the Federal Districts," PONARS Policy Memo no. 284, October 2002.

Tedstrom, John E., "The Reemergence of Soviet Cooperatives," in *Socialism, Perestroika, and the Dilemmas of Soviet Economic Reform*, ed. John E. Tedstrom (Boulder, CO: Westview Press, 1990).

Telitsyna, Irina, Irina Kuz'menko, and Vladislav Kovalenko, "Zaroite vashi denezhki," *Kompaniia*, no. 237 (October 28, 2002), via www.apkmarket.ru/content.html?n=153, accessed September 16, 2003.

Thornhill, John, and Andrew Jack, "Assets Battle Hits Gazprom Offer for Media Most," *Financial Times* (September 18, 2000), via *JRL* no. 4521.

Tikhomirov, Vladimir, "Capital Flight from Post-Soviet Russia," *Europe-Asia Studies* (June 1997).

Timofeev, Lev, *Institutsional'naia korruptsiia: ocherki teorii* (Moscow: Rossiiskii gosudarstvennyi gumanitarnyi universitet, 2000).

Titova, Irina, "Court Bailiffs Arrive at Yukos' Office," *AP* (July 1, 2004), via *JRL* no. 8277.

"TNK Chief Quits Post to Chair Yukos Board," *Moscow Times* (June 19, 2003)

Tolkacheva, Julie, "Food Industry Is Feeding Russian Economic Growth," *Reuters* (January 13, 2002), via *JRL* no. 6074.

——, "Russia to Sell YUKOS Unit on Sunday," *Reuters* (December 18, 2004), via *JRL* no. 8505.

Tompson, William, "Old Habits Die Hard: Fiscal Imperatives, State Regulation, and the Role of Russia's Banks," *Europe-Asia Studies* 49 (1997): 1159–85.

——, "Nothing Learned, Nothing Forgotten: Restructuring without Reform in Russia's Banking Sector," in *Shaping the Economic Space in Russia*, ed. Stefanie Harter and Gerald Easter (Aldershot, UK: Ashgate, 2000).

Traynor, Ian, "Russia Puts Its Farmland on the Market," *The Guardian* (June 27, 2002), via *JRL* no. 6325.

Treisman, Daniel, "The Politics of Intergovernmental Transfers in Post-Soviet Russia," *British Journal of Political Science* 23 (July 1996): 299–335.

——, *After the Deluge: Regional Crises and Political Consolidation in Russia* (Ann Arbor: University of Michigan Press, 1999).

——, "Inter-Enterprise Arrears and Barter in the Russian Economy," *Post-Soviet Affairs* 16 (July–September 2000): 225–56.

——, "Russia Renewed?" *Foreign Affairs* 81 (November–December 2002): 58–72.

Tsentr politicheskoi informatsii, *Federal'naia i regional'naia elita Rossii, kto est' kto v politike i ekonomike: Ezhegodnyi biograficheskii spravochnik* (Moscow: Izdatel'stvo GNOM i D, 2001, 2002).

TsK VKP(b) [Central Committee of the All-Union Communist Party (Bolshevik)], *Short Course on the History of the Communist Party of the Soviet Union (Bolsheviks)* (New York: International Publishers, 1939).

Tsygankov, V., "Mezhdu nami, direktorami . . . ," *Gorodskie vesti* (December 8, 1994): 1.

Tucker, Robert C., "The Image of Dual Russia," in his *The Soviet Political Mind* (New York: W. W. Norton, 1971).

——, *Stalin in Power: The Revolution from Above, 1928–1941* (New York: W. W. Norton, 1990).

Utkin, E. A., and M. A. Eskindarov, *Finansovo promyshlennye gruppy* (Moscow: EKMOS, 1998).

Vacroux, Alexandra, "Privatization in the Regions: Primorsky Krai," in *Russia: Creating Private Enterprises and Efficient Markets*, ed. Ira W. Lieberman and John Nellis with Enna Karlova, Joyita Mukherjee, and Suhail Rahuja (Washington, DC: World Bank, 1995).

Vaknin, Sam, "A Russian Roulette—Agriculture," *UPI* (March 6, 2002), via *JRL* no. 6119.

Vaksberg, Arkady, *The Soviet Mafia* (New York: St. Martin's, 1991).

Van Atta, Don, "Russian Agriculture between Plan and Market," in *The "Farmer Threat,"* ed. Van Atta (1993a).

——, "Russian Food Supplies in 1992," in *The "Farmer Threat,"* ed. Van Atta (1993b).

Van Atta, Don, ed., *The "Farmer Threat": The Political Economy of Agrarian Reform in Post-Soviet Russia* (Boulder, CO: Westview, 1993c).

Vas'kin, V. F., "Reformirovanie predpriiatii agropromyshlennogo kompleksa," *Ekonomika sel'skokhoziaistvennykh i pererabatyvaiushchikh predpriiatii*, no. 3 (1996): 29–30.

Vdovin, V., "Aktsionery keramicheskogo doveriaiut sovladel'tsam 'Al'fa-Kapitala,'" *Delovye vesti* (October 15, 1993).

Verdery, Katherine, *What Was Socialism, and What Comes Next?* (Princeton, NJ: Princeton University Press, 1996).

Vin'kov, Andrei, "Okhota za den'gami Chubaisa," *Ekspert* (February 4, 2002a): 26.

——, "Bestsennyi 'Korall,'" *Ekspert* (February 18, 2002b): 24.

——, "Gavan' dlia magnata," *Ekspert* (April 15, 2002c): 40–47.

Vin'kov, Andrei, and Dmitrii Sivakov, "Piat' ugol'nykh dram," *Ekspert* (May 21, 2001): 30–36.

Vinton, Louisa, "Yeltsin Issues Privatization Ultimatum," *RFE/RL Daily Report* (July 20, 1994).

Viola, Lynne A., *The Best Sons of the Fatherland: Workers in the Vanguard of Soviet Collectivization* (New York: Oxford University Press, 1987).

Vlasova, Ekaterina, and Vladimir Kuz'min, "A oligarkhi—to ne te!" *Nezavisimaia gazeta*, August 9, 2002, via ng.ru/economics/2002–08–09/1_oligarh.html, accessed November 12, 2002.

Volkov, Aleksandr, Ta'tiana Rurova, and Viktor Titov, "Sanitary i marodery," *Ekspert* (March 1, 1999): 19–25.

Volkov, Vadim, *Violent Entrepreneurs: The Use of Force in the Making of Russian Capitalism* (Ithaca, NY: Cornell University Press 2002).

Volodin, V. M., "Opyt preobrazovaniia aktsionernogo obshchestva zakrytogo tipa v sel'skokhoziaistvennyi proizvodstvennyi kooperativ," *Ekonomika sel'skokhoziaistvennykh i pererabatyvaiushchikh predpriiatii*, no. 10 (1997): 10–14.

von Hagen, Mark, "The NEP, *Perestroika*, and the Problem of Alternatives," in *Socialism, Perestroika, and the Dilemmas of Soviet Economic Reform*, ed. Tedstrom (1990).

von Laue, Theodore H., *Sergei Witte and the Industrialization of Russia* (New York: Columbia University Press, 1963).

Vorob'ev, A. V., "Spravka o khode zemel'noi reformy v Volgogradskoi oblasti," Volgograd, mimeo (June 1992a).

——, "Spravka o khode zemel'noi reformy v Volgogradskoi oblasti," Volgograd, mimeo (August 1992b).

——, "Dokladnaia zapiska o khode zemel'noi reformy i ee itogakh za 1991–1992 gg. v Volgogradskoi oblasti," Volgograd, mimeo (September 21, 1992c).

——, "Puti razvitiia fermerstva," *Vestnik APK*, no. 2 (1995).

Voslensky, Michael, *Nomenklatura: The Soviet Ruling Class* (Garden City, NY: Doubleday, 1984).

Vysshii arbitrazhnyi sud Rossiiskoi Federatsii, "APK 'Agros' Vykhodit iz sostava aktsionerov Taganskogo Miasokombinata," *MK-Novosti* (February 15, 2004), via www.garweb.ru/project/vas/news/smi/04/02/20040215/8439436.htm, accessed July 13, 2004.

Wädekin, Karl-Eugen, *The Private Sector in Soviet Agriculture*, ed. George Karcz, trans. Keith Bush (Berkeley: University of California Press, 1973).

Wandel, Jürgen, "Vertical Integration in the Russian Agro-food Sector," in *Russia's Agro-Food Sector: Towards Truly Functioning Markets*, ed. Peter Wehrheim, Klaus Frohberg, Eugenia Serova, and Joachim von Braun (Boston: Kluwer, 2000).

Wegren, Stephen K., "Dilemmas of Agrarian Reform in the Soviet Union," *Soviet Studies* 44 (1992a): 3–36.

——, "Private Farming and Agrarian Reform in Russia," *Problems of Communism* 41 (May-June 1992b).

——, "Rural Reform in Russia," *RFE/RL Research Report* 2 (October 29, 1993).

——, "Building Market Institutions: Agricultural Commodity Exchanges in Post-Communist Russia," *Communist and Post-Communist Studies* 27 (1994a).

——, "Farm Privatization in Nizhnii Novgorod: A Model for Russia?" *RFE/RL Research Report* 3 (May 27, 1994b): 16–27.

——, "Rural Reform and Political Culture in Russia," *Europe-Asia Studies* 46 (1994c): 215–41.

——, "From Farm to Table: The Food System in Post-Communist Russia," *Communist Economies and Economic Transformation* 8 (1996): 149–83.

——, *Agriculture and the State in Soviet and Post-Soviet Russia* (Pittsburgh: University of Pittsburgh Press, 1998a).

——, "Russian Agrarian Reform and Rural Capitalism Reconsidered," *Journal of Peasant Studies* 1 (October 1998b): 82–111.

——, "Socioeconomic Transformation in Russia: Where Is the Rural Elite?" *Europe-Asia Studies* 52 (2000): 237–71.

——, "Observations on Russia's New Agricultural Land Legislation," *Eurasian Geography and Economics* 43 (December 2002): 651–60.

Whalen, Jeanne, "Gas Guzzler? Russian Monopoly Faces Scrutiny," *Wall Street Journal* (October 24, 2000).

——, "Putin Works to Increase Transparency at Russia's Clannish State Companies," *Wall Street Journal* (January 11, 2002).

Whalen, Jeanne, and Bhushan Bahree, "How BP Learned to Trust Ally That Once Burned It," *Wall Street Journal* (February 27, 2003).

White, Gregory L., "Moscow Restricts West's Oil Titans," *Wall Street Journal* (February 11, 2005), via *JRL* no. 9058.

White, Gregory, and Bhushan Bahree, "Russian Government Sets Plans to Nationalize Yukos's Chief Unit," *Wall Street Journal* (December 31, 2004), via *JRL* no. 8522.

White, Gregory L., and Matt Pottinger, "Rosneft Takes Control of Yukos, But Fate of Unit Remains Unclear," *Wall Street Journal* (January 2, 2005), via *JRL* no. 9002.

White, Gregory L., and Guy Chazan, "Yukos Is Further Squeezed by Ban," *Wall Street Journal* (April 19, 2004), via *JRL* no. 8173.

White, Stephen, *After Gorbachev* (Cambridge: Cambridge University Press, 1993).

White, Stephen, Graeme Gill, and Darrell Slider, *The Politics of Transition: Shaping a Post-Soviet Future* (Cambridge: Cambridge University Press, 1993).

Whitefield, Stephen, *Industrial Power and the Soviet State* (Oxford: Clarendon, 1993).

Williamson, John, ed., *The Political Economy of Policy Reform* (Washington, DC: Institute for International Economics, 1994).

Woodruff, David, *Money Unmade: Barter and the Fate of Russian Capitalism* (Ithaca, NY: Cornell University Press, 1999).

——, "Rules for Followers: Institutional Theory and the New Politics of Economic Backwardness in Russia," *Politics and Society* 28 (December 2000): 437–82.

——, "Property Rights in Context: Privatization's Legacy for Corporate Legality in Poland and Russia," *Studies in Comparative International Development* 38 (Winter 2004): 82–108.

World Bank, *Russian Economic Reform: Crossing the Threshold of Structural Change* (Washington, DC: International Bank for Reconstruction and Development, 1992).

Yanov, Alexander, *The Drama of the Soviet 1960s: A Lost Reform* (Berkeley, CA: Institute of International Studies, 1984).

Yenukov, Mikhail, "YUKOS in Loan Default, Shares Drop," *Reuters* (July 5, 2004), via *JRL* no. 8281.

——, "China Lends Russia's Rosneft $6 Billion for Future Oil," *Reuters* (February 1, 2005), via *JRL* no. 9044.

Yorke, Andrew, "Business and Politics in Krasnoyarsk *Krai*," *Europe-Asia Studies* 5 (2003): 241–62.

"Yukos Buys 68 Percent of Artikgas and Gains Foothold in Yamal-Nenets," *Energy Day* (March 7, 2002), via LEXIS-NEXIS.

Yurova, Yana, "What Made the Audit Chamber Doubt Privatization Results?" *RIA Novosti* (December 2, 2004), via *JRL* no. 8479.

Zakharova, N., and T. Antonova, "Nazad puti net. A vpered?" *Volgogradskaia pravda* (March 30, 1995): 3.

Zasurskii, Ivan, interview with the author, Moscow (October 28, 1994).

Zavarskii, Leonid, "Rosaviakonsortsium predlozhil sebia gosudarstvu," *Kommersant"-Daily* (February 22, 1997).

Zemel'naia reforma na opyte Nizhegorodskoi oblasti (Moscow: Rossiiskaia gazeta and Sotsial'naia zashchita, 1994).

Zhdannikov, Dmitry, "Russian Oil Firms on Buying Spree Abroad," *Reuters* (September 3, 2002), via *JRL* no. 6419.

——, "China May Get Piece of YUKOS Spoils," *Reuters* (December 30, 2004), via *JRL* no. 8521.

Zhdannikov, Dmitry, and Douglas Busvine, "YUKOS Seeks U.S. Bankruptcy to Stop Key Unit's Sale," *Reuters* (December 15, 2004), via *JRL* no. 8500.

Zhurek, Stefan Y., "Transforming Russian Agriculture: Why Is It So Difficult?" *Soviet and Post-Soviet Review* 21 (1994): 253–81.

——, "Food Exchanges Information Network: New Marketing Opportunities in Russia," paper for the Strengthening Democratic Institutions Project, John F. Kennedy School of Government, Harvard University (October 1995).

Zlobin, E. F., *Rynochnaia model' agrarnogo sektora regiona* (Moscow: AgriPress, 2000).

Zolotov, Andrei, Jr., "TV6 Sidelined as the Games Begin," *Moscow Times* (January 23, 2002), via www.internews.ru/article/tv6/tv6games.html, accessed July 21, 2004.

Zudin, Aleksei, "Biznes i gosudarstvo pri Putine: granitsy vozmozhnogo" (2002) via www.politcom.ru/2002/aaa_c_b2.php, accessed December 27, 2002.

INDEX

Page numbers in italics refer to tables in the text.